One and Many in Aristotle's *Metaphysics*

One and Many in Aristotle's *Metaphysics*

The Central Books

EDWARD C. HALPER

Ohio State University Press: Columbus

Library of Congress Cataloging-in-Publication Data

Halper, Edward C., 1951–
  One and many in Aristotle's Metaphysics. The central books.

  Bibliography: p.
  Includes index.
  1. Aristotle. Metaphysics. 2. One (The one in philosophy) 3. Many
(Philosophy)
  I. Title.
  B434.H35 1989   110   88-22496
  ISBN 0-8142-0456-2
The paper in this book meets the guidelines for permanence and durability of
the Committee on Production Guidelines for Book Longevity of the Council on
Library Resources.
Printed in the U.S.A.
9 8 7 6 5 4 3 2 1

To Slavka

Contents

Analytical Table of Contents

an addition is not the formula of one thing. Attributes and composites not only lack unity, they lack being.

2.4.5 Secondary Essences
Aristotle's reason for denying that non-*ousiai* have essences and definitions is also his reason for saying that they have essences and definitions in a secondary way. Non-*ousiai* lack essences and definitions because they are not properly one, but they have essences and definitions because they are one in a way; they are one by the "addition and subtraction" of *ousia,* just the reason that they are beings.

2.4.6 Addition, Subtraction, and *Ousia*
The method of Z 4-5 looks like the method Aristotle uses in Z 3. The former seeks to avoid additions, the latter subtracts accretions. Both assume that *ousia* is one. But, unlike the latter method, the former succeeds because it is applied to the formula. In arguing that only *ousia* properly has an essence, Z 4-5 set the stage for Z 6's arguments that *ousia* is essence.

2.5 Z 6: The Identity of Thing and Essence
Although an investigation of an identity might not seem to be an instance of the problem of the one and the many, Aristotle's arguments for the identity depend on showing that thing and essence cannot be two. Thus, these arguments draw upon and explore the unity of *ousia.*

2.5.1 1031a19–28: What Is Said Accidentally
The first part of Z 6 argues that what is said accidentally is not one with its essence. The argument is valid, and the conclusion follows because what is said accidentally is not one at all. In this argument Aristotle takes essence in the strict sense. What is said accidentally is one with its secondary essence because both are pluralities of the same sort.

2.5.2 1031a28–1032a11: What Is Said *Per Se*
Aristotle describes what is said *per se* as what is primary. Here "primary" includes only a part of what it means in Z 4, but it is still a kind of unity. Since the thing is one, and since essence is one, if they are not one and the same, then they are a plurality. On the other hand, Aristotle argues, in effect, that each must possess the unity associated with the other. The consequence of this argument is the identity of essence and another candidate for *ousia,* form (or formal substrate).

2.6 Z 7-9: The Physical Treatment of Essence
In this section Aristotle argues that neither form nor matter is generated in the generation of the composite. Were form generated, it would be a plurality. So to show that form is not generated is to show that it is one. Here, essence or form is one in formula, and it can only be such if it does not include physical matter. Aristotle also argues that form cannot exist apart like the Platonic form; this is tantamount to arguing that it cannot have the numeric unity that the Platonic form is supposed to have.

2.6.1 Some Objections
Although Z 9 seems to be a loosely organized appendix to Z 7-8, considered from the perspective of unity, it answers objections to the conclusions argued in Z 7-8. Since the analysis of change presented in Z 7-8 seems to apply equally well to instances of other categories besides *ousia,* they too seem to be

count of form in the central books resolves these problems by showing how form can have seemingly contrary types of unity.

4.4 *The Nature of Ousia*

Although the problems about *ousia* that the central books address are mainly problems about unity, to resolve them Aristotle needs to identify form as actuality. What ultimately emerges is the character of actuality as an entity with a peculiar mode of existence.

Glossary

The problems in translating Aristotle's key terms are well known. A large part of the difficulty is that Aristotle is often engaged in sorting out different terms and deciding their proper or primary senses. Since the central questions of the *Metaphysics* are, τί τὸ ὄν? (what is being?) and τίς ἡ οὐσία? (what is *ousia*?) particular care should be taken with these terms. Accordingly, I have adopted the conventional "being" for τὸ ὄν and merely transliterated οὐσία. I have also transliterated several other important Greek terms. It may be disconcerting to some to see both Greek and transliterated Greek. However, there are advantages to this path. I think that readers unable to read Greek will be able to follow the text and identify key concepts more easily than if I had left them in Greek. Also, I hope that my translations (or lack of translations, as the case may be) will direct attention away from the concepts toward the arguments through which Aristotle delimits them.

Aristotle uses the following as technical terms:

accident (τὸ κατὰ συμβεβηκός)   Usually, an accident is anything that does not belong to a thing's essence or does not belong to a thing in virtue of its essence. But Aristotle often uses this term to refer to any instance of a category other than *ousia*. Although the traditional view is that all non-*ousiai* are accidental, many commentators think that some non-*ousiai* are not accidents. I do not take a position on this issue here. Since Aristotle refers to non-*ousiai* as the accidental categories, I use "accident" to refer to any non-*ousia*.

actuality (also activity) [*energeia* (ἐνέργεια) or *entelechia* (ἐντελέχεια)]   *Energeia* comes from the word that means work or function (*ergon*). Actuality is the proper function of a thing. The other term for actuality, *entelechia,* comes from the word *telos*, end. It refers to the internal completion or end of the thing. Aristotle uses the terms interchangeably because he identifies the proper function of a thing with its internal completion. The central books identify actuality with form and essence.

addition   Aristotle uses several different terms for this important concept, but they seem to have no difference in meaning. "Addition" is an all purpose term for any combination. It resembles predication, but lacks the metaphysical baggage.

analogy   Aristotle's analogy has four terms: a/b :: c/d. Analogy is a tool for comparing things in distinct genera (see Δ 6, 1016b32–1017a3). Thomas Aquinas refers to *pros hen* as a kind of analogy, but this represents an extension of Aristotelian usage.

aporia   Literally, "lack of passage." An *aporia* is a deadlock that results from apparently sound arguments that support contrary conclusions. It is an antinomy.

attribute   A being that is said of another. Although Aristotle also speaks of words as being said of things, attributes are beings; that is, they are things that are said of other things. He distinguishes between essential (*per se*) attributes and accidental (*per accidens*) attributes.

being (τὸ ὄν)   This term could mean either (1) something which is or (2) the character which such things possess, depending on whether the term is a participle or a gerund. Often Aristotle's meaning seems to approach both: being is the nature a thing has which makes it be in the process of "ising"; it is both the universal and the thing with the universal character. But these characterizations make it seem as if that which makes a thing be is the same in each case and as if the process of ising were an act distinct from, say, the process of living. Being is not properly a single nature, but neither is the term entirely equivocal. Instead, all beings are related to a single nature, *ousia*; that is, they are *pros hen*.

categorial being   The being of the categories. This schema is one of the four ways being is said.

category   This term means predicate, and it can refer to the classes of predicates that Aristotle describes in the *Categories*. More often Aristotle uses the term "category" to refer to the genera these predicates name. The categorial genera are the most universal genera of beings.

cause (αἴτια)   Aristotle uses this term in a more general way than we usually do. In English, a cause is usually what Aristotle calls a "moving cause" and was later called an "efficient cause." Many philosophers refer to Aristotle's other causes as "explanatory principles." This has the unfortunate consequence of suggesting a subjective aspect to cause that is foreign to Aristotle's thinking. His causes are things. Despite its deficiencies, "cause" captures the objectivity of αἴτια. So I render the term as "cause."

composite (τὰ σύνθετα)   A variety of composites appear in the *Metaphysics:* (1) material composite—a form in a matter, a particular individual; also called a composite nature; (2) accidental composite—an instance of an *ousia* and an instance of some other category, including natural composites such as white man and north wind, and artifacts such as a bed or a book; (3) *per se* composite—an instance of an *ousia* or some substrate and one of its *per se* attributes; for example, snub nose. Although *ousia* is a constituent of the latter two types of composites, Aristotle often illustrates these composites with a substrate that is not properly an *ousia*, like nose.

definition   The formula of a thing's essence. Obviously, things without essences lack proper definitions as well. They have formulae, and these are definitions of a sort.

diairesis **(διαίρεσις)**   Division. The Platonic mode of arriving at definition is to divide a genus.

differentia   (1) A character that divides a genus. The differentia is the form of the genus, and the genus is its intelligible matter. (2) Probably by extension, Aristotle also applies the term differentia to attributes that characterize matter, such as being in a particular position or being glued. These latter differentiae are the forms of accidental composites.

eidos **(τὸ εἶδος)**   This term is rendered either as "form" or "species" depending on the context. Sometimes Aristotle uses it like shape (μορφή), as a principle contained in a composite. Then it should be rendered "form." In passages where he uses the term as a universal predicate, it should be rendered "species." Though traditional, this dual rendering has been questioned partly because Aristotle does not draw the distinction himself and partly because it conflicts with a particular view of form, that form is universal. Although the two senses sometimes slur together, I think the distinction should be made.

element (τὸ στοιχεῖον)   A constituent. Usually Aristotle reserves this term for material constituents of a thing. By extension he refers to some genera as elements because they are constituents of other genera and species. An element is a kind of principle.

essence (τὸ τί ἦν εἶναι)   Aristotle coined this phrase to indicate the character of a thing by which it is what it is. The essence is the thing's nature, its form. A phrase that is usually equivalent is τὸ X εἶναι (where X is in the dative). The essence is what is defined by a definition, though it is not identical with the definition. Sometimes Aristotle also refers to an essence as a τί ἐστιν because we answer this question with the definition of an essence.

essential   A standard translation of *per se,* q.v.

form (τὸ εἶδος)   Often this term means shape (μορφή) in contrast with what has the shape, but Aristotle apparently extends it, by analogy, to anything that resembles shape in relation to what has shape. It is the latter that he identifies with essence.

formula (ὁ λόγος)   Properly, a group of words that characterizes something's nature. A formula may or may not be a definition. It is a definition only when it is the formula of an essence, and it can be such only if the thing of which it is the formula has an essence. Because language is closely tied to thinking, Aristotle sometimes uses formula when he means rational.

function (τὸ ἔργον)   The work that defines a thing. Here a function is not just what something does—that would suggest that the thing could do something else. A thing's function is what makes it what it is.

genus   (1) A predicate that defines a class broader than a species. (2) The class so defined. (3) A category or the class of entities that fall under the category. Aristotle speaks of a genus in respect of a species, so that the genus for one species could be the species for another genus.

***kath' hen* (καθ' ἕν)**   Literally "in respect of one." This describes the instances of a genus or a species. For example, individual animals are called animals "in respect of one" nature, the nature of animal which they all share. Cf. *pros hen.*

individual (καθ' ἕκαστον)   Also translated as "particular." Usually Aristotle uses this term for sensible composites. But he sometimes applies it more broadly, using it of species and, I maintain, anything that is numerically one.

indivisible   Aristotle uses two terms that are translated as "indivisible," ἄτομον and ἀδιαίρετον. The former is literally "without a cut" and the latter "without a division."

"is it?"   This is one of Aristotle's four scientific questions, and he also uses the phrase to refer to the answer to this question. Although the question can be raised about simples, the question only serves to guide inquiry when asking it amounts to asking whether one thing belongs to another.

matter (ὕλη)   What underlies a form, but not matter as the inert stuff of modern physics. Matter is always defined relative to some form so that what is the matter in one respect may be form in another. Even a logical entity such as a genus can function as matter. Matter is potentiality.

motion (κίνησις)   Aristotle defines motion as the actualization of a potentiality *qua* potential. This definition is more general than that of modern physics for it admits not only local motion but also change in quality or quantity. Sometimes Aristotle also calls change in *ousia*, generation or destruction, a motion; on other occasions he calls each a change (μεταβολή), a term he also applies to motions.

nature   In the *Physics* Aristotle defines a nature as an internal principle of motion or of rest, and he goes on to argue that this principle is both the thing's form and its matter but primarily the form. A nature is an *ousia* or the form of an *ousia*.

one (τὸ ἕν)   In Greek this term could refer to the one itself (if there is such an entity), the unity possessed by a particular thing, the thing that possesses this unity, or the property of oneness or unity in general. Because the proper interpretation is often a point of contention, I have usually rendered the term simply as "one." As he does for most of his important philosophical terms, Aristotle describes the many ways that "one" is said, but this term is more complex than the others. He distinguishes two main groups of ones, one in number and one in species. Something can be one in number by having a continuous matter, by being an instance of a species, or even by lacking matter altogether. Aristotle equates one in species with one in formula, and something has this type of unity if its formula is not divisible into constituents that signify the same thing. There are other ways of being one that do not fall under either head, such as one in genus and one by analogy. All these are predicative uses of the term "one." Aristotle also discusses cases where the term functions as a subject, such as, the essence of one and the number one.

organically united (σύμφυσις, συμπέφυκεν)   Grown together. Aristotle uses these terms to describe the strongest type of continuity.

ousia **(ἡ οὐσία)**   A noun formed from the participle "being." "Substance" is the usual translation, and it does capture Aristotle's use of the term in the *Categories*. In the *Metaphysics,* though, Aristotle denies that the *ousia* of the *Categories* is primary; so "substance" no longer seems appropriate. Since the central books seek its nature, I have left the term transliterated.

per accidens **(κατὰ συμβεβηκός)**   An attribute is *per accidens* if that to which it belongs could lose it without altering its nature.

per se **(καθ' αὐτό)**   Literally "in respect of itself." Attributes belong to a thing *per se* if the thing has them in virtue of its nature. The thing's nature or essence is also *per se*.

potentiality (ἡ δύναμις)   The correlate of actuality. A potentiality is either (1) what comes to be actualized through some generation or (2) what underlies the form or actuality in a composite.

predicate (ἡ κατηγορία)   Although a predicate is anything said of another, there is a great deal of ontology packed into predication. Only an *ousia* or what is treated as *ousia* can receive a predicate, and the existence of predicates depends on *ousiai*. Though Aristotle sometimes speaks as if predicates were terms, they are things; but they differ from the things of which they (or their names) are said.

primary   (1) The primary instance of something is both that which is most properly the thing and that in respect of which the other instances of something are so called. (2) In Z 4 Aristotle describes something as primary if it is "not said by something's being said of something else." (3) In Z 6 Aristotle describes something as primary if it is not said of something else.

principle (ἡ ἀρχή)   Like cause, but more general. Among the principles are not only the four causes but also the principles of demonstration; for example, the principle of noncontradiction.

proper differentia   A differentia uniquely associated with the genus it differentiates.

proper function   That activity which makes a thing what it is. Although I speak of performing one's proper function, the latter is not an activity that one can choose to perform or not perform. It is the form that makes a thing be.

proper matter   The matter that is nearest to the form in that it receives the form directly: the proximate matter. This matter is peculiar to the form. Although there are some difficult cases, in *ousiai* and natural composites one matter is proper to one form. Proper matter is both the first matter and the last matter: it is first because it is closest to the form, and last because it is furthest from the least determinate matter.

proper sense   My way of speaking about the primary instance, the instance to which other lesser instances are related and through which they are defined as instances.

pros hen **(πρὸς ἕν)**   Literally "in relation to one." A character is *pros hen* if it belongs to things by virtue of their (different) relations to one primary nature. For example, things are called medical because they are all related, albeit in different ways, to health in a body. A *pros hen* is usually broader than a genus. Cf. *kath' hen.*

proximate matter   *See* proper matter.

said in many ways (λέγεται πολλαχῶς)   Most of the important Aristotelian terms are said in many ways, and this is often taken to mean that they have multiple definitions. What Aristotle means, however, is that many different things are called by the same term.

same (ταὐτά)   "Same" parallels one: it is said in as many ways as one. But it is a unity of many things or of what is treated as many.

science (ἡ ἐπιστήμη)   A branch of demonstrative knowledge. Alternative translations of this Greek term include "knowledge" and "discipline." None of these renderings is entirely apt. (1) To us the word "science" suggests a body of knowledge supported by observation and experiment; Aristotle applies the Greek term to metaphysics. (2) In its current usage, the English word "knowledge" does not admit a plural; but Aristotle frequently uses the Greek word in the plural. (3) The word "discipline" connotes a loosely organized area of knowledge; Aristotle insists that each ἐπιστήμη concerns a single genus and demonstrates the attributes that belong to that genus. Because this structure is so important for understanding the Aristotelian ἐπιστήμη, I have often rendered the term as "science."

soul (ἡ ψυχή)   The form of a living thing. For Aristotle, "soul" has none of the religious or mystical connotations that the term has in English. Soul is the difference between a living thing and a corpse. So there is no question that it exists. The problem is to determine what it is.

species   (1) The lowest (least general) predicate of individuals. (2) Any portion of a genus defined by differentiating the genus. According to the *Categories,* only species and genera are properly predicated of individuals. Qualities, quantities, and the other categories are "present in" individuals, though there are also individuals and species in these other categories.

substrate (τὸ ὑποκείμενον)   The substrate is the subject of predications; since predicates are things, so is their substrate. Aristotle distinguishes three kinds of substrate, matter, form, and composite. The last is primary *ousia* in the *Categories*. In the *Metaphysics*, the formal substrate, the form, is primary.

summa **genera**   The most inclusive and, thus, the highest genera. Since neither being nor one is a genus, the categorial genera are the *summa* genera.

thing (ἕκαστον)   "Thing" is a standard translation for the term that means "each." The thing is what has an essence, and Aristotle argues that it is its essence. Thing is usually identified as composite, but nothing in the text requires this. What it is needs to be decided, and the result of Aristotle's analysis is, I argue, that it is form. There is another term that is sometimes rendered as thing, τὸ πρᾶγμα. Occasionally, Aristotle uses this latter term in the same way as the former, but often it has a broader nontechnical usage.

this (τόδε τι)   "This" is often the distinguishing mark of *ousia*, but Aristotle never explicitly defines it. A this is something but not something else, a description that immediately excludes accidents and composites. I argue that a this is numerically one.

ultimate differentia   The last differentia of a genus; the differentia that defines a species which cannot be further differentiated.

universal (τὸ καθόλου)   An Aristotelian coinage for "predicate." Literally the term means "in respect of the whole." A universal is said in respect of some whole. Aristotle defines it as a "one over many."

unmoved mover   Aristotle's first principle. He identifies the unmoved mover with both the cause of motion of the heavenly spheres and with thinking about thinking. From the former identification, he infers that there must be forty-seven or fifty-five unmoved movers. Each is a pure actuality.

"what it is," "what is it?" (τί ἐστιν)   The Greek for both is the same. This is a stock Aristotelian phrase for: (1) one of the four scientific questions which ought to be raised in any inquiry, the question whose answer is (or should be) the formula of the essence of the thing; (2) the answer to that question, whether it is the definition or simply the formula of the thing.

Preface

This book is part of a larger study of the problem of the one and the many in Aristotle's *Metaphysics*. Although this portion can be read and understood on its own, some remarks about the contents of the two sister volumes will be helpful for two reasons. First, several important distinctions that emerge from the first part of the study are used here with little or no explanation or justification. Second, a detailed study of one and many in the central books may raise suspicions in the minds of readers who are well acquainted with Aristotle's text. Why, it will be asked, does the author pay close attention to portions of the *Metaphysics* where unity seems to play little if any role and virtually ignore portions where Aristotle explicitly treats unity, such as Δ 6 and the whole of book I? An answer is that I do deal with these sections elsewhere. It is possible to treat the role of unity in the central books with little reference to these other sections because Aristotle distinguishes many ones, and different ones are pertinent to different sections of the *Metaphysics*. Aristotle's treatment of one in book I does not bear directly on the central books. Book I concerns the essence of one and what is one in respect of a genus. The central books use other ones to examine being, particularly one in species and one in number. The opening books of the *Metaphysics* have a variety of other uses for one. Even though Aristotle often starts from the problem of the one and the many, he regards unity as subsidiary. It can even be misleading to speak of *the* problem of the one and the many. This is a rubric for a broad spectrum of problems, united more by the method Aristotle uses to consider them than by any common content. Although the central books contribute to a project begun and completed elsewhere in the *Metaphysics*, they can be fruitfully considered by themselves.

My study of the problem of the one and the many in the *Metaphysics* begins with a discussion of the problem and its various manifestations in the Aristotelian corpus. Aristotle often refers to the problem when treating his predecessors, a good sign that he himself is interested in it. Presocratic philosophers apparently thought of the problem as a single one: are all things one or many? Aristotle, however, recognizes that "one" is said in many ways. It follows that the problem of the one and the many immediately divides into many problems. He can, and generally does, ask about each object of interest in each work, is it one or many? It follows that to get a complete hold on the problem of the one and the many in Aristotle it is necessary to examine the many ways "one" is said. Aristotle has three discussions of the things said to be one: Δ 6, I 1, and *Physics* A 2. An important point that is frequently overlooked is that each entry in the schema of ones is itself a schema. Among what is one by continuity, for example, Aristotle distinguishes what is continuous by nature from what is continuous by art. Also, a key distinction, one that Aristotle himself makes in I 1, is between those things that are numerically one, such as composite individuals, and things that are one in formula, such as species. The same thing can be one in various ways. So Aristotle's treatment of the ways "one" is said is really an account of the different respects in which things can be called one. Besides this variety of ones, Aristotle distinguishes the essence of one (τὸ ἑνὶ εἶναι) from things that are one (Δ 6, 1016b17–21; I 1, 1052b1–20). Also, he describes qualitative and quantitative series of ones (1016b23–1017a2). Thus, his exposition of ones has a complexity without parallel in book Δ.

This complex treatment of one is the key, I argue, to understanding Aristotle's metaphysical *aporiai,* the antinomies that constitute book B. Most of these result from the contrary claims of competing unities. The first group of *aporiai* concern the subject matter of metaphysics, and they turn on the question of whether or not that subject matter can be one. The second group arise because principles seem to require contrary types of unity, and the third group consist of arguments for and against competing candidates for the first principles often based on whether or not they have requisite unities. Although the central books make no reference to the *aporiai,* they address and resolve the second set, or so I argue at the end of the present volume.

The problem of the one and the many is implicit in both of Aristotle's introductory books. In book A he addresses the question of the number of causes. It is clear that this is a way for him to investigate their nature. In book α he argues that the causes cannot be infinite if there is to be knowledge. Implicit here is the idea that unity is the principle of knowledge.

Book Γ begins with the assertion that a science of metaphysics exists. This, I argue, is a conclusion that hinges on the demonstration that the subject matter that ought to be treated by metaphysics possesses sufficient unity to belong to a single science. Aristotle advances seven arguments for the unity of the subject matter in the first three chapters of book Γ. (These arguments effectively resolve the first set of *aporiai.*) The most important of them includes Aristotle's well-known assertion that things are said to be by virtue of their relation to some primary nature; in other words, that being is *pros hen.* That this is a kind of unity can be inferred from Aristotle's comparison of it with the unity he ascribes to species and genera. The latter are said in respect of one nature; they are *kath' hen.* Most scholars make too much of the failure of being to be a genus. In the context of the *Metaphysics* it is more significant that being possesses a kind of unity that resembles the unity of a genus. It is in virtue of this unity, *pros hen* unity, that being can be treated by one science. Thus, it is through unity that Aristotle answers what the *Posterior Analytics* terms the "is it?" question in regard to being.

The present volume begins with Aristotle's inquiry into the second question of the *Posterior Analytics,* "what is it?" That is, it begins with Aristotle's investigation of the nature of being. This occupies the whole of the central books, E–Θ. Answering this question depends on resolving various forms of the problem of the one and the many.

My third and final volume begins with a lengthy examination of the inquiry into the one that comprises book I. This inquiry parallels the central books, but an important aim is to show the subsidiary character of one. A thing and what it is are the same, but a thing and its unity differ. What is one is always some other nature. In general, Aristotle describes one as what is indivisible in a genus. Thus, one differs in each species and it is defined by analogy: one is to genus as the indivisible is to the divisible. The ambiguities in interpreting this analogy generate diverse ones.

In book Λ Aristotle compares the analogy he uses to define one with the *pros hen* structure he uses to describe being, and he argues for the primacy of the latter. He then goes on to argue for the existence of the unmoved movers as the first principles and to characterize their nature. Books M–N consider and reject other candidates for the first principle: mathematicals, forms, forms-numbers, and (Academic) elements (one and the indefinite dyad). Each of these is a candidate because each is a kind of unity. Nevertheless, each fails to be the most successful candidate because it lacks the pertinent unity.

It is widely believed that one and being are both *pros hen.* My study shows that they differ. A second, related fallacy is that Aristotle's one is or resembles what medieval philosophers termed a transcendental. This notion can be dispelled by analysis of Aristotle's definition of one as a measure. This treatment of the nature of one shows how it is possible to have the function it does in the *Metaphysics.*

Although the one and the many are central for the problematic that Aristotle addresses in the *Metaphysics,* they are mostly peripheral to the doctrines that he advances to solve these problems, doctrines traditionally identified as Aristotelianism. Paying close attention to the one and the many allows us to see the *Metaphysics* as something more than a compilation of doctrine. Aristotle's positions take on a deeper significance when we see them as solutions to problems. Many of these problems are, I argue, manifestations of the problem of the one and the many.

One reason that the problem of the one and the many is so important to the *Metaphysics* is that Aristotle regards the world as a collection of individuals and he seeks, as his first principle, some particular nature. The problem of the one and the many reflects Aristotle's concern with individual things and his attempt to make some particular thing the cause of all other things. His pursuit of the nature of these individuals leads him to recognize the existence of something which lacks the character of individuality as usually conceived, something which possesses its own kind of individuality. The central books make a key move in this redefinition of individuality. Although they are intelligible in themselves, as the present volume aims to show, they contribute to the inquiry into being that constitutes the entire *Metaphysics*.

* * * * *

My work on the *Metaphysics* began—longer ago than I care to remember—at the University of Toronto, where I wrote a dissertation on the role of unity. This is an opportunity to express my thanks to Father Joseph Owens for his supervision. His own work has been both a model and an inspiration. I am also indebted to John Rist for reading my dissertation with care, correcting many mistakes, and eventually serving as the internal examiner. Reg Allen's course on the *Parmenides* got me interested in the one, and he continued to encourage my work on the *Metaphysics*. My view of the function and significance of unity in the *Metaphysics* has not changed over the years, but in depth, detail, and understanding the present work far surpasses my dissertation.

This is also an opportunity to thank others who have written on Aristotle. Although most of my references to secondary works are critical, the present endeavor would not be possible without them.

Earlier versions of parts of this book were delivered to a variety of audiences, and I am grateful for the comments I received on those occasions. I want to thank Russ Dancy, who served as my commentator for an American Philosophical Association presentation on Z 4-5.

Three portions from this text have been published earlier as: "*Metaphysics* Z 12 and H 6: The Unity of Form and Composite," *Ancient Philosophy* IV (1984): 146-59; "*Metaphysics* Z 4-5: An Argument from Addition," *Ancient Philosophy* VI (1986): 91-122; and "Aristotle's Solution to the Problem of Sensible Substance," *Journal of Philosophy* LXXXIV (1987): 666-72. The two articles that appeared in *Ancient Philosophy* were reviewed, and the reviewers made several helpful suggestions. I gratefully acknowledge the permission of Mathesis Publications to reprint portions of these two articles here. The third article is a condensed version of the final chapter of this book, and I am also grateful to the editors of the *Journal of Philosophy* for allowing it to be reprinted here.

Work on the final stages of this manuscript was supported by summer grants from the University of Georgia's Department of Philosophy.

An anonymous reviewer for Ohio State University Press caught several mistakes and made some helpful suggestions. I would also like to thank Robert Turnbull for his helpful suggestions.

Above all, I would like to thank my wife, Slavka, to whom this book is dedicated.

A Note to the Reader

The central books of Aristotle's *Metaphysics* are extremely dense and their interpretation is highly controversial. Unfortunately, the complexity stems not merely from Aristotle's cryptic style, but is inherent in the subject matter. To develop and defend an interpretation I have had to look closely at many textual details. My chief concern is reconstructing Aristotle's arguments. Those whose leisure or interest will not allow them to peruse the entire discussion with the attention it will likely require are advised to proceed immediately to the final chapter. There I address the classical scholarly problem of the central books and argue for a resolution. Also, I explain the nature of form or essence that emerges from the central books. The final chapter is not a substitute for the whole, but I hope that, besides tying together the preceding results, it may help readers who might otherwise be lost in a forest of detail.

Why dwell on the detail? Contemporary commentaries divide into those who see the text of the *Metaphysics* as the exposition of a doctrine and those, lately more numerous, who see it as a collection of interesting but often inconsistent explorations of various related subjects. The present work falls into neither of these camps. Instead, I take Aristotle to be conducting an investigation, an inquiry, into the nature of being. His text aims to arrive at and to justify an account of being. The emphasis is on discovery, not exposition. But this process of discovery is so carefully arranged and systematically organized, at least in the form in which it has come to us, that I find it extremely implausible that its author had failed to reach a conclusion or to sustain it. The central books of the *Metaphysics* inquire into the nature of being by seeking the nature that is primary in each of the four ways "being" is said. The inquiry is a carefully laid out search for causes. To be sure, it does not occur along the lines Aristotle describes in the second book of the *Posterior Analytics*, but the discrepancy is due to the character of the inquiry into being rather than to Aristotle's having abandoned his view of scientific inquiry. The *Metaphysics* exhibits the process of finding the causes, and the present book traces this process of inquiry.

Introduction

Should the study of a great work of philosophy such as Aristotle's *Metaphysics* seek to understand the text in its own terms or to understand the text in terms of contemporary problems and developments? There is much to be said for both alternatives. It is clear that Aristotle's work was written in a particular context, that it makes assumptions consonant with other works in the same tradition, and that it addresses problems that were peculiar to a particular period. It is hard to see how we could examine it in terms of contemporary problems without distorting the intentions and doctrines of the author. On the other side, when faced with a difficult text like the *Metaphysics,* should we not use everything at our disposal to try to understand it? Philosophy has made great strides in recent years in the development of logical techniques for the assessment of arguments and in the study of important distinctions. To fail to use these developments seems like an unjustified restraint. Conversely, philosophers studying contemporary problems have much to learn from past masters like Aristotle. A study of his text that shows what light it sheds on contemporary issues performs a valuable service.

Like many scholarly disputes, this one springs from a divergence in philosophical positions. The history of philosophy is sometimes seen as consisting of distinct periods, each with its own assumptions and perspective. On this view, it makes no sense to use current distinctions and assumptions to aid in the study of Aristotle's work. On the other hand, the history of philosophy has also been seen as a succession of attempts to treat the same problems, a view which clearly encourages the use of contemporary work in understanding Aristotle.

While there is something to be said for both approaches, there are also dangers inherent in each. The attempt to study the history of philosophy in the terms in which it is formulated can easily become stale and sterile. It can result in the mere repetition of well-known, and not so well understood, doctrines; mere scholarship as opposed to philosophy. On the other side, studying texts in the light of current problems, we risk importing alien ideas into the text and so distorting it beyond recognition and intelligibility.

A dialectic between these two perspectives has played itself out in the history of twentieth century scholarship on Aristotle's *Metaphysics*. On one side, we have seen attempts to baptize Aristotle as a proponent of the reigning orthodoxy. In this century, he has been an empiricist, a Deweyan naturalist, an ordinary language philosopher, a Heideggerian, and an essentialist. In each case the motive is entirely laudable: to use a classic text to shed light on current problems and to use the latter to help explain the text. Each movement has spurred close attention to particular textual details that seemed to be relevant to the overall perspective, and each has generated new insights into the text and the problems it treats. It is a tribute to the profundity of the text that it admits of such a variety of interpretations.

At the same time, there is little doubt that current philosophical movements go far beyond anything that we can find directly in the text. To consider Aristotle as an ordinary language philosopher, for example, we need to import a perspective at which the text, at best, only hints. The criticism of Aristotle that arises after taking this perspective is always suspect. We need to decide whether it reflects a failure in Aristotle's philosophy or simply failure of his philosophy to fit squarely into the prescribed perspective.

Confronted with various, conflicting attempts to treat Aristotle in terms of current problems, many scholars have retreated to the close study of brief passages. We cannot merely assume that the text is a unity, the reasoning goes. Let us then examine a sentence or two, present the possible interpretations, and decide on a case by case basis which interpretation is the most plausible. In this way, we will avoid importing global hypotheses about the text, avoid succumbing to the tyranny of earlier, possibly unfounded ways of interpreting the text, and perhaps be able to construct a coherent picture of the whole from the details. Moreover, by focusing attention on small bits of text, we can examine just those doctrines that are philosophically most interesting. This seems to me the approach to the text that is currently most popular. Initially, it is conceived as a way to avoid introducing alien hypotheses. However, such is the dialectic of Aristotelian scholarship that it, too, is pressed into the service of scholars interested in contemporary questions. For divorced from its context, a sentence or two of Aristotle's crabbed text often does seem to bear on current problems. If we are indeed justified in viewing bits of text by themselves, then it makes sense to inquire into Aristotle's views on, say, modal semantics, in a particular passage from book Θ without paying much attention to other passages that may or may not have been written at the same time and from the same stance.

The important lesson that has emerged from the close scrutiny given to brief passages is how little support traditional interpretations have in the text. It is not that the text is inconsistent with these interpretations, but that the interpretations require reading a great deal into the text that is not stated explicitly. Looking closely at a particular sentence, many scholars have found it possible to understand the text in ways quite different from the traditional ways.

The method that I shall employ in this study is a kind of synthesis of the method of close textual analysis with the method of viewing the text in terms of a particular perspective. To avoid the pitfalls of these approaches, I have chosen a perspective which is characteristically Greek, and I examine the details of the text in terms of this perspective. I am concerned throughout with Aristotle's treatment of the problem of the one and the many. This problem is an issue that Aristotle mentions often in conjunction with a critique of his predecessors and only occasionally when expounding his own metaphysical doctrines. It comes up repeatedly in different contexts and in different forms. To argue that the problem has the significance that I think it has in the *Metaphysics,* I need to show that it is implied or presupposed in many places where Aristotle does not mention it explicitly. Taken individually, such interpretations are highly suspect. However, when we see the possibility of reading many passages in this way, the approach becomes more plausible. Often I need to go beyond claims that appear in the text, but I hope to avoid the usual distortions inherent in such a procedure by focusing on a problem with which Aristotle is clearly concerned.

Why should we think that Aristotle's concern with the problem of the one and the many is greater than what is indicated explicitly in the text and greater than what has traditionally been ascribed to him? Part of the reason is that many of the traditional readings of the text stem from Aristotle's Greek commentators. It has become a commonplace that their interpretations should not be taken as authoritative. Where in particular do they go astray? Where does their own Neo-Platonism interfere with their understanding of the text? Their commentaries focus on the details of the text and do not contain any overt claims to indicate the Neo-Platonic perspective of their authors. We can surmise that if they err anywhere, these commentaries err in assessing the role that unity plays in Aristotle's philosophy. As Philip Merlan has pointed out, whatever Aristotle's merits as an interpreter of Plato, the doctrine that he ascribes to Plato was, in fact, adopted by later Platonists.[1] The claims that the one is the highest principle and that the forms are somehow generated from it constitute important elements in Neo-Platonic doctrine. We should be suspicious of the treatment that Aristotle's views on unity and his criticism of Plato's view of unity receive from his Neo-Platonic commentators. Let us suppose, for the moment, that a central, but subtle, aim of Aristotle's *Metaphysics* is to refute the Platonic or Neo-Platonic view of unity. We would surely expect these commentators to de-emphasize this aspect of the work. They might be anxious to pass over it quickly or to ignore it. It is precisely on questions about unity that the Neo-Platonistic commentators really have an ax to grind. Could they have written their commentaries in order to show that Aristotle's views on unity are not essential for an understanding of his doctrine? We know that the Neo-Platonists took Aristotle's doctrine to be of a piece with Plato's. Perhaps their motive in commenting upon Aristotle was just to show the convergence in doctrine between Plato and Aristotle, an end that they could only have achieved by reinterpreting texts that seemed inconsistent with the primacy of unity. All of this is, of course, speculation, but it shows that the indifference to the problem of the one and the many manifested by the tradition of interpretation of the *Metaphysics* may reflect the motives of Aristotle's earliest interpreters rather than the text.

Perhaps another reason for the scant attention given to the problem of the one and the many is Aristotle's own success. After all, he regards questions about unity as subsidiary, and at one point in the *Metaphysics* he refers to an instance of the problem of the one and the many as "archaic" (N 2, 1088b35–1089a6). Philosophers who accept his conclusions may well have been deterred from a thorough study of this problem. As far as the doctrine that Aristotle enunciates in the *Metaphysics* is concerned, unity and the problem of the one and the many are relatively unimportant. My contention is that they often provide Aristotle with justification for his doctrines. In the context of Greek philosophy, the problem of the one and the many is central. Aristotle examines the problem in its various manifestations, and he shows that, in each case, the problem can be resolved by the introduction of another doctrine. These other doctrines are what we now regard as Aristotle's philosophy. Attention to unity and to the problem of the one and the many can, I propose, explain how Aristotle arrives at and justifies his doctrine.

The problem of the one and the many is not thought to be terribly important by most current philosophers. To those with little interest in the question, a detailed analysis of Aristotle's treatment of it may well seem a tedious exercise. Let me confess to what may be only my own prejudices: I find the problem of the one and the many in all of its manifestations thoroughly fascinating. I also think that it is of central importance for physics and for philosophy. This is a minority opinion. However, I hope that my exploration of the various formulations and solutions of this problem in the *Metaphysics* will not only show the basis of some of Aristotle's metaphysical doctrine but also generate some interest in the problem itself.

Most scholars take it for granted that Aristotle's work shows some type of development. The text of the *Metaphysics* contains many claims that certainly seem inconsistent. Though it is clearly a mistake to allow a reverential awe of Aristotle to deter one from entertaining the possibility that some passages are inconsistent or mistaken, it seems to me that a student of an ancient text like the *Metaphysics* should begin by striving to reconcile apparent inconsistencies. Although this has not always been possible, the problem of the one and the many provides a context which enables us to piece together much of the text in a reasonably consistent and coherent way. What began as a study of unity *in* the *Metaphysics* became a study showing the unity *of* the *Metaphysics*. Because the structure and the content of the work seem clearer when viewed from this perspective, there is reason to think that Aristotle himself shares it. He does not indicate his intentions very clearly, but this is a disadvantage that all interpretations share. We know from Aristotle's accounts of his predecessors that the problem of the one and the many is a central issue for Greek metaphysics. It is a problem that we would expect him to address. Yet, where in the *Metaphysics* does he treat it? Can it be that Aristotle treats it nearly everywhere in the *Metaphysics?*

One and Many in
Aristotle's *Metaphysics*
The Central Books

Chapter 1

Book E: What Is Being?

1.1 THE CENTRAL BOOKS

Traditionally, the phrase "central books" refers to books Z–H–Θ of the *Metaphysics*. They occupy a central position in the work, and they all pursue an inquiry into being and, particularly, into sensible *ousia*. Other books of the *Metaphysics* conceive of the science differently. In books A, B, and Γ, metaphysics is the science of first causes and highest principles, and book Λ undertakes an investigation into the unmoved movers. Since Z–H–Θ contain no explicit reference to the earlier books and only a few references to what appears to be book Λ, they have been thought to constitute a distinct investigation stemming from a distinct period of Aristotle's development.[1] More recent writers tend to see the central books as somewhat tentative and inconclusive investigations into scattered topics loosely connected with sensible *ousiai*. There is no need to assess proposed accounts of the relation of the central books to the rest of the work, for most of these are predicated on the assumption of major inconsistencies between the central books and other portions of the *Metaphysics*. We should show the existence of these inconsistencies before looking at developmental hypotheses. My own view is that these supposed inconsistencies lie not in the work but in the perspective from which the *Metaphysics* has been approached. Many of the usual problems vanish if we consider the text in terms of the classical problem of the one and the many. In the following treatment of the central books, I shall use the problem of the one and the many to reconstruct the structure and the arguments of the text. The result sheds some light on several difficult areas in Aristotle's philosophy, and my study also constitutes an exploration of a problem that is intrinsically interesting in its own right.

Which books are the "central books"? Since the first chapter of book E repeats material that appears in the first two chapters of book Γ, it is generally grouped with books A, B, and Γ.[2] In terms of its argument, however, E 1 belongs with the central books. While book Γ argues for the existence of a science of metaphysics by showing how the topics that it ought to treat— topics that, as book B shows, do not seem amenable to a treatment by a single science—can fall under one science, book E begins an inquiry into the nature of being. As we will see, books Z–H–Θ pursue this inquiry; they investigate the "what is being" question by examining *ousia* and actuality.

1

The first chapter of E shows its concern with the nature of being in several passages. First, the book opens with remarks that characterize the science of metaphysics by contrasting it with the particular sciences, and Aristotle emphasizes the distinctive role of the "what it is" in metaphysics and other sciences (1025b3–18). The other sciences (1) do not give an account of the "what it is" of their respective genera; instead, they each make clear by sensation a "what it is" or assume a "what it is," and then demonstrate its *per se* attributes (1025b10–13). Likewise, (2) these other sciences do not ask whether the genus they study exists because it belongs to the same thought (διανοίας) to show what it is (τί ἐστι) and if it is (εἰ ἔστιν) and because they do not show the former (1025b16–18). Since, in the lines that immediately precede these, Aristotle contrasts metaphysics with the other sciences by the universal scope of its subject matter, just as he did in book Γ, these two claims about the other sciences should express two additional contrasts.[3] They imply that metaphysics *does* give an account of the "what it is" of its subject and that it *does* ask of its subject if it is besides asking what it is. Since the subject of metaphysics is all beings (1025b3–10), this science should seek the "what it is" of being. To make clear the "what it is" of being amounts to expounding the nature or essence of being. Moreover, even if I were mistaken in taking (1) and (2) as intended contrasts, even if Aristotle intended these claims to hold for metaphysics as well as the other sciences, this text would still enjoin the metaphysician to make clear the "what it is" of his subject matter, the nature of being.

A second indication of Aristotle's concern with the nature of being is his assertion, a bit further in the chapter, that "it is necessary not to overlook how the essence and the formula exists,[4] since, without this, to inquire is to do nothing" (1025b28–29). He speaks here about the essences treated by physics; but the claim is even more true of metaphysics, which, unlike the other sciences, is able to give an account of an essence, as I just said. Again, for metaphysics to consider how the essence and formula of its subject matter exist is for it to consider the essence and nature of being. Third, concern with the essence and formula is evident in the injunction with which the first chapter closes: "and it belongs to this science to investigate in regard to being *qua* being both what it is (τί ἐστι) and what belongs to it *qua* being" (1026a31–32). This sentence parallels claims made in Γ (1003a31–32; 1003b15–19; 1005a13–18), but it contains what they lack, reference to the "what it is."

In sum, E 1 raises what the *Posterior Analytics* calls the "what is it" question (B 1, 89b24–25). Book Γ, on the other hand, aims only to show that there is a science that studies all beings and what belongs to them *qua being:* it examines only the "is it" question.[5] As we saw, Aristotle himself mentions these two questions in the opening lines of book E (1025b16–18).[6] Since a particular science assumes the "what it is" of its subject genus and since to know the latter "belongs to the same thought" as to know the "is it" of the subject, particular sciences must also assume the "is it." Aristotelian metaphysics, on the other hand, inquires into the nature of being. We should expect Aristotle also to inquire into the "is it" of the subject of metaphysics; but, in virtue of the contrast between metaphysics and the particular sciences, we need not expect metaphysics to treat them together. In fact, the *Metaphysics* relegates these questions to distinct books.

It is the examination of the "what is being" question that marks off the central books from the rest of the *Metaphysics*. After an introductory chapter that distinguishes metaphysics from other sciences partly on the ground that metaphysics must inquire into the nature of its subject matter, book E proceeds to inquire into the nature of being in its second chapter. Its first lines (E 2, 1027a33–b2) list the ways "being" is said under the same four heads that appear in Δ 7: accidental being, the true and the false, the categories, and the potential and actual. Aristotle treats accidental being in E 2–3, truth in E 4 and Θ 10, the categories in books Z–H, and actuality in book Θ 1–9. Book Z's interest in the question "what is being?" is well known. Early in the book, Aristotle reduces it to the question "what is *ousia?*" (1028b4; 1028b31–32), and he asserts the necessity of investigating "most of all, primarily and even exclusively about being of this sort [i.e., *ousia*], what is it?" (1028b6–7). Most of book Z is taken up with examining alternative answers. Although it is often overlooked, the discussions of other ways being is said exhibit a parallel interest in the "what is being" question. E 2 concludes with the remark that "what the accidental is . . . has been said" (1027a26–27; also 1026b24–26). Likewise, Aristotle's account of being as true examines the nature of truth, "for it is necessary to consider what (τί) we say this is" (1051b6). Aristotle explains truth for both composites (E 4, 1027b20–23; Θ 10, 1051b11–13) and incomposites (1052a1–2). Finally, in regard to actuality, Aristotle claims that his discussion makes clear its "what it is" (Θ 6, 1048b35–36). Since "being" is said in many ways, he must consider the "what is being" question for *each* way "being" is said. Thus, when he explains what truth is, Aristotle is giving an answer to the "what is being" question. The various examinations of this question in E–Θ constitute what I shall call the central books.

Is there anything in common to these four investigations of the "what is being" question? According to book Γ, being is *pros hen* (2, 1003a33–34). Thus, we would expect an account into the nature of being to explain how all beings are related to the primary being and to explain the nature of the primary being. Since we have what amounts to four inquiries into the nature of being, we would expect each of them to locate a primary being. Are there then four distinct primary beings? To anticipate the result of Aristotle's analysis, the being that emerges as primary in each of the four cases is *ousia*. Most discussions of the investigation into being focus on the inquiry into categorial being in Z–H and miss the significance of the other ways "being" is said. In order to understand Aristotle's view of the nature of being, we need to consider all the ways "being" is said. Z–H do constitute the most difficult and interesting portion of the discussion, and I shall devote much attention to them, but we still need to understand them in connection with the treatments of the other three ways of being.

Although the central books contain few references to the problem of the one and the many, my contention here is that Aristotle attacks the "what is being" problem by treating it as a particular kind of one-many problem. Not only is "being" said in many ways, but "one" is also said in many ways. So just as the "what is being" question turns into four questions, the problem of the one and the many quickly turns into many problems, and each of these has a variety of formulations. For most of Aristotle's predecessors the problem of the one and the many is the problem of whether all things are one or many. They all agree that each being is one, but they differ on whether there are many different types of being. As we will see, in the central books Aristotle focuses his attention on a different formulation of the problem: how can an individual being be one? He assumes that each being and each *ousia* is one. He then proceeds to determine the nature of being and of *ousia* by finding something that is itself one and that can account for the unity of each being and each *ousia*.

This broad sketch of the argument needs considerable elaboration. Let me note in advance that the doctrine of the central books that will emerge from my analysis does not differ very much from some traditional accounts. My discussion serves to defend traditional interpretations from the recent onslaught of alternatives. More important, though, focusing on Aristotle's use of the problem of the one and the many in the central books allows us to grasp the structure of the work and to understand its arguments.

1.2 THE THEORETICAL SCIENCES: E 1

After drawing the distinction between metaphysics and other sciences in the opening lines of E 1 (1025b3–18), Aristotle goes on to compare three theoretical sciences: physics, mathematics, and theology. His aim here is also to distinguish metaphysics from other sciences, but he devotes much of the discussion to showing that it, mathematics, and physics are each theoretical sciences.

The chapter provides two reasons to think that physics is a theoretical science. The first is simply that it is neither practical nor productive. It is not a productive science because its principles do not lie in the maker, nor is it a practical science because its principles do not lie in choice. Since these three are the only types of sciences, physics must be a theoretical science (1025b21-26). This text does not say where the principles of the objects of physics lie, but the *Physics* indicates that they lie in the things themselves: nature is an internal principle of motion and rest (B 1, 192b12-15). In the latter work, Aristotle goes on to argue that, although the physicist needs to investigate matter besides form, the principle is primarily the form (B 1-2; e.g., 193b3-5).

A second argument points to the formulae that physics treats. Definitions of the objects of physics are like the definition of snub: they cannot be separated from matter. The formulae of physical objects must include motion, and motion belongs to things that have matter (1026a2-3).[7] From this, Aristotle infers that physics must be a theoretical science (1025b26-1026a7). What is the argument? Physics is not a theoretical science because the formulae of its objects express motions; insofar as its objects are in motion there is some doubt whether physics is a science at all. Aristotle's point is that even though its objects are in motion, physics seeks to know their formulae. The assumption is that a theoretical science treats formulae and definitions, in contrast with practical and productive sciences which treat, respectively, actions and objects of art. Since the end of a theoretical science is knowledge (cf. A 2, 982b11-12, with 24-27), and since knowledge is a grasp of formulae of essences, theoretical sciences must be fundamentally concerned with formulae. Because the objects of physics are material composites, there could be some doubt that physics is a theoretical science. Accordingly, Aristotle's second argument explains how the physicist "seeks and defines the 'what it is'" (1026a4). Physics is a theoretical science because it aims at knowledge of formulae and essences.

Mathematics also treats formulae. Whether the formulae of mathematicals are separate from matter is unclear at this point (1026a8-9). However, mathematics treats its objects as if they were separate and immobile (1026a9-10). This is, I think, the basis for Aristotle's claim that mathematics is also a theoretical science (a7-8). The point is that mathematics, like physics, seeks to know formulae. If the inseparability of the formulae of physics from matter is not an objection to physics being a theoretical science, then the possible inseparability of mathematical formulae is even less of an objection to mathematics being a theoretical science; for mathematics, at least, treats its formulae as if they were separate. There should be no question that mathematics aims at knowledge of formulae.

Why does Aristotle devote so much attention to arguing that physics and mathematics are theoretical sciences? This material belongs in a discussion of metaphysics if the grounds for claiming that physics and mathematics are theoretical sciences are also grounds for claiming that metaphysics is a theoretical science and if these grounds show metaphysics to be the primary theoretical science. Is this the case?

The rest of E 1 (1026a10–32) examines the possibility of a third theoretical science, theology. Aristotle begins by raising the possibility that there might be something eternal, separate, and immobile (1026a10–11). If it exists, it will be treated by a theoretical science different from and prior to physics and mathematics (a10–13). It will be divine (a20–22) and the science of it will be a theology (a19) and a first philosophy (a29–30). All these claims are hypothetical; they begin with "if" (εἰ). In E 1 Aristotle never asserts the existence of eternal, immobile, and separate *ousiai*. (For him to do so would be inconsistent with his earlier indication that metaphysics must prove the existence and nature of its subject matter.) Here, Aristotle's point is only that *if* such *ousiai* do exist, they are prior and they—rather than physical *ousiai* or mathematicals—ought to be the subject of first philosophy (cf. 1026a27–29).

Why is the science of immobile, eternal, and separate *ousiai* a theoretical science and why is it prior to physics and mathematics? Aristotle's answer, as it appears in the manuscripts, is the following:

> If there is something that is eternal, immobile and separate, it is clear that knowledge of it belongs to a theoretical science, neither to physics (for physics concerns what moves)[8] nor to mathematics, but to a science prior to both. For physics concerns what is inseparable[9] but not immobile; some [branches] of mathematics treat what is immobile, though perhaps not separate but in matter. The first [theoretical science] treats things that are separate and immobile (1026a13–16).

The first sentence, obviously the conclusion of the passage, asserts that given the existence of a certain subject matter, the science of it is a theoretical science that is prior to mathematics and to physics (cf. 1026a18–22). To prove this, Aristotle characterizes the subject matter of this theoretical science, theology, and compares it with the subjects of the other two theoretical sciences. Just how does this characterization and comparison support the conclusion?

The immediate context of the text under discussion is Aristotle's arguments that mathematics and physics are theoretical sciences. Somehow, that these latter are theoretical sciences tells us that theology is also a theoretical science. As we saw, the reason that physics is a theoretical science is that it aims at knowledge of formulae and essences even though these essences do not exist apart from matter and even though what has them is in motion. Again, mathematics is a theoretical science despite its objects' not being separate from matter. That is to say, Aristotle has argued that physics is theoretical *even though* its essences are "neither inseparable nor immobile"[10] and that mathematics is theoretical *even though* its objects, which are immobile, are probably also inseparable. If the inseparability and mobility of these objects do not prevent them from falling under a theoretical science, then there is no reason to doubt that objects which do not have such defects, objects which are separate from matter and immobile also fall under theoretical science. It is obvious that the aim of a science of these objects is knowledge of their formulae and essences: here action or production is out of the question. What sense could it make to speak of the principles of what is eternal as possibly lying in a maker or a doer? Thus, Aristotle's characterization of physics and mathematics in 1026a13–15 is not a direct reason for concluding that theology is a theoretical science; it is a reason for dismissing doubts about theology's being theoretical. This accounts for the troubling word order in the manuscripts. I gloss the text as follows: theology is a theoretical science because physics, which concerns objects that are "neither inseparable nor immobile," is theoretical and because mathematics, whose objects, though they are immobile, are not separable but in matter, is also theoretical. *A fortiori*, theology is also a theoretical science.

As for the justification of priority, the reason that theology is a theoretical science is also a reason that it is prior to the other theoretical sciences. Because the objects of theology are more obviously objects of theoretical science than the objects of mathematics and physics, the science of theology should be prior to those other sciences. Moreover, the subject matter of theology is prior to that of the other theoretical sciences, for Aristotle assumes that the immobile is prior to the mobile and the separate prior to the inseparable.[11] In sum, Aristotle's distinction of theology from mathematics and physics, quoted above, justifies both theology's being a theoretical science and its being prior to the other theoretical sciences.

Is this science of what is immobile and separate the science of being *qua* being that Aristotle discusses at the beginning of E 1? The final portion of the chapter (1026a23–32) identifies both descriptions. However, at the beginning of this text, Aristotle raises the issue as an *aporia* about whether first philosophy is "universal or about some genus and some one nature" (a23–25). His answer presumes the priority of what is immobile. If there is no nonphysical *ousia*,

> physics will be the first science; but if there is some immobile *ousia*, this [science] is prior and [it is] first philosophy, and it is universal in this way because it is primary (1026a27–31).

In other words, there is nothing contradictory in a universal science that treats one genus or one nature. A science of immobile *ousiai* will treat things that are prior to, and apparently presupposed by, all other beings. It will be a universal science because it is a primary science.

How, though, do we know that the objects of the other sciences do presuppose immobile *ousiai?* E 1 does not answer this question, but we can surmise what Aristotle's answer would be at this point. Metaphysics is the science of all beings, of being simply (ἁπλῶς); and being, as we know from Γ, is *pros hen.* Other things are called beings by virtue of their relation to primary being. They depend on this primary being, and this latter, Aristotle now suggests, is immobile and separate being. A science which treats all things by treating one primary thing is consistent with Aristotle's claim that being is *pros hen,* for the primary object of a *pros hen* science is the one object to which the others are related.

Of course, all this is hypothetical. It remains to be shown that there is an *ousia* that is immobile and separate. While E 1 has stated how the treatment of such an *ousia* could be identified with the universal science of metaphysics, Aristotle still needs to prove that immobile *ousiai* do indeed exist and possess a character that is presupposed by all sensible *ousiai.* If he can somehow show that the nature of being is ultimately immobile *ousia,* then the objects of theology will possess in the highest degree a character that is shared by all things; namely, being. Accordingly, it is entirely appropriate to end E 1 with an injunction to investigate the nature and the attributes of being.

Though the first chapter of book E seems to be a major step, it does not advance the inquiry very far. W. D. Ross thinks that it resolves the third *aporia,* whether the same science treats all the *ousiai.* [12] But the obstacle to be overcome in that *aporia* is how to avoid a single science that demonstrates all the attributes of all *ousiai,* and E 1 does not discuss the attributes of *ousiai.* What this chapter does do is to inaugurate an inquiry into the nature of being. Further, it explains how the study of primary being can be the universal study of all beings. This is a lesson put into practice in the discussion of the four ways of being that constitutes the remainder of the central books. As I said earlier, in each case Aristotle seeks the primary being. E 1 justifies Aristotle's method of inquiring into the nature of being by seeking the primary being.

1.3   ACCIDENTAL BEING: E 2-3

1.3.1   E 2: *Knowledge of Accidents*

A central concern in the discussion of accidental being is to show that there is no science (or knowledge) of what is accidental (1026b3-4; 1026b25-26; 1027a27-28). A sign that accidents are unknowable is that no science considers accidents (1026b4-5). They do not belong to productive sciences because the maker of a house, for example, does not make the accidents along with the house; he could not because the accidents are indefinite in number (b6–10). Nor do the accidents belong to theoretical sciences because a geometer, for example, knows the essential attributes of triangles but not accidents like whether the triangle and the triangle whose angles equal two right angles differ (b10–14). Another argument against there being a science of what is accidental begins from the definition of accidental as what is neither always nor for the most part (1026b31–33). Science concerns what *is* always or for the most part (1027a20–21). Hence, there can be no science of the accidental (1027a27–28).

A puzzling feature of these arguments is that among the accidents that Aristotle mentions to illustrate his conclusion appear the difference or identity of triangle and triangle with angles that equal two right angles (1026b11–12) and of Coriscus and musical Coriscus (1026b16–18). The first of these is puzzling because the identity of triangle and triangle having angles equal to two right angles does not seem accidental: it always obtains. Probably Aristotle has in mind the identity of a particular composite and the geometrical triangle (cf. *An. Po.* A 1, 71a17–b8); this would be an accidental identity.[13] The second illustration, the identity of Coriscus and musical Coriscus, is puzzling because it seems to be the very same sort of identity that Γ 2 argues must be included in metaphysics, the identity of Socrates and sitting Socrates (1004b1–8). How can it be consistent to argue that the accidents must belong to metaphysics and then to turn around and deny that they can be known?[14] If they fall under a science, are they not knowable by that science? As we would expect of a text that takes these attributes to be knowable, book Γ refers to them as "proper attributes" (ἴδια πάθη—1004b11, b15–16); but E 2 treats them as accidents that do not belong to any science. Can the two discussions possibly be consistent?

A path of reconciliation may lie in making a distinction between attributes of individuals and attributes of genera or of being. In book Γ, Aristotle calls the identity of Socrates and sitting Socrates a "proper attribute" of being *qua* being, but in book E he denies that a similar identity is a knowable attribute of Socrates. (Analogously, I 9 declares that male and female are "proper attributes" of a genus [1058a37]. They are not proper attributes of individuals.) Socrates may or may not be sitting; so the identity of himself and himself sitting may or may not hold. Since the identity depends on Socrates' possessing an accident, the identity itself is an accident of Socrates. It is a matter of chance and thus unknowable. On the other hand, any being must be identical to the same being with its accidental attributes. Here, too, identity is an attribute, but here the identity is necessary. Of course, the two identities differ. The former is: Socrates = (Socrates + sitting); it depends on whether Socrates happens to be sitting. The latter is: Socrates = the Socrates (who is sitting), a necessary identity which can be known by metaphysics. There is no textual support for applying this distinction here, but it does afford a way to avoid inconsistency between E 2 and Γ. The former declares identity an accident because it conceives of the identity that belongs to individuals. Such identities would not belong to the investigation envisioned in book Γ of identity as a proper attribute of being *qua* being; that discussion of identity probably appears in book I. In contrast, E 2–3 treat identities as accidental beings, one of the ways of being. These latter fall under metaphysics not because they are necessary attributes, as the former identities are, but because they are beings.

An even simpler way of reconciling E 2 with book Γ lies in understanding the identity of Coriscus and musical Coriscus that Aristotle mentions in E 2 as the same sort of accidental identity as that between triangle and triangle with angles equal to two right angles. That is, the former may be an identity between a particular individual (Coriscus) and a type of nature, the musical: is this particular person the musical Coriscus? A reason for thinking that Aristotle has questions of this kind in mind is that he mentions the Coriscus identity in the same breadth as the identity between the musical (man) and the grammatical (man) (1026b16–18), and the latter identity does depend on finding a particular individual in which they both inhere (cf. Δ 7, 1017a13–18). The identity of Coriscus and musical Coriscus resembles the identity of musical and grammatical in that both depend on inherence in a substrate. Further, Aristotle compares the absence of such an inherence to not-being (1026b21; 1017a18–19). The accidents at issue in E 2 are those that depend on a particular substrate. Again, they seem to differ from those that Γ 2 insists must be included in metaphysics.

The problem with both of these attempts at reconciling Γ and E 2 is that the two texts declare the identities to be those that troubled the sophists (1026b15–16; 1004b22–26). How, then, can Aristotle insist in one place that these identities fall under metaphysics and yet deny that they can be known? One approach to this question is to distinguish between treating the accidents and knowing the accidents. The passage from Γ only insists that they be treated by metaphysics. This treatment occurs in book E, and it shows them to be unknowable.

This distinction resolves the problem, but it points to another, more troubling puzzle: how can a treatment of the accidents prove that they are unknowable? Do we not need to know what the accidents are before we can know that they are unknowable? E 2 attempts to define the nature of what has no nature, and to find the cause of something that cannot be known through its cause. The very idea of a treatment of accidents that shows their unknowability seems contradictory.

That Aristotle intends E 2 to provide the nature of the accidental is clear from the last line of the chapter.

What the accidental is, through what cause it is, and that there is no knowledge of it has been stated (1027a26–28).

The "what it is" or nature of the accidental to which this passage refers is that an accident is what occurs neither always nor for the most part (1026b31-33). The cause indicated here is matter which is capable of being other than it usually is (1027a13-15). Does this knowledge of the nature of accidents belie the claim that they are unknowable? According to Aquinas, E 2 describes the nature of the accidental but does not provide knowledge of any particular accidents much in the way that *Physics* Γ explains the nature of the infinite even though it cannot be known.[15] Unfortunately, the similarities between the two cases do not explain either one. We still need to ask, why is the nature of the accidental not the nature of particular accidents? Why do we still lack knowledge of accidents even when we know what it is to be an accident? Let me propose that the answer to these questions lies in the negative character of the accidents. An accident is what does *not* occur always or for the most part. It is a kind of privation; it is an indeterminate negation. All that we can know about the nature of an accident is what it is not, and we cannot even determine precisely the character of this negation. The nature of the accidental is not like the nature of a horse. Rather, as Aristotle explains, an accident is like non-being. Because it is indeterminate, it is not properly knowable.

As mentioned, Aristotle's treatment of accidents in E 2 consists largely of showing that, because of what they are, accidents are unknowable. How does this discussion contribute to his overall inquiry into being? What I want to propose here is that Aristotle's aim here is to show the dependence of the accidents on *ousia*. It will help my case to continue with a discussion of E 3.

1.3.2 E 3: Causes of Accidents

The biggest puzzle about E 3 is why it has been included in the text at all. The discussion of accidental being seems to be complete when E 2 describes its nature and its cause. The next chapter seems at first to be an afterthought. It addresses the question why everything that happens does not occur of necessity; that is, the question why accidents exist. Aristotle argues that to avoid the conclusion that everything happens of necessity we need to recognize the existence of causes whose generation is not caused by something else. What occurs accidentally depends on some principle which does not in turn lead to another principle:

> Accordingly, it is clear that [the causal process] goes back to some principle [beginning], and this no longer goes back to something else. This principle will be the cause of the fortuitous, but nothing else will be the cause of its coming to be (1027b11-14).

These first principles of accidents are generated or destroyed without being in the process of coming to be or being destroyed (1027a29-30). E 3 does not indicate what the first principles are; the chapter ends only with the injunction to investigate "into what sort of principle and what sort of cause this 'leading back' [ἀναγωγή] is, whether it is into a matter, final cause, or moving cause" (1027b14–16).

Why should the existence of a first cause be the mark of accidental being? Does this mean that nonaccidental beings do not have a first cause? It cannot if this passage is consistent with other portions of the corpus, for Aristotle argues at some length in α 2 that there cannot be an infinite sequence of causes. What, then, distinguishes accidents from non-accidents? Because it is consistent with common views of accidents and because alternatives are hard to conceive, it is tempting to accept Richard Sorabji's contention that accidents are uncaused.[16] This would provide a clear-cut distinction between accidents and events that are necessary. The objection to this position is that it has no real support in the text. Aristotle does not, after all, say that accidents have *no* principles or causes. Quite the contrary, he emphasizes the importance of tracing the accident to its causes. The closing injunction to seek the principles of the accident would make no sense at all if Sorabji were right. Likewise, the opening sentence asserts the existence of causes that are not in the process of being generated or being destroyed (1027a29–30): these are the causes of accidents. Sorabji thinks that the ultimate cause of the accidental is an uncaused accident; but, for reasons that will be clear soon, I think this is a mistake.

What sort of cause does an accident have? Aristotle declares that its cause must be accidental (1027a7–8). This does not mean that its cause is another accident: to be accidental is not necessarily to be an accident. Were accidents always caused by other accidents, we would face the possibility of an infinite sequence of causes. Rather, a cause is accidental if it does not always or for the most part produce its effect. The cause of my meeting my creditor in the marketplace may be my going to the marketplace for the sake of purchasing food. The cause of this meeting is a final cause, purchasing food, only it has gone awry.[17] The result is different from what usually occurs (cf. *Phys.* B 5, 196b29–197a6). Purchasing food does not ordinarily lead to encounters with creditors. This cause may or may not lead to this effect. An accidental cause is only tenuously connected with what it brings about. That this is what Aristotle means when he calls the cause of an accident accidental follows from the inferences he draws from this claim, "to accidental results, there corresponds no determinate art or faculty" (1027a6–7, Oxford trans.), and also from his characterization of an accident as what is neither always nor for the most part but sometimes. A cause is accidental if it brings about an effect sometimes but not always or usually.

An important point made in E 3 is that something becomes or ceases to be an accidental cause without being in the processes of becoming or of ceasing to be an accidental cause. Accidental causes are nontemporal. Aristotle's argument for this claim is a *reductio* that runs nearly the whole length of the chapter.[18] That there are principles which are nontemporal must be true, he argues. "For if it were not, all things will be from necessity" (1027a30–31). In other words, Aristotle assumes that (1) everything which is a cause or a principle comes to be such or ceases to be such through a process, and he then proves the presumably absurd conclusion that everything is of necessity. In addition to the premise that he assumes for the purpose of refuting, Aristotle also assumes that (2) whatever is in the process of coming to be or ceasing to be "must have some nonaccidental cause" (1027a31–32). Aristotle does not support this latter assumption, and its resemblance to the conclusion may raise some eyebrows. Since it is crucial to the argument, let us assume for now that it is true and return to it later. Aristotle begins with some event in the present, and asks whether it exists (1027a32–33). It does if something else exists, he answers, referring to its cause (1027b33). And this cause exists if something else exists. Both assumptions come into play here: if the first event exists, it must have come to be through a process (assumption 1); this event must have some nonaccidental cause (assumption 2). Further, this cause comes to be through a process; so it, too, has a nonaccidental cause, and so on. If we start from some determinate amount of past time and subtract time intervals from it, we will eventually come to the present. For example, someone eats spicy food, he gets thirsty, goes to the well, and so forth. Each event occurs in time, each causes the next, and eventually we get to the present. Because each event necessarily causes the next, and because each is in time, after some finite period of time, we eventually arrive at the present. Since each event has been caused by what precedes, the present is necessary. So the person who dies a violent death at the well had to have died in this way; and, by the parallel reasoning, past and future are determined as well. All will be of necessity (1027a34–b10). This is absurd. Hence, the first assumption is wrong: there must be some causes that come to be and cease being without being in the process of coming to be or of ceasing to be. This, the claim made in the very first lines of the chapter (1027a29–30), is, I think, what Aristotle intends to assert when he draws the conclusion of the argument at 1027b11–14, a passage quoted earlier. But he states the conclusion in terms slightly different from those he uses at the beginning. He says in the conclusion that the cause of what is fortuitous does not have another principle; it "has no other cause of its coming to be." It has no other cause of its coming to be because it is not in the process of coming to be; it just is or is not. Aristotle's point here is not that the cause of an accident is uncaused but that it is ungenerated, that is, that it does not become a cause through a process of generation. So this conclusion does make the same point as the first line. If this interpretation is correct, E 3 does not argue against determinism. It assumes that determinism is false and infers, from this, that there are causes that are not in the process of becoming or ceasing to be.

Is there any support for Aristotle's second premise? A process of generation or destruction is a physical process. Its causes are physical, and it occurs
in a determinate way. Dropping a tea kettle full of boiling water on my foot
may be accidental, but the way the kettle falls, the spilling of water from the
upside down vessel, and the burning of my foot are all processes that occur
not accidentally, but in accordance with nature. The second premise asserts
only the uniform operation of physical causes, a claim Aristotle accepts even
though he rejects determinism. E 3 explains how it is possible to avoid determinism while accepting the uniformity of nature. There must be causes
which are not in the process of becoming. Since they do not themselves come
to be or cease to be, such causes do not require other causes. They can serve
as the end of a sequence of causes. To return to an earlier example, my
encounter with my creditor was caused by my going to the marketplace and
this latter was, in turn, caused, let us say, by my seeking food for a dinner
party. The dinner party is the cause of my going to the market. It is not an
accidental cause of the trip because it does typically bring about a trip to the
market and because it comes to be a cause. The dinner party was contem-
plated, decided upon, and planned. Its causing the trip does occur over time.
In contrast, the dinner party does not ordinarily bring about an encounter
with a creditor, and the dinner party becomes the cause of this encounter not
over a period of time but all at once, at the instant the encounter occurs. It
becomes a cause without being in the process of becoming a cause.

The foregoing explains E 3's treatment of the causes of accidents, but it
suggests another problem: E 2 also describes the cause of accidents; it declares that matter is their cause. Why does Aristotle provide two discussions
of the cause of accidents? Are the two treatments consistent? Matter is the
cause of accidents in the sense that in order for there to be accidents, there
must be matter; and this is what E 2 means when it calls matter the cause of
accidents. On the other hand, we can still ask what causes matter to assume
the accidental form that it has. The answer could be another form (acting as
efficient or final cause) or, of course, the privations of these forms; and the
matter itself is the material cause of this transformation. So any or all of the
three types of cause could be given as the cause of an accident. At the very
end of E 3, Aristotle raises and leaves open this question about the causes of
an accident (1027b14–16). It is not our text that is incomplete. Rather, one
reason he leaves the question open is that accidents are indeterminate. Some
accidents have one type of cause; other accidents have another type of cause.
Some accidents have all three causes. Each case differs. We need to look for
the particular first cause of each accident by itself.

Indefiniteness (or infinity—ἄπειρον) is an important aspect of individual
accidents and of the totality of accidents (1026b7).[19] Although Aristotle accounts for the possibility of accidental causes by arguing that some causes
must be nontemporal, he could also have accounted for this possibility by

referring to the numeric plurality of accidental causes. One reason that my encounter with my creditor is accidental is that it has at least two causes: the decisions each of us made to go to the market. This plurality of causes makes an accident possible. The encounter belongs to neither of us by nature, nor is it an expected result of either decision. It results from the interaction of the two actions. Most interactions between natures are not *per se* attributes of either nature, but indeterminate consequences of the one nature impinging on the other. A plurality of things, each governed by its own nature, would interact in an indefinite number of ways: these interactions are the accidental beings. The plurality of causes even explains why an individual composite like pale man is an accidental being: a pale man has at least two causes, the nature of man and the absence of sunlight. Matter is necessary for accidents; it is one cause. The accident must, though, have some other cause. The idea that accidents are uncaused is a mistake: one reason that accidents are possible is that some things have a plurality of causes. However, it is not the plurality of causes that Aristotle chooses to emphasize in E 3. Instead, he emphasizes the non-temporality of accidental causes.

With this discussion we can return to a question raised earlier, how does Aristotle's treatment of accidents contribute to his inquiry into the nature of being? From what we have seen in E 1, we would expect Aristotle to describe the nature of accidents, and this is what we saw him doing in E 2. We also saw that an adequate account of accidents is impossible because they are unknowable. I suggest that E 3's injunction to trace the cause of accidents to first principles stands in lieu of complete knowledge of the nature of accidents. Ordinarily, knowing the nature of a thing involves knowing that upon which it depends (Γ 2, 1003b16–17): to know a thing is to know its cause (α 2, 994b29–30). It is for this reason that the subsequent inquiries into the other ways that "being" is said seek a primary being. In these cases, the primary being is both the cause of being and the nature of being. Aristotle's treatment of accidental being separates what is normally a single inquiry into two parts. E 2 describes the nature of accidents, only this nature is unknowable and not properly a nature at all. Because the "nature" that E 2 ascribes to accidents is not their cause, a distinct inquiry into the causes of accidents is necessary. E 2 begins this inquiry by discussing matter, but mainly it is E 3 that undertakes the inquiry.[20] Unfortunately, though, the text of E 3 does not arrive at any conclusions about what the causes of accidents are. As mentioned, one reason it is inconclusive is probably that each case differs.

Another, and more important, reason is that a complete determination of the causes of accidents waits upon the treatment of *ousia*. In other words, I propose that the cause of accidents which Aristotle seeks at the end of E 3 is *ousia*. If this interpretation seems implausible, it is because of the widespread assumption that an accidental cause is an accident that is a cause.[21] What Aristotle claims, however, is that the causes of accidents are accidental

(1027a7-8), that these causes are ungenerated (1027a29-30), and that accidents are ungenerated (1026a22-24). To be sure, all this is consistent with
the view that an accident is a cause, but it is also consistent with other
causes. A cause is accidental not because it is an accident, but because of its
tenuous connection with what it causes; eating spicy food, in Aristotle's
example, is an accidental cause of violent death because it does not usually
result in violent death. It becomes an accidental cause at the instant the death
occurs; it is never in the process of becoming an accidental cause. In short,
eating spicy food is not an accidental cause because it is an accident or an
uncaused accident, but because it causes without being in the process of
causing. There are several accidental causes of this violent death besides
eating spicy food. One of them is the nature of the person who dies. He could
not suffer a violent death unless he had the nature he has, and this nature
does not ordinarily bring about a violent death. The nature is never in the
process of bringing about the violent death; it becomes an accidental cause
instantaneously when the death occurs. Thus, even in Aristotle's own example, an *ousia* is an accidental cause, a material accidental cause. The perpe-
trator of the crime is also an *ousia,* and he too may be an accidental cause
(e.g., in a case where the victim was mistaken for someone else), an efficient
accidental cause. *Ousia* could also be a final accidental cause. The only type
of accidental cause *ousia* could not be is formal, and just this one is absent
from Aristotle's suggestions for accidental causes at the end of E 3
(1027b14-16), an indication that he has *ousia* in mind.

It is obvious that an *ousia* is a constituent of all accidental beings, for an
accidental being is a kind of conjunction of attributes or of attribute and
ousia, and there can be no attribute without an *ousia* in which it inheres (cf.
Δ 7, 1017a13-18). The causes of any accident must always include some
ousia (cf. I 9, 1058b18-24). Also the agent by which an accident comes to
be must be an *ousia.* He had argued in the *Physics* that chance and fortune
presuppose some intelligence or nature (B 6, 198a9-13). In either case, an
ousia is the causal agent; and it can cause accidents not only through its
presence but also through its absence (*Phys.* B 3, 195a11-14). Furthermore,
given the aim of his inquiry into being, Aristotle needs to trace accidents to
ousiai in some way, for only if *ousia* is the cause of accidental being can he
show that it is primary among *all* the ways of being. His claim that being is
pros hen requires that even accidental beings be related to some *ousia.* There
may be a hint of the significance of *ousia* implicit in Aristotle's comparison
of accidents to non-being (1026b21). In Γ 2 he had declared that a non-being
is a kind of being because it is related to primary being, *ousia* (1003b10).
Insofar as they are similar to non-being, accidents should also be related to
primary being (cf. Δ 7, 1017a18-19).

If, though, Aristotle's aim in E 3 is to suggest that a cause of accidents
must be an *ousia,* why does he not say so directly? One possibility is that he

wishes to wait until his investigation of *ousia* in the next books. Against this it may be objected that the priority of *ousia* is so fundamental for Aristotle that it is hard to imagine him setting it aside. Perhaps, however, it is just because the priority of *ousia* is so fundamental that Aristotle need not mention *ousia* in E 3. Perhaps he thought it would be obvious to his listeners that *ousia* is the cause of accidents that he seeks.

Another problem is that there are no later texts that investigate the causes of accidents in the way that E 3 enjoins. This is a problem for any interpretation of E 3, but it is less disturbing if Aristotle's aim is to point to the priority of *ousia* because this priority emerges clearly from the subsequent investigation of *ousia*. In Z 1 Aristotle argues for the priority of *ousia* to other categories, and in Z 4 he argues that the formulae of composites of accidental attributes and *ousiai* contain the formula of *ousia*. Z 9 shows that the matter and form of these composites must exist prior to the generation of the composite (though the form need only exist potentially), and *ousia* is the matter of accidental composites. The agent who causes the accident is also an *ousia* in whose mind the form of the accidental composite exists. In short, the investigation of the causes of accidental beings does occur implicitly in book Z.

This solution points to yet another problem: how can Z 4's assertion of formulae and essences of accidents be consistent with E 2's denial that accidents are knowable? Insofar as accidents and accidental composites have formulae and essences, they are knowable. What, then, are we to make of the arguments that accidental beings are not knowable? Aristotle's characterizations of accidental beings seem inconsistent. Someone might try to avoid inconsistency by pointing out that accidents do not have essences in the proper sense; at best, they have secondary essences. So they remain unknowable in one respect even if they are knowable in another. This response will not do, for the arguments of E 2 show the impossibility of any knowledge of accidents. Let me propose a different way to save Aristotle from inconsistency. E 2 shows that there cannot be any demonstrative knowledge of accidents. We cannot demonstrate that an accident belongs to a nature. We can give an essential formula of an accidental being, for example, a musical carpenter, but a particular musical carpenter is a fluke that does not fall under any branch of knowledge because there is no nature of which it is a *per se* attribute. There is no unity between being musical and being a carpenter; the two are simply conjoined in an accident. Neither follows from the other or from the nature of man. The kind of knowledge of accidents that E 2 rejects is knowledge of them as attributes of natures, and the reason they are unknowable is that there is no way to determine from the character of the nature what accidents it may have, for the number of possible accidents is indefinite.

Book Z shows that accidents depend on sensible *ousiai*. Because Aristotle claims that the cause of accidents is ungenerated (E 3, 1027a29–30), someone could wonder whether the unmoved mover were not the principle of accidents (cf. 2, 1027a17–19).[22] An unmoved mover is the indirect cause of the accidents because it is the cause of the sensible *ousiai* that cause them, but its direct agency could not bring about accidents. For it is always the same and accidents are *not* always or for the most part. It is not even the cause in the sense that its absence brings about the accident: this type of causality can be ascribed only to something that *could* be an agent. On the other hand, since both matter and form of sensible *ousiai* are ungenerated (as Aristotle argues in Z 8—1033a28–b19), sensible *ousia* in either of these two senses meets Aristotle's requirement that the first cause of accidents be ungenerated. Thus, *ousiai* are ungenerated causes not only in the sense that they become causes of accidents instantaneously but also in the sense that as matter or as form, they are themselves ungenerated. This provides further support for my interpretation of E 3.

The treatment of accidental being in E 2–3 does not refer explicitly to the problem of the one and the many. The only hint of the problem lies in Aristotle's claim that the number of accidents of a thing is indefinite or infinite (ἄπειρον) (1026b7). Because the accidents of a thing are infinite, they cannot be known even by the person who knows how to make the thing. The assumptions are that there is no knowledge of an infinity (see α 2, 994b21–23), and that no one can deliberately produce an infinite number of products. Although this is the only unity argument in E 2–3, Aristotle could have advanced others. It is clear, for example, that no individual accident can be known because it, by itself, is a kind of plurality. The characterization of accidental beings in Δ 7 shows them as mere conjunctions, such as the musical grammatical (1017a7–22, esp. a19–22). Since they lack unity, and since unity is a principle of knowledge (B 4, 999a28–29), they cannot be known.[23] Perhaps the reason that Aristotle does not advance this argument is that he will argue in Z 4 that, despite their plurality, accidental beings have a kind of unity and thus can be known through their formulae though not demonstratively (a discussion to which I referred earlier in this section). To argue in terms of unity would introduce still more confusion into what is already a difficult subject.

Aristotle could also have advanced unity arguments in E 3. As I suggested, the possibility of accidents rests on the existence of a plurality of individual natures each acting in accordance with its own nature. Accidents arise from the interactions of these natures, interactions that cannot be derived from the individual natures by Aristotelian science. This path of argumentation would, though, lead Aristotle into a discussion of *ousia,* a topic he reserves for later. The argument for the possibility of accidents that appears in the text points only to the peculiar nontemporal nature of accidental causes.

In sum, considerations about the unity of accidents and their causes could have played a prominent role in Aristotle's treatment of accidental being.

Aristotle may have avoided them here in discussing a topic whose significance to the investigation of being is slight in order to avoid confusion with his discussions of other ways of being, discussions where such unity considerations are, I shall argue, central.

Metaphysics E concludes with a chapter on truth. Since Aristotle considers this way of being again in more detail at the end of book Θ, I shall defer my discussion of E 4 until later (3.3).

Chapter 2

Categorial Being: Z–H

Books Z–H constitute an extended treatment of categorial being, one of the four ways that "being" is said. For reasons that become clear in Z 1, Aristotle's chief concern is the question "What is *ousia?*" The analysis is tortuously complex and many of its details are controversial. It is best to begin my discussion by pointing out some structural features of the text that are widely acknowledged. First, Aristotle lists four candidates for *ousia* at the beginning of Z 3 and most of the rest of the book consists of an examination of their merits. He treats the substrate in Z 3, essence (τὸ τί ἦν εἶναι) in Z 4–11 (and in Z 12, as I shall argue in 2.8), and the genus together with the universal in Z 13–16. In Z 17 Aristotle takes a new approach to the problem by assuming that *ousia* is a cause. Book H treats another candidate for *ousia,* the composite.[1] It is generally recognized that Aristotle regards essence as the most successful candidate and that in the course of Z–H he identifies it with form and with actuality.

Whether Aristotle succeeds in giving a consistent and coherent account of *ousia* is a matter of disagreement. An objection raised often is that he maintains that essence is *ousia* and that the many instances of a species have the same essence, but denies that *ousia* is universal.[2] A variety of expedients have been proposed to avoid the apparent inconsistency in these claims. Although it is not apparent from its formulation, the problem of how to avoid a contradiction is a version of the problem of the one and the many. Despite the importance of the latter in the central books, this particular version is not one that Aristotle addresses here. Accordingly, I shall defer discussion of it until later (chapter 4). After examining the details of the text, we will be in a better position to consider it.

Although my concern here is the role of the problem of the one and the many, this problem, in its various manifestations, is so significant in Z–H that the following discussion will examine most of the text of these two books. In order to evaluate candidates for *ousia,* Aristotle clearly needs some criteria. Though there are other criteria, I shall show that the unity of *ousia* plays an important role in Aristotle's argumentation. I argue that Aristotle determines the nature of *ousia* by determining what has the unity possessed by *ousiai* and what can cause unity in a composite. To show that substrate, genus, and universal are not *ousiai,* Aristotle shows that they are not one in pertinent ways. On the other hand, most of the complex analysis of essence in Z 4–12 centers on showing that, despite appearances, essence is one. The rest of Z–H explains how essence can be one and also be the cause of unity in the composite. As we will see, the attempt to account for unity leads Aristotle to identify essence as form and actuality. All this serves to determine the nature of categorial being and, thereby, to advance the treatment of the nature of being begun in E. In short, Aristotle justifies his characteristic doctrines about *ousia* by showing that they enable *ousia* to fulfill assumed unity conditions. The analysis that follows is lengthy and complex, but it is able to make more sense of the details of the text than any other interpretation of which I am aware. The key idea throughout is that whatever else *ousia* may be, it must also be one.

2.1 Z 1: THE PRIMACY OF OUSIA

Book Z begins with the claim that "being" is said in many ways (1028a10). It justifies this by referring to an earlier discussion (apparently Δ 7) and by noting that being signifies "the what is and this something, quality, quantity, and each of the other things that are predicated in this way" (a10–13). At first glance, it looks as if Aristotle means to say that the categories constitute the plurality of ways that "being" is said. But Δ 7's presentation of the ways that "being" is said mentions the categories collectively as one of the ways "being" is said in contrast with three other ways (one accidental and two *per se*). Z 1 is either listing only some of the ways that "being" is said, or, more likely, the "being" that it describes as said in many ways is categorial being. Whichever is correct, its opening lines signal Aristotle's intention to focus on categorial being.

Immediately following these remarks, Aristotle states what I think is the thesis of the first chapter.

> Since being is said in these many ways, it is clear that primary being is the "what it is," the very thing which signifies *ousia* (1028a13–15).

He makes nearly the same claim later at 1028a30–31. The rest of the chapter adduces arguments to explain why and how *ousia* is primary. It is clear from these arguments that Aristotle means to assert merely that *ousia* is primary among categorial beings. Only after he considers the other ways of being will he be entitled to assert the primacy of *ousia* absolutely.

The first bit of support Aristotle offers for the primacy of *ousia* is the claim that whenever we ask "what sort [of thing is this]?" we answer by saying "good" or "bad" but not "three cubits" or "man"; and whenever we ask "what is it?" of something, we do not answer "white" or "hot" or "three cubits," but "man" or "god" (1028a15–17). This claim should be an argument because it follows the assertion of the primacy of *ousia* in a14–15 and begins with "for" (γάρ—a15).[3] But what is the reasoning? It seems to be: since we answer a "what is it" question by giving an *ousia* (like man or god), *ousia* is the "what it is."

This scarcely seems correct. For we also ask, "what is good?" "what is three-feet?" and so forth. These "what is it" questions are not usually answered by an instance of the category of *ousia*.[4] But neither red, three-feet, nor any other instance of a category other than *ousia* occurs without an *ousia*. The *ousia* in which these inhere is properly the "what," in contrast with the "how much," the "what sort," and so forth. So whenever we ask "what is it?" about something we encounter in nature, the proper answer is an instance of the category of *ousia*. The other categories are answers that we would make to other questions about what we encounter in nature. We could ask the "what is it" question of an attribute, but to do so we would need to somehow separate it from its *ousia*. Aristotle's point is that the attribute does not exist apart from an *ousia*. It is always an attribute *of something,* and when we explain the nature of the attribute we need to mention that it can only exist in some *ousia*. Since red, for example, is a color of something, its inherence in an *ousia* belongs to its nature. Thus, even attempts to ask the "what is it" question of separated attributes only confirm the point of the argument, that *ousia* is the primary being. This point is expressed in the very next sentence:

> The others are called "beings" by being quantities, qualities, affections, etc. of what is in this way [i.e., *ousia*] (1028a17–20).

A very interesting claim. It expresses the doctrine of the *Categories* that everything else is present in or said of *ousia* (5, 2a34–35). At the same time, it asserts Γ's *pros hen* doctrine of being, that other things are said to be in virtue of their relation to primary being.

The claim that all beings are *ousiai* or attributes of *ousiai* raises a question about actions like walking, being healthy, and sitting (1028a20–22). Are they beings or not?

> Therefore someone might be in *aporia* whether walking, being healthy, and sitting are each beings or not beings, and the same problem pertains to others like them. For none of these is either *per se* by nature[5] or able to be separated from *ousia*, but rather if anything is a being, it is the walker, the sitter and the one who is healthy. These latter are more beings because there is a determinate substrate for them; this is the individual *ousia*, the very thing that appears in such a categorial predication (τῇ κατηγορίᾳ). For neither "good" nor "sitter" is said without this. Accordingly, it is clear that each of these exists through this [i.e.,

ousia]; so that *ousia* is the primary being; it is not some being but simple (ἁπλῶς) being (1028a20–31).

The *aporia*, as usually understood, is whether walking, being healthy, and so forth are really beings at all if they are merely attributes of *ousia*.[6] They are neither *per se* nor separable from *ousia*. To walk does not exist by itself. There is always something that walks. Consequently, the walker has a better claim to be called a being than walking because he or she is some determinate substrate, an *ousia*. This *ousia* "appears" whenever the verb "walk" is predicated. (For the verb is always equivalent to a participle [see also Δ 7, 1017a27–30].) So, walking and other categorial predicates are beings through *ousia*. They exist only insofar as they inhere in some *ousia*. *Ousia* is primary and unqualified (or simple) being.

This equation of *ousia* with simple being (ὄν ἁπλῶς) in contrast with particular being (τὶ ὄν) amounts to the identification of the subject matter of metaphysics as *ousia*.[7] In E 1 Aristotle describes the subject matter of metaphysics as simple being and as being *qua* being (1025b7–10). Since the present passage identifies simple being and *ousia*, we are justified in equating all three, simple being, being *qua* being, and *ousia*. This identification is reflected in the claim with which Z 1 closes, that the inquiry into what being is (i.e., into the nature of being) reduces to an inquiry into the nature of *ousia* (1028b4, 6–7). The science of being *qua* being is thus the science of *ousia*.

In the remaining portion of the first chapter (1028a31–b2), the portion that precedes Aristotle's assertion of the reduction of the inquiry into being to an inquiry into *ousia*, Aristotle describes ways in which *ousia* is prior to the other categories. *Ousia* is primary in all ways: it is primary in time (apparently) because it alone of the categories can exist separately; it is primary in formula because its formula is contained in all the other formulae; and it is primary in knowledge because we know each thing when we know the "what it is" of the thing (1028a31–b2).

A problem with this discussion is that the three kinds of priority mentioned here do not correspond very well to the ways that "prior" is said sketched in Δ 11.[8] There are no indications in Z 1 about the significance of these three kinds of priority.[9] It is helpful to recall that the priority of *ousia* to other beings has been Aristotle's theme throughout the first chapter. The description of the three types of priority at 1028a31–b2 further supports the identification of *ousia* as simple being (1028a30–31; 1028b4).

Aristotle does not describe the three types of priority in terms of unity, but two of them can be understood as instances of the priority of a one to a many. *Ousia* is prior in formula because "it is necessary that the formula of the *ousia* be present in the formula of each thing" (1028a35–36). This is a case of the priority of a constituent or element to that of which it is an element (cf. Δ 3, 1014b14–15; 25, 1023b22–24). Insofar as the formula of *ousia* is a constituent of other formulae it is more of a unity than they are. It is prior to them because unity is prior to plurality.

Likewise, priority in knowledge is also a kind of priority by virtue of unity, but this is a bit more difficult to see. *Ousia* is prior in knowledge, Aristotle claims, because

> we think we know most of all whenever we know what is the man or what is the fire, more so than [when we know] the quantity, the quality, or the place [of the man or the fire], since we know each of these also whenever we know what is quantity or what is quality (1028a36–b2).

Clearly, this passage can only justify the priority of *ousia* if to know the "what it is" of a thing is to know its *ousia*. Aristotle means to say that *ousia* is prior because when we know something we know its *ousia*. Even so the argument seems to rely on equivocation: Aristotle argues for the priority of the *ousia* of a thing but infers the priority of the category of *ousia*.[10] For the argument supports the priority of *ousia* by pointing to the priority of the essence (or *ousia*) of quantity. Yet, this objection misconstrues the argument. Aristotle does not say that the essence of quantity is prior to the quantity or that we know the former *before* the latter. He claims that we know the essence or *ousia* of quantity *just when* we know the quantity. To know a quantity, or an instance of any other category, is just to know its "what it is" or its *ousia*. How does this show the priority of the category of *ousia*, the "what it is"? Aristotle's point here is that the "what is it" question is always prior in knowledge to the "how much" question, the "what sort" question, and so forth, because it is what we ask when we wish to know a thing. Answering another question does not give us knowledge of what the thing is; it can only tell us what character it has. An indication that the "what is it" question is what we ask when we wish to know something is that when we wish to know a quantity or quality or other category, we ask, "what is the quantity?" and so forth. How, though, do we get from the claim that we know a "what it is" when we have knowledge to the priority of the category of *ousia*? Since the formula is the definition of the thing's essence (Δ 8, 1017b21–22), we know the thing when we grasp its formula. We already know from the last argument that formulae of the other categories contain the formula of *ousia*. Consequently, to know the "what it is" we must know what an *ousia* is, and knowing *ousia* is prior to the knowledge of the other categories. *Ousia* is prior in knowledge because it is a constituent of the knowledge of other categories. Thus, *ousia* is prior in knowledge for the same reason that it is prior in formula. Knowledge of *ousia* is prior in knowledge because it is more of a unity than the knowledge of something of which it is a constituent.

The notion that *ousia* is somehow contained in the formulae and in the knowledge of the other categories certainly seems to be at odds with the distinct categorial genera that Aristotle describes in his *Categories*. More needs to be said about this puzzle; I shall return to it later. Even apart from this issue, Aristotle should say more here to justify ascribing both types of priority to *ousia*. On what basis does Aristotle assume that *ousia* is a constituent in the formulae of the other categories? Later on we will see that Z 4 provides some support for this assumption (1030a17–32) and for the assertion that knowledge of *ousia* is a constituent of other knowledge (2.4.4).

The remaining type of priority, priority in time, is the most difficult on any interpretation. Aristotle seems to think that *ousia* is prior in time because it is more separate (or, perhaps, more separable) than the other categories (1028a33–34). What does he mean by calling *ousia* separate, and what does this character have to do with *ousia*'s temporal priority? The discussion of temporal priority in Δ 11 does not mention anything about separation (1018b14–19). How could separation justify temporal priority? Let me start with the meaning of separation in this passage. First, separation should have the same sense here as it does earlier in Z 1 in the claim, "none of the others are able to be separate from *ousia*" (1028a23–24). The other categories cannot be separate because they inhere in *ousia*. It is also plausible to think that the priority that Aristotle ascribes to *ousia* because of its separation at 1028a32–34 has something to do with inherence because the other two types of priority mentioned here do not concern the physical status of *ousia*. That is, since Aristotle is about to refer to the priority of *ousia* in respect of formula and knowledge, we would expect him to say at this point that *ousia* is prior because the other categories inhere in it.[11] What he says is that *ousia* is prior (in time) because it is separate and the other categories are not (1028a33–34). That these two claims are closely related is clear from a text in the *Physics:* "None of the others [the categories] is separate, except *ousia;* for the others are said in respect of a substrate *ousia*" (A 1, 185a31). That is to say, the reason that *ousia* is separate is that it does not inhere in anything else. And from its separation, so understood, Aristotle infers that *ousia* is temporally prior. What does Aristotle mean by temporal priority? Clearly, it cannot refer to an *ousia*'s existing before acquiring *any* quality, quantity, relation, or place. No sensible *ousia* exists without any of these.[12] On the other hand, if we consider a particular instance of a category other than *ousia*, it must exist in some individual *ousia,* and the *ousia* must have existed before it acquired the instance of the other category.[13] As we learn later in book Z, the latter could not have existed before the *ousia* in which it is present, though one like it could have existed in another *ousia* (cf. Z 9, 1034b16–19). However, this is still not enough to prove that *ousia* is prior in time to the other categories: what about those qualities, quantities, etc., that the *ousia* is born with?[14] One response to this question is to stress the modal character of *ousia*'s separation: an *ousia* *could* exist before acquiring any particular attribute, even those it happens to be born with. Since Aristotle says that none of the other categories can exist separate from *ousia* (1028a22–24), *ousia* should be separate because it can exist separate from the other categories. It would follow that an *ousia* could exist before acquiring any particular attribute from another category. Why, though, it will be objected, can we not say the same thing about the other categories? Could not pale also exist before Socrates becomes pale? Someone else could be pale before Socrates becomes pale. It would then appear to follow that pale is temporally prior to Socrates. This objection will not work for the reason stated earlier: the pale in Socrates and the pale in someone else are distinct instances of pale. The existence of the latter prior to Socrates' existence does not show the priority of pale to Socrates. Even so, to call *ousia* temporally prior to its attributes because it *might have* existed without them seems like an abuse of language. If *ousia* is temporally prior, it needs to exist before they do. Again, it is a later discussion that provides a way to understand how this can be. In Θ 8 Aristotle argues that actuality is temporally prior to matter (1049b17–1050a3). Since *ousia* is actuality, *ousia* is prior in time to any particular matter. Since instances of the other categories inhere in composites of matter and form, *ousia* is temporally prior to the other categories. Thus, *ousia* is temporally prior to the other categories because it exists before coming into any particular composite and acquiring any particular attributes. In this way, even an *ousia* that always exists with other categories can be prior in time to them.

Assuming that these interpretations of "separate" and "prior in time" are correct, we can see at a glance why the former implies the latter. Individual instances of categories other than *ousia* have no existence separate from some particular *ousia* because they are always said of some substrate *ousia*. The particular *ousia*, though, exists before coming to be in some matter, and thus before acquiring the attributes it comes to have. Of course, this reasoning takes us far beyond what we have in Z 1, but so do the arguments which justify the other two types of priority. In all three cases, the priority of *ousia* is not established until later. 1028a31–b2 is thus a promissory note, but it still plays an important role in Z 1. If *ousia* is primary in all three ways, then metaphysics' concern with it is justified.

The appearance of temporal priority in this list is initially surprising because this type of priority does not seem particularly significant. We might have expected to see what Aristotle elsewhere calls priority in *ousia* or in nature (Δ 11, 1019a2–4), a priority that belongs to "something which can exist without the others but the others cannot exist without it." This is the priority that Plato is supposed to have ascribed to his forms, and it is the priority that Aristotle gives to the unmoved mover. Sensible *ousia* does not, however, meet this requirement because it cannot exist without the other categories. Neither *ousia* nor its attributes can exist without each other. Under the circumstances, temporal priority is appropriate to mention here.

In referring to separation to support the priority of *ousia*, Aristotle draws on a character that he often ascribes to *ousia*. Separation is widely recognized as one of Aristotle's criteria of *ousia*. He uses it in his arguments (e.g., 3, 1029a27; 16, 1040b6–7), and he uses it to describe *ousia* in important passages (e.g., H 1, 1042a28–31). Separation is important, but often it is a red herring. Compare, for example, Aristotle's well-known criticism of Plato's separation of his forms (M 4, 1078b31 ff.; 10, 1087a4–7) with his praise of the Platonists for separating forms at Z 16, 1040b27–29. While he insists that *ousia* should be separate, he points out the impossible consequences of such a separation. Moreover, his own primary sensible *ousia* is form that is immanent in matter (Z 11, 1037a29) and separate only in formula (H 1, 1042a29). The reason separation is confusing is that its meaning slides from the absolute separation of the sensible composite and of the Platonic form to the lesser degree of separation characteristic of Aristotle's own form.[15] Moreover, absolute separation could refer to separation from matter (cf. E 1, 1025b20–1026a6, a10–12, and my earlier discussion in 1.2), or to the separate existence of a sensible composite (H 1, 1042a29–31). The two passages in Z 1 that refer to *ousia* as separate are ambiguous, probably intentionally so. They assume that *ousia* is separate because it does not inhere in a substrate, but whether *ousia* is separate absolutely remains to be determined later. Because the precise kind of separation which *ousia* has is undecided, separation is not a good criterion of *ousia*. It needs to be determined along with *ousia*. Further, absolute separation seems inconsistent with unity, at least in sensibles, for the composite is most separate but, as we will see, the form or essence is most one. In choosing the form as primary, Aristotle assumes that unity is more fundamental as a criterion than separation.

The preceding remarks anticipate some of what is to come. This study focuses on unity because it is more important than, and accounts for, separation. There is no doubt that separation remains a criterion of *ousia*. However, Aristotle often uses another criterion to do its work in the argument. This other criterion is unity. In Z 1 *ousia* is separate because the other categories are not able to exist separately from it; that is, they inhere in it or are said of it while *ousia* is not said of another substrate. Later in book Z, he describes things that are "primary" in much the same terms; they are things that are not said of other things but other things are said of them (4, 1030a7–11; 6, 1031b13–14). Since only the formula of what is primary is a definition, and since only what is one has a formula that is a definition (1030b7–9), what is primary is what is one. In other words, the character on the basis of which Aristotle terms *ousia* "separate" in Z 1 is just the character that he has in mind when he calls *ousia* "one" later on. The later arguments are mainly posed in terms of one. As we will see, Aristotle's softening of the separation requirement to "separation in formula" is the result of determining the unity possessed by form. In general, Aristotle treats separation as a kind of unity.[16]

Although most of what is to be gained from concentrating on unity will be apparent later, there is one important advantage apparent in Z 1. It helps us to understand the significance of Aristotle's arguments for the priority of *ousia*. What we have seen in Z 1 is a version of the *pros hen* doctrine of being. Qualities, quantities, and so forth are called beings by virtue of their relation to *ousia* (1028a18–20). Unlike the initial statement of the doctrine in book Γ (1003a33–b10), Z 1 asserts definitively that *ousia* is the nature to which all others are related, and it takes those other beings to be only the categories other than *ousia*. [17] The latter should be the *hen* of the *pros hen,* even if Z 1 does not use the phrase *pros hen.* Not only is *ousia* one, but it is prior because it is one—if, that is, the section under discussion (1028a31–b2) should be understood in terms of unity, as I think it should. The first part of Z 1 (1028a13–31) argues that *ousia* is primary. The part under discussion (1028a31–b2) shows the ways that *ousia* is prior to the other beings. If *ousia* is prior because it is one, as it seems to be, then the entire chapter aims to establish a consistent and coherent picture of *ousia* as the primary nature of being, the one of the *pros hen.*

Having stated the ways in which *ousia* is prior, Aristotle concludes Z 1 with the famous reduction of the problem of being to the problem of *ousia* to which I referred earlier:

> And indeed what was sought long ago, and is sought now and always, and is always puzzling, "what is being?" is just [the question], "what is *ousia?*" . . . Therefore, it is necessary for us to investigate most of all, first, and only, concerning what is said to be in this way, what is it? (1028b2–7).

The plain sense of these words is that the inquiry into the nature of being is just an inquiry into the nature of *ousia.* And, as mentioned earlier, this reduction is implicit in the identification of *ousia* as simple being. Since only categorial being has been under discussion, Z 1 has justified only the reduction of the inquiry into categorial being to an inquiry into *ousia*—if, that is, it has justified any reduction at all.

Has Z 1 really justified the reduction? An inquiry into *ousia* is part of an investigation of being, but is there not more to the latter? Are other beings not included in metaphysics? These questions arise from a misunderstanding of the kind of reduction Aristotle makes in Z 1. At issue here is not the scope of the science but the character of its subject matter. In Γ 2 Aristotle uses the *pros hen* doctrine of being to show that a single science of metaphysics could treat all beings. Just as medicine treats health and everything related to health, metaphysics can treat the primary being and everything related to it (Γ 2, 1003a34–b10). Thus, all beings can fall under a single science even though they do not belong to a single genus. The issue in the central books is not what falls under the science, but what is the nature of its subject matter;

this is what Aristotle seeks when he asks, what is being? (1028b4). Z 1 invokes the *pros hen* doctrine of being and the priority of *ousia* in order to reduce *this* question to an inquiry into the nature of *ousia*. Just as a science of a *kath' hen* studies the one common nature, a science that studies a *pros hen* studies the one nature that is somehow common to all, health in the case of medicine and *ousia* in the case of metaphysics (Γ 2, 1003b12–19). Later in book Z, Aristotle claims that health is the *ousia* of disease because the latter is the absence of health (7, 1032b2–6). Likewise, the primary being is, in some sense, the nature of every instance of being. This is just what Z 1 has argued. Since *ousia* appears in every categorial predication, and since the others are beings through *ousia*, *ousia* is simple being (1028a27–31). Whenever we ask of any particular being "what is it?", we answer by indicating its *ousia* (1028a15–18; a36–b1). By analogy, when we ask, "what is it?" of being in general, simple being, we should answer by explaining the nature of *ousia*. Thus, the first answer to the question about the nature of being, "what is being?", is *ousia*. Having recognized this, we are led to inquire into the nature of *ousia*, "what is *ousia*?" (1028b4).

Although the reduction of the inquiry into the nature of being to an inquiry into the nature of *ousia* may seem surprising, it is no more (nor less) puzzling than the subsequent reduction of the nature of an *ousia* to its form. *Ousia* is a part of being, but it is also, in some way, the nature of all beings; so too, while form is a part of the composite, it is somehow the nature of the whole composite. Aristotle's moves may be difficult to understand, but they are consistent. In each case an inquiry into the nature of a whole becomes an inquiry into the nature of its primary part. In knowing the latter, we know the nature that all the other parts somehow possess.

To speak of the nature of all beings surely sounds suspicious in an Aristotelian context. But what else could Aristotle be seeking when he asks "What is being?" Z 1 would be truly surprising if it suggested that there were some single nature possessed by all beings (a *kath' hen*). The claim that *ousia* is the nature of being avoids such a Platonic common nature. At the same time, Aristotle's identification of *ousia* as the nature of being leaves the nature of being open because the nature of *ousia* is as yet undetermined. Z 1 does characterize *ousia*, but it does so without presenting its nature. Aristotle describes it as a determinate substrate and as "the what it is" (1028a11–12). *Ousia* is the answer to a "what is it" question (1028a13–18). Such a description may help us to pick out an *ousia*, but it does not explain what makes it an *ousia*.

Aristotle's characterization of *ousia* in Z 1 does, however, have an intriguing consequence. Since *ousia* is the answer to a "what is it" question, to ask "what is being?" is to inquire into the *ousia* of being. Z 1 thus argues in effect that the *ousia* of being is *ousia*. Its concluding injunction to investigate "what is *ousia*?" amounts to the demand to seek the *ousia* of *ousia*.

If these formulations are correct, the inquiry in Z 1 is inherently reflexive. At first glance, however, they seem to be based on an equivocation. In the expression "*ousia* of being," the term "*ousia*" refers to the essence of being; but the *ousia* that this essence is identified with is the category of *ousia*.[18] This criticism is unjustified. At this point in Aristotle's inquiry, the nature of *ousia* has not been determined. His description of *ousia* as the "what it is" does not presuppose that *ousia* is essence; it reflects preliminary ignorance about the character of *ousia*. *Ousia* is the "what it is" of something; it is the answer to a "what is it" question, whatever that happens to be. All that Z 1 asserts is the truism that the answer to the question "what is being?" is just the "what it is." Something analogous obtains in the other categories: the answer to the question "what sort [of thing is it]?" is just the "what sort," the quality; and the answer to the question "how many [is it]?" is just the "how many," the quantity. Z 1 does not equivocate because the nature of *ousia*, the answer to the "what is it" question, has not been decided. It remains unclear just what is being sought when the question is asked. This is what Z-H aims to determine.

When viewed retrospectively in light of the rest of the book, Z 1 can be seen to use *ousia* in two different ways, as essence and as the first category. But this is not a sign of equivocation. It reflects Aristotelian arguments that essence is, in some way, the nature of the category of *ousia*. If Z 1 assumed this result, Aristotle's reasoning would be circular; if it could not be understood in terms of this result, his reasoning would be inconsistent.

Dwelling on the possibility of equivocation, we risk missing Aristotle's method of exploiting for the sake of his own inquiry the reflexivities inherent in an inquiry into being. He is, as it were, trying to determine what being is at the same time that he is trying to find what one would need to know in order to determine what being is. How is it possible to determine the nature or *ousia* of being when this requires that we also determine what it is to be the nature or *ousia* of anything? Among the few tools at Aristotle's disposal to answer this question is being. He uses being as a tool of inquiry when he pursues what the *Posterior Analytics* calls ways of inquiring (B 1, 89b23–25). To ask the questions "is it?" or "what is it?" is to inquire into the being of something. Here, the something is being. So the ways of inquiry concern the being of being. As noted, Aristotle considers "whether being is" in book Γ when he asks whether being can be treated by a single science. Now, in book Z, his attention turns to what the being of being is, that is, to the nature of being. So far from being a mere play on words, these formulations show one reason that metaphysics has a special status as the first Aristotelian science. Metaphysics is a truly self-subsistent science just because it uses its own subject matter to determine itself. To inquire into being is to seek the being and the nature of being; to seek the nature of being is to seek the nature of *ousia*, the *ousia* of *ousia*.

The character of the inquiry into being seems to account for some of Aristotle's conclusions. First, because Aristotle seeks to determine the nature of being, he can dismiss any characteristics without which being would still be being. That is to say, Aristotle seeks only what makes being what it is, not anything that is inessential to being. But the categories other than *ousia* are such inessential characteristics. So the nature of being should be what underlies these other categories; it should be the category of *ousia*. Since the essence of a thing is what makes it be what it is, the foregoing reasoning implies that the category of *ousia* is the essence of being. So the identification of *ousia* as the nature of being amounts to making an essence also be a substrate. To put it a bit differently, because of the special character of an inquiry into being, the primary being must be both the substrate for accidents and the essence of all things. Insofar as *ousia* is both substrate and essence, it is both the principle of knowledge (for we know the essence) and the principle of the being or existence of all beings (for the other categories exist only because they are present in some *ousia*).

This dual character of *ousia* emerges later in book Z when Aristotle examines the candidates for *ousia*. The discussion of being in the first chapter of this book proceeds without any explicit references to the inherent reflexivity of the inquiry. Instead, the tool that Aristotle uses more directly to advance his inquiry here and elsewhere in the *Metaphysics* is unity. Unity affords Aristotle a means of reasoning about being and *ousia* because there is a unity that is associated with being and another unity that is associated with *ousia*. To show that something is a non-being Aristotle need only show that it lacks the unity associated with being. Indeed, how else could he show the non-existence of something?

Even in a text like Z 1 where unity is scarcely mentioned, it is unity that does the work of the argument. As we have seen, Aristotle justifies the primacy of *ousia* on the ground that other things derive their being through their relation to *ousia*. The latter is the *hen* to which the other beings are related. As such, *ousia* is the one nature studied by metaphysics. In describing further ways in which *ousia* is primary, Aristotle enhances the claims of *ousia* to be the subject matter of metaphysics, and I have suggested that behind those other ascriptions of primacy to *ousia* lies the notion that it is more one.

The plurality of ways that *ousia* is one is, though, not only indicative of its primacy; it is the source of the problematic of the rest of Z–H. For, insofar as *ousia* is more knowable and prior in formula, it is one in formula. But, insofar as it is the substrate for accidents, it is one in substrate, a kind of numeric unity. These two types of unity seem to be incompatible. The former is a principle of knowledge and the latter is a principle of individual composites. In M 8 Aristotle accuses the Platonists of ascribing what appear to be the same two incompatible types of unity to their principles (1084b2–32). If his *ousia* is to be both the nature of being and the substrate of all beings, it seems to be subject to the same criticism. He needs to explain how *ousia* can have both types of unity. Although Aristotle does not pose the problem in these terms, the reasoning in much of Z–H centers on showing how *ousia* can be one. These books assume that *ousia* is one in both ways. The problem is to find something that can satisfy these unity requirements.

This last formulation of the issue is exactly analogous to the question raised earlier about how *ousia* can be both a substrate and an essence. Thus, Aristotle's use of unity disguises the reflexive character of the inquiry. It does not abrogate the reflexivity. Because unity is so closely tied to being and to *ousia*, to consider the pertinent unities is tantamount to considering being and *ousia*. Like the reflexive character of the inquiry, the unity of being and *ousia* usually remains implicit in Z 1. However, unlike the former, the unity assumptions are, I shall argue, necessary for understanding the arguments in the text. If these assumptions are necessary, then we will have reason to believe that Aristotle himself thinks of the problem of the determination of the nature of being and of *ousia* as a problem of accounting for the unity of *ousia*. As we will see, it is in this guise that the assumption that *ousia* is one plays a central role in Z–H.

A possible obstacle to this interpretation is a passage that occurs in the midst of Aristotle's assertion that the problem of the nature of being is a problem about *ousia*.

> For it is this [*ousia*] that some say is one, others more than one, and that some say is limited, others unlimited. Therefore it is necessary for us to investigate most of all, first, and only, concerning what is said to be in this way, what is it? (1028b4–7).

Since Aristotle steers us away from questions about unity and insists that the inquiry examine *ousia* exclusively, it might seem as if I am making too much of an implicit ascription of unity to *ousia*. Aristotle's point in the foregoing passage is that it is necessary to determine the nature of *ousia* before we consider its attributes. In Γ he had ascribed the mistakes of sophists and dialecticians to their failure to consider *ousia* (2, 1004b6–8). To consider whether *ousia* is one or many is to ask about the number of different *ousiai*, a question that Aristotle broaches in Z 2 (1028b18–27) and treats in books Λ (e.g., 1, 1069a30–b2) and M. But such an inquiry into the number of *ousiai* only makes sense if we already know that each *ousia* is one. (And Aristotle claims that anything that is must be one—Γ 2, 1003b22–25.) Conversely, the assumption that *each ousia* is one still leaves open the question whether the number of *all ousiai* is one or many. In short, the passage under discussion is not at all antithetical to the assumption that each *ousia* is one. It may, though, be partly responsible for the failure of commentators to recognize the significance of unity in Z-H. Perhaps the use of one by Aristotle's predecessors to which this passage refers is also the reason that Z 1 does not explicitly ascribe unity to *ousia*.

2.1.1 One and This

Although Z 1 does not explicitly describe *ousia* as one, there are grounds for identifying a characterization of *ousia* that it does use, "this something" or "this" (τόδε τι—1028b12), with one in number. If this identification does obtain, Z 1 and other texts would be more explicit about the fundamental role of unity as a characteristic of *ousia*. Since this identification may be controversial, and since the importance of unity in Z-H is clear without it, I shall not rely on this identification later.[19] Nevertheless, it is worth noting some reasons for the identification and explaining its significance in the investigation of categorial being which comprises these two books.

The identity of one and this is presupposed in the *Categories*. At 3b10 Aristotle asserts that a composite is a this because it is "one in number and indivisible [ἄτομον]." On the other hand, a universal is not a this because it is not one (3b16-18). Apparently, to be numerically one is a necessary and sufficient condition of being a this.

Similarly, in discussing the final *aporia*,[20] *Metaphysics* B 6 denies that a universal can be a principle because it signifies a such instead of a this (1003a7-9; cf. Z 8, 1033b21-26). If the universal did signify a this, then Socrates would be many because he falls under many universals (1003a9-12). Why does falling under many universals make Socrates many if each of those universals would be a this? Socrates would only be many if each universal were numerically one; so, to be a this must be to be one. Further, this passage expresses this supposition about the universal by saying both that it is a this (a9-10) and that it is "a this and a one" (a12).

If the καί in this last passage is explicative, as I think it is, the identity between "one" and "this" is not merely extensional but intensional as well. However, this text and the preceding one from the *Categories* could be interpreted as assuming only an extensional identity. A similar passage from Z 12 is even more likely to be asserting an intensional connection. There Aristotle claims that *ousia* signifies "something one and a this" (1037b27). Since this chapter goes on to consider the number of constituents in the essential formula of an *ousia*, the unity here must be numeric, and "this" neither adds anything to one nor means anything other than numeric unity.

Additional support for intensional identity can be garnered by comparing texts that state the same doctrine in terms of either one or this. For example, Z 16 claims that material elements are not ones but heaps that can be made into unities (1040a8-9), and H 1 summarizes what appears to be the same point by saying that matter is potentially a this (1042a27-28). A similar doctrine is repeated at Θ 7, 1049a27 when Aristotle claims that fire is the first matter because it is not a this. Along the same lines, Λ 3 declares that matter only appears to be a this, "for those things which are by contact but are not united by nature [συμφύσει] are matter and substrate" (1070a9–11). Apparently, it makes no difference whether we say that fire and the other elements are potentially one or potentially a this. One and this seem to be identical.

In general, the early chapters of book Z describe *ousia* as a this, and the rest of Z–H tends to characterize it as one. The transition point seems to be the end of Z 4, where Aristotle asserts that there is a one in each category, including the first category, the this (1030a10–12). After this passage the references to the unity of *ousia* are more explicit. Perhaps the opening chapters avoid characterizing *ousia* as one because the one associated with *ousia* differs from the one associated with being (as at 1003b22–25). After Z 4 explains that there are ones in each category, it is possible to speak of the unity of *ousia* with less risk of confusion.

That unity does not appear explicitly in the opening chapter of book Z is no ground for neglecting to consider it. As we look at Aristotle's argumentation in later chapters, we will see ample evidence of his assumption that *ousia* is one. Accepting the identification of one and this makes it easier to see the significance of one; but were I to rely upon it, my analysis would rest on what may be a vulnerable foundation. My case for the importance of unity in Z will be stronger if I do not exploit the identity but instead show how assumptions about unity are at work in Aristotle's arguments. The role of unity and its importance are manifest without relying on the identification of one and this.

2.2 Z 2–3, 1028b36: INSTANCES OF OUSIA

Aristotle begins his inquiry into the nature of *ousia* by listing the *ousiai*. The problem is that there are two lists, one in Z 2 and the other at the beginning of the following chapter. The first of these includes the things to which *ousia* seems to belong (ὑπάρχειν). Later, they are called the "agreed upon *ousiai*" (H 1, 1042a7–11; a24–25). All are bodies (σώματα) of one sort or another: plants, animals, the parts of plants and animals, the simple bodies (fire, water, etc.), the heavens, and the parts of the heavens (stars, moon, and sun) (1028b8–13). In addition, Pythagorean and Academic philosophers have proposed other instances of *ousia*: limits of bodies, such as, planes, lines, points, and units (b16–18); forms (b20); mathematicals (b20); and souls (b24–25). There is some question about which if any of these are genuine *ousiai* (1028a13–15). While describing these proposed *ousiai*, Aristotle mentions briefly some of the different views held by members of the Academy on the number of *ousiai* (b18–27). The question of how many *ousiai* there are is part of the fifth *aporia* of book B (997a35–b2), and Z 2 concludes by mentioning what I take to be a formulation of this *aporia:* are there any *ousiai* beyond and apart from sensible bodies? (1028b27–32).

The list that appears at the beginning of Z 3 contains four ways in which *ousia* is said "most of all": essence (τὸ τί ἦν εἶναι), substrate, genus, and universal (1028b33–36). All of these are expressions that Aristotle himself uses to signify *ousia.*[21] Essence and substrate appear in book Δ's discussion of *ousia:* essence is what the definition defines (1017b21–22), and the substrate is the subject of predications (1017b13–14; b23–24). The substrate is also the primary *ousia* of the *Categories* (2b15–17; 2b37–3a1). In the same work Aristotle calls genera and species secondary *ousiai* (2a14–19). Since both genera and species are universals (even if the *Categories* does not use this term), all four entries on the second list are Aristotelian *ousiai*.

Why does Aristotle list genus and universal as distinct entries? Joseph Owens maintains that in this context Aristotle uses "universal" to refer to the species in order to avoid confusing the species with the essence, both of which are designated with the same Greek word, τὸ εἶδος.[22] But the species are already included in the list under the heading of "genus." The seventh *aporia* of book B asks whether "the first genera" or "the last genera predicated of individuals" are principles (B 3, 998b15–16). Later in the discussion, Aristotle calls these "last genera" "species" (999a3–5). So Aristotle does not need a distinct term for species to include them in the list of Z 3; they are already included under "genus." I think it is more likely that Aristotle adds "universal" to the list in order to include universals that he does not ordinarily regard as genera. The discussion of the seventh *aporia* also argues that neither one nor being can be a genus (998b22–27). So it is more in line with the usage and results of book B for Aristotle to use the term "genus" for both species and genus and to use "universal" of these and of one and being. In support of this interpretation, I note that book Z does consider one and being as candidates for *ousia* (16, 1040b16–19). Since one and being do not fall under any of the other entries in the list of Z 3, if "universal" in this list referred to species, there would be candidates for *ousia* that were not mentioned on the list. Consequently, "universal" should refer to genera, species, and nongeneric universals like one and being. Since Aristotle is engaged in an inquiry into the nature or *ousia* of being, there is even some Aristotelian basis for calling being a kind of *ousia,* though it is, of course, weak.

Why are there two lists of *ousiai?* How are these *ousiai* connected? The first list contains the things to which *ousia* belongs. Socrates could appear on this list, but not on the other list. Instead, the second list contains the ways in which or the reason for which we could call Socrates an *ousia*. He is an *ousia* because he is a substrate for attributes, because he has an essence, because he falls under a genus, or because he is a being. These entries in the second list are all characters or aspects of the things on the first list, characters in respect of which they could be called *ousiai*. All the items on the second list specify legitimate respects in which something could be called an *ousia*. At issue in Aristotle's examination of this list is, in virtue of which entry is something *most properly* called an *ousia?* and the ensuing discussion chooses one entry. An examination of the first list would not aim at finding the single best entry but at delimiting all entries on the list. Though Aristotle pays some attention to the first list in Z–H (e.g., Z 16, 1040b5–16), the examination of some of the putative entries is left for the final books. Usually, he just assumes that at least some of these bodies must be *ousiai* and seeks to determine in virtue of what they are most properly called *ousiai*. Significantly, none of the entries on the second list is self-subsistent. All exist with something else. However, through most of book Z, Aristotle examines the entries on the second list independently. He treats them as if they alone were the *ousiai*.

This picture of the connection of the two lists is consistent with the discussion of *ousia* in Δ 8. There, too, Aristotle offers two lists. The first includes: (1) things with bodies, (2) causes of being such as soul, (3) parts which define the thing, such as, planes, lines, and numbers, and (4) the essence that is defined by a definition (1017b10–23). The second list contains only two entries: (a) the last substrate which is not predicated of anything else and (b) the form (b23–27). This second list is generally regarded as a summary or distillation of the first list: the first entry on the first list is thought to correspond with the first entry on the second list, and the other three entries on the first list are supposed to fall under the second entry on the second list.[23] However, Aristotle's remarks on why the first entry appears on the list suggest a different relation.

> All these [things with bodies] are said to be *ousiai* because they are not said in respect of a substrate but the others are said in respect of them (1017b13–14).

This sentence does not identify substrate and body. Instead, it refers to substrate to justify calling a body an *ousia*. A body is an *ousia* because others are said of it, that is, because it is a substrate for others. The relation between substrate and body here is just the relation that holds between the first and second lists in book Z. An entry from the second list indicates that in respect of which an entry on the first list is called an *ousia*. The last three items on the first list of Δ 8 comprise an abbreviated description of the Pythagorean and Academic *ousiai* listed in Z 2. All of them are called *ousiai* by virtue of the remaining entry from the second list, the form;[24] for Aristotle's description (in Δ 8) of why these are called *ousiai* mentions functions performed by form: causing being, delimiting, being defined. Thus, these instances of *ousia* are such in respect of form. In Z 3 Aristotle refers to form with another name, essence, and he adds universal and genus to the second list. (It is unclear why these latter were omitted from Δ 8.) In sum, the functions of the two lists in Δ 8 are the same as the corresponding lists in Z 2–3.

A possible objection to this correlation of the two dual listings of *ousiai* is that essence appears on the first list in Δ 8 but on the second list of Z. But this will not stand, for Z's first list of *ousiai* includes the forms advanced as *ousiai* by Platonists and Pythagoreans. In other words, where the first and second lists of Δ 8 speak of essence and form, respectively, the first and second lists in Z have form and essence, respectively. Since Aristotle eventually equates these two anyway, their interchange does not count against the correlations of the two sets of lists.

Another challenge to my interpretation is that in Z 2 Aristotle calls plants, animals, and others things *ousiai* not because they are substrates, but because they are bodies (1028b8–10). Thus, body should be the character in respect of which these things are called *ousiai,* and if the second list did contain the justification for including items on the first list, it would include body. This objection is easily answered. Bodies are *ousiai,* and plants and other things may be *ousiai* because they are bodies, but in respect of what are bodies *ousiai?* As the passage from Δ 8 quoted above explains, bodies are *ousiai* because they are substrates for attributes. Likewise, mathematicals may be *ousiai* because they are the limits of bodies, but these limits in turn are (perhaps) *ousiai* because they are (perhaps) the essences or forms of the bodies. Even though the entries on the first list are mentioned in Z 2 along with some account of why they are on the list, the entries on the second list still justify the entries on the first list being called *ousiai.* All bodies may be *ousiai,* but if so, they are not *ousiai* just because they are bodies. Thus, there is no good reason to doubt that the second list consists of the aspects or characters of the things we call *ousiai* in respect of which we call them *ousiai.*

It is the second list that plays the central role in book Z. The book proceeds to examine its entries in detail, and Z answers the question "what is *ousia?*" by choosing an item from this list.

What precisely is at issue in this examination of the second list? If all the items on the second list have some claim to be called *ousia,* how is it possible to decide the nature of *ousia* by choosing one of them? Since the *ousia* Aristotle seeks here cannot be the only *ousia,* it must be the *best ousia,* that candidate with the characteristics of *ousia* in the highest degree. In other words, the aim of the inquiry is to find the primary *ousia.* Denials that a candidate is *ousia* ought to be understood as denying that it is primary *ousia.*

Just as the answer to the "what is being" question is primary being (as we saw in Z 1—1029a29-31, b4), so too the answer to the "what is *ousia*" question is primary *ousia*. It is primary *ousia* that Aristotle seeks in Z–H.

What are those characteristics of *ousia* that the primary *ousia* possesses most of all? What are the criteria for *ousia* that Aristotle uses to evaluate the four candidates on the second list? As usual Aristotle is not explicit, and different commentators have fastened on different criteria at work in his arguments.[25] We would expect the criteria to be drawn from the characteristics of *ousia* that Aristotle mentions in Z 1 (esp. 1028a22-29). For the criteria should be established before the lists are presented in Z 2-3 and examined in most of the rest of book Z.

Some of the characterizations made in Z 1 are, in fact, mentioned later as criteria of *ousia*. For example, Aristotle uses separation (1028a33-34; a23) and "thisness" (τόδε τι—1028a12) to exclude substrate (3, 1029a26-30). Separation is also mentioned with unity (e.g., Z 16, 1040a6-9). However, as I said earlier, what Aristotle refers to as separate in one text he will, with apparently the same character in mind, elsewhere term one. Something that exists by itself (e.g., form without matter) is separate because it is one; something that exists only with another thing fails to be separate because it lacks unity. Thus, Aristotle often seems to think of separation as a result of unity or even as a kind of unity. But, of course, this needs to be shown, and this will be done through a careful examination of the arguments in the text. My contention is that the criterion that proves most important in Aristotle's argumentation is unity. Unless my identification of one and "this something" is accepted, the unity of *ousia* is merely implicit in Z 1. Later, Aristotle is explicit and, as we will soon see, unity figures prominently in his valuation of candidates for primary *ousia* (e.g., Z 12, 1037b27; 13, 1039a7-8; 16, 1040b5-8).

Besides possessing the characteristics of *ousia* in the highest degree, the primary *ousia* ought to be the cause in respect of which the other candidates are called *ousiai*. As noted earlier, all the entries on the second list are answers to the question, in respect of what is a particular thing an *ousia?* We can also ask of each entry itself, in respect of what does *it* make something else an *ousia?* This is equivalent to asking what makes it an *ousia* or why is it included on the list of Z 3. The item in respect of which the other entries are *ousiai* is the primary *ousia*. Further, if unity is a criterion of *ousia,* the item that is the primary *ousia* and the cause of *ousia* to the others should also be the cause of unity to the others. This later constitutes an additional criterion of *ousia*. Whereas Aristotle's efforts in Z are taken up with showing that all but one of the candidates is not one, book H shows that the successful candidate is also a cause of unity. As we will see, most of Z aims to evaluate the items on the second list and, in the process, assumes that some portion of the first list is correct. I shall argue that much of this evaluation turns on assumptions about the unity of *ousia*.

2.3 Z 3: THE SUBSTRATE

Of the four candidates for primary *ousia*, Aristotle declares that the substrate must be investigated first because it—or rather the "first substrate"—seems to have the best claim to be *ousia* (1028b37–1029a2). Let me suggest that the reason for its priority is that bodies seem to be *ousiai* most of all (2, 1028b8–9), and bodies are called *ousiai* in virtue of being substrates.

What, though, does Aristotle mean by the first substrate? He goes on to mention three ways that "substrate" is said: matter, form, and the composite of form and matter are all called substrates (1029a2–5). Just as each of the many ways of being is itself a schema, the substrate, a way of being an *ousia*, is also a kind of schema; "substrate" is said in many ways. The first substrate should be exactly analogous to the primary *ousia*: it should be the substrate that is most of all substrate and that in virtue of which the others are called substrates. Which of the three substrates is first?[26] This is the central question of Z 3. However, the chapter does not ask, which is the primary substrate? but, what probably amounts to the same thing, which is the primary being? It is clear from the start that "if the form is prior to the matter and more of a being, it will be prior to the composite for the same reason" (1029b5–7). Much of Z 3 aims to show that form is "more *ousia* than matter" (1029a29–30). From this it follows that form is the primary substrate. Thus, Z 3 does not show that no substrate is *ousia;* it shows that the material substrate is not the primary *ousia*.

A source of obscurity in this argument is that Aristotle uses "matter" in two different ways. At first, it is a kind of substrate (1029a2) (and thus an *ousia*), but later in the argument "matter" refers to the result of the process of stripping away attributes, an entity that belongs in none of the categories (1029a20–21). The bronze of the statute is Aristotle's example of the former matter (a3–5), but neither bronze nor any other determinate thing could be called matter in the second sense.[27] What we see here, I maintain, is Aristotle using instances from the two lists together. To consider an item from the second list, substrate, Aristotle points out the examples from the first list of *ousiai* that it would sanction. The source of the confusion is his labeling both substrate and the instances of substrate matter, but this is consistent with his labeling instances from both lists as *ousiai*. The dichotomy between these two types of matter parallels the dichotomy between the first and the second list of *ousiai*. The matter that is a substrate is that in respect of which something could be called an *ousia*. The other matter mentioned here is the result of the application of this character.

Given this distinction we can look at the argument. It begins by repeating the idea that the substrate is something of which the others are predicated while not being itself predicated of anything else (1029a7–9). This characterization suggests a way of arriving at the primary substrate, the substrate that would be *ousia* if any substrate were (1029a1–2; a15–16). We need simply strip away all predicates, and we will arrive at what cannot be predicated of anything else. Accordingly, Aristotle undertakes the thought experiment of subtracting (ἀφαιρουμένου)[28] away everything predicated of a thing. Not only are the affections, products, and capacities removed, but also length, depth and breadth (a12–15). What remains is the ultimate material substrate, something that should be *ousia* most of all (a15–16). But once all these determinations are subtracted, what remains is only what they delimited (a16–18; cf. Δ 8, 1017b17–18). This is completely undetermined matter, and this is what the argument leads us to identify as *ousia* (a18–19, a10).

This undetermined matter should not be identified with the substrate that appears on the second list and is under consideration in Z 3. Things are not called *ousiai* in respect of their ultimate matter. Rather, it is the ultimate matter that is called *ousia* (at least according to this argument) in respect of its being a material substrate. In other words, if the undetermined matter could be an *ousia*, it would be one which would appear on the *first* list. The portion of the argument of Z 3 discussed so far locates a particular thing, the undetermined matter, that would have to be on the first list if material substrate were the primary entry on the second list. The remainder of Z 3 (a20–30) argues that this matter cannot be *ousia*.

The reason is that the matter arrived at by the process of subtracting all attributes would not itself fall under any of the categories. This is obvious, for the categories are predicates, and the matter under consideration lacks all predicates. As Aristotle explains, the other categories are predicated of *ousia*, and *ousia* is predicated of the matter (a23–24). Consequently, the being or essence of matter differs from that of the categories, the predicates (a22–23). How could matter be *ousia* if *ousia* is one of the categories? Further, lacking all predicates, matter loses determination; it is neither separate nor a "this," two characteristics of *ousia* (a27–28). So, matter cannot be *ousia*.

This conclusion scarcely seems justified. The argument shows only that completely undetermined matter cannot be *ousia*. Does not the possibility remain open that bronze, wood, or some other material substrate could still be *ousia*? The answer to this question is that this possibility does remain open; Z 16 closes it (1040b5–10). However, to raise a question like this is to miss the point of the argument. The issue in Z 3 is whether things are said to be *ousiai* primarily because of their substrates. What Aristotle argues is that were this so, completely undetermined matter would be the primary instance of *ousia* because such a matter is said to be a substrate most of all. But this matter lacks the characteristics of *ousiai*. So the material substrate cannot be the primary nature in respect of which things are called *ousiai*.

As I understand it, the argument does not aim to delimit the contents of the first list. Aristotle's argument that undetermined matter is not *ousia* does, in effect, exclude undetermined matter from the first list. But his aim here is to examine whether an entry on the second list, the material substrate, is the primary nature in respect of which things are called *ousiai*. After the argument of Z 3, we still do not know whether bronze or wood are *ousiai*. But we do know that if they are *ousiai,* it is not because they are material substrates.

The material substrate is not the primary *ousia* because the thing that is an instance of material substrate most of all is not an *ousia*. Not only is this thing neither separate nor a "this," material substrate is neither separate nor a "this" (cf. 1029a26-28). Accordingly, as I mentioned earlier, Aristotle concludes that the formal substrate is the primary substrate and that it needs to be examined (1029a29-33).

Aristotle describes *ousia* here as what is not said of another but that of which the others are said (1028b36-37; 1029a8-9). Why does being said of a substrate exclude an entity from being an *ousia?* What is said of a substrate depends upon the substrate; it could not exist apart from that, or some other, substrate. Anything that is said of a substrate thus fails to be *ousia* because it fails to be separate (cf. *Phys.* A 2, 184b31-32). Accordingly, the material substrate looks like an attractive candidate for *ousia* because, insofar as it is the substrate for predication and not itself predicated, it seems more separate than the predicates are. The problem is how to find the material substrate, and Aristotle proposes the method of subtracting whatever is predicated. Implicit in this method is the assumption that something which is one will be separate. For the process of subtraction is only possible if we begin from a plurality; the material substrate and what is said of it constitute such a plurality. The process ends when we reach something from which nothing more can be subtracted, something which is one. So what the process of subtraction actually produces—or, better, should produce—is something which is one. Aristotle just assumes that this unity must also be separate and thus be an *ousia*. This assumption is well founded since insofar as anything is one, it is not predicated of any substrate. Contrariwise, the predicates lack unity because they depend on the substrate; their nature includes a reference to something else, to the substrate in which they inhere. Removing all of these added predicates, Aristotle should reach the one nature to which they have been added.

The problem, of course, is that instead of something one, the result of the subtractions is something that lacks all determination, a nothing.[29] The process of subtraction goes awry because it removes too much. Without any determination, what remains lacks unity; it lacks "separation and the 'this' which belong to *ousia* most of all" (1029a28). As a result of the argument, Aristotle rejects the assumption that things are called *ousiai* (primarily) in virtue of their material substrates. The assumption that *ousia*, whatever it is, must be one remains in force, as does the assumption that what is one will also be separate. If, though, we are to determine *ousia* further, we must rely on some other technique besides subtraction.

2.3.1 1029b3–12

According to the manuscripts, Z 3 ends with an injunction to look at sensibles first because some of them are agreed to be *ousiai* (1029a33–34). Although 1029b3–12 occurs in the manuscripts near the beginning of Z 4, most editors and commentators append it to Z 3. It asserts that learning proceeds from what is less knowable by nature to what is more knowable by nature. Since "less knowable by nature" seems to refer to the sensibles, this passage is placed after Aristotle's injunction to investigate sensibles.[30]

This rearrangement is unnecessary. First, the sentence of Z 3 that the manuscripts have as the last line of the chapter (a33–34) makes good sense in its context. The chapter shows that the material substrate is not *ousia*, and the penultimate sentence of the chapter in the manuscripts (a32–33) expresses the need to investigate another substrate, form. But "form" is ambiguous. It could refer to Platonic separate forms and perhaps even to Aristotle's unmoved movers. Accordingly, it is appropriate for Aristotle to remind us that we should begin our investigation with the agreed upon *ousiai*, as he does in the last sentence. This amounts to an injunction to examine the forms of sensibles before supersensible forms.

Likewise, the text of 1029b3–12 also makes sense in Z 4 where it appears in the manuscripts. At the beginning of Z 4, Aristotle announces that he will investigate essence, one of the entries on the second list (1029b1–3). In the position it occupies in the manuscripts, 1029b3–12 justifies this investigation by claiming that knowledge proceeds from what is less knowable but more known to us to what is more knowable by nature. Is there any reason to think that an investigation of essence concerns something that is known in only a small degree? There is indeed. The discussion of essence runs from Z 4 through Z 12. It not only occupies the bulk of book Z but also includes some of the most difficult argumentation in the entire corpus. Essence is, of course, knowable in itself. It is just not known by us, at least not at the start of the analysis. As the discussion proceeds, Aristotle identifies essence as form and eventually as actuality; during the inquiry essence becomes more known to us. The initial stage of this inquiry begins in Z 4 immediately after the passage under consideration. Aristotle announces that he will consider essence from a logical perspective (*logikōs*—1029b13). Taking this together with 1029b3-12's claim that we must begin from what is more known to us, we can understand Aristotle to assert that the logical perspective on essence focuses on what is more known to us but less knowable in nature. This perspective provides the first but not the best grasp of essence.

The next section will look more closely at what this perspective involves. Anticipating its results, I note that the logical grasp of essence concerns definitions and predications and that it depends to a large extent on grasping essence as one. As the treatment of essence develops, Aristotle shows that other characters are the source of the unity of essence. These other characters are form and, most properly, actuality. Once we grasp essence through them, we have come closer to knowing essence "by nature." Accordingly, the transition from the less knowable to the more knowable is the transition from viewing essence as simply one to viewing it as actuality.[31] This transition occurs during Z-H, unlike the transition from sensibles to supersensibles to which 1029b3-12 is usually taken to refer. I shall fill out the details of this picture and justify it in what follows. For the time being it suffices to conclude that 1029b3-12 can make good sense in Z 4 where it appears in the manuscripts.

2.4 Z 4-5: ESSENCE

From the results of Z 3 we would expect to find a treatment of the formal substrate in Z 4. Instead, the opening sentence of the chapter announces an investigation of another candidate for *ousia* from the second list, essence. Since, though, Aristotle later identifies essence and form (7, 1032b1-2; 10, 1035b32), this treatment of essence amounts to a continuation of the treatment of substrate.[32] It is widely accepted that essence is the most successful candidate for *ousia* and that Z 4 marks the beginning of the justification for this choice. What contribution do Z 4-5 make? How do they investigate essence?

Early in Z 4 Aristotle announces that he will investigate essence *logikōs* (1029b13). This term should refer to some use of language, but precisely what method of investigation does he intend to describe? In what other way could we investigate essence? A question closely connected to these is precisely where in the text Aristotle investigates *logikōs*. According to Ross, this type of investigation is a merely plausible linguistic discussion that occurs between 1029b13 and 1030a27; after that the "real" or "factual" inquiry begins.[33] This cannot be correct, for (1) the putatively "linguistic" section includes "factual" considerations (e.g., 1029b26-27), (2) the sentence that Ross supposes to make the transition (1030a27-28) is in the middle of an argument from which Aristotle draws conclusions about essence (1030a28-29), and (3) Ross's purely linguistic investigation would not support the conclusions about essence that Aristotle draws from it.[34] A purely linguistic inquiry of the sort that Ross envisions is not to be found in Z 4–5. Nevertheless, formulae and definitions do play an important role in this section. It seems that to investigate essence *logikōs* Aristotle uses formulae (*logoi*) to determine the character of essence. To pursue this line of thought further we need to look closely at the details of Aristotle's analysis. So let us temporarily set aside questions about the nature of investigating essence *logikōs* and turn to the text.

The investigation of essence begins in 1029b13–14 with the following claim: "The essence of each thing is what is said [of it] *per se.* "[35] That is to say, anything that is said of (λέγεται) something *per se* belongs to its essence. To find the essence of a thing, we need only determine what is said of it *per se*. Are there not, though, *per se* attributes of a thing that do not belong to its essence? Aristotle will need to refine the claim that anything said *per se* belongs to an essence; he does this in 1029b16–18 and in Z 5. For now, a more pressing concern is, how can we determine what is said *per se*? Rather than tackling this question directly, Aristotle turns his attention to showing when things fail to be said *per se*. For example, immediately after the passage quoted he denies that to be you (τὸ σοὶ εἶναι) is to be musical, on the ground that "you are not musical in respect of yourself" (1029b14–15). In other words, the essence of musical does not belong to your essence because you are not musical by nature. Apparently, what does belong to you *per se* are things for which to be is the same as for you to be (τὸ σοὶ εἶναι). But rather than explaining how to tell when the being of something is the same as the being of something else, Aristotle first goes on, in lines 1029b16–22, to consider cases in which something belongs *per se* but does not belong to an essence. Because syntactic ambiguities make this section difficult to interpret, it is best to return to it later when we can compare it with other portions of Z 4. For the present we need only notice that one of Aristotle's concerns in these lines is composites like white surface.

Concern with composites of *ousiai* and instances of other categories generate what seems to be the central questions of the chapter. (I shall call such composites [σύνθετα] "accidental composites.")[36] Aristotle's problem here is whether these accidental composites have essences.

> It is necessary to inquire [1] whether there is a formula of the essence of each of them and [2] whether essence belongs to each composite, for example, to white man (1029b25–27).

Since the "formula of the essence" is the definition (5, 1031a12), the first question can also be expressed as, does a composite have a definition? (1030a6–7). If the formula of the composite does express an essence, that is, if the composite does have a definition, then it surely has an essence.[37] So answering the first question could also answer the second. But how can we tell if the formula expresses an essence? How can we tell if the formula of an accidental composite is a definition? The very suggestion that something's formula might not define it is striking. Under what circumstances could a formula fail to be a definition?

Immediately after posing the two questions quoted above, Aristotle goes on to describe two ways in which something could fail to be *per se:* (1) "by addition" (ἐκ προσθέσεως) and (2) "not by addition" (1029b29–31). He characterizes the first case as follows:

> In the one case, what is defined is said [λέγεται] by adding [τῷ . . . προσκεῖσθαι] it to something else; for example, if the person who is defining white were to give the formula of white man (1029b31–33).

A formula that expressed the nature of man in addition to the nature of white would not define white. It would express too much, for it would add something that does not belong to the thing being defined.

Something fails to be *per se* in the second way also because of an unwarranted addition to a formula:

> In the other case, [what is defined is said by adding] something else to it; for example, if cloak signifies white man and someone defines cloak as white. The white man is white, but his essence[38] is not to be white (1029b33–1030a2).

This type of failure is usually understood to arise when a formula omits something that it ought to include.[39] This is probably part of what Aristotle means to describe but it cannot be entirely correct. The first objection to it is that in the description quoted Aristotle does not point to a defect in the formula; he speaks of the addition of something to the thing being defined.[40] Further, such a defect in the formula could be corrected simply by adding something to the formula of white. But the last line quoted above implies that even such a formula would fail to define white man. Since the essence of white does not belong to the white man, and since the essence of white man consists of what does belong to it *per se* (1029b13–16), the formula of white should never be included in any way in the formula of white man. Thus, the problem with trying to define white man with the formula of white is not just that the latter omits something, as it does, but that it includes something illegitimate. In offering the formula of white as the formula of white man, we would, in effect, be adding something to the essence of white man, namely, white. Thus, it is appropriate to understand the second type of failure to arise for just the reason that Aristotle provides, the addition of something to the thing being defined. As Aristotle describes them, both types of failure involve additions: in the one case, the addition occurs when the formula adds the thing to be defined to something else; in the other case, the addition occurs when the formula adds something else to the thing defined. So stated the two failures sound equivalent, but the first addition occurs when someone who defines white adds the formula of white to the formula of man, and the second case occurs when someone who defines white man gives the formula of white. Only in the first case is the addition reflected in the formula and by itself the source of the error. So it is properly designated as a failure "by addition."

From these descriptions it is clear that the failure to be *per se* refers, at least in part, to the formula. Something fails to be *per se* when its formula fails to define it. Conversely, something is *per se* when its formula does define it. A defining formula expresses an essence and, as noted earlier, the essence of a thing is what is said to belong to it *per se* (1029b13–14). It is, thus, appropriate to speak of the formula as being *per se* if it expresses an essence and as not being *per se* if it expresses an addition of the essence to something else or of something else to that essence. Whatever else it may be, the failure to be *per se* is the failure of a formula to express an essence.

The question is whether there is anything more to a failure to be *per se*. Are the failures of formulae to be definitions due to the character of the formula or to the thing defined? The answer given by Ross and all subsequent commentators is that they spring from errors in the proper formulation of definitions. A good definition (1) ought not to include its definiendum and (2) ought to define the whole thing rather than just a part of it.[41] Failure to observe these guides arises from the incompetence of the definer; and it is, Ross supposes, in principle, correctable. He reads 1029b28–29 as an interlocutor's objection that a composite like white man cannot have an essence because white fails to belong to man *per se*. Aristotle answers this objector, Ross maintains, when he describes the two types of failure; for the formula of the composite white man need not fail to be *per se* in either way, though, of course, it could fail if it were incorrectly formulated in either of the two ways.[42] But Aristotle's defense is only temporary. For, Ross continues, white man does fail to have a *per se* formula for another reason: it is not a this (τόδε τι) and only what is a this has a *per se* formula (cf. 1030a2–7).[43]

This interpretation is weak on several grounds. First, it requires that formulae be capable of failing to be *per se* in more than the two ways Aristotle describes in 1029b29–1030a2. But this latter passage begins with the words, "not *per se* is said in two ways." If there are not more than two ways in which a formula can fail to be *per se*, then the failure that Aristotle describes in 1030a2–7 must be one of the two described earlier. Second, there is no indication that Aristotle intends the description of the two ways that formulae fail to be *per se* as an answer to someone denying that accidental composites have *per se* formulae. There is no hint in this text that any objections are being answered or that we should think that formulae of white man can escape these types of failure. Quite the contrary, we have seen that Aristotle objects to including white in any formula of white man. Moreover, the passage that Ross thinks raises the objection these lines answer, 1029b28–29, expresses Aristotle's own view. It asserts that accidental composites like white man are not said *per se*. In 1030a14–17, a passage that expresses the conclusion of the entire discussion, Aristotle claims that though composites can have formulae expressing that one part belongs to another, they lack definitions and essences. Since the essence of something is what it is said to be *per se* (1029b13–14), 1030a14–17 is equivalent to 1029b28–29. So far from raising an objection that is subsequently answered, the latter passage states the conclusion of the discussion.

Furthermore, the supposition that the failures that Aristotle describes in 1029b29–1030a2 stem from an incompetent definer and are correctable renders these failures trivial and only minimally relevant for the inquiry into essence. After all, the conclusion of Aristotle's discussion is that composites lack essences and definitions (in the most proper sense). Any formula of an accidental composite must fail to be *per se*. Since, according to Ross, it does not fail for either of the two reasons described, the description of these two ways does not directly help to explain why formulae of composites are not *per se*. What relevance, then, do they have to the point at issue? On the other hand, Ross's account of how Aristotle does argue that composites lack *per se* formulae assumes what needs to be proven, as we will see shortly (2.4.1). Something is clearly wrong with his view of the two ways that formulae fail to be definitions.

Perhaps part of the motivation for thinking that the two ways formulae fail to be *per se* stem from the incompetence of a definer is that this supposition seems to be a way to avoid some sticky questions. If the failure were due only to the definer, it would have no metaphysical significance. The definer would merely have failed to give the correct formula of the thing. Suppose, on the other hand, that formulae of composites failed to be *per se* not because of some correctable mistake in formulation but inherently because of the nature of composites—Aristotle's position, I maintain. It then follows that there are things which have formulae that inevitably fail to be definitions. How can something have a formula and yet not admit of a definition? Furthermore, composites also lack essences. How can something have a formula and yet lack an essence? Indeed, can there be anything that inherently lacks an essence and a definition? The idea that these last two questions might be avoided by interpreting 1029b29–1030a2 as errors made by an incompetent definer is a mistake. For later in the chapter Aristotle declares that the formula of each composite contains one constituent which belongs to another, and that the composite has neither definition nor essence (1030a14–17). However we interpret the two types of failure, we need to face Aristotle's view that the formula of a composite will fail to express its essence, no matter how carefully it is formulated. How can this be?

The problem is that we tend to regard an essence as a kind of hypostatized formula. The idea that something can have a formula but lack an essence is then absurd. It makes even less sense to speak of something as having a secondary essence. How can an essence ever fail to be primary? If, though, this assumption about the nature of essence makes nonsense of Aristotle's claims about essence, we have good reason for rejecting it. To make sense of Aristotle's claim that things have formulae but fail to have either definitions or essences we need to recognize essence as ontologically distinct from formula. This doctrine is clearly at odds with current linguistic philosophies. Indeed, it undermines linguistic philosophies. I do not intend to defend Aristotle's view here, but it is important to understand what it is if we are to make any sense of his arguments. A formula expresses what a thing is, and this may or may not define the thing and express its essence. Something which has no essence could still have a formula. The question at issue in Z 4 is not how to avoid errors in formulating definitions but whether properly formulated formulae of composites can ever express essences. This is the plain sense of Aristotle's query "whether there will be a formula of the essence of each of them" (1029b25–26). That there are *formulae* is not at issue. The question is whether or not these formulae are definitions.

The key idea in both the description of the ways that formulae fail to be *per se* and the subsequent discussion in this section is addition. Terms for addition are ubiquitous in Z 4–5: πρόσεστιν (1029b19), πρόσθεσις (1029b30; 1030b15, b16; 1031a2–4), προσκεῖσθαι (1029b31), and προστιθέντας (1030a33). I do not discern any differences among Aristotle's use of these terms in this section. Here, as elsewhere, they are all opposed to αφαίρεσις, a word usually translated as "abstraction" but in this context more appropriately rendered as "subtraction." Elsewhere in the corpus, Aristotle uses these terms in a variety of ways. All can signify additions of things, such as the addition of an attribute to an *ousia,* and also additions of formulae, such as the addition of the formula of white to the formula of man. For example, πρόσθεσις is used of the addition of attributes to an *ousia* (*Topics* B 11, 115a26–29; Γ 5, 119a22–25) and the addition of the formula of an *ousia* to the formula of an attribute (*Met.* M 2, 1077b10–11).[44] This last example shows that the notion of addition is general enough to include a variety of different sorts of combinations. Not only can attributes be added to *ousiai,* but *ousiai* can be added to attributes. Addition allows Aristotle to discuss attributes that are "present in" *ousiai* (to use the expression of *Categories* 2) and the *ousiai* in which they are present without drawing ontological distinctions between them. Predication is asymmetrical: attributes can be predicated of *ousiai,* but *ousiai* cannot be predicated of attributes. In contrast, Aristotle can speak indifferently of adding attributes to *ousiai* or adding *ousiai* to attributes. In a context like Z 4–5, where ontological priority is at issue, the priority of *ousiai* to attributes that is implicit in a discussion of predication cannot be taken for granted. Here, addition is a useful alternative.

Aristotle also uses addition often in the *Topics* (e.g., H 2, 152b37–38), but there his concerns are different. He proposes addition and subtraction as ways to test whether a formula adequately defines a word (cf. A 5, 102a11–17—the term for "addition" here is πρόσθεσις). A good way to dispute a proposed definition is to add or subtract the same expression from both the term and the proposed formula and then to show that the result is not the same (see H 1, 152b10–16). This procedure is supposed to help decide whether a formula and the term it defines are the same (A 5, 102a11–17). On the contrary, the issue in Z 4 is whether it is possible to define certain things, composites. The procedure described in the *Topics* will not help us with this question.

The only place in Z 4–5 where Aristotle considers the question of whether a formula defines a term is a passage that dismisses it:

> There is not a definition when a name signifies the same as a formula, for then all formulae could be definitions. For there will be a name for a particular formula; so that even the *Iliad* will be a definition. Rather, there is a definition if the name is of something primary (1030a7–10).

Apparently, the test proposed in the *Topics* has limited value. The name "*Iliad*" does signify the same as the group of words that is its formula (λόγος), the poem; and both would signify the same even with additions and subtractions. But the *Iliad* is still not the formula of an essence because it is not the formula of something primary. As Aristotle puts it later in the chapter, the *Iliad* is not something one, but words placed together by an artist (1030b9–10).[45] A group of words may constitute a formula, but they are not thereby a definition. This dismissal of the *Iliad* as a definition ought to lay to rest the idea that the definitions under considerations in Z 4 are formulae that define words. Whereas the *Topics* speaks of using addition to dispute attempts to define terms with formulae, the point at issue in *Metaphysics* Z 4 is whether a formula expresses what a thing is. At issue here are definitions of things, real definitions;[46] and Aristotle uses addition and subtraction to examine whether a formula expresses the essence of a particular kind of thing, an accidental composite.

2.4.1 *Accidents and Accidental Composites*

With this discussion, we can look more closely at the two ways in which a formula can fail to express an essence. I have argued against the usual view that this passage describes errors that someone might make in formulating a definition, and I have claimed that in Z 4 addition refers to both relations of things and relations of formulae. Now the first type of failure ("by addition") occurs when something is defined by adding it to another, when, for example, someone defines white by adding the formula of this attribute to the formula of man. The second type of failure ("not by addition") occurs when someone defines something by adding another to it, such as when someone defines white man by giving the formula of white. In my view, Aristotle's choice of examples to describe each type of failure is significant.

Let us consider the first type of failure. Why would anyone mistakenly add the formula of man when attempting to define white? The formula of white ought to express what it is to be white. But white is always an accident of some *ousia*. As Aristotle explains in Z 1, beings other than *ousiai* are qualities, quantities, affections, and so forth **of** *ousiai* (1028a18–20); and the other categories do not exist separately from some *ousia* (1028a33–34). Ontological dependence is part of the nature of white. It follows that a formula expressing completely what white is would have to mention that white always belongs to some *ousia*. This is not to say that someone defining white would have to give the formula of white man; it is not necessary that man be the *ousia* to which white is added. What we would need to include in the formula of white is the general expression for *ousia* and some indication that white cannot exist apart from *ousia*. The very expression of the dependence of white on *ousia* would amount to including something besides white in the formula of white. A complete formula of white would add an expression for the quality white to the general expression for *ousia*. This inclusion of *ousia* is what Aristotle must have in mind when he says of instances of categories other than *ousia*, in the first chapter of book Z, "it is necessary for the formula of *ousia* to be present in the formula of each" (1028a35–36). Accordingly, Aristotle's example of defining white with the formula of white man represents not a careless error but an instance of an inevitable addition. Since the formula of any accident necessarily includes some reference to *ousia*, it necessarily fails to be *per se* in the first way. Any attempt to give a *per se* formula of white or any other accident fails because the formula inevitably adds the attribute to some substrate.[47] Such a formula fails to define only the attribute.

What we usually find in Aristotle's work seems, however, somewhat different. He does give a genus-differentia formula of white that contains no explicit reference to *ousia*: white is a "piercing color" (I 7, 1057b8–9; cf. *Timaeus* 67e). Is such a definition at odds with the preceding analysis? No. The preceding discussion assumes that it is possible to give a formula of the attribute white; this is what is added to the general formula of *ousia*. As I noted, this formula is incomplete. Color is a quality (*Cat.* 8, 9a28–31), and quality inheres in *ousia* (*Cat.* 5, 2b1–6c). The genus of quality is ordinarily omitted from statements of white's formula, even though a complete formula would need to include it. So too, inherence in an *ousia* is usually omitted even though it would belong in a complete formula of white. Nearly always, interest in a formula centers on its differentia because it is what uniquely distinguishes this thing from other beings. The differentia "piercing" distinguishes white from other colors; the formula "piercing color" distinguishes white from other beings. It is unnecessary to mention quality in the formula of white because it is implicit in the other terms (cf. Z 12, 1038a28–33). Dependence on *ousia* is also something implicit in the other terms. Moreover, dependence on *ousia* is something white shares with all beings. Only in metaphysical contexts like Z 4–5 is it important to emphasize the presence of *ousia* in the complete formula of white. The complete formula of white must, to use Aristotle's language, add white to *ousia*. A parallel claim holds for any other instance of a category other than *ousia*, that is, for any other accidental attribute.

While the first type of failure applies to formulae of attributes, the second type of failure applies to formulae of accidental composites. Attempts to define an accident like white necessarily involve an addition; attempts to define accidental composites necessarily fail in the other way. Consider Aristotle's description of the second type of failure: someone who defined white man with the formula of white would make the mistake of adding something else to the thing to be defined (1029b33–34). The thing to be defined here is the composite white man. Why would the formula of white constitute an addition to it? Because white does not belong to the white man *per se*. As we saw earlier, though the white man is white, it does not belong to his essence to be white (1030a1–2). Hence, a formula that expresses the essence of white man ought not to include white; it should simply express what it is to be a man (see 6, 1031a20–24). A formula of white man that also included the formula of white would contain an unwarranted addition. It follows from this reasoning that although a composite does have a *per se* formula that expresses what its substrate is, the whole composite never admits of a *per se* formula. A formula of the composite that included an expression for the accident would inevitably add something to the thing defined, and thus necessarily fail to be *per se* in the second way. If the formula included *both* the substrate and the accident (cf. 1030a14–16), it would express what the composite is, but it too would add something that does not belong *per se* to the thing being defined. Only the formula of the substrate, for example, the formula of man, would belong to the composite *per se*. But it does not express the nature of the *whole* composite. In sum, the formula that does express what the whole composite is does not belong to it *per se* because it adds the accident to the thing defined, and the formula that does belong to the composite *per se,* the formula of the substrate, does not express what the whole composite is. Therefore, an accidental composite cannot have a *per se* formula that expresses the nature of the entire composite.

According to the foregoing interpretation, the failure of formulae to be *per se* lies not in an incompetent definer but in the nature of the things whose formulae they are. Even well formulated formulae of accidents and accidental composites fail to be *per se* in one of the two ways Aristotle describes.[48] The formula of a composite that included an expression for an accidental attribute would fail to be *per se* by adding something to the thing defined. Likewise, the formula of an accidental attribute by itself would fail to be *per se* because it would inevitably add the attribute to something else, a substrate *ousia.* These formulae express the "what it is" of accidents and accidental composites, but they *still* fail to be *per se,* and their failure is not correctable. The two ways in which a formula can fail to be *per se* are precisely the ways in which formulae of accidents and accidental composites inevitably fail to be *per se.*

One advantage of this interpretation is that it shows why accidents and accidental composites must fail to have *per se* formulae. Another advantage is that it fits perfectly with Aristotle's description of the two types of failure. Yet, this description has troubled commentators. The problem is that, at first glance, the statement of the two ways in which formulae can fail to be *per se* seems to be inconsistent. According to the usual view, the first type of failure arises when what is being defined is added into the formula and the second failure arises when there is an addition in the thing defined (e.g., a white man) but the formula omits a constituent of the thing. The symmetrical formulation of these failures in the text (1029b31-33) is "misleadingly stated," Ross claims, because the addition in the first case lies in a formula, while the addition in the second case lies in the thing.[49] If my account is correct, both types of failure arise because of the characters of the things. In the first case, the thing to be defined exists added to something else; thus, its formula must contain an addition. In the second case, the thing to be defined exists with something else added to it; so the formula that expresses what it is contains something that does not belong to it *per se.* The problem vanishes. Both types of failure are due to an addition. Aristotle may term the first failure "by addition" because the thing to be defined implicitly contains an addition. The second failure is "not by addition" because, though the thing to be defined may be some sort of composite, it does not contain an addition in its nature. Significantly, the formulae of both accidents and accidental composites involve additions, just as Aristotle indicates at 1030a14-16.

Furthermore, on my interpretation the discussion of the two ways in which formulae fail to be *per se* contributes directly to answering the question that it follows in the text, whether accidental composites have definitions and essences (1029b25-27). First, since no formula of an accidental composite is *per se,* it is fairly clear that no formula will succeed in defining the composite. As Aristotle puts it, a formula will be a definition not when it signifies the same as a term (for then even the *Iliad* would be a definition) but when it is the formula of something primary (1030a7–10—quoted earlier). What things are primary? Things in which one element is not said of another (1030a10–11). That is to say, a formula will be a definition when it is *not* the formula of something which contains an addition. What justifies this claim? The discussion of the two ways that formulae fail to be *per se.* Formulae fail to be *per se* just when that of which they are the formulae contain additions. Aristotle just assumes that a formula which is *per se* is a definition, a reasonable assumption because the essence is what belongs *per se* and the definition is the formula of an essence. In sum, Aristotle's discussion of the two ways that formulae are not *per se* shows when a formula would be *per se,* when it is the formula of something which does not contain an addition. Such a formula is a definition.

It follows from this that accidental composites do not have definitions. Further, it follows that accidents also lack definitions because they too, in a sense, contain an addition; they are added to an *ousia.* Only *ousiai* have definitions because they alone do not contain additions. They are primary; that is to say, they are one.

The preceding argument that accidental composites have no definitions is embedded in Aristotle's discussion of why accidental composites lack essences. The discussion starts in 1030a2 with the question whether "to be a cloak" (i.e., "to be a white man"—"cloak" is the term he uses for this composite) is an essence.[50] No, Aristotle answers. In the manuscripts, his reason is: ὅπερ γάρ τί ἐστι τὸ τί ἦν εἶναι (1030a3), a sentence difficult to render.[51] Ross translates, "for the essence is precisely what something *is.*"[52] An alternative that I think is more helpful is, "for essence is something in itself." In other words, ὅπερ here might be equivalent to *per se* in 1029b13–14, in which case the two sentences would also be equivalent. Let me return to this. In any case, the passage continues with the claim that whenever something is said of something else, it is not a this, since (εἴπερ) "this" belongs only to *ousiai* (1030a3–4). It follows, Aristotle concludes, that there is an essence for just those things whose formulae are definitions (1030a6–7). At this point in the text, in a passage discussed in his preceding paragraph (1030a7–11), Aristotle explains that only what is not said of something else has a formula which is a definition. From all this it somehow follows that only the species of a genus has an essence (1030a11–13) and, eventually, that composites have neither essences nor definitions (1030a16–17).

On one interpretation (Ross's), Aristotle's reasoning here seems dogmatic. He apparently argues: since (1) only an *ousia* has a this (1030a5–6),[53] and (2) a composite like white man is not an *ousia,* then (3) a composite is not a this. Since, further, (4) only a this is an essence (1030a3–5), it follows [from (3) and (4)] that (5) a composite is not an essence.[54] Since Aristotle consistently characterizes *ousia* as a this (e.g., 1028a12; 1029a28; 1030b11), (1) and (2) are unproblematic. How, though, does he justify (4)? That only a this is an essence surely needs to be shown, for if we grant that (1) and (2) are obvious, (4) is nearly a part of the conclusion of the entire discussion (5, 1031a11–14). In effect Aristotle would be assuming that only *ousia* has an essence in order to prove that only an *ousia* has an essence. Unless this discussion is an exercise in question begging, something must be wrong with this interpretation.

Let me propose instead that the argument turns on claims about composites that consist of one element said of another, that is, claims about things that contain an addition. Aristotle makes parallel claims about such composites here: "Whenever one thing is said in respect of another, there is not just [ὅπερ] a this something" (1030a3–4), and "These primary things are just those which are not said one in respect of another" (1030a10–11). From these claims Aristotle infers, respectively, that things which contain additions lack essences and that they lack definitions. It is because of the parallel between these conclusions that Aristotle identifies the things which have essences as just those that have definitions (1030a6–7). I have already spoken about the reason that things with additions lack definitions. Why do things with additions also lack essences?

Aristotle could answer this question by drawing on the parallel between essences and definitions. A definition is the formula of an essence. If things with additions lack definitions, it is unlikely that they will also have essences, for if they did, their essence would be ineffable. Aristotle could take this approach, but the structure of the text suggests something different. Rather than starting with the argument about definitions, he begins with essences and then turns to definitions. The argument that things with additions lack essences should be complete before Aristotle draws the parallel between essences and definitions in 1030a6–7 and begins to discuss definitions. It should be contained in 1030a2–6. As we have seen, the main claims in a2–6 are that essence is ὅπερ τι and that things that contains additions are not ὅπερ τόδε τι. Unfortunately, this passage does not explain or justify these claims. Nor can we expect much help from an analysis of other uses of ὅπερ. For, though Aristotle often uses this term in contrast with the accidental (e.g., Γ 4, 1007a32–33; *Phys.* A 2, 186a32–b10),[55] it is difficult to give it any sense more precise than essential. The term is generally rendered as "just," "precisely," or "the very." Any of these ordinary senses of the term suffices here. Something which contains an addition is not *just* a this; it includes something else as well. An *ousia* is a this, and it is *just* a this. A composite, though, is an *ousia* and something else. Why does a composite lack an essence? Because, Aristotle answers, the essence is just something (1030a3); it is just what the thing is. But the composite is not just anything; it is two things. How could it have *an* essence? Since an *ousia* is neither something said of something else, nor is it itself said of another, there is no reason to doubt that it has an essence. As stated, accidental composites and accidents both contain additions. Neither can have an essence.

Although the argument of 1030a2–6 should now be clear, two further details will help us to fit it into its context. First, as I suggested earlier, Aristotle's claim that essence is just something expresses much the same idea as his assertion at 1029b13–14 that the essence of a thing is what is said of it *per se*. It is nearly the same to say that essence is what it is in virtue of itself and to say that essence is just itself. The difference between these two formulations is that 1029b13–14 includes "is said"; this allows it to apply to formulae as well as things. At 1030a3 Aristotle speaks about things in contrast with definitions and formulae. ὅπερ here avoids any ambiguity. A second point about this argument is that it assumes that only what is one has an essence. This assumption is explicit if "this" means one, as I argued earlier. But even without this equation, the assumption is clear: on what other ground could Aristotle deny that what contains an addition has an essence? Something with an addition lacks an essence because it is not one but two. Indeed, a composite is not really a thing at all.

That this assumption about unity is really Aristotle's is also apparent from his later formulation of the result of the present argument. Near the end of Z 4 he says that though definitions and essences belong primarily to *ousiai*, anything that is one will have a definition (1030b4–10). Since a definition is a formula of an essence, whatever has a definition must also have an essence. Hence, whatever is one would have an essence. Anything without addition, that is, anything that is primary (1030a10–11), should have an essence.

These remarks help to clarify the final portion of Aristotle's argument that what has an addition lacks an essence or a definition. In 1030a11–17 Aristotle insists that only the species of a genus has an essence but that an attribute, an accident, or what is by participation does not because the formulae of these latter ascribe something to something else. An attribute or an accident lacks unity because it contains an addition, as I said earlier. Participation is often mentioned as an example of what causes unity, but Aristotle explains it as a conjunction of two things (Z 12, 1037b14–18). He thinks that participation requires a cause partly because what is by participation is not just one (H 6, 1045b5–11). A species is one, even though it falls under a genus, a claim that Aristotle will argue in Z 12.

In sum, Z 4, 1029b22–1030a17 is a consistent and cogent treatment of the question whether accidental composites have definitions or essences. Although they have formulae, these formulae fail to be definitions because they are not *per se,* and they are not *per se* because what is defined contains an addition. Likewise, accidental composites lack essences because an essence is just what a thing is, and composites are pluralities. The same analysis shows that no accidental attribute could ever have an essence or a definition either because it, too, contains an addition. An attribute is always added to an *ousia*. It also follows that only an *ousia* can have an essence and be defined because only an *ousia* does not contain an addition. Only an *ousia* has a definition and essence because only it is one.

2.4.2 The Opening Lines of Z 4: 1029b13–22

With this analysis we can return to the lines near the beginning of Z 4 that we skipped over earlier, 1029b13–22. This text is terse, and portions of it are difficult to construe. Aristotle begins to investigate essence *logikōs* with a claim that played an important role in the analysis of the preceding section: "The essence of each is what is said [of it] *per se*" (1029b13–14). He supports this with an example: "To be you is not to be musical because you are not musical in respect of yourself [κατὰ σαυτόν]" (1029b14–15). That is to say, things like musical do not belong to your essence because they do not belong to you in respect of what you are. Contrariwise, things that do belong to you in respect of what you are do belong to your essence.

As we saw earlier, to apply this principle, Aristotle needs to explain just what does and does not belong to something *per se*. The opening lines mention some things which are said to belong *per se* that are not part of an essence: though a surface can be called white *per se*, white is not a part of its essence because "to be a surface" is not "to be white" (1029b16–18). Presumably, Aristotle has in mind that a surface is white *per se* because white is "received in it first" (Δ 18, 1022a29–31; cf. 1022a16–19).[56] In this sense, an attribute belongs to a substrate *per se* if there is nothing else besides the substrate in which the attribute inheres. A man could be white in virtue of his surface, but his surface could be white in respect of nothing besides itself. The surface would then be white *per se*, but whiteness would not belong to it in virtue of its essence. The same surface could be blue *per se*. The reason that Aristotle mentions this type of *per se* is to exclude it. The essence of a thing is what belongs to it *per se*, but not in every sense of *per se*. What belongs to a substrate *per se* because that substrate is its first recipient is not included in the essence of the substrate. This type of *per se* is not directly pertinent to the discussion of essence.

What is the pertinent sense of *per se*? The obvious answer is that it is the *per se* that Δ 18 describes as follows: "In one way the essence of each thing is *per se*; for example, Callias *per se* is Callias or the essence of Callias" (1022a25–27).[57] There is, though, another *per se* that looks as though it might be pertinent, the *per se* that characterizes the elements of a thing's formula. This is the sense of *per se* in which animal belongs to Callias *per se* (1022a27–29). Since this *per se* apparently differs from the former *per se*, the elements of a formula, or at least not all of them, are not the essence. But this point remains undeveloped in Δ 18, nor does Z 4 explicitly exclude the *per se* in formula from the *per se* that characterizes essence. The latter chapter leaves it open whether a genus is said of an individual *per se*. Presumably, though, Aristotle would say that animal is not the essence of Callias because to be Callias is not (precisely) to be animal. Be this as it may, Aristotle's chief interest in 1029b13–19 is attributes. Since to be a surface is not to be white, white does not belong to the surface *per se* in the pertinent sense of this phrase. An analogous claim holds of all accidental attributes.

The two final sentences of the passage under consideration are ambiguous. Both clearly concern composites like white surface. The first (1029b18–19) is usually taken to deny that to be a surface is to be a white surface because the latter adds something (αὐτό).[58] Alternatively, the sentence may be denying that to be a white surface is to be white.[59] Still a third possibility is that the sentence denies that to be a composite (the essence of the composite) is to be a white surface because the latter adds white.

The next sentence (1029b19–22) is particularly difficult:

ἐν ᾧ ἄρα μὴ ἐνέσται λόγῳ αὐτό, λέγοντι αὐτό, οὗτος ὁ λόγος
τοῦ τί ἦν εἶναι ἑκάστῳ, ὥστ᾽ εἰ τὸ ἐπιφανείᾳ λευκῇ εἶναί ἐστι τὸ
ἐπιφανείᾳ εἶναι λεία, τὸ λευκῷ καὶ λείῳ εἶναι τὸ αὐτὸ καὶ ἕν.

Along with the preceding sentence, it is usually understood as an exhortation to avoid including the definiendum in the definiens.[60] Ross renders it,

The formula, therefore, in which the term itself is not present but its meaning is expressed, this is the formula of the essence of each thing.

All the objections that I raised earlier against interpreting 1029b29–1030a2 as rules for formulating good definitions apply here, and more besides. Such rules are even less relevant at this point in Z 4 than they would be later. Suppose that these rules were violated by defining white surface as white. What would follow from this? Could we infer that white surface does not belong to surface *per se,* that white does not belong to surface *per se,* or that white surface has no *per se* formula? Could we infer anything at all about the point at issue in this portion of Z 4, that is, about what belongs *per se?* How could a rule for formulating good definitions help us to decide what belongs *per se?* Aristotle thinks the supposed rule at 1029b19–20 follows from what has gone before (notice ἄρα in b19). But a rule about how to formulate good definitions does not follow from the preceding discussion of what belongs *per se.*[61] The rule is not even pertinent to this discussion.

Ross's (implicit) supposition that 1029b18–22 anticipates the discussion of the two ways formulae fail to be *per se* in 1029b29–1030a2 is plausible. The mistake lies in thinking that either passage presents rules for formulating good definitions. I intend to draw on my discussion of the latter passage to advance an interpretation of the former. The first few lines of Z 4 (1029b15–18) deny that accidents belong to substrata *per se*, and 1029b18–22 clearly concern composites. This dichotomy between accidents and composites parallels the two types of examples of things that fail to have *per se* formulae in 1029b29–1030a2. Not only is addition mentioned in both passages, but the language that Aristotle uses to explain the second type of failure is similar to the problematic sentence at 1029b18–19. The second type of failure occurs when white man is defined by adding white to it; but white is not a *per se* formula of white man because though "white man is white, its essence is not to be white" (1030a1–2). This assertion is very close to one of the possible interpretations of 1029b18–19 mentioned earlier, the one that denies that white belongs to white surface *per se* because to be a white surface is not to be white. Let us accept this interpretation because it illuminates both 1029b18–19 and 1029b33–1030a2. The former denies that white belongs to white surface *per se*. The latter draws the inference that the formula of white man does not include the formula of white. So understood, 1029b18–19 explains why formulae of composites fail to be *per se* if they add the formula of the accident. Analogously, the argument in the preceding lines (1029b15–18) that white does not belong to surface *per se* explains the first type of failure of a formula to be *per se*. Since an accident does not belong to an *ousia per se*, to mention the *ousia* in the formula of the accident is to define the accident by adding it to something else.

What about the problematic 1029b19–22? Since white does not belong to white surface *per se*, a definition of a white thing ought to omit white. The formula that expresses the essence of a white thing is the formula that omits white and expresses the essence of the thing that is white. This, I think, is what Aristotle intends to assert in 1029b19–20. The word αὐτό here refers to white just as it does in the preceding sentence.[62] Thus, I interpret the first part of the passage as follows:

> The formula in which it [white] is not present, but which expresses it, is the formula of the essence of each [white thing].

This requires that in its first instance αὐτό refer to white and in its second instance to the white thing, but this merely reflects the ambiguity of the Greek τὸ λευκόν (see Z 6, 1031b22–28). So interpreted, the sentence expresses a consequence for definitions of composites that follows from the fact that accidents do not belong *per se*, presumably the claim being made at 1029b18–19.

This interpretation immediately explains the rest of the sentence. Since the essence of a white surface is the essence of a surface, it follows that the essence of smooth surface will also be the essence of surface. Hence, to be a white surface is to be a smooth surface. But since subtracting equals from equals yields equals, the identity remains after we take the being of surface from both sides. Consequently, to be white and to be smooth are identical. As Aristotle puts it:

> . . . so that if to be a white surface is to be a smooth surface, to be white and to be smooth are one and the same.

The identity in the consequent is meant to be an absurdity. A similar argument at Z 6, 1031a21–28 draws out the reasoning in greater detail. In both, deriving an absurd identity is supposed to refute the initial assumption. In Z 4 the assumption that we are to reject is the assertion of first part of the sentence, that the formula of the essence of an accidental composite should not include the formula of the accident. At first glance this assumption seems unexceptionable. It follows from the preceding claim that an accident does not belong to a composite *per se*. Or better, it would follow if we could assume that the accidental composite has an essence and that an accident has an essence. Of course, it is exactly these assumptions that Aristotle goes on to question and to reject (1029b25–27; 1030a16–17).

If this interpretation is correct, the opening lines of Z 4 prepare the way for the discussion of the two ways in which a formula can fail to be *per se* in 1029a25–1030a2. Examining the case of the white surface enables Aristotle to generalize the results, and it also shows the inadequacy of supposing that an accidental composite can be understood only in terms of what belongs to it *per se*. The difference between πρόσεστιν and μὴ ἐνέστιν in line 19 resembles the difference between προσκεῖσθαι (implicit in 1029b33) and οὐκ ἐκ προσθέσεως (in ll. 30–31); and the discussion of accidents and composites in the opening lines parallels the treatment of them in 1029b33–1030a2. The interpretation I advance here is not the only one possible, but it has the advantage of making sense of the opening of Z 4. If my analysis is correct, the text contains a coherent and insightful development.

What emerges from the opening of chapter 4 is that accidents belong *per se* to neither *ousiai* nor accidental composites. This conclusion is a fitting preamble to the analysis of the ways in which formulae fail to be *per se* that follows it. Apparently, neither accidents nor accidental composites have essences because they contain additions. Only *ousiai* have essences in the proper sense (1030b4–6).

2.4.3 Z 5: Coupled Things

Z 4's assertion that only *ousiai* have essences in the proper sense (1030b4–6) is a bit premature because Z 5 goes on to consider whether there are definitions and essences of something else, coupled things. The first problem of chapter 5 is posed in its opening lines:

> If someone denies that the formula from addition can be a definition, it is an *aporia* whether there are definitions of what is not simple but coupled (1030b14–16).

Snub is Aristotle's paradigmatic example of what is coupled. It is coupled because it cannot be made clear without the particular substrate in which it inheres, nose (1030b23–25). Snub belongs to nose *per se* in the second sense distinguished in the *Posterior Analytics* (73a37–b3): its formula includes the formula of nose.[63] Is the formula of a coupled thing a definition? Does a coupled thing have an essence at all (1031a7–11)?

Coupled things are *per se* attributes (1030b18–20). Since accidental attributes lack definitions and essences because they contain additions, the same should be true *a fortiori* of coupled things. All Aristotle needs to do here is to show that the formula of a *per se* attribute does contain an addition. This he does in 1030b16–26 by showing that snub is concavity in a nose. From this he immediately infers that coupled things either have no definitions or essences or have them in another (secondary) way (1030b26–27). Aristotle could only derive this result by applying the reasoning of Z 4.

A second *aporia,* posed later in the chapter (1030b28–1031a2), concerns composites of coupled things and the substrata to which they are coupled, composites like snub nose.[64] The *aporia* is that there are arguments against identifying snub nose with concave nose and also against denying this identity. First, if they are the same, then snub will be the same as concave (1030b29–30). But this is false because the former is a *per se* attribute and the latter is not. If, on the other hand, the two are not identical because snub cannot be said without nose,[65] then there is a problem with snub nose. Either snub nose cannot be said or someone saying it will say the same thing twice (1030b32–33). That is, since snub is concavity in a nose, a nose that is snub will be a nose that is a concave nose: snub nose will be concave nose nose (1030b34–35). Thus, Aristotle claims that there will be an infinite regress of noses (1030b35–1031a1).

From this dilemma Aristotle draws two conclusions: "it is absurd that there be essences of these things" (1030b34–35), and definition belongs only to *ousia* (1031a1–2). The first of these must refer to composites like snub nose, not to snub as usually thought,[66] for it is snub nose that Aristotle argues cannot be said. Clearly, the purpose of this passage is to show that these composites lack definitions and essences. But precisely how does this conclusion follow?

To answer this question it is helpful to recognize the parallel between Z 4 and Z 5: the former examines accidental attributes and accidental composites, the latter *per se* attributes and, what are usually overlooked, *per se* composites. The first part of Z 5 denies that *per se* attributes have definitions and essences on the same ground that Z 4 denies accidental attributes have definitions and essences. Z 5's discussion of *per se* composites also bears some similarity to Z 4's treatment of accidental composites. Both texts point to the absurdity of identifying composites that have the same substrate: Z 4 notes that if to be a white surface is to be a smooth surface, to be smooth will be to be white (1029b21–22); Z 5 contends that if snub nose is concave nose, concave will be snub (1030b28–30). In the former, the absurdity results from assuming that the essence of a composite is the essence of its substrate.

Z 4 also denies that the formula that adds the accident defines a composite in the proper sense; and, as we will see, it maintains that such a formula constitutes a secondary kind of definition. At Z 5, 1030b30–1031a1 Aristotle makes, I propose, an analogous point. At issue here is the formulae of *per se* composites like snub nose. Is the formula of snub nose just the formula of concave nose? That would result in an absurdity. Then let us assume that snub nose is different from concave nose (1030b30). In this case, the formula of snub nose should differ from the formula of concave nose. What would the formula of snub nose be? The problem is that either (1) it has no formula or (2) its formula contains the substrate twice. Because the formula of snub already refers to nose, the formula of snub nose will refer to nose twice. This formula necessarily contains an addition; thus, it necessarily fails to be *per se* or to be a definition. From this Aristotle infers, without additional argument, that snub nose cannot have an essence (1030b34–35). He apparently relies on the principle shown in Z 4 that things with essences are just those that have definitions (1030a6–7). He could have argued for this by pointing out once again that there is no one thing which is just snub nose (cf. 1030a2–6), but this is obvious from the doubling of the noses in the formula. What, though, about the expression that appears with (is added to) the two noses in the formula of snub nose? For the same reasons that we earlier rejected the identification of snub and concave, this expression cannot be concave; it must be a character peculiar to noses, a character that implicitly contains nose. Hence, the formula of the composite will need to repeat nose still another time, and so on *ad infinitum*. On this reasoning, the formula of snub nose cannot even be said (the first alternative above).[67] It follows *a fortiori* that snub nose lacks an essence and a definition. Accordingly, Aristotle can conclude in 1031a1–2 that only *ousiai* have (proper) definitions. Since, on the other hand, snub nose contains additions, it should also possess a definition and an essence of a sort "by addition" (1031a1–5), for reasons I shall explore shortly. We will also see that accidental composites have secondary definitions and essences for analogous reasons, though the essences and definitions of the two types of composites differ.

Why does Aristotle not simply use the same argument to deny that *per se* composites have definitions and essences that he used in Z 4 to deny that accidental composites have essences? Since an accidental attribute does not belong to the substrate *per se*, to offer the formula of the accident as a definition of a composite is to add something to it. It is less clear that the formula of a *per se* attribute would be an addition to the thing defined; for a *per se* attribute does, by definition, belong *per se* to its substrate, and according to Z 4 what belongs *per se* constitutes the essence. In other words, because the *per se* attribute meets Z 4's criterion for essence, its formula seems not to be an addition to the thing defined. (Of course, this shows that Z 4's criterion needs to be refined, for a *per se* attribute does not belong to the essence.) So the argument of Z 4 will not do here. Instead, Aristotle shows that any attempt to give a formula of a *per se* composite will necessarily result in a formula that contains an addition and that thus fails to be *per se* in the first way. From this it follows that what belongs to something *per se* in the second of the senses distinguished in the *Posterior Analytics* does not belong to the essence of the thing. Thus, the argument of Z 5 enables Aristotle to distinguish between the *per se* that marks off constituents in an essence (as in 1029b13–14) and the *per se* that characterizes an attribute. Although Aristotle does not say so, Z 5 shows that the sense in which an attribute is *per se* must not be the sense of *per se* which marks off the essence. This chapter helps to refine further Z 4's claim that a thing's essence is what belongs to it *per se* (1029b13–14).

Ross denies the validity of the regress argument on the ground that it collapses the distinction Aristotle draws at *De Sophisticis Elenchis* 182a4 between snubness and that which is snub.[68] In the expression "snub nose," the term "snub" signifies a quality of a nose; but, he maintains, in the regress argument Aristotle takes it to signify the *nose* that is snub. This charge is easily dismissed: the regress comes about just because it is impossible to express the quality that snub is without mentioning that it inheres in a nose.[69] A *per se* attribute includes its substrate in its formula.

A more serious objection to Aristotle's argument is that the regress is not pernicious because Aristotle nowhere shows that the noses are distinct from each other. The repetition of nose in a formula would be troublesome only if we could assume the non-identity of the noses.[70] The first point to notice in response is that the plurality of noses that Aristotle speaks about is a plurality that exists in a formula. The formula of snub nose seems to contain the expression for nose twice. This point is quite different from saying that there are many noses. The problem is that we cannot give a well-constructed formula of snub because we cannot explain the quality of snubness without repeating nose. It does not really make sense to ask whether the nose that is contained in the formula of snub is the same as the nose contained in the formula of snub nose: the *formula* of nose is always the same. The difficulty here is that it is repeated. This argument differs from the third man regresses of *Parmenides* 132a–133a because the latter imply the existence of a plurality of things, forms of largeness. The regress here lies in formulae.

What, though, is wrong with a formula that repeats an element? As long as the plurality of elements in the definition are the same, why is there a problem? If we would have to repeat nose infinitely many times to explain what a snub nose is, then snub nose would not have a formula at all (it would be impossible to say it—1030b32). Suppose, though, that the formula of snub nose repeats nose only twice. In which of the two ways described in Z 4 will it fail to be *per se?* As I said earlier, it seems to fail "by addition" because its formula adds an extra nose. ("By addition I mean a case where the same thing is said twice"—1030a4–5.) Z 4 describes this failure as occurring when what is to be defined is added to something else (1029b31–33). Apparently, the problem here is that a part of snub nose is added to something and this addition is included in the formula of snub nose. But if this addition is merely an element contained in the formula already, where is the problem? Could we not just clean up the formula by leaving out the second nose? Would not the formula of snub nose say the same thing with just one nose? The answer is no. The formula of snub nose that repeats nose is concave nose nose (or the formula of concave nose nose). If we do remove the second nose from this formula, the result will be concave nose. But Aristotle has already argued that snub nose is not the same as concave nose (1030b28–30), so this will not do as the formula of snub nose. Any formula that expresses what snub nose is will, it seems, repeat nose at least twice and so fail by addition to be a definition.

This failure in formula occurs because of the character of the composite snub nose. One of the constituents of this composite, snub, cannot be separated from the other. Snub is not simply the mathematical shape, concavity; it is a concavity that inheres in a nose. Since the formula of the composite snub nose will consist of the formula of snub and the formula of nose, it will repeat nose. This repetition in formula expresses the inseparability of the attribute snub from its substrate, nose. All attempts to separate the attribute from nose fail. The infinite regress is a way of expressing this inseparability. Let us try to separate snub and nose by subtracting nose from the composite snub nose. What is the result? It seems to be just concavity, but snubness is not just concavity. Snubness is concavity *in a nose,* and the formula of the separated attribute will need to include the formula of the substrate. We just attempted to consider snub apart from nose, but upon further examination nose appeared again. If we once again subtract nose from this new composite, the result will be the same: nose will appear again implicitly in snub, and so on *ad infinitum.* Are the noses different in each case? Of course not. To speak of an infinite regress here is merely to express the impossibility of separating snub from nose. No matter how many times we try to consider the formula of snub apart from the formula of nose, the latter reappears. The addition in the formula of snub nose reflects the mode of existence of the attribute snub as an addition to nose. The composite is inevitably an indeterminate plurality.

Understood in this way, the infinite regress is just a way of expressing the necessary dependence of snub on nose. It is, I think, a characteristically Greek mode of argumentation.[71] Using an infinite regress to assert the inseparability of two constituents may strike us as a peculiar way to make the point, but this is hardly grounds to criticize the analysis.

In sum, Z 5 shows that *per se* attributes like snub fail to have definitions and essences because their formulae fail to be *per se* "by addition" and that *per se* composites like snub nose also fail to have definitions and essences because they either have no formulae or have formulae that repeat the substrate twice. Putting these results together with those from Z 4, we can infer that only *ousiai* have essences and definitions.

2.4.4 Addition and Essence

Although Aristotle's reasoning seems clear enough, it remains puzzling why an addition in a formula should prevent that formula from being a definition. A formula of an accident fails to be *per se* by addition because it adds the accident to *ousia*. The formula contains an addition, but it does express what an accident is. Likewise, though a formula of an accidental composite that includes the accident adds something to what is being defined, it does express what the composite is. A *per se* attribute can also be given a formula that expresses what it is, though it too contains an addition. Why does Aristotle deny that formulae that express the nature of accidents, composites, and *per se* attributes are definitions? Clearly, Aristotle thinks that a formula must do more than just express what something is if that formula is to be a definition. A formula that is a definition must express what a thing is without including any additions. It must express just what the thing is.

Is this stipulation legitimate? Again, why should the presence of an addition in a formula prevent it from being a definition? Aristotle's reasoning makes sense if he also assumes that unity is a criterion of whether a formula is a definition. Then, a formula with an addition would not be a definition because it is not one and thus not the formula of one thing. Likewise, the reason that composites containing one element predicated of another lack definitions is that they are not one. Does Aristotle make this assumption? Even if it did not appear in the text, we would have good reason to ascribe it to Aristotle because it is difficult to make sense of his argument without it.

Further, the assumption fits perfectly with the Greek tradition of concern with the one and the many. Aristotle's apparent insistence that what has an essence or a definition must be one is an instance of the idea that whatever exists is one (see, e.g., Γ 2, 1003b19–22). A similar assumption is at work when Presocratic philosophers inquire whether all is one or many, for there can only be a plurality of beings if each being is one. We can also see assumptions about the unity of being at work in Plato's *Parmenides*. This understanding of Aristotle's assumptions may not make his reasoning any more plausible to us, but it does allow us to understand his arguments in the context of the Greek tradition. Because assumptions about unity are foreign to current thinking, it is easy to overlook the arguments.

The only explicit expression of the assumption that what has a definition is one occurs near the end of Z 4 in a passage that summarizes the results of the entire chapter.

> It is not necessary . . . that there be a definition of a thing when it signifies the same as a formula but when it is the same as some [type of] formula. This occurs if the formula is of something one—not one by continuity as the *Iliad* is or things that are one by being bound, but one in any of the [main] ways one is said (1030b7–11).

There is only a definition of something that is one. Since a definition expresses an essence, only what is one has an essence.

This passage is similar both in content and examples to 1030a7–11 (a passage quoted above), except that in the latter a formula is a definition if it is the formula of something primary (πρώτου τινός) rather than the formula of something one. Something is primary if it does not contain one component that is said of another component (1030a10–11). That is, something that is primary is also one. While most of Z 4 speaks of being primary as the condition of a thing's having a definition and essence, the passage near the end expresses the same thought when it presents unity as the condition of something's having a definition. We could say that accidents, accidental composites, *per se* attributes, and *per se* composites all fail to have definitions and essences because they are not primary or that they fail to have definitions and essences because they are not one. Apparently, Aristotle equates being primary with being one.

Why is unity so important here? Aristotle assumes that whatever is is one. Hence, something that lacks unity does not exist, or exists in some lesser sense. An addition in formula arises because the thing of which it is the formula contains an addition, a thing that contains an addition is not one, and what is not one is not. Since the formulae of accidents, accidental composites, *per se* attributes and *per se* composites contain additions, none of these things is one, and it follows that none of them exists in the full sense. What lacks being in the full sense lacks an essence in the full sense. Obviously, the formula of something without an essence cannot express an essence. So something that is not one cannot have a definition (cf. Z 12, 1037b25–27). While this reasoning is not explicit, it allows us to account for what we do find in the text. How else could we explain Aristotle's insistence that only what is one has a definition (1030b7–11) and his mention here that qualities, quantities, and so forth are said to be in a lesser way (1030a32–b2)?

Can anything be truly one? It seems that any formula would contain an addition because it would be composed of genus and differentia (cf. Δ 6, 1016a34–35).[72] It would follow that each thing is a plurality composed of at least two constituents. On this reasoning no genus-differentia formula could be a definition, and no thing with such a formula could have an essence. Aristotle recognizes the problem, and he addresses it in Z 12. In brief, he maintains that genus and differentia constitute a special case. Even though the differentia falls outside of the genus it differentiates, it forms a unity with that genus. Thus, a species is one (cf. B 3, 999a1–6). As I said earlier, Aristotle seems to have this result in mind when he declares that essence belongs only to the species (1030a11–13).

If attributes and composites lack essences and definitions because they are not one, then it follows by elimination that only *ousiai* have essences (cf. 1030b5–6). The analysis that I have advanced allows us to make sense of Z 4–5's project of examining *ousia* through essence and also to understand just what it means to investigate essence *logikōs*. Z 4–5 examine essence by considering formulae and definitions. Aristotle shows that something has an essence if its formula does not contain an addition. Since only *ousiai* have formulae without additions, only *ousiai* have essences. Z 6 also considers essence by means of formulae and definitions. The way essence is investigated *logikōs* in these three chapters stands in sharp contrast with the analysis of form (i.e., essence) and physical change in Z 7–9.[73]

2.4.5 Secondary Essences

Thus far I have focused my attention on the negative results of Z 4–5, the denial of essences to accidents, accidental composites, *per se* attributes, and *per se* composites. At the end of Z 4, though, Aristotle claims that while only *ousiai* have essences in the primary sense, accidents and composites do have essences in a lesser sense: essence, "what it is," and definition belong primarily to *ousia* and then to instances of the other categorial genera. The final sentence of the chapter concludes:

> Therefore there will be a formula and definition of white man but in different way from the formula and the definition of white and of *ousia* (1030b12–13).

Likewise, at the end of Z 5, Aristotle indicates that though *ousiai* have definitions and essences "most of all, primarily, and simply," other things have them in other ways (1031a7–14). How does he justify the ascription of essences to non-*ousiai*? The beauty of Aristotle's analysis is that the very reason that attributes and composites lack essences and definitions in a primary way is also the reason that they have essences and definitions in a lesser way. In this section I shall show that they have essences and definitions because they are one by addition.

The pertinent text is the portion of Z 4 that we have not yet examined, 1030a17–b13. Much of this section consists of an extended parallel between essence, definition, "what it is" (τὸ τί ἐστιν), and "is" (τὸ ἔστιν).[74] All are said in many ways, but not equivocally; each belongs primarily to *ousia* and in lesser ways to the other categories. The expressions "what it is" and "is" do not appear elsewhere in Z 4–5. The latter is apparently the same as the participial phrase τὸ ὄν, for Aristotle uses ὄντα and ἐστι virtually in apposition later in the chapter (1030a32–b1).[75] He does not explain the significance of "what it is" here, but in this context it should refer to the formula. For we answer a "what is it" question by giving a formula, Aristotle seems to have such an answer in mind here (esp. 1030a23–27), and formula is the only major term from the first part of Z 4 that does not appear here.[76] One of the issues under investigation in Z 4 is whether, or in what circumstances, a formula is a definition. By distinguishing "what it is" from definition and essence, Aristotle can speak of formulae that express what a thing is but may not be definitions in the proper sense.

How does Aristotle establish the parallel between all of these? First, he takes it for granted that "is" belongs to all things, but primarily to *ousiai* and in a lesser way to the other categories (1030a21–22). This illustrates and, perhaps, supports ascribing the same relation to "what it is" (1030a21–23). Aristotle further justifies the latter as follows:

> For even of quality we might ask, what is it? So quality is also among the "what it is" but not in a simple way. Rather, just as some say about what is not that in respect of formula (*logikōs*) non-being is, not in a simple way but not *being*, so too with quality (1030a23–27).

In other words, quality has a "what it is" because we can ask "what is it" of it. But quality does not have a "what it is" in the primary sense because the "what it is" of quality is not simple. There is nothing in this passage that explains what this means, but following my suggestion that "what it is" refers to the formula, we can make good sense of it. As we saw, the formula of a quality includes one thing said of something else. (1030a14–16 expresses the same idea.) The second thing here, that of which the first is said, is *ousia*. Just as non-being can be discussed because of its relation to *ousia*

(Γ 2, 1003b10), qualities and instances of other categories have formulae by virtue of their relation to *ousiai*.[77] Thus, their formulae are not simple but complex, and *ousia* is contained in their formulae. Aristotle seems to have this result in mind in Z 1 when he speaks of the priority of *ousia* in knowledge (1028a36–b2), and also when he speaks of the priority of *ousia* in formula. In a sentence I quoted earlier, he says that the formula of non-*ousia* contains the formula of *ousia* (1028a35–36). The analysis in Z 4–5 justifies both types of priority.

Aristotle uses this discussion of "what it is" to to draw a parallel inference about essence. His discussion of essence opens with the claim that it is necessary to consider not only what is said about things, but how they exist (1030a27–28). This is not a transition from a linguistic inquiry to a factual one,[78] but the transition from a discussion of formula to a discussion of essence. For the next sentence draws an inference about essence from the discussion of formula:

> Therefore [διό], since what is said is now clear, it is also true that essence belongs primarily and simply to *ousia* and then to the others, just as the "what it is" does; not essence simply, but the essence of quality or the essence of quantity (1030a28–32).

That is to say, because the "what it is" belongs primarily to *ousia* and then to the others, essence must do likewise. This is certainly a surprising argument. Until this point Z 4 had been arguing that only *ousiai* have *per se* formulae and essences. These earlier arguments assume that a being other than *ousia* has a "what it is" or a formula. Indeed, they use such formulae to show that other beings lack essences and definitions. How can Aristotle now say that the other beings have essences *because* they each have a "what it is"? Part of the answer is that the first portion of Z 4 denies essences to everything but *ousiai* whereas the present passage ascribes secondary essences to non-*ousiai*: essence belongs to *ousiai* primarily and to other beings in a lesser way. Secondary essences are inevitably ambiguous because in a way they are essences, but in another way they are not (properly) essences at all. Still, how can Aristotle ascribe essences to non-*ousiai* in any sense at all, given the arguments of Z 4's first part? The text goes on to answer this question.

> For [γάρ] these [instances of other categories] must be called beings [ὄντα] either equivocally or by adding and subtracting (just as the unknown is known); however,[79] since it is right to call [them beings] neither equivocally nor univocally; but, just as medical, it [being] is said in relation to one and the same thing [τῷ πρὸς τὸ αὐτὸ μὲν καὶ ἕν]; but it [being] is neither one and the same nor equivocal; for neither is a body, an act or an instrument called medical equivocally or in respect of one nature [καθ'ἕν—*kath' hen*] but in relation to one nature [πρὸς ἕν—*pros hen*] (1030a32–b3).

The first word here indicates that the entire passage is supposed to be offering support for the preceding sentence, the claim that non-*ousiai* have essences in a secondary way. How is this discussion of being supposed to support this claim?

First, we need to be clear about what it says. The point of the passage is that non-*ousiai* are said to be neither equivocally nor univocally but in relation to one nature; that is, being (τὸ ὄν) is a *pros hen*. Aristotle makes the same claim at Γ 2, 1003a33–b10. Here, though, he also expresses it by saying that these non-*ousiai* are beings by "addition and subtraction."[80] Lest there be any doubts that the latter expression means the same as the former, we have only to notice that the above passage contrasts addition and subtraction with univocal and with equivocal (a32–33) in precisely the same way as it contrasts *pros hen* with *kath' hen* and with equivocal (a35–b2). Instances of categories other than *ousia* are beings by "addition and subtraction."

Addition and subtraction of what? The obvious answer is *ousia*, for *ousia* is the one nature in relation to which they are said to be (Γ 2, 1003b5–10). Further, being (τὸ ὄν) here is just the "is" (τὸ ἔστιν) that Aristotle discussed earlier in the passage, and "is" belongs primarily to *ousia* (1030a21–22).[81] Precisely how are qualities, quantities, and so forth beings "by addition and subtraction"? While the text does not spell this out, Aristotle probably has in mind that qualities and the others exist only because they are added to (or said of) *ousiai*. He may mention subtraction here because we distinguish qualities and other accidental attributes by subtracting (or leaving out) *ousia*, or subtraction may be included here because accidental composites are related to *ousiai* by subtraction. The conjunction between addition and subtraction at 1030a33 need not imply that both are needed to account for the being of qualities or of other non-*ousiai*. Addition may refer to attributes and subtraction to composites. Despite the uncertainty of the details here, there is no difficulty in understanding the claim that qualities and the others are beings by virtue of the addition and subtraction of *ousia*, and it is consistent with the use of addition earlier in this chapter.

How does this account of the *pros hen* character of being help to support the ascription of essences in a secondary sense to non-*ousiai*? Since *ousiai* have essences and since the other beings derive their being through their relation with *ousia*, it is plausible to ascribe some sort of essence to these other beings. However, this reasoning is inadequate because it does not answer the earlier arguments that only what is primary has an essence and a definition. Thus, what we see in the passage quoted is a seeming *non sequitur*: Aristotle asserts that *essence* belongs primarily to *ousiai* and then to non-*ousiai* because *being* belongs primarily to *ousiai* and then, "by addition and subtraction," to non-*ousiai*. There is nothing in the text that explicitly tells us how to get from being to essence, and this move is particularly problematic because of Aristotle's earlier argument that only beings that are primary have essences. Let me suggest that the reason that that argument does not apply here lies in Aristotle's claim that non-*ousiai* derive their being from *ousia* by "addition and subtraction." To grasp why we need to look at what follows in the text.

The remaining portion of the passage under discussion (1030b3–13) concerns definition. Since essence belongs "primarily and simply" to *ousiai,* Aristotle infers that definition (the formula of the essence) will also belong "primarily and simply" to *ousiai* (1030b4–6). And just as essence belongs to other beings in a secondary way, so too the formulae of these other beings are also definitions of a sort (1030b6–7). It is in the justification of this latter claim (1030b7–13) that Aristotle states what has been the guiding assumption all along: only what is one has a definition. I discussed this claim earlier (2.4.1, 2.4.4), and I showed how it supports the conclusion that only *ousia* has a definition. Only *ousia* is one because it is neither added to anything nor has anything added to it. In the present context, however, Aristotle uses the unity requirement for exactly the opposite end: he uses it to justify ascribing definitions to non-*ousiai.* He notes that one is said in as many ways as being and mentions the different ones in each category (1030b10–12). "Therefore," Aristotle concludes, "there will be a formula and a definition of white man but in a different way from that of white and of *ousia*" (1030b12–13). If something must only be one to have a definition, then anything that is one should have a definition. Since each category has its own peculiar type of unity, instances of each admit of some sort of definition. Because the composite is also a unity of a sort, it too admits of a definition. Thus, the stipulation that only what is one has a definition justifies ascribing a definition not only to what is most one, *ousia,* but also to non-*ousiai* that are one in different and lesser ways.

In discussing essences Aristotle had declared that instances of accidental categories are beings by addition and subtraction. Now in explaining why they have definitions, he claims that, as beings of some sort, they have a corresponding kind of unity. These two descriptions are closely connected, for whatever is is one. If accidents are beings by addition and subtraction, then they are one by addition and subtraction. Since addition and subtraction are mathematical operations, it is easy to see why accidents have a kind of unity through them. Accidents are beings by virtue of their addition to *ousiai,* and this addition forms a kind of composite. The latter is not one in the way that an *ousia* is one; it is not simple. But it does have a unity that results from addition, a unity that resembles the unity of a number. The number five, though not simple, is one number by virtue of the addition of units. So too a quality which is a being by virtue of its addition to an *ousia* is one by the same addition.

As far-fetched as this reasoning may appear, Aristotle himself speaks in very similar terms at H 3, 1043b34–1044a9. This passage compares definition to number: (1) like a number, a definition is divisible into indivisible parts (1043b34–36); (2) the addition or subtraction of something alters both number and definition (1043b36–1044a2); and (3) number and definition are each unities composed of a plurality of parts united by some principle (1044a2–6). In the strict sense neither number nor definition is one, but each is a plurality that is somehow one. While the immediate context of this passage from H 3 is the definition of accidental composites, it illuminates the unity of all secondary definitions and the same comparisons hold of what these definitions define, accidental composites and accidents.

With this analysis, we can return to the question of why qualities and other accidents have essences of a sort. Earlier in Z 4 Aristotle had denied that they have essences and definitions on the ground that they are not primary, that is, not one (1030a3–4; a7–11). Their formulae contain additions and so are not formulae of something one. In the section now under consideration, he asserts that they do have essences because they are beings by "addition and subtraction" and that they have definitions because they are one in ways that correspond to their being. Thus, non-*ousiai* lack essences because they are not one, but they have essences of a sort because they are one in a way. Non-*ousiai* lack the degree of unity possessed by *ousiai*, but they have a lesser sort of unity, unity "by addition and subtraction." This lesser unity is at once a relation of non-*ousiai* to *ousiai,* and thus the source of being for the former, and also the means of distinguishing them from *ousia.* Since formulae of these non-*ousiai* will necessarily contain additions, they are not properly definitions; but, since what they define is one by addition and subtraction, they express essences and are definitions of a sort. Just as Aristotle says, non-*ousiai* have essences of a sort because they are beings by addition and subtraction (1030a29–b1).

If this analysis is correct, 1030a16–b13 is a carefully organized argument. The passage begins with the comparison of definition and "what it is" (1030b17–18). It continues with a discussion of "what it is" that draws on what has been said in Γ about "is" (1030a18–27). From this latter and also from the character of being, Aristotle infers that essence has the same character: it too belongs primarily to *ousiai* and in a lesser sense to the others (1030a27–b3). From this, Aristotle draws parallel conclusions about definition (1030b3–13), thus confirming the claim made in 1030b16–17.

The purpose of the passage is to show *that* non-*ousiai* have definitions and essences of some sort; it provides little explanation of *how* we are to find those definitions. Since non-*ousiai* are beings because they are one by addition and subtraction, we can expect them to have definitions also by addition and subtraction. My analysis of Z 4–5 suggests procedures for constructing such definitions. Let us begin with Aristotle's standard definition of the quality white, "piercing color." As I said earlier, a complete definition of white contains *ousia* implicitly because color is a quality and qualities always inhere in an *ousia.* Thus understood, the formula contains an addition. However, with this addition what is supposed to be the formula of white is actually the general formula of an accidental composite that is white. To arrive at the formula of white by itself, we must subtract the general expression for *ousia* that is implicit in the formula of white. The result of this addition and subtraction is just the formula "piercing color," the formula of white that Aristotle regularly mentions. The definition of white is thus constructed by the addition and subtraction of *ousia*. Other attributes could receive definitions by a similar process (cf. 1030a29–33).

This account seems both superfluous and circular. We already know that white is "piercing color"; what is gained by adding it to *ousia* and then subtracting *ousia?* If white together with *ousia* constitutes a plurality, are not white and *ousia* each one? Thus, the addition of white to *ousia* seems entirely unnecessary to account for its unity. These objections rest on two mistakes. First, they take the analogy between number and accidental composite too far. Numbers are composed of units; the accidental composite is composed of something one (*ousia*) and something added to it. Because the latter has no existence apart from *ousia,* it lacks unity.[82] So piercing color is not one independently of *ousia;* it is one only as part of a composite. The second mistake here is the expectation that the procedure of defining an attribute by reference to *ousia* will alter the formula. The purpose of Z 4–5 is not to produce definitions, but to explain the possibility of definitions. The formula of white is already clear without the addition and subtraction of *ousia.* An account of this addition and subtraction should explain only how this formula can signify one thing. Further, recognition of the implicit presence of *ousia* in the definitions of attributes does not enhance any of the logical functions that we sometimes associate with definitions. Accordingly, that the addition and subtraction of *ousia* does not produce a new formula of an attribute is not an argument against the need for this procedure or against my account of it.

Like the accidental attributes just discussed, accidental composites, *per se* attributes, and *per se* composites can all be defined through their relation to *ousia. Per se* attributes have formulae that necessarily add *ousia.* To explain what snub is, it is necessary to include the formula of nose (1030b23–25). In this case, though, it is impossible to subtract the formula of the substrate. For the source of the infinite regress, as I explained it, is that attempts to subtract the substrate fail and what remains is always found to have the substrate within it. Thus, the definitions of *per se* attributes are constructed not by addition and subtraction, like those of accidental attributes, but by addition alone. In virtue of this addition, they lack the unity that would make them definitions in the most proper sense; but, also by virtue of the addition, they have a kind of unity and thereby are definitions of a sort and express essences of a sort.

Per se composites lack definitions in the proper sense because their formulae say the same thing at least twice, but Aristotle claims that they have definitions "by addition" (1030b1–5). Even though the formula of snub nose repeats nose, Aristotle seems to think that it contains enough unity to be some sort of definition. Similarly, accidental composites have formulae that are constructed by addition. While definitions of accidents are constructed by adding something to the general formula of an *ousia* and then subtracting the latter, the definition of an accidental composite adds the definition of an accident to the definition of a specific *ousia*.[83] Again, addition is both a reason to deny that a formula is a definition in the most proper sense and also a reason to recognize it as a kind of definition (1030b12–13).

In this way it is possible to construct definitions of accidents, accidental composites, *per se* attributes and *per se* composites by the addition and subtraction of *ousia*. This account shows how all of these formulae depend on *ousia*. It would have been better if Aristotle were more explicit about these constructions, but my account is suggested by his remarks on addition and subtraction and on unity at the end of Z 4. Further, it allows us to make sense of his parallel between "is," "what it is," definition, and essence. Just as accidents and composites depend on *ousia* in order to be, so too they depend on *ousia* in order to be what they are. Thus, *ousia* is included or implicit in their definitions and essences. It is in this way that we should understand the claim made in Z 1 that *ousia* is prior to the other categories "in formula" (1028a23–33): the formula of *ousia* must be present in the formulae of each thing (1028a35–36). Like "is," formula, definition, and essence are all *pros hen*.

2.4.6 *Addition, Subtraction, and* Ousia

The argument from addition that appears in Z 4–5 stands in striking contrast with the analysis of Z 3. There Aristotle attempts to arrive at the primary substrate by stripping away or subtracting (περιαιρουμένων— 1029a11–12; ἀφαιρουμένου—1029a16–17) all the attributes predicated of a substrate. As I explained earlier, this procedure is a reasonable way of arriving at the primary *ousia* only if Aristotle assumes that *ousia* is one, for subtracting all the attributes should yield a unity underlying the accretions. The difficulty with this method is that it removes too much. What remains is neither separate nor a this, characters that seem to belong to *ousiai* (1029a27–28): what remains is not one at all.

The method of Z 4–5 remedies this deficiency by a very simple move. Instead of subtracting all attributes, it seeks a formula that contains no additions. Again, this procedure makes sense only on the assumption that an *ousia* is one. Since it is possible to subtract only from something that has or can have parts, that is, from something that is constituted by an addition, subtracting and not adding would seem to amount to the same operation. Here, though, they differ. Z 3 seeks to find something from which nothing can be removed, and the only such thing is completely undetermined matter. Z 4–5 seek something with no additions. They succeed in finding *ousia* because they assume that what receives additions has some integrity as a thing; it is something with an indivisible formula. Another reason for the difference between subtracting and not adding is that the latter operation is applied mainly to formulae. Besides assuming that *ousia* is one, the argument also assumes that a formula that contains no additions yet expresses everything that is in the thing is the formula of something one. Such a formula expresses the essence of an *ousia*.

That Aristotle distinguishes accidents, composites and *per se* attributes from *ousiai* is well known. What we see in Z 4–5 is the argument that supports this bit of Aristotelian doctrine. It is an argument from addition, for Aristotle shows that the formulae of non-*ousiai* contain additions, and he infers from this that non-*ousiai* lack proper essences and definitions. A central premise of Aristotle's argument is that *ousia* and essence are each one. So interpreted, Z 4–5 is not simply a statement of doctrine but an argument.

How, though, does this argument contribute to the inquiry into *ousia?* In particular, how does the conclusion that only *ousiai have* essences in the most proper sense advance what is supposed to be an examination of whether *ousia is* essence? Should not Z 4–5 elucidate essence rather than *ousia?* Aristotle examines essence because it is a candidate for *ousia,* but the result of this examination is that *ousia* has an essence. What begins as a treatment of essence to elucidate *ousia* ends by using *ousia* to elucidate essence. Z 4–5 seems to go in a circle.

These objections may look serious, but they are easily removed. The purpose of Z 4–5 and the seven chapters that follow them is to show that *ousia* is essence. To establish this conclusion, Aristotle cannot point to something prior to either *ousia* or essence and then infer their identity from it. There is nothing prior. The only conceivable procedure is to show that essence and *ousia* have the same characteristics. This he does by showing that essence belongs primarily in the first category. The things which have essences in the most proper way are *ousiai*. The relation between essence and *ousia* in Z 4–5 is some sort of possession; essences belong to *ousiai*. While this is different from saying that the two are identical, it serves as a first step for Z 6's demonstration of their identity.

2.5 Z 6: THE IDENTITY OF THING AND ESSENCE

The sixth chapter opens with the assertion that "it is necessary to consider whether each thing and its essence are the same or different" (1031a15–16). The conclusion of this examination appears several times during the chapter: for things said *per se,* thing and essence must be one (1031b11–12; b21–22;

1032a4–6). At issue in the chapter is the unity or sameness of the thing and its essence.

Sameness is a kind of unity (Δ 9, 1018a4–9), and the chapter uses the terms "same" and "one" indifferently. But does this type of one, the identity of an apparent plurality, have anything to do with the assumption that *ousia* is one or with the problem of the one and the many? Contemporary philosophers usually think of identity as a logical relation existing in abstraction from what falls under it. Were this what Aristotle had in mind when he argued for the identity of a thing and its essence, Z 6 would not concern unity in the senses we have seen so far. What we find in Z 6, however, are arguments showing that thing and essence cannot be two things. Such arguments make sense only if we assume in advance that thing and essence are each one. The issue is whether together they make two or they are one and the same. This *is* an instance of the problem of the one and the many. We could have gathered as much from Aristotle's view of sameness: "It is clear that sameness is a kind of unity either of what is many or of what is treated as many, as when someone says that something is the same as itself" (Δ 9, 1018a7–9). For things to be the same, they must be or be treated as a plurality; but for things to be or be treated as a plurality, each must be one. Thus, in order for essence and thing to be the same, each must be one. And they are the same when they are one rather than two.

The assumption that the thing (ἕκαστον) is one is familiar from Z 4–5. Aristotle claims that essence is what belongs to each thing *per se* (1029b13–14), and we later see that only what is one has an essence and a definition. It follows that the thing which has an essence is one. Is its essence also one? This is also implicit in Z 4, for Aristotle denies that a formula expresses an essence if it contains an addition. Since to be a definition a formula must be one, the essence it defines should also be one. As I said, the overt issue in Z 6 is whether essence and thing together are one or two. By considering this question Aristotle also further determines the character of essence. Further, these arguments also help to explain what the thing is. In Z 4 there was at least a suggestion that the thing is a composite individual, for immediately after speaking of the thing which has the essence Aristotle speaks of "the being of you" (1029b13–15). Most readers assume that the thing in Z 6 is also a composite. To decide whether this is so, we need to look closely at the arguments in Z 6.

At first glance, the question of the identity of thing and essence seems peripheral to the inquiry into *ousia* that is Aristotle's chief concern in Z–H. But Aristotle makes a point of telling us right at the beginning of Z 6 that this identity is important for the inquiry into *ousia*,

> For each thing seems to be no other than its *ousia*, and the essence is said to be the *ousia* of each thing (1031a17–18).

Here *ousia* is the middle term of a three way identity. We might think that by identifying the extremes, thing and essence, Z 6 supports both legs, the identity of thing and *ousia* and of essence and *ousia*. (The latter is, of course, the most interesting and pertinent at this point in the inquiry into *ousia*.) However, Aristotle actually asserts that the second leg, the identity of essence and *ousia*, is presupposed at two crucial points in the argument for the identity of thing and essence (1031b2–3; b31–32). We need to look more closely at the arguments if we are to understand how the considerations in Z 6 help Aristotle to evaluate the candidates for *ousia*.

The chapter contains two sections. The first (1031a19–28) considers things said accidentally; the second (1031a28–1032a11), things said *per se*. Focusing on the role of one enables us to get a handle on the main arguments of both sections.

2.5.1 1031a19–28: What Is Said Accidentally

Aristotle begins with a paradigmatic instance of something said accidentally, white man; he assumes that it is identical with its essence; and he draws one or two absurd consequences. As I construe the text, the argument goes as follows:

> (1) White man and the essence[84] of white man are the same (a20–21).
>
> (2) Man and white man are the same (a22–23).

Therefore,

> (3) The essence of man is the same as the essence of white man (a21–22, 23–24).

By parallel reasoning:

> (4) The essence of musical man is the same as the essence of man.

From (3) and (4):

> (5) The essence of musical man is the same as the essence of white man.

Hence:

> (6) The essence of musical is the same as the essence of white (a27–28).   Absurdity!

The first problem is how statement (3) is derived. From (1) and (2), it follows that man and the essence of white man are the same. (3) requires an additional assumption. The obvious candidate is (2a) man and the essence of man are the same.[85] Apparently, Aristotle assumes that if thing and essence are the same in what is said accidentally, they must surely be the same in what is said *per se*. That is, he assumes that statement (2a) is true *a fortiori* if (2) is true.

Reasoning parallel to what generates (3) gives rise to (4). Together these imply (5). Starting with (5) and taking equals from equals yields the absurdity in (6). It follows that the initial assumption of the identity of white man and its essence must have been incorrect.

Besides this argument, the passage is usually thought to offer a second *reductio* argument. Ross and most other commentators think that (3) is also an absurdity.[86] On this interpretation, the first argument lies in 1031a20-24 while the second argument includes the first and the text through 1031a28. Is it absurd to identify the essence of man and the essence of white man as statement (3) does? No. Quite the contrary, there are ample grounds to affirm this identity from the reasoning of Z 4. According to that chapter, the essence of a thing includes only what belongs to it *per se* (1029b13-14). Since white does not belong to man *per se,* it is not included in the essence of man. Hence, the essence of a white man *is* just the essence of man. Z 4 goes on to use this identity to draw virtually the same absurdity that appears in (6) above (Z 4, 1029b19-22): since the essence of white man is the same as the essence of man, the essence of white is the same as the essences of all the other attributes of man. Thus, statement (3) is not absurd by itself. The essence of an accidental composite like white man is just the essence of its substrate *ousia,* man. Statement (3) is a step in the single *reductio* argument that culminates with the absurdity of (6).

Z 4 draws the same absurdity for a somewhat different purpose. As we saw, there Aristotle advances the argument to show the inadequacy of trying to understand an accidental composite through what belongs to it *per se.* Later in the chapter he argues for secondary essences of composites. The possibility of secondary essences introduces an ambiguity into the references in Z 6 to the essence of what is said accidentally. When Aristotle speaks of the essence of an accidental composite in this argument does he have in mind the proper essence of the composite or the secondary essence? The argument under consideration seems to trade on the ambiguity between these two types of essences. Later in Z 6, Aristotle points out how another ambiguity precludes the simple identification of an accident with its essence.

> On account of the accident's signifying two [things], it is not true to say that it and [its] essence are the same: for both that to which it belongs and the accident are white. So that in a way the essence and the thing are the same and in a way they are not, for the essence of white is not the same as man or the white man,[87] but it is the same as the attribute (1031b23-25).

This passage emphasizes the ambiguity of the thing. If "thing" is construed narrowly as the attribute, thing and essence are one; but if the thing is the substrate, this identity fails. The essence that this passage equates with the thing is obviously the secondary essence of the attribute. In the strict sense, the attribute has no essence.

The opening argument of Z 6 seems to draw on a similar ambiguity in the accidental composite, an ambiguity not in the thing, but in the essence. As we saw, (3) is plausible because the essence of the composite is just the essence of its substrate *ousia*. This is the strict or proper essence of the composite. Statements (4) and (5) also presume the same essence. In contrast, the subtraction that yields (6) seems to make sense only if the essences that appear in (5) are secondary essences, for only these essences would include a component for the attribute in addition to the component for the substrate *ousia*. Only from such essences would it be possible to subtract the essence of man and have something remain. The result of subtracting the essence of man from the *primary* essence of white man would be nothing, in which case (6) could only be true as the identity of two zeros. Apparently, the interpretation of essence needed to make (6) more than an identity of zeros would make (3)–(5) false: the secondary essence of white man is not the same as the secondary essence of musical man.

What about the argument Aristotle uses to infer (3)? As I have construed it, the argument rests on a series of identifications; the conclusion identifies the first and last members of the series. The reasoning is unproblematic as long as the "same" in each of the premises indicates a numerical identity. Man and white man in (2) are numerically the same. Likewise, the man and the essence of man in (2a) are also numerically one. All Aristotle needs to derive the numerical identity of the essence of man and the essence of white man in (3) is the numerical identity of the identification in (1). That is to say, white man and the essence of white man need to be numerically the same for (3) to follow. This must be the type of sameness that Aristotle assumes in (1). Understood in this way, the argument for (3) is legitimate.

The problem is that, as I said, (3) is true only if the essence of white man in (1) is the primary essence. But it seems that if (6) is more than an identity of zeros, to derive it from (5) by subtraction, the essence of white man in (1) must be the secondary essence.

The preceding analysis suggests that Aristotle could block the absurdity asserted in (6) simply by specifying which essence of white man he intends to identify with white man. No absurdity would follow if it were the secondary essence, and it seems to be correct to say that an accidental composite is the same as its secondary essence. As I said, Aristotle's argument trades on the ambiguity of the essence of white man. Why, though, does Aristotle insist that the accidental composite is not identical with its essence when, on one interpretation of these terms, they can be identical? Is Aristotle's point that they are not in general identical, that they are not identical unless we specify which essence we mean? If this were his point, then the aim of the argument would be to point out the ambiguity in essence.

Against this interpretation of the aim of the argument stands the absence of any reference here to cases when the identity does hold. Aristotle does nothing here to tell us about the ambiguity or about how to correct it. Further, there would be no need for another discussion of this ambiguity: Aristotle has said enough about secondary essences in Z 4. Finally, this interpretation makes Aristotle guilty of an intentionally illegitimate argument that he does not retract.

The apparent alternative is that essence is always the primary essence, essence in the narrow sense, and (6) is what I have called an identity of zeros. This too leads to problems. First, (6) becomes vacuous but not absurd. In the strict sense neither white nor musical has an essence; so there is no objection to equating their essences. If, though, the conclusion of the passage were not absurd, there would be no argument for denying the initial assumption; there would be no argument for the claim that for what is said accidentally thing and essence are not the same. This interpretation is no better than the preceding one.

Let me propose still another way of understanding Aristotle's argument. First, I suggest that the essence of the accidental composite pertinent to this argument is always the primary essence. We have seen that this is the essence in (3)–(5). The problem is how to get (6) without assuming that essence in (5) is the secondary essence. To draw the inference that the essence of white is the essence of musical, Aristotle could rely on the initial assumption, that white man is the essence of white man. Since man is a part of white man, and man = the essence of man and since white man = the essence of white man, the essence of man is a part of the essence of white man. By the same reasoning, the essence of man is a part of the essence of musical man. These equations enable us to subtract equals from equals and thus to infer (6) from (5) without assuming that secondary essence is meant in (5). There is no reason to think that the essence of white in (6) is empty. On the contrary, the initial assumption implies that it has some content. It is thus because of the initial assumption that it is absurd to equate the essence of white and essence of musical, and the absurdity of the latter shows that the assumption is false. An accidental composite and its primary essence are not one.

So construed, Aristotle's argument at 1031a19–28 is valid. Most commentators have come to the opposite conclusion. Ross rejects it because the identity of white man and man [in (2)] is only *per accidens*.[88] This is backwards. *Per accidens*, a man and a white man *differ*. They would be the same *per se* because white does not belong to the man *per se*. Man and white man differ, but their differences are accidental.

Aristotle's argument has also been criticized for committing a "fallacy of subtraction." According to the contributors to *Notes on Book Zeta*, it is a mistake to subtract the essence of man from the essence of white man and from the essence of musical man and then to infer the identity of what remains.[89] They maintain that this is comparable to identifying equilateral triangle and equiangular triangle and then inferring that equilateral is the same as equiangular. Since equilateral and equiangular are *per se* attributes of figures, this example is poorly chosen. Like snub, their formulae include the substrate in which they inhere. Accordingly, attempts to subtract figure from equilateral figure and equiangular figure will prove unsuccessful because what remains implicitly contains figure. Since figure is also a part of the formula of a triangle, at least some portion of triangle cannot be subtracted from equilateral triangle and equiangular triangle. A feature that distinguishes *per se* attributes from accidents is that substrates of the latter can be subtracted. Is there anything illegitimate about applying subtraction to accidental composites? Let us start with the identity of two accidental composites, such as white man and musical man. This is an extensional identity. When we subtract man from both sides we get an identity between white and musical. This looks absurd if we take it as intensional, but it is a mistake to do so. The attributes should have exactly the same sort of identity as the composites, extensional identity. In the present argument, Aristotle asserts the identity between the essences of these two composites. As I have said, this identity holds only in the strict sense of essence because in the strict sense neither white nor musical adds anything to the essence of the composite. Here, too, it is not illegitimate to subtract the essence of man from both the essence of white man and the essence of musical man, and the result is just the essence of white and the essence of musical. As I said, these are vacuously identical because neither has an essence in the strict sense. However, because Aristotle assumes that white man is identical with the essence of white man, there is, as we saw, some reason to think that the essences of musical and of white are not empty. This is the reason that the equation of these two essences is absurd. Just as we would expect, it is the assumption which Aristotle wants us to reject that generates the absurd conclusion. There is nothing in this argument that constitutes an abuse of subtraction.

In sum, the argument that what is said accidentally and its essence are not one is a valid argument so long as essence is understood here in the strict sense. This conclusion should not be surprising. How could both be one together when neither is one individually? On the other hand, the accidental composite and its *secondary* essence are one. The unity they possess together is, of course, a lesser unity than would be required if the primary essence were at stake. Just as the accidental composite is less one than the *ousia*, the unity it has with its essence is less than the unity of *ousia* and its essence.

2.5.2 *1031a28–1032a11: What Is Said* Per Se

Most of the rest of Z 6 argues that in the case of what is said *per se*, the thing and its essence are one. I distinguish two main groups of arguments.

(The first μέν of 1031b3 is, I propose, answered by the second δέ of 1031b28.⁹⁰) Both contain *reductio* arguments that begin with the assumption that the thing and its essence differ; that is, they assume that the thing and its essence are "severed" from each other.

The first group (1031a28–b22) argues against this separation by showing the absurd consequences for the severed constituents. "There is knowledge of each thing whenever we know its essence" (1031b6–7; see also 1031b20–21). If, then, the thing could be somehow severed from its essence, it would be unknowable. Further, the essence that was severed from the thing would not exist (1031b4).

Aristotle seems to support this last claim by example and analogy. Suppose that being were separated from the essence of being. Then the latter would lack being and would not exist. But being is similar to good, one, and the others of this sort. So none of them would exist either (1031b7–10). Further, since anything to which the essence of good did not belong would not be good, the essence of good and good should be one (b11–12). Since all are similar, it follows that everything which is *per se* and primary should be identical with its essence (b11–14).

These arguments against the severing of things from their essences presuppose the existence of Platonic forms like good, one, and being. Some even rely on the character of particular Platonic forms. Does Aristotle need to make Platonic assumptions to support his thesis? No; the Platonic forms provide ready examples of things that are *per se*, and Aristotle is anxious to show that the identity of thing and essence holds for them because it provides a basis to criticize them. In a brief remark after the first group of arguments, Aristotle suggests that Plato pays a high price for the identity: he needs to separate the forms from material particulars which partake of them (1031b15–18).⁹¹ That is, Plato identifies the form and its essence only at the expense of severing the material thing and its essence. I shall return to this text a bit later. For the moment all we need to realize is that Aristotle's disagreement with Plato concerns not whether the thing that is primary and its essence are one but only which things are primary.

The second group of arguments begins at 1031b28. While the first group explores the consequences for each of the severed constituents, the second group shows that the severing leads to an infinite regress. Again, Aristotle begins by assuming that thing and essence are severed. If the essence exists separate from the thing, it too is a kind of thing; and, as such, it has its own essence.

The absurdity [of severing] would be clear if someone were to give a name to each of the essences, for there will be another essence besides each essence; for example, there will be another essence of the essence of horse (1031b28–30).

This second essence should also be severed from the thing of which it is the essence, that is, from the first essence. Hence, it too will be a thing with an essence severed from it, and so on *ad infinitum* (1031b32–1032a4).[92] To avoid an infinite regress, something must be identified with its essence. But if this will be necessary at some point, why not immediately identify thing and essence (1033a31–32)?

To illustrate these arguments Aristotle again refers to Platonic forms, specifically to the form of the one. But once again, the analysis he supplies undercuts the Platonic form. It is the Platonic form that exists severed from the material things whose essence it is; for, according to Aristotle, it is the essence of the sensibles, and the one is the essence of the forms (A 7, 988b4–6). Aristotle apparently thinks that the Platonists are committed to just the sort of regress that he describes here. To bring the sequence to an end they must recognize something which is its own essence. If Aristotle is right, this is the Platonic one. If, though, it is ultimately necessary for Plato to identify the essence with the thing whose essence it is, then why not make this identification right from the start? Why not simply identify the sensible thing with its essence? Further, whatever argument there is for distinguishing essence and thing in the case of sensibles and forms seems to apply equally well to the Platonic one; so that the regress should continue. Thus, even though Aristotle uses Platonic forms to illustrate his arguments against severing, these arguments speak against Platonic forms.

Although Aristotle's use of the Platonic one in the two groups of arguments is obvious, the real significance of one in Z 6 lies in something more obscure, the mode of argumentation that it makes possible. Both groups of arguments rely on the assumptions that the essence is one and that the thing is one, and both argue against the plurality that would result if these unities differed.

The second group of arguments contain what are obviously unity arguments. As we saw, Aristotle declares that severing thing and essence would result in an infinity of essences. He could derive this consequence only by assuming that each essence is one. Moreover, it is because each essence is one that an essence is a kind of thing and thus possesses its own essence. The unacceptable consequence of severing is that what should have one essence seems to have an infinite number of essences.[93] Why is this unacceptable? The answer must be that Aristotle assumes that essence is one. Again, part of the reason that Aristotle illustrates this argument with the Platonic one is that its essence is clearly one.

The first group of arguments also contains unity arguments; or, at least, they can be construed as unity arguments. My suggestion is that Aristotle's description of thing and essence shows them each to be one in different ways. Thus, the effect of the arguments that thing and essence are one is that each must possess the unity which is properly associated with the other. Since thing and essence each need to be one in order for them to be one together, I think that Aristotle must have something like this in mind even though he does not express it clearly in the text. Moreover, this interpretation has the advantage of making clear what Aristotle means here by "thing," and it allows us to see the relation of Z 6 to other parts of his treatment of essence.

What sort of unity does essence possess? Aristotle declares that a thing severed from its essence would be unknowable. He must be assuming here that the object of knowledge is always an essence. This is scarcely surprising, for we know a thing when we grasp its definition or formula (in the case of what has no definition), and a definition is a formula of an essence. In other words, to know something is to grasp a formula, and the formula expresses an essence. If, then, there could somehow be a thing without an essence it would be unknowable. We know already that a formula with an addition is not properly a definition. Such a formula is not the formula of what is one. It follows from these considerations, all extracted from Z 4-5, that essence is "one in formula." Something is one in formula if its formula cannot be divided into parts that signify the same thing (Δ 6, 1016a32-b1, b31-33). Unity in formula is clearly the unity that is most pertinent to knowledge. Aristotle often calls one the principle of knowledge (e.g., B 4, 999a28-29, Δ 6, 1016b19-21). By this he means that we know a plurality of particular individuals through their common formula. This formula is a "one over many." Likewise, the essence it expresses, if the formula is a definition, is also one; that is, it is one in formula.

There is no question that the thing is also one in some way. It must be one by itself if it is to be one with its essence. Also, since Aristotle argues that an essence severed from the thing of which it is the essence would lack being, unity, and goodness, we can infer that a thing must be one. By the same reasoning, the thing has being. This argument's association of being and one suggests that Aristotle has in mind the being and one that he connects in book Γ (2, 1003b22-24). But this need not be the case, and it would not help even if it were true until we had settled on which being and which one are at issue in the Γ passage. A more promising place to look for indications of the type of unity possessed by the thing is Z 6. Aristotle's discussion of things that are said *per se* begins with the question:

> In regard to what is said *per se,* is it necessary that [thing and essence] be the same; for example, if there are some *ousiai* to which other *ousiai* or other natures are not prior, as some say the forms to be? (1031a28-31).

Here Aristotle assumes that Platonic forms are *per se* and he asks whether thing and essence are the same for them. However, the reason that the forms are *per se* is that they are (supposedly) things to which nothing else is prior. This description is important, for later in Z 6 Aristotle speaks of,

> things that are not said in respect of another but are *per se* and primary (1031b13–14; cf. 1032a4–6).

That is to say, the key example of things that are *per se* is something which is prior because it is not said of anything else. Such things are "primary." This latter term is familiar from Z 4, where it is equivalent to unity, as we saw. Here, though, it is described slightly differently. In Z 4 "primary" refers to what does not contain an addition, to things "not said by something's being said of something else" (1030a10–11). The things that Z 6 calls primary are not said of something else. The latter is nearly the same as Aristotle's description of substrate, "that in respect of which the others are said, but which is not itself said of another" (3, 1028b36–37; cf. 4, 1030a10–11). To be primary in Z 6 is just to be a substrate.

Are these two descriptions of "primary" equivalent? Since something said of something else is added to it, something that is not a substrate (something which is said of or added to something else) is also something which is not one (something that is said by something's being said of something else). So what fails to meet Z 6's requirements for "primary" would also fail to meet Z 4's. Can we say, though, that what fails to meet Z 4's requirements would also fail to meet those of Z 6? There is no question that both descriptions of primary exclude attributes. We have also seen that accidental composites are not primary in Z 4. But it is unclear whether these composites would also fail to meet the requirements of Z 6. At first glance, they seem to be primary because they are not said of another. On the other hand, it is surely strange to call an accidental composite a substrate. How can it be a substrate if nothing is predicated of it? Attributes are not predicated of it; they are predicated of part of it, the *ousia*. Nevertheless, Aristotle must regard both descriptions of primary as equivalent, for later in book Z, while summarizing Z 6's results, he uses a description that includes Z 4's description of "primary."

> Essence and thing are sometimes the same, as in primary *ousiai* such as curvature and the essence of curvature, if this is primary; and I call primary what is not said by something's being in something else as in some substrate or matter (11, 1037a33–b4).[94]

Curvature is a poor example of what is primary, but Aristotle often chooses imperfect illustrations. (Neither a nose nor a statue is properly an *ousia;* curvature here contrasts with snub—1037a30–32.) Nevertheless, this passage makes it clear that any composite of form and matter—be it an accidental composite or a composite of form and physical matter—is not one with its essence. Thus, the "primary" things, the things which Z 6 argues are one with their essences, are the primary things in Z 4, just the things that have essences in the proper sense.

This equation of "primary" in both discussions must hold, for Z 4 argues that only what is primary has an essence. Obviously, it is only possible to equate a thing and its essence if the thing has an essence. To have an essence, a thing must meet more stringent requirements than Aristotle gives for being one with an essence: it must be one in the sense that Z 4 explains, it must neither be said of another nor consist of something said of something else. Anything one in this respect is also primary in the sense of Z 6; it is not said of another. Thus, the result of Z 6 holds of what Z 4 terms "primary" or one. The thing which this chapter equates with essence must be one.

This conclusion makes troubling Aristotle's assertion that an attribute like white is one with its essence, provided that "white" refers to the attribute and not the thing that is white (1031b22–28). Since white has no primary essence, this passage can only be referring to the identity of white with its secondary essence, as I said earlier. For attributes, both thing and essence are pluralities of a sort.[95] White is not properly *per se*; but because we can ask, "what is white?" just as we ask, "what is a man?" we can speak of what belongs to white *per se* (cf. 4, 1030a23–27). Recognizing the existence of things that are *per se* in a secondary way does not invalidate the argument of Z 6; it helps us to see it in the context of Z 4–5. That what is properly *per se* is properly one remains true.

Although the thing must be one in this strong sense, Z 6 ascribes to it only a portion of this unity: its example of a thing that is primary and *per se* is something which is not said of another. Following the lead of Z 4, I want to suggest that this "primary" is also a type of unity. Something that is said of another depends on that other and is posterior to the other. Because it is dependent, it contains a kind of addition. What contains any sort of addition is not one. So anything said of another is not properly one. In contrast, what is *per se* is not said of another; there is no such obstacle to its unity. What is *per se* is one in the sense that it is a substrate for others. We can call it one in respect of its substrate; it has a kind of numeric unity. Apparently, the argument of Z 6 requires that the thing have only this type of unity.

With this characterization of the unity of thing and the earlier description of the unity of essence, we can return to the first group of arguments. I said that they could be construed in terms of unity. Aristotle begins by supposing, *per impossibile,* that thing and essence are severed. A thing severed from its essence would be a substrate that was one in number but not one in formula. Without the latter kind of unity, the thing would be unknowable. Since the thing is knowable, it must be one in formula. On the other hand, were the essence severed from the thing it would not be a substrate, for it would be the essence *of* the thing. As such, essence would be added to the thing; it would be said in respect of another, the thing. Insofar as it depends upon another, essence would not be said in respect of itself (*per se*). An essence which depends upon another is surely no *ousia*. Assuming that the essence is *ousia*, as Aristotle does here (1031b1–2), the essence must be a substrate. It must be one in number. In short, each has a characteristic unity and each must have the unity that is characteristic of the other. Either they could not be severed or, if they could be severed, they would be indistinguishable. Thus, what is one in substrate is also one in formula.

At first glance, formulating this argument in terms of unity seems to be a pointless endeavor. It might be justified if it provided us with some special insight into the text. Does it? An essence that is severed from a thing would be said of it or, equivalently, added to it. From Z 4 we know that such an essence would fail to have a *per se* formula. Further, the addition of essence makes thing and essence a plurality, and opens the possibility for an infinite number of further additions of essence. Considering the argument in terms of unity allows us to see it in the context of Z 4–5. Moreover, it enables us to identify what Z 6 calls a *per se* thing with what Z 4 terms one and primary. According to the latter, only such things *have* essences. Z 6 argues that they *are* essences. What things are one, primary or *per se*? We know from Z 4–5 that neither accidents, accidental composites, *per se* attributes, nor *per se* composites are properly one because they contain additions; only *ousiai* can be one and have essences in the most proper sense. Symmetry leads us to expect Aristotle to maintain in Z 6 that only *ousiai* are said *per se*. He does not say this explicitly, but he does speak of what is *ousiai* as being *per se* (1031a29–30). How, though, could *per se* attributes and *per se* composites not be *per se*? We have already seen that Z 5 excludes them from the essence of a thing even though Z 4 defines the essence as what is said *per se*. *Per se* attributes and composites are not *per se* in the relevant sense because they are not one. Aristotle mentions *per se* as a characteristic of *ousia* in Z 1 (1028a23). We can now see that to be *per se*, *ousia* must be one. Z 6 argues that a thing which is *per se* is an essence (cf. Δ 18, 1022a25–27).

Formulating Aristotle's arguments in terms of unity also helps us to understand his remarks on Plato. In Z 6 Aristotle usually speaks as if the Platonic forms were prime examples of things that are identical with their essences. At one point, though, he claims that the existence of Platonic forms is inconsistent with the existence of material *ousiai*.

> And at the same time it is also clear that if there are ideas, as some say, the substrate will not be *ousia;* for it is necessary that these ideas be *ousiai,* and they would not be if they were said in respect of a substrate because they would then be by participation (1031b15–18).

Why would the Platonic forms not be *ousiai* if they were predicated of substrates? For just the reason that essence would not be *ousia* if it were severed from the thing: something would be prior to them and they would not be primary. Plato tries to avoid the difficulty by denying that material things are *ousiai* and by denying that forms are said of a substrate. In effect, he separates the forms from the sensibles in order to enable them to be one with their essences. If the material substrates are *ousiai,* as Aristotle thinks, then Plato's forms cannot be *per se* or one. Moreover, Plato's attempt to make the form both thing and essence is, I think, what Aristotle refers to when he accuses Plato of making form both individual and universal (M 9, 1086a32–34). Equivalently, he could say the Platonic form is supposed to be one in number and one in formula (see B 3, 999b33–1000a1). These latter are, of course, just the two types of unity that a form has by virtue of being both thing and essence. A problem with the Platonic form is that an essence separated from sensible things cannot have both kinds of unity. The reason is usually thought to be the incompatibility of individual and universal, but there is another reason: Plato regards his forms as the essences of sensible things. Thus, the Platonic form is just an essence severed from the things of which it is an essence and posited as itself a thing. Insofar as it is the nature of sensibles, it lacks the unity it is supposed to possess.

Does Aristotle fare any better in finding an *ousia* with both unities? Can anything be one in both ways? There are two difficulties here. The first is whether the two types of one are compatible. Of course, it would be absurd to identify the two *types* of unity—as absurd as identifying apples and oranges. But the two kinds of one could be compatible without being identical. All we need is some *thing* that is one in both ways, something that is one in substrate and one in formula. If such a thing exists, then the two types of one are compatible. Thus, the second difficulty is whether there is something that is one in both ways. There is no question that Aristotle recognizes such things. For he claims that whatever is one in number is also one in formula; and since he defines one in number as having a single material substrate (Δ 6, 1016b31–36), he must think that what is one in substrate is also one in formula. Aristotle has in mind here individual composites, like Socrates, that are numerically one because they each have a single substrate and one in formula by virtue of being instances of a species. From the existence of such things, it follows that the two types of one are compatible.

This reasoning removes an obstacle to Aristotle's position, but it does not show that essence or *ousia* is one in both ways. It should be clear that essence cannot have both types of unity in the way that a composite does. Socrates is one in substrate because he *has* one substrate. Essence is one in substrate because it *is* a substrate. From a composite's being one in formula, it does not follow that its substrate, or any other substrate, must be one in formula. So the link between unity in substrate and unity in formula that exists in composites does not hold for essence. Nevertheless, if my analysis of Z 6 is correct, that chapter argues, in effect, that essence is one in both ways. What remains to be explained is just how it has both sorts of unity.

What is the significance of Z 6 for the larger questions of being and *ousia?* In Z 3 Aristotle dismisses the material substrate as a candidate for *ousia* and concludes the chapter with a discussion of the need to examine the formal substrate. Surprisingly, though, Z 4 begins an examination of another candidate, essence. In Z 6 Aristotle considers what is *per se*; and, as we saw, this is the substrate. The thing which is *per se* is just the formal substrate. Hence, Z 6's identification of thing and essence is tantamount to the identification of formal substrate and essence. There is no doubt that Aristotle equates formal substrate (or form) and essence, for he says so in later chapters of book Z (7, 1032b1–2; 10, 1035b32). If my interpretation is correct, the arguments of Z 6 justify this identification.

Is it clear, though, that Z 6 justifies the identity of essence and *formal* substrate? It is sometimes supposed that what the chapter supports is the identity of essence and composite. Since this latter is also a substrate, it might conform to Z 6's characterization of *per se* and primary.[96] The third type of substrate, material substrate, cannot be the substrate Z 6 identifies with essence because the material substrate is the substrate *for* the essence (cf. 13, 1038b3–6). What about the composite? Could it and its essence be one? There are obvious problems. Socrates is a composite of form and matter and his form is his essence. How could he be one with his essence? How could the physical matter and the essence possibly be one with the composite's essence. Furthermore, when Aristotle states the results of Z 6 elsewhere (11, 1037a33–b4—quoted earlier), he describes the things which are one with their essences as primary and defines the latter to exclude composites which contain one part in a matter; and he continues, "all those which are either matter or composites with matter are not the same" (1037b4–6). Other passages in Z also distinguish the thing that is one with its essence from the composite and from the matter (10, 1035b31–1036a12). Also, later Aristotle appears to refer to form as the substrate of attributes (13, 1038b3–6).

It should be clear that the material composite is not the substrate that Aristotle intends to identify with the essence in Z 6. However, we still need to ask whether there is anything in the chapter's argumentation that prevents its conclusion from applying to composite substrates. As I said earlier, the way that this chapter describes "primary" suggests that the term refers to any type of substrate. The characterization of "primary" in Z 4 seems to exclude material composites, though this is perhaps not entirely clear. According to Z 4, only what is one has an essence. Is the material composite one? Is the essence the essence of the composite or is it properly the essence of the form? These questions call for a discussion of physical matter, not surprisingly the very topic that Aristotle turns to next. If he can show that the physical matter cannot belong to the essence without drawing on the results of Z 6, he will have removed all suspicions that the substrate which Z 6 identifies with the essence could be the composite substrate. At the end of

Z 6, Aristotle notes that the Sophists were concerned with questions such as whether Socrates and his essence are one, and he indicates that the analysis of this chapter helps to answer them (1032a6–8). However, he regards this as a different question from what the chapter addresses, and he apparently does not think it has already been answered.

Like much of the discussion of the central books, Z 6 pays more attention to the requirements for *ousia* than to what meets those requirements. It speaks of what is *per se,* primary, and one with its essence. Nearly nothing is said about which beings, if any, have these characteristics. Not much more is said about the candidates for *ousia* from the second list which Aristotle is supposed to be examining. Z 4–5 show that only *ousiai* have essences and that things with essences must be one. Z 6 delineates the requirements for *ousiai* further, and it shows that essence can meet them only if it and the thing or formal substrate are one. *Ousiai* are said *per se* (1, 1028a23), and they are both knowable and substrates (1028a26–27). If essence is to be *ousia,* a condition Aristotle reminds us of twice in Z 6 (1031b2–3; b31–32), then it must be both knowable and a substrate. It is obviously knowable; it can be a substrate if it is also the form. Since essence can meet these requirements for *ousia,* and since nothing else seems able to do so, there is some reason to think that essence does meet these requirements. Aristotle can strengthen his case for essence by showing that nothing else can meet the requirements and that objections against essence can be answered. This is the path he takes in the rest of Z–H.

Z 6 explains the consequences of logical requirements of *ousia.* By exploiting the assumption that *ousia* is one as a substrate of predication, Aristotle shows that it must be identical with its essence. This identity enables *ousia* to be both one in substrate and one in formula. The immediate problem Aristotle faces is to explain how a sensible *ousia* can have this unity if it contains matter. Accordingly, he goes on to consider the relation of form and matter in the next three chapters of Z. Here his aim is to exclude matter from essence. As we will see, these chapters explain the physical requirements for *ousia.*

2.6 Z 7–9: THE PHYSICAL TREATMENT OF ESSENCE

There are no passages explicitly connecting Z 7–9 with the surrounding text, and most commentators think that they interrupt the treatment of essence in Z 4–12.[97] In my view, they constitute a physical treatment of essence, and Z 4 alerted us to expect something like them when it described its own treatment of essence as *logikōs* (1029b13).[98] While the logical treatment of essence in Z 4–6 concerns definitions and formulae, the physical treatment focuses on change and the physical matter necessary for change. My claim is that Aristotle's chief problem in these chapters is how essence can be one if the thing whose essence it is changes. I shall argue that attention to questions of unity allows us to make sense of Z 7–9 in the context in which it occurs.

Z 7 begins by describing the principles of change: in each process of becoming, there is something from which (ἐκ) the thing becomes, something by which (ὑπό) it becomes, and the thing that it comes to be (τί) (1032a13–15). Aristotle spends some time describing these moments of change in both natural and artificial changes, but the purpose of this discussion clearly lies in the support it lends to the claim that neither form nor matter is generated in the generation of a composite, a point argued in Z 8. A composite is generated when a form comes to be present in a matter. The question is whether, when the composite is generated, the matter and form are also generated along with it. According to Aristotle, the form and the matter must exist before the generation. Otherwise, the process of generation will involve an infinite regress.

> If, accordingly, he [the artisan] makes this [the matter? the form?],[99] it will also be made in the same way, and the process will continue to infinity (1033b3–5).

The argument draws on the universality of Aristotle's analysis of change. The composite comes from the matter when the matter acquires a form. If the form or the matter were themselves to be generated while the composite was being generated, each of them would also come from a matter when that matter acquired a form. Thus, the form of the initial composite would itself be constituted from another matter and another form. What about these latter? If they too have come to be, each of them is constituted from still another form and matter. To avoid an infinite regress, some form and some matter must be ungenerated in the generation of a composite.

What I take to be a second argument for the same conclusion follows in the text:

> If there will be generation of the essence of a sphere, something will be from something, for the thing that becomes will always be divisible and [a part] will be a this and [another part] also a this; I mean that the one is matter and the other is form (1033b11–13).

In other words, a generated essence would retain parts, and each of these parts would be a this. By way of illustration, Aristotle explains that if the essence of the sphere were generated, one part would be the matter, the other part would be in the matter, and the entire essence would be like[100] a composite (1033b14–16).

What would be wrong if essence were like a composite? It would be divisible, Aristotle claims. But what is wrong with the essence being divisible? The text does not answer this question; it assumes that the answer is obvious.

And indeed it is; if, that is, Aristotle assumes here what we have seen him assuming all along, that essence must be one. Unless he makes this assumption, it is hard to see what could be wrong with an essence that is divisible. Aristotle explains that if the essence were generated, it would be "a this and a this" (1033b12–13). Essence should, it seems, be *one* this, not two thises. An essence that is generated or divisible would not be one this. If "this" means one, as I argued earlier, then the text is explicit about the requirement that essence be one. But even if we cannot count on "this" meaning one, the text must be assuming that essence is one because it dismisses the possibility that essence be two thises. Since essence or form cannot be a plurality, it does not resemble the composite. The latter is a plurality, a this in a this, because it is generated (1033b16–19).

The assumption that what changes is a plurality goes back to Plato. In the so-called affinity argument of the *Phaedo,* he describes a form as what is always the same, an unchanging unit, and he contrasts it with the sensible which is always changing and never the same as itself (78d–79a). A form cannot change because it is one. Because the sensibles are always changing, they are pluralities. To meet these specifications Plato locates the forms in a realm separate from the sensibles. Interestingly, Aristotle accepts Plato's assumption that the form must be one and therefore unchanging, but he explains how form can fulfill these stipulations without being separated from sensibles. Even though the form is in sensibles, Aristotle argues that it remains ungenerated. As we saw, the composite is generated when form comes to be present in matter, but the form itself does not come to be in the process. Z 7–9 show how form can remain ungenerated and one despite being present in changing things.

What sort of unity does form possess? According to Z 8, the form is one in species but not one in number (1033b31–32). This claim seems to be inconsistent with the conclusion I drew from earlier chapters in Z that essence is one in number. The text in which the claim appears is problematic and bears scrutiny. The passage begins at 1033b19 with the question whether form exists apart from the composite (as Plato thought), or whether there could ever be generation if form is a this:

Is there a sphere apart from [παρά] these or a house apart from the bricks? Or would there be no coming to be if form were, in this way, a this? (1033b19–21).

This formulation of the question suggests that being apart is the same as being a this. The answer, Aristotle seems to think, is that form is neither a this nor apart from sensibles, but a such. Generation occurs when a this becomes a such; for example, when some particular thing, a this, comes to be a particular bronze sphere. The composite that is generated is a this such.

An individual man is generated when *this* particular flesh and bones acquires *such* a character, the human form (1034a5–7). Aristotle also calls the generated composite a this.

> The whole this, Callias or Socrates, is like a particular bronze sphere, but man and animal are like bronze sphere in general (1033b24–26).

The main aim of this passage seems to be to criticize the Platonic forms. Aristotle contends that the this acquires its character not from a form existing apart—it would be difficult to see how such a form could be an agent—but from something that already has the character itself: man generates man (1033b27–32). It is in this context that Aristotle insists that the agent and the thing generated are one in species though they differ numerically.

Can the denial that form is a this possibly be consistent with the assertions earlier in Z 8 (1033b2–3; b10; b16–19) that form *is* a this?[101] In denying that form is a this, Aristotle disputes what he takes to be the Platonic view of form. Aristotle's form is not a this in the way that Plato's form is, or is supposed to be, a this. We need to look not only for differences in their views of form, but also for differences in their views of this. In the texts where he denies that form is a this, Aristotle applies the term "this" to the matter and the composite. He calls the latter the "whole this." Here a this is a separately existing individual. Given this meaning of "this," Aristotle's denial that form is a this is not surprising. This denial is inconsistent with the earlier assertion that form is a this only if "this" has the same meaning in both texts. But in the earlier passages, "this" could not refer to a separate individual because Aristotle speaks of the form as a this and the matter as another this (1033b2–3). It makes no sense to speak of both form and matter as thises because they are separate while also saying that they are not separate but exist together in a composite. In short, Aristotle's assertion and denial in Z 8 that form is a this are not inconsistent because "this" cannot have the same meaning in the assertion as it has in the denial.

We can understand the two different kinds of this as different kinds of one, and this understanding helps us to make sense of the unity that Aristotle ascribes to his form at the end of Z 8. When Aristotle denies that form is a this in the passage under consideration, he intends to deny that form is an individual, as I said. Form is not an individual because it is not apart. The individual is just something that is one in number (B 4, 999b33–34), and something is one in number because it has a single matter (cf. Δ 6, 1016b31–33). It is obvious that form could not be one in this way, and that a composite would be one in this way. Since matter like bricks can exist separately, since it has its own material substrate, and since this latter substrate is one, it also makes sense to speak of the matter as one in number. When Aristotle calls form a this (e.g., 1033b12–13; b19), he also intends to assert that form is one. As argued earlier, form must be one in these passages because Aristotle objects that a composite of form and matter is a plurality. However, this is a different sort of unity than the numeric unity possessed by composite or matter. What sort of unity does the form have? Since form and matter together are many, they must each be numerically one. But how can form be numerically one if it does not have matter? Form is one in the sense that it is distinguishable from other forms and from matter; it has its own distinct nature. That is to say, form has a kind of numeric unity by virtue of being form. This may be what Aristotle means when he claims at the end of Z 8 that form is indivisible (ἄτομον—1034a8). Composites such as Socrates and Callias differ because of their matter, but they are the same in species (1034a7–8). The form itself is one in species, that is, one in formula (Δ 6, 1016b31–33), but it is also a particular form distinguishable from other forms. It is numerically one, at least in some sense.

We need not dwell on this latter sense of unity just yet. It will be important later. For the present we need simply notice two points: (1) to exist apart is to be a this or one, and Plato's forms are (supposed to be) one in this way; (2) Aristotle's form is not numerically one in the way that the Platonic form is supposed to be numerically one, as an individual that exists separately. Aristotle's form exists in many different composite individuals. It is made many by the matter, but it remains one in species or one in formula despite a plurality of instances.

How does Z 7–9's discussion of physical change in the composite contribute to the treatment of essence begun in Z 4? As we saw, Aristotle assumes that whatever else *ousia* is, it must be one. The logical discussion of essence in Z 4–6 shows that the essence of an *ousia* does not contain any additions and that the essence must be identical with that of which it is the essence if it is to be one. The physical treatment of essence in Z 7–9 also shows what needs to be true of essence if it is to be one. In order to be one, essence must be unchanging; but it cannot be separate. Essence must be in physical matter, but it cannot contain physical matter. Were essence to come to be, it would need parts. Instead, change occurs when the essence comes to be present or ceases to be present in a matter, but essence is not generated or altered in this process. It remains one despite the generation of the composite. In order to preserve the unity of essence, Aristotle needs to exclude physical matter from it. The essence of man, for example, can be one only if the particular flesh and bones of Callias are not part of it. In sum, Z 7–9 show how essence can be one despite being in changing things, and in doing so they delimit and define the character of essence.

Z 7–9 emphasize the universal character of essence. Is this consistent with Z 6's identification of essence and thing? The problem is that Z 6 equates essence and substrate while Z 7–9 seem to treat essence as a universal. Further, in Z 6 essence is one in substrate (a numerical unity) and one in formula, but Z 7–9 emphasize its unity in formula in contrast with the material substrate in which it exists. Near the end of the preceding section, I raised the question whether the substrate which Aristotle identifies with essence in Z 6 is the formal substrate or the composite. Although the former is surely what Aristotle means, the argument does not exclude the composite. After Z 7–9, there can be no doubt that the substrate which is one with its essence is the form, for these chapters show that essence cannot include the physical matter. Thus, the characterizations of essence in these two sections are consistent. Z 6 identifies essence with form, and Z 7–9 show that this form can be present in different matters and can come to be and cease to be present in them without being many. Both explore the unity of essence. Z 6 shows that essence is one in formula and that it is one in substrate; we know from Z 4–5 that essence is also one in the sense that it lacks additions and is not itself added to something else. Z 7–9 show that essence can be one in formula only if it excludes physical matter, and they show that essence cannot be one as a distinct individual, like the Platonic form is supposed to be.

The treatment of generation contributes to the investigation of essence by showing how it can be one. The reasoning implicit here should be familiar by now: since essence can be one if it does not include physical matter, since nothing else seems able to be one in this way and in the other ways, and since *ousia* is one, we have good reason for thinking that essence does not include physical matter.

These discussions make progress toward delimiting the nature of form or essence, but they do not suffice. For one, some matter seems to belong to essence. This is an issue that Aristotle addresses in the next two chapters of book Z and also one that he returns to in book H. Another inadequacy of his discussion is that it treats form as a universal. As we will see, he qualifies this conception of form after his treatment of universals.

2.6.1 Some Objections

A potential difficulty with this interpretation is Aristotle's insistence that not only are the forms of *ousiai* one in species despite generation by nature, but that all forms are one in species regardless of how they are generated. Things that come to be by art have forms that are one in species with forms present in the mind of the artist, and even things which come to be by chance sometimes share forms with their agents. A chance generation occurs when something which could be generated by art comes about through some other cause, as when heat is produced in a body by some other means than by a physician rubbing the body (1032b21–26). Apparently, even in this case the form that is in the agent comes to be in the thing acted upon: the form of heat that is present in the motion of rubbing comes to be present in the body; and heat is also the form of health or of a part of health (9, 1034a26–30).[102] Thus, even forms produced by chance are one in species with forms existing elsewhere.

According to the interpretation I have advanced, Z 7–9 show how essence can be one as a part of Aristotle's account of how essence is *ousia*. Can Aristotle really be interested in showing the unity of *ousia* in Z 7–9 if he devotes so much attention to showing that forms of non-*ousiai* are also one despite change?

First, Aristotle has not yet offered reasons to doubt that what is generated by art or by chance is an *ousia*. More important, he discusses the products of art and chance because he wants to establish as a general principle that what comes to be comes from some matter, comes by some agency, and comes to be something. He needs these moments of change to be universal in order to argue that form is ungenerated. Were form generated, it would come from something, by some agency, etc., and thus would follow the absurd consequences that we saw earlier.

Besides helping to establish the universality of the moments, the discussion of artistic change helps to illustrate the case of natural change. The artist has the form in his mind before he brings it about in nature; form in a natural change already exists in the parents. In some sense, form exists prior to generation in both cases. Thus, Aristotle's discussion of other types of generation contributes to his treatment of natural generation.

Both natural generation and generation by art and chance preserve the unity of essence. So unity in formula does not characterize *ousia* exclusively. But there is no reason that it should. Z 4–6 have already distinguished *ousiai* from attributes and composites. There is no need to repeat this here. Instead, Aristotle's aim in Z 7–9 is to distinguish *ousia* from matter. The physical matter of a particular individual cannot belong to its essence if the essence is to be one.

Another potential difficulty with my analysis, and with Aristotle's, concerns the possibility of new forms. In order to show that essence is one, Aristotle maintains that a form which comes to be in a matter already exists in some other matter, but this seems often to be false: new substantial forms arise through evolution and other new forms are generated by inventors, artists, and artisans. Since they are generated, such forms should not be one. It is easy to see how Aristotle would respond to part of this difficulty. He would deny the possibility of evolution, and Z 7–9 shows why: a form that evolved would be a plurality.[103] Aristotle recognizes the existence of hybrids like mules, but these do not have new forms; they possess characteristics common to both parents, characteristics proper to the genus to which both parents belong (1033b33–1034a2).[104]

The part of the difficulty that concerns the generation of new forms by artists and inventors is more difficult. I think that some of Aristotle's remarks in Z 9 bear indirectly on the problem. This chapter begins by asking why some things come to be by both art and chance while others come to be only by art (1034a9–10). Aristotle's answer is that some materials have the potential to move themselves in the right way, but others do not (1034a10–16; b4–6). Let us suppose then that something comes to possess a form by moving itself; say, a wound heals spontaneously and health is restored. Has the form of health been produced? No, it was present in the man all along, only potentially. It must have been present potentially in order to be realized without external interference. Similarly, suppose that an artist produces a new shape. This is no longer a case of generation by chance, but the same analysis should apply. Only the actual existence of the form is new. It was already present potentially in the matter or in the mind of the artist or both. In short, there need be no invention of the forms of accidents because these forms were present at least potentially before they came to be.

The introduction of a distinction between actuality and potentiality at this point weakens the universality of Aristotle's claim that the form of the agent is shared by the form of what comes to be. Both the agent and the patient may possess the form of an accident only potentially. We might think that this point would also weaken Aristotle's arguments that the forms or essences of *ousiai* are ungenerated, but it actually provides additional support for ungenerated forms of *ousiai*. For Z 9 distinguishes between forms of *ousiai* and forms in other categories (1034b7–19). The former are unique in that before an *ousia* is generated, another form of the same nature must exist in actuality. Forms of accidents need exist only potentially before the accidents are generated (1034b16–19). In other words, a house can become white even if the form white does not exist in actuality; sand and metal can become a computer even if no such artifact had previously existed in actuality. But a human being cannot come to be without another human being. Forms of accidents that never existed in actuality could come to be realized (though they are not absolutely new because they always existed potentially), but new forms of *ousiai* cannot come to be realized. Aristotle has more to say about why this is so later.

Since the form of an *ousia* must always exist in actuality for there to be composite *ousiai* of the same nature, it is temporally prior to the forms of accidents.[105] The form of an accident need not always exist in actuality. For this reason the form of an *ousia* is one in actuality, while the form of an accident is not.

Thus, Z 9 shows in effect that the essence of an *ousia* is one in actuality. Although the chapter seems to be a loosely organized appendix to Z 7–8, when we consider it from the perspective of unity, we can see that it provides answers to objections and further reasons to think that forms of *ousiai* are one despite their role in the generation of composites. Only the forms of *ousiai* are one in species as actualities. They can be one only insofar as they do not include the matter of particular composites.

Z 7-9 consider only the particular physical matter of composites, just as we would expect of a discussion of physical change. This is the matter which receives or loses a form. There are other kinds of matter, some of which are not so easily separated from the form. Though the unity of form requires that the matter of individuals be excluded from form, it is not yet clear whether all matter needs to be excluded from form. The next three chapters of book Z examine this problem.

2.7 Z 10-11: THE PARTS OF *OUSIA*

Z 10-11 examine questions about the parts of the formulae of *ousiai* and the parts of the *ousiai* they define. Since these chapters concern formulae, they have been tied to Z 4-6 in contrast with Z 7-9.[106] However, Z 10-11 differ from Z 4-6 in considering physical matter, also a concern of Z 7-9. While Z 4-5 show that only *ousiai* have definitions and essences, Z 7-9 eliminate physical matter from the essence or form. The problem of Z 10-11 is whether the formula of an essence should include parts and, in particular, whether it should include material parts. Since these chapters consider formulae, they do return to the perspective of Z 4-5, but they do so in order to consider the topic treated in Z 7-9. In this way, all three sections cohere. My discussion will show how Aristotle's problematic arises from the same assumptions about the unity of *ousia* that we saw in the preceding sections. Besides explaining the details of the text, this approach also ties this section even more closely to what precedes.

2.7.1 Z 10

Z 10 addresses two problems. The first appears in the following *aporia* with which the chapter opens:

> Since a definition is a formula, and every formula has parts, and since the formula stands with respect to the thing just as the parts of the formula stand to the parts of the thing, someone might wonder whether or not it is necessary to include the formula of the parts in the formula of the whole (1034b24).

The difficulty is that sometimes the formulae of the parts are not included in the formula of the whole, but sometimes they are. The formulae of the segments of a circle, for example, are not included in the formula of the circle, but the formulae of the letters are included in the formula of the syllable (1034b24-26). While considering when the formula of the whole includes the formulae of the parts, Aristotle raises a second, closely connected problem: if the parts are prior to the whole, are parts like the acute and the finger also prior to their wholes, the right and the human being (1034b28–31)? It might seem as though this question should be answered first, but Aristotle uses the formula to determine whether whole or parts are prior (1034b31–32). Thus, he goes on to solve the first problem (1034b34–1035b3) and then returns to address the second (1035b4 ff.).[107]

Aristotle's answer to the first problem is fairly straightforward. He begins by distinguishing three senses of *ousia:* form, matter, and composite (1035a1–2). Matter is a part of the composite *ousia,* but it is not a part of the form (1035a2–7). Accordingly, the formula of the form ought not to include material parts though the formula of the composite will include matter. The formula of the form can include the parts of the form, but not the parts of the composite (1035a11). The proportion that generates the first problem (formula/thing :: parts of formula/parts of thing) is ambiguous because the thing could be either the form or the composite. Most properly, the thing (τὸ πρᾶγμα) is the form, the same sense thing (ἕκαστον) has in Z 6; and the formula of the thing is the formula of the form. Accordingly, the formulae of the segments do not belong to the formula of the circle because they are not parts of the form, while the formulae of the letters do belong to the formula of the syllable, because the letters are parts of its form.

This relatively simple solution needs some refinement. Since the segments are not parts of the form, the preceding analysis suggests that they must be parts of the composite. A circle could exist as a composite; for example, a bronze circle. But the segments are not parts of the composite circle because they are not material parts. The segments are mathematicals, and they are parts of the mathematical circle. On what basis, then, can Aristotle say that the segments are not parts of the formula of the circle? I think that Aristotle is responding to this problem when he declares that mathematicals are intelligible matter (1036a9–12). The segments of a circle do not belong to the matter of the composite circle; but they do belong to the matter of the mathematical circle, not to its sensible matter—it has no sensible matter—but to its intelligible matter (cf. 1035a12–14). Aristotle indicates another reason for recognizing the existence of intelligible matter. A thing is destroyed into its matter. Just as man is destroyed into flesh and bones and a statue is destroyed into its matter, the circle is destroyed into its segments (1035a31–b1). Since the segments do not belong to the physical matter of the circle, they can only constitute some sort of intelligible matter. It is just because the segments can remain after the destruction of the circle that we know that the they do not belong to the form of the circle. For this reason, the formulae of the segments are not parts of the formula of the form.

Aristotle's other example, the syllable, is also problematic. He maintains that the letters do belong to the formula of its form (1035a10–11). Apparently, the letters do not remain when the syllable is destroyed; they do not belong to its physical or intelligible matter. There is, though, something that does remain after the destruction of a particular spoken or written syllable, the wax or air in which it is present (1035a14–17). These are the sensible matter of the syllable. They are part of the composite, but not part of the form. So some types of letters are included in the formula of the form, but physical letters are not. (Later in book Z, however, Aristotle refers to the nonphysical letters as "elements" of the syllable and distinguishes them from the cause or *ousia* of the syllable, presumably its form [17, 1041b11–27].)

The second part of Z 10 (1035b3–1036a12) elaborates on this analysis by considering the issue of priority. Here Aristotle declares that material parts of the composite are posterior to the parts of the form (1035b11–14). He supports this conclusion by pointing out first that the parts into which a formula is divided are prior to the whole formula (1035b4–6). This principle would seem to imply that a part is prior to the whole. But the converse is true, for often the formula of a part includes the formula of a whole. The definition of an acute angle, for example, includes the definition of the right angle, and the definition of a finger includes that of a human being. The acute angle and the finger are material parts of their respective wholes. (The acute angle belongs to the intelligible matter of a right triangle because the latter could be destroyed into the former. Only as intelligible matter could the acute angle serve as an illustration of material parts [1035b11–12].[108]) Since the formula of the whole thing is just the formula of the form, it follows that the formula of a part of the form is included in the formula of a material part. Hence, the parts of the form, some or all, are prior to the material parts.

Again, there are problems with this analysis. First, it will not work for all material parts: although the definition of the headboard of a bed includes the definition of the bed, the definition of the wood does not. Perhaps the formula of the whole is not always included in the formulae of the parts for artifacts. This seems like a way to avoid a problem, and it is supported by the fact that the text here focuses on natural *ousiai* and mathematicals. But even for these latter, difficulties arise. A natural *ousia* is not destroyed into its material parts because the dead finger is not really a finger at all (1035b22–25). Such parts cease to exist when the whole does. Furthermore, some material parts, such as the heart and the head are closely tied to the form: they are that in which the form of a man is primarily (1035b25–27). When the man is destroyed, these are also destroyed, and *vice versa*. More remains to be said about the relation of form and matter. Nevertheless, despite these difficulties, Aristotle insists that the formula of an *ousia* is the formula of its form (1035b33–34), that in such cases the essence and the thing are the same (1036a1–2), and that the composite does not have a (primary) definition (1036a5).

2.7.2 Z 11

Whereas Z 10 considers mainly the parts of matter, Z 11 seeks criteria to identify the parts of form (1036a26–27). What it actually proposes are criteria for removing the matter from the form, an approach that has made this issue seem (erroneously) to be the same as that of Z 10.[109] When a form can occur in different materials, none of the various materials belong to it because it can exist separately from any of them (1036a31–34). Since a circle can exist separated from bronze, stone, and wood, these ought not to be included in its formula, even if the particular circle whose formula it is happens to be present in one of them. In other words, the form ought not to include what might not be present with it. Applying this criterion to man, however, would imply that flesh and bones *do* belong to the form of man because man does not occur without them. But, Aristotle insists, this is not the case: flesh and bones do not belong to the form of man because they can be "subtracted" or separated "in thought" (1036b2–7). This latter is a stronger criterion for form that Aristotle also endorses later (see H 1, 1042a29): the form of a thing includes whatever cannot be subtracted in thought.

This stronger criterion seems to generate absurd consequences. Can we not remove all matter by thought? It seems that the only things that cannot be removed in thought are numbers and the one itself. So a form which consisted of what cannot be removed in thought would seem to be a number or the one (1036b7–17). It would follow that (1) different things would have the same form, and (2) all would be one (1036b17–20). Both consequences are absurd.

The problem is how to set a limit to the matter that is abstracted or subtracted from the composite *ousia*. If the matter consisted only of what might not be present with the form, then the *ousia* or form of man would include flesh and bones. If, on the other hand, everything that can be subtracted in thought does not belong to the form, then the form of man would be just the one itself. Neither alternative is plausible.

Aristotle blocks the second alternative by pointing out the necessity of defining sensible things by their motions (1036b28–30). But what does he mean by this? As usually understood, such a definition would include at least some matter.[110] Since the definition is the formula of the form, this would mean that the form includes some matter. There are problems with this interpretation. First, including motions and matter in definitions is clearly insufficient to exclude abstraction in all cases. Mathematicals, for example, are not in motion. Aristotle still needs to explain how to avoid the conclusion that the forms of mathematicals are all numbers or the one, for he denies that their forms or definitions include matter.[111] Furthermore, to include any matter in the form is inconsistent with the argument of Z 10 that matter belongs to the composite rather than to the form (I shall return to this latter problem in

2.7.4). In view of these difficulties, when Aristotle speaks of defining a thing through its motion, it is unlikely that he means to include matter in the formula of the form. We need to find another way to understand why defining sensible things by their motions blocks excessive abstraction. There is not far to look. Aristotle claims that a definition through a motion should express the work or function of the thing defined (1036b30–32). The functions of sensible things presuppose matter; but they do not include it. On the other hand, the products of complete subtraction, the one and a number, cannot be the function of man or any other sensible *ousia* because they are not functions. Insisting that form be a function ties it closely to matter and thus prevents the subtraction of everything but number and one.

2.7.3 Wholes, Parts, and Unity

Thus far I have given a brief summary of the contents of Z 10–11. As traditionally understood, the conclusions reached by these two chapters make reasonable sense; they refine our understanding of essence. The problem is that so understood they relate to the main concern of book Z only tangentially. With some reflection, however, we can connect the conclusions of Z 10–11 with the inquiry into essence. We learn in these two chapters that essence does not include material parts, which are nevertheless part of the composite, and that it is prior to the composite. Clearly, this primacy of the form or essence is part of the motivation for identifying it as primary among sensible *ousiai*.[112] But why should Aristotle consider essence or form by examining the parts of composite *ousiai?* We can surmise that had the formulae of the material parts been included in the formula of the thing, that is, had the query with which Z 10 opens been answered differently, there would have been reason to deny that form or essence is primary. If the formulae of the material parts belonged to the formula of the form, the form would be composed of material parts and the matter would be prior to essence. In this way, it is possible to connect the problems of Z 10–11 with the central issue of Z; but this only helps us to understand Aristotle's conclusion. The reasoning remains baffling. The details of particular passages continue to puzzle even after recognizing how the results of both chapters bolster the claims of essence to be primary *ousia*.

So long as we retain the traditional approach, Z 10–11 remain problematic. My contention is that once we consider the issues in terms of the assumption about the unity of *ousia* that we saw at work in the preceding sections, the argumentation of these chapters becomes more intelligible and the doctrine more coherent. In the rest of this section, I shall explain the argumentation of Z 10–11 in terms of unity by working systematically through the two chapters. Of necessity, I shall repeat some of what I have already said, but we will now be able to understand Aristotle's claims in their context.

Let us return to the two opening questions of Z 10. Why is Aristotle concerned about the parts of *ousia* and the formulae of those parts? The text not only gives us no reason, but the assumption that motivates the initial *aporia,* the assumption that the formula stands to the thing as the parts of the formula stand to the parts of the thing, is interpreted during the discussion. (Initially it looks as though the thing Aristotle has in mind is the composite; but, as I said earlier, Z 10 argues that the formula of the thing is properly the formula of its form, not the formula of the entire composite.) Let us suppose that, like the earlier sections, Z 10 also assumes that *ousia* must be one. Can we make more sense of why Aristotle raises this opening question? At issue since Z 4 is whether essence is *ousia.* Since *ousia* is one, Aristotle needs to show that essence is one to show that it is *ousia.* If the thing has a plurality of parts and if those parts are contained in the formula that expresses the thing's essence, then the essence is a plurality. Accordingly, in excluding matter from the parts of the essence, Aristotle removes a reason to think that essence is a plurality, and thereby supports the conclusion that essence is primary *ousia.* Suppose, on the contrary, that matter were contained in the formula of a sensible thing. Then matter would belong to the essence. Since sensible things generally contain many material parts, the essence of a sensible thing would be a plurality. Even if the essence contained only a single material constituent, essence would still be a plurality because it would consist of form and matter. (The four elements do not contain a plurality of material parts, nor do they have a form that is distinct from their matter, but Aristotle denies they are *ousiai* later on other grounds.) In short, if the formula of a sensible thing included the formulae of its material parts, the sensible thing would not be one and thus not be an *ousia.* (On similar grounds, Plato distinguishes forms and sensibles in the *Phaedo* [80b].) Accordingly, Aristotle's efforts to exclude matter from the formula of the form are perfectly intelligible if he is assuming that *ousia* must be one.

Aristotle also assumes that there is some sort of correspondence between the thing, its essence, and the formula of its essence. If there is a plurality of parts in the thing, there should be a plurality in its essence and in the formula of that essence. Conversely, if the formula contains a plurality of parts, then so does the essence. If essence is to be one, Aristotle must insist that the formula be one and also that the thing be one. The existence of parts of a thing is an obvious obstacle to its unity and to the unity of the two others. Z 10 maintains that such parts belong to the matter and excludes them from the thing (the form) and from the essence. In excluding parts in the thing, Aristotle preserves unity in the essence. Only if essence is one can it be *ousia.* Of course, excluding material parts from the essence does not by itself show that essence is primary *ousia;* it merely removes a ground for doubt, an objection to its being one. The existence of a plurality of material parts is not a legitimate objection to essence being *ousia* because these parts do not belong to essence. Showing that material parts do not make essence many does not by itself show that formal parts do not make it many. It remains for Z 12 to examine formal parts and to explain how to preserve the unity of essence despite them, an entirely appropriate task on this interpretation. I shall soon discuss how Z 11 contributes to this end.

If, though, the first problem of Z 10 concerns the unity of essence, why does Aristotle not explicitly mention unity? The answer is that to pose a question about whether something has parts is *obviously* to ask about its unity. Even without direct testimony from Aristotle that the first problem of Z 10 is a problem about the unity of essence, we can infer as much from the way that he reasons. To support his claim that the material parts do not belong to the form, he notes that a thing is destroyed into its matter. The text uses "destruction" (φθείρεται) (1035a18, a25, a27, a29, a32) virtually interchangeably with "division" (διαιρεῖται) (1035a17, b12, b21). Why is a division a destruction? Because both involve the loss of unity, and whatever is is one. Furthermore, the reason that the material parts do not belong to the form is that the destruction of an *ousia* is the separation of form and matter. What remains after the destruction is thus matter that could not have belonged to the form. Insofar as the form is one, it remains undivided.

This argument from Z 10 is an appropriate sequel to Z 7-9. The latter argues that form is ungenerated in the generation of a composite; Z 10 argues that what remains after destruction is not part of the form. If form is not generated from parts, then it has no parts into which it could be destroyed. Z 10-11 do not quite say that form has no parts or that form is not destroyed, but they remove a reason to think that form is destroyed at the destruction of the composite. In so doing, they remove another reason to doubt that form is one. Taken together, Z 7-9 and 10-11 show that form neither comes to be nor ceases to be. That is to say, they show that form is neither assembled from parts nor broken down into parts. In Ross's language, we could say that form cannot be in the process of generation or in the process of destruction. Both processes require a plurality.

Likewise, Aristotle's arguments about the priority of form to material parts also rely on assumptions about unity. As we saw, he claims that the parts of the formula into which it is "divided" are prior to the whole formula (1035b4-6), and on this basis he argues that the formal parts are prior to the material parts (1035b11-14). A part into which a formula is divided is prior to the whole formula because it is more one; the whole formula is a plurality because it is composed of parts. In particular, the formula of a material part is a plurality because it includes as a constituent the formula of the whole thing, that is, the formula of the form. (The formula of a hand, for example, refers to the whole of which the hand is a part, and the formula of the whole is the formula of its form.) The formula of the form is thus more one than the formula of a material part because the formula of the material part contains it. Consequently, the form is more one than the material constituent: it is more one in formula. Thus, the priority of the form to the matter is the priority of what is more one to what is less one.

In short, both of the questions of Z 10 concern the unity of form, and the answers to both remove obstacles to asserting that form is one: the apparent presence of the formulae of material parts in the formula of the form and the apparent priority of the material parts. In neither discussion does Aristotle argue directly that form is one; he argues against reasons to think that form is many.

As I mentioned earlier, there is some indication in Z 10 (1035b14–18) and in Z 11 (1036b28–32) that the form or essence is, or is closely related to, the function of the matter. Aristotle's remarks on the finger and the heart show the close connection of form and matter that results from identifying form as function. The composite animal is, in general, prior to its material parts because, cut off from the composite, a part like the finger cannot function and thereby ceases to exist as a part. The composite can exist without many of the material parts, but not without all of them. Parts like the heart and the head are so closely tied to the functioning of the composite that they cannot be cut off without destroying the composite. So the composite is neither prior nor posterior to such parts (1035b22–27).[113] Parts are prior to a whole when they are more one than the whole that is composed of them. The composite, however, is a whole that is prior to many of its parts because those parts could not exist without it. This, too, is a priority of a one to a many, though the pertinent type of one here is the whole (Δ 6, 1016b11–13; I 1, 1052a22–23). The parts are posterior because, insofar as they presuppose the whole, they are pluralities. That they are pluralities is apparent from their formulae which, as we saw, include the formula of the whole within them.

The final portions of Z 10 (1035b27–1036a25) are difficult. Part of what occurs here is a reformulation of previous claims in the language of "universal and individual." Aristotle now speaks of the formula of the universal and the individual composites known through it (1035b33–1036a8). The matter is unknowable in itself (1036a8–9), and composites lack definitions (1036a5–6). They are known through the formula of the form. Apparently, the form is universal and the composite is individual. The problem here is that form and composite are not exactly equivalent to universal and individual. At 1035b27–30 Aristotle speaks of a universal man or horse as some sort of *composite* of a formula and a matter taken universally. (He seems to have the same thing in mind at 1037a9–10.) How can we reconcile this with his comparison of the universal and form? Is the universal a composite of form and matter or just the form? Is the universal man the species man or this species plus a universal matter? I suggest that the universal man which Aristotle considers at 1035b27–30 includes the matter only secondarily. He describes it as composed of *some formula* and a matter taken universally. The formula must be that of the form, and the formula of the form is the species of man.[114] This species is itself a universal, but one that does not include matter, a point that Aristotle also makes elsewhere (I 9, 1058b3–11). Nevertheless, it is appropriate to ask, "what is its matter?" about an instance of this species and to answer by referring to flesh, bones, and so forth. These latter are the material constituents of all men; in grasping them, we are taking matter universally. The universal man that Aristotle mentions in the final portion of Z 10 consists of the species and this universal matter. It is, I think, a universalized composite.

This reasoning, however, raises another question: why does Aristotle say that matter is unknowable? All through Z 10 he speaks of the formulae of material parts. Indeed, even while denying that matter can be known, he describes it as bronze or wood (1036a10). Prime matter, if it exists, is perhaps unknowable, but this is not what Aristotle is talking about here. He means to say that the matter of a composite, the bronze of the bronze statue, is unknowable. But the very assertion of this claim seems inconsistent: we need to know that the matter is bronze before we can say that the bronze is what is unknowable. A solution of this difficulty would begin from the observation that the text does not claim that bronze is unknowable in all ways. Matter is unknowable *per se*; it is unknowable *qua* matter. To speak of something as bronze requires that we know it, but not that we know it as matter. We know the bronze through its form, the form of bronze. We may also know that bronze can be made into good statues, but none of this constitutes knowing matter in itself. Form is one, and unity is the principle of knowledge. Because matter is always the matter for some form, it depends on the form. It is not one; at least, it is not one insofar as it is matter. It is knowable as matter only through a form, as potentiality for the form. But what is knowable only through another is unknowable in itself. We can provide a universal formula for each matter. As I have suggested, this is just what Aristotle means when he speaks of taking matter universally (1035b29–30). We can know the matter as an instance of bronze, wood, or something else; but to know the formulae of these is not to know just the matter as matter. The matter remains unintelligible insofar as it is matter because matter as such lacks the unity required of what is knowable.

Since the sensible composite contains an unknowable constituent, it too is not properly knowable. On one hand, Aristotle claims that it is known through the formula of its form. On the other, he recognizes a formula that includes the formula of the form and the matter taken universally. Only the form is properly one, and its formula expresses what belongs to the composite *per se,* the essence of the composite in the strict sense. The formula of the composite that is composed of the formulae of its form and of its matter is an instance of what Aristotle earlier called a "formula by addition." Just as we can construct a formula of an accidental composite by adding an expression for an attribute to the formula of the *ousia,* we can construct a formula of a sensible composite by adding the universal formula of the physical matter to the formula of the form. A formula of this latter sort expresses the secondary essence of the composite. Lacking unity, this formula does not express a proper essence. It is easy to see that grasping it does not properly constitute having knowledge of an individual composite. We still do not know the particular matter that happens to be present with the form. At best, grasping the secondary essence of the composite amounts to knowing all composites universally. The particular individual remains unknowable. Later in H 2 Aristotle discusses in more detail the formulae of material composites that are formed by an addition of the formula of the form and the formula of the matter (1043a14–18).

The existence of a formula "by addition" of a material composite has important consequences for the question whether Aristotle recognizes forms of individuals. Is there, for example, a form of Socrates that is unique to him? We can now see that there are no obstacles to a unique essence of Socrates. It would consist of his form, his matter, and any accidental attributes he has (cf. 1030b12–13). Lacking unity, this essence could not be primary, a qualification that will likely rob individual essences of much of their appeal. The real issue should not be whether there is a form of Socrates, but whether this form is one and thus primary or whether it is a composite.

2.7.4 One and Subtraction

The assumption that *ousia* is one also sheds light on Z 11. It explains why form does not include the matter that might not be present with it. Since the form can exist separately from this matter, the form must come to exist with it through some sort of addition. Together, form and matter seem to constitute a kind of plurality. In regard to matter such as flesh and bones, apart from which a form (like man) does not exist, Aristotle claims we can "subtract (ἀφελεῖν) it in thought" (1036b2–3; also b23). If flesh and bones can be subtracted from man and if the form of man is one, flesh and bones cannot belong to this form. The unity of form requires that all matter be excluded from it. On the other hand, it is just the continued application of this principle that leads to absurdities. Circle is defined through continuity and line, but these themselves contain matter that can be subtracted (1036b8–10); lines, for example, are sometimes said to be just instances of two (b13–14). If we continue to subtract (or abstract) matter from the circle, we arrive first at a number and ultimately at the one itself. Is the latter the form of the circle? If it were, the same reasoning would show it to be the form of everything else. Thus, there would be one form of everything and all would be one, both of which are absurd (1036b16–20). Yet, on the assumption that form is one, it seems difficult to avoid the conclusion that form is just the one itself.

In Z 11 the analysis of *ousia* has come full circle from Z 3. There Aristotle attempted to arrive at *ousia* by subtracting or stripping away all accretions to matter. Here, in Z 11, he tries to determine the *ousia* (the form) by subtracting all matter. Neither is successful, but both are motivated by the assumption that *ousia* is one.

How does Aristotle avoid the conclusion that one is the form of all things? To point out an absurd consequence is not to explain how to avoid it, and avoiding this absurdity is particularly difficult when Aristotle continues to accept the assumption that generates it. He does not deny that we can arrive at the form by subtracting the matter; instead, he tries to limit what is subtracted. The reason it is a mistake to subtract all matter, he claims, is that sometimes "a this is in a this or has some this" (1036b23–24). He means, of course, that the form is in a matter. But just what effect does this have on the form? As I said before, most interpreters have thought that Aristotle means here to include some matter in the form.[115] He is after all trying to avoid the absurdity of subtracting all matter from the form (1036b22–23), and elsewhere he maintains that the formula of a natural *ousia* must include matter (E 1, 1026a2–3). Further, Aristotle contends that a sensible nature should be defined by its motion, and that such a definition must include its parts, apparently its matter (1036b28–29). Finally, the matter of an animal ceases to be what it is when it is cut off from the animal because it can no longer fulfill its function (1036b30–32; 1035b23–25), but the matter of an artifact retains its character even when it loses the form of the artifact. For all these reasons, it seems that the forms of natures should include matter in some way.

However, for the reasons mentioned earlier, it is unlikely that Aristotle means to include matter in the form here. Throughout Z 10 he argued that matter must be excluded from the *ousia* or essence if the latter is to be one. Has matter somehow crept back into the form in Z 11? This would overturn the earlier arguments. Aristotle does not say that the form includes matter. Rather, it is because the forms of man and other natural *ousiai* are always *in* matter that the subtraction of all matter is useless. We do not arrive at the form of a thing by taking away all its sensible and intelligible matter, but by finding the characteristic function of that matter (1036b30–32; 1035b16–18).[116] Aristotle's point here is not that such a function necessarily contains some kind of matter, but that in physical *ousiai* it exists *in* some matter (1036b23–24). The reason that it is a mistake to try to arrive at a form by subtracting all sensible and intelligible matter is that the motion that defines an *ousia* requires matter; it cannot exist nor can it be understood apart from matter. The form of a physical *ousia* is a function (ἔργον) or actuality (ἐντελέχεια) of a matter (1035b17; 1036a7); but as the form of a matter, it is still distinct from that matter. The "parts" that Aristotle includes in the form are not the material parts but their functions; for example, the function of the hand is a part of the function of man. Later in the chapter, Aristotle speaks of the form as "indwelling" and compares it to the curvature in a snub nose (1037a29–30). The curvature is a mathematical shape. If he had intended to say that the form included matter, he would have compared it to snub rather than to curvature.

Further, if in 1036b21–32 Aristotle intended to include the matter of animals in their forms, it would be puzzling why he accepts the principle that flesh and bones are not part of the form of man because they can be subtracted in thought (1036b2–4). Are they not as necessary for the motion of the animal as the hand? If Aristotle meant to include the matter in the form somehow, he should include flesh and bones in the form of man. The sensible flesh and bones of a particular individual do not belong to the form of man, even though it is an important fact about that form that it is present in this matter.

Aristotle's rejection of attempts to subtract all matter in thought and arrive at number or at the one is a rejection of Pythagorean and Platonic forms. He is not insisting that their forms include matter, but that they be capable of being in matter and of being the actuality of matter. Only in the case of mathematical forms do the Pythagoreans seem to be on good ground. Thus, it is appropriate, on my interpretation, that Aristotle examines this case immediately after his claim that the form is a function (1036b32–1037b5). There is no need to assume, as is usually done, that the question he raises here is the one with which Z 10 opens.[117] Considering the problem at issue in Z 11, we should render the question here as,

In regard to the mathematicals, why are the formulae [of their matter] not parts of the formulae [of their forms]; for example, [why is the] semicircle [not part of the formula] of the circle? (1036b32–33).[118]

This question is pertinent. In the case of mathematicals, Aristotle cannot avoid Pythagorean and Platonic subtraction by insisting that a definition indicate the thing's motion: the figures of plane geometry have no motion. Can the formulae of matter, such as a semicircle, be excluded from the formula of the form of the circle on the ground that the matter, that is, the semicircle, is sensible? No, Aristotle answers, for the semicircle is not sensible (1036b34). Why should being sensible be relevant here? Because it is the presence of the form of animal in sensible matter that makes it wrong to subtract all matter (1036b28–29). Even if the mathematicals do not move, it makes sense to try to block the Pythagorean subtraction by referring to something that was effective in the preceding discussion of natural *ousiai*. But, Aristotle declares, "it makes no difference" (1036b35): the same reasoning *does* apply because circles have intelligible matter. The form of the circle is always present in particular line segments in an individual circle (1037a1–2); the circle is present in intelligible matter. Attempts to identify the form of the circle with numbers would remove the form from this intelligible matter. But mathematical form cannot exist without such matter. Thus, subtraction is a mistake even for mathematicals.

This analysis of Z 11 shows it to be consistent with Z 10, and it allows us to make sense of Aristotle's continuing insistence that forms are distinct from matter (1037a5–10, a24–25). It also shows that there are special relationships between the forms of sensible *ousiai* and their matter and between mathematical forms and their intelligible matters. In contrast, the material of an artifact is more independent of its form. Simply put, the artifact is less one. But this is a line that is developed in greater detail in book H. Here in Z 10–11 the emphasis is on the unity and priority of form in contrast with the duality and posteriority of the composite.

Z 11 concludes with a summary of its results (1037a27–b7) and with injunctions to consider (1) whether there are any *ousiai* that exist apart from matter (1037a10–13), and (2) why the definition is one formula (1037a18–20). If Z 10–11 are understood in the traditional way, this mention of the need for further investigation into the unity of the definition is unconnected with the discussion. It would be reasonable to accept Werner Jaeger's view that these lines are a later addition made to refer to H 6 but, in their present position, referring to Z 12.[119] However, if my interpretation of the text is correct, these lines are entirely apt. The problem that Z 10–11 address is how the *ousia* can be one if the thing whose *ousia* it is has parts. The answer that some of the parts are material parts of the composite but that the *ousia* of the thing is its form removes some obstacles to the *ousia*'s being one. Aristotle supports this answer by examining the formulae of individual *ousiai* and of their parts. As we saw, the formulae of the material parts are not included in the formula of the form, and the latter is the formula of the *ousia*. But this very solution raises another problem: how do we know that the formula of the form does not contain parts? If this formula has parts, then the form too should have parts. Since Aristotle assumes that *ousia* is one, he needs to prove the unity of form if he is to show that form is *ousia*. Thus, he also needs to show that the formula of the form is not a plurality. This latter is precisely the task of Z 12. As Aristotle explains at the end of Z 11, the reason to consider the unity of the definition is that "it is clear that the thing is one, but by what will it be one if it has parts?" (1037a18–20).

The summary with which Z 11 concludes (1037a21–b7) repeats the main points of the section, emphasizing in particular the necessity that form be distinct from matter. Insofar as form is distinct from matter, the identity for which Z 6 argues can obtain: the thing (i.e., the form) and its essence are one and the same if the essence is *ousia* (1036a33–b4). If, on the other hand, the form has matter, it cannot be identified with its essence, and the two will be only "accidentally one" (1037b4–6). With matter, the thing would be a plurality; it and essence could not be one. In order to meet the criteria for *ousia,* the thing must be one, and this unity obtains among what is primary; that is, among forms (1037b3–5). Understood in this way, the discussion of matter and formulae in Z 10–11 contributes to the investigation of essence begun in Z 4 by removing reasons for doubting that the essence or form has the unity required of *ousia.* As in the previous sections, this discussion indicates what essence must be like for it to have this unity.[120] Since essence seems to be the only candidate that could have the requisite unity, there is good reason to think that it does possess those characteristics which will enable it to have this unity. The characteristic pertinent to Z 10–11 is that essence must not include the parts of sensible or intelligible matter. An important objection to essence's being one remains to be removed, but Aristotle's discussion of essence has made substantial progress toward showing that essence has the unity required of *ousia.*

2.8 Z 12: THE UNITY OF FORM

Z 12 begins with a question also posed in the *Posterior Analytics* (B 6, 92a29–33), "Why is that whose formula we call a definition one?" (1037b11–12). The "that" here is the form or essence; for the definition is properly of the essence or form (Z 4, 1030a6–8; cf. Z 7, 1032b1–2), and there is no reason to suppose a secondary usage here. Since Aristotle assumes that *ousia* is one, he needs to show that form or essence is one in order to identify it as the primary *ousia.* As we saw, Z 10–11 argue that only the parts of the form are expressed as parts of the essential formula (1035b31–34). It seems to follow that if the formula of something contains a plurality of parts, the thing of which it is the formula will also contain a plurality of parts. However, the formula that is a definition of a form consists of a genus and a differentia. It should follow that the form also consists of a plurality of parts. To show that form satisfies the criterion of primary *ousia,* Aristotle needs to show that it is not a plurality. Thus, it is the connection of form and formula established in Z 10–11 that leads Aristotle to examine the unity of form by considering the unity of its formula, and this examination is a crucially important part of book Z.

In contrast, for more traditional interpretations of book Z, the discussion of the unity of form is, at best, peripheral to the main concerns of the book. Jaeger maintains that this chapter, and its "doublet" H 6, were later additions to the main body of Z–H.[121] Even scholars who dispute Jaeger's developmentalism accept his view that Z 12 and H 6 are parallel treatments of the problem of the unity of definition.[122] On the other hand, once we recognize the importance that the assumption about the unity of *ousia* plays in the preceding sections of Z–H, the treatment of Z 12 becomes easily distinguishable from H 6 and quite pertinent to the treatment of essence.

Although the presence of the unity assumption is often implicit elsewhere in Z–H, Z 12 invokes this principle clearly: "An *ousia* is something that is one and a this" (1037b27). Moreover, it makes this claim to justify precisely the connection between the unity of the formula and the unity of the thing that we saw at work in Z 10–11:

> Everything in the definition must be one because the definition is some one formula of an *ousia,* so that it must be the formula of something one (1037b25–27).

Because the *ousia* is one, its formula must also be one. On the other hand, since Aristotle assumes that the parts of a formula express the parts of that of which it is the formula, if a formula contains parts, that of which it is the formula will also have parts and thus not be an *ousia.* As we saw, Z 10–11 exclude material parts from the form, thereby preserving its unity. The problem in Z 12 is whether form contains formal parts. As I said earlier, form seems to be a plurality because its formula contains a genus and a differentia. To remove a reason for doubting that form is one, Aristotle needs to show that the formula of a form is not really a plurality. In arguing for the unity of form, Aristotle is, in effect, supporting its claim to be *ousia.*

How, then, does the text of Z 12 account for the unity of form? Ross divides the argument into two steps. After recognizing that a definition consists of a first genus and a series of successive differentiae (1037b29–1038a4), Aristotle begins the argument by identifying the genus as matter for the differentiae (1038a5–8). Without separate existence apart from the differentiae, the genus "offers no obstacle to the unity of the definition, and accordingly the definition may be considered as if it consisted only of differentiae." The second step of the argument (1038a9–34) reduces these differentiae to the ultimate differentia. So Ross.[123]

A nice interpretation, and it is consistent with Aristotle's other claims that genus is matter (Δ 6, 1016a24–28; I 8, 1058a23–24). Nevertheless, two difficulties tell decisively against it. First, 1038a5–8 does not assert that genus is matter. It merely raises this as a hypothetical possibility.

> *If* the genus does not exist absolutely apart from its species, or *if* it does but as matter . . . , then it is clear that the definition is the formula of the differentiae (1038a5–8).

The mere statement of the conditional hardly suffices to justify inferring the content of the *apodosis* (nor does the remark on sounds at 1038a6–7). There is no question that Aristotle regards the genus as a kind of matter, but he does not express this view at 1038a5–8, as Ross thinks. That the genus has not been eliminated from the definition at this point is evident because the subsequent discussion continues to refer to differentiating the genus animal.

The second difficulty is more subtle. Let us suppose, for the moment, that Ross is right about 1038a5–8. Perhaps Aristotle does simply assume a doctrine that he states categorically elsewhere, that genus is matter. Suppose that, as such, genus "offers no obstacle to the unity of the definition." Then much of Z 12 would be useless labor. There would be no need for Aristotle to divide the definition into a first genus and a string of differentiae; for the doctrine that genus is matter applies not only to the first genus but to *any* genus. All he would need to do in Z 12 is to point out that a definition consists of a genus and a differentia and that the former is matter for the latter. Were Ross right about what the argument of Z 12 assumes, the problem of Z 12 would be quickly resolved. The distinction of the first genus from successive differentiae (1037b29–1038a4) and the lengthy discussion of differentiae (1038a9–34) would be superfluous.

Though initially appealing, Ross's interpretation is quite difficult to reconcile with the order of the text. Aristotle does, in fact, assert the *apodosis* of 1038a5–8, that the definition is the formula of differentiae, but it comes at 1038a28–30 as a part of the conclusion of the entire argument. Z 12 establishes that the definition consists of differentiae at the same time that it shows that the definition consists only of the ultimate differentia. The argument does not have two steps, as Ross supposes, but one.

Why, though, is the number of steps in Aristotle's argument significant? Ross and I agree about the outcome of the argument and about most of Aristotle's assumptions. The point of dispute is what Aristotle needs to prove to arrive at his conclusion. Ross thinks that the chief step is the identification of genus as matter for the differentiae. He emphasizes this point because he thinks that it is also crucial to H 6 and because he subscribes to Jaeger's view that Z 12 is merely an incomplete version of H 6.[124] What Ross does not explain is why form and matter (differentia and genus) are one. On my view, Aristotle needs to show why the form and matter of a definition are one, and he does this with the same doctrine that explains why all the differentiae reduce to the ultimate differentia, the doctrine of proper differentiation.

Z 12 devotes a great deal of attention to the doctrine of proper differentiation. In the manuscripts, the discussion begins as follows:

> But it is also necessary to divide the differentia of the differentia; for example, footed is a differentia of animal. Again, it is necessary to know the differentia of footed animal *qua* footed (1038a9–11).[125]

Later in the chapter, Aristotle speaks of "dividing by the proper [οἰκεία] division" (1038a24). Winged and lacking wings fail to divide footed animal properly because they do not divide it *qua* footed. They divide this genus in much the way that white and non-white divide the class of tall men. Winged, footed animal (like white, tall man) is one only by chance concurrence of attributes; it is only accidentally one (cf. 1037b21-24). In contrast, the proper differentia bears an essential (καθ' αὐτὸ) relation to the generic character it differentiates: cloven-footed and noncloven-footed properly differentiate footed animal because cloven-footedness is a kind of footedness (1038a15). A differentia that has been properly differentiated can be predicated of its proper differentia.

Unlike the differentiae, the first genus fails to satisfy this criterion for being properly differentiated: it cannot be predicated of its differentiae (*Topics* Z 6, 144a36-b3). In fact, Z 12 does not supply a criterion of proper differentiation that would enable us to decide if the first differentia properly differentiated its genus. It does, however, assert that the process of proper differentiation "wants" to continue to indivisible differentiae (1038a16): "At that time there will be as many species of foot as differentiae" (1038a17). These ultimate differentiae divide the first genus completely. Because of this thorough division, the first genus has no existence apart from its species. Where or in what could it exist? The species contain the entire content of the genus as their matter. Freaks like mules may come under more than one species, but even they have no characteristics that do not belong to a species of the genus (8, 1033b33-1034a2). Accordingly, the condition enunciated in the *protasis* of the hypothetical of 1038a5-8 is met: the genus does not exist apart from the species. From this and the entire hypothetical, it follows that a definition contains only differentiae. Significantly, the basis of this inference lies in the doctrine of proper differentiation. It is because the genus and its differentia can be properly divided that the first genus is completely divided into indivisible species.

A further consequence of the doctrine of proper differentiation is the reduction of the series of differentiae to the final or ultimate one. The ultimate proper differentia implicitly includes all the others in the series. Since two-footed is a kind of footedness, to mention the latter in addition to the former is to say the same thing twice. It follows that a definition need only include the ultimate differentia.

> It is clear that the ultimate differentia will be the *ousia* and definition of the thing, unless we are to say the same term many times in a definition; this would be superfluous (1038a18-20).

Despite appearances, the definition or essential formula contains only a single constituent, the ultimate differentia.

With this conclusion the problem of Z 12 is solved. Since the formula has only one constituent and since the parts of the form are parts of the formula, there is no ground for denying that the form is one. To use Aristotle's standard example, the form of man is simply two-footed. If animal is the capacity for self-caused local motion (at present it matters little whether this is the best definition), the mention of an organ for local motion, for example, two feet, makes it unnecessary to state as well the genus animal and the other differentiae. The ultimate differentia implicitly includes everything in the whole series of differentiae and also the genus.

The key move in Aristotle's analysis is the doctrine of proper differentiation. With it he eliminates from the definition the first genus and all but the last differentia. However, this doctrine of Z 12 seems to be at odds with Aristotle's insistence in *De Partibus Animalium* A 3 that a single differentia cannot constitute the essence of a genus (643b13–17; 643b28–644a10). Yet, this latter text does not call into question Z 12's doctrine of proper differentiation or its consequence that a series of differentiae reduces to its ultimate differentia. Quite the contrary, it is precisely because *De Partibus Animalium* A 3 presupposes this doctrine that it considers the possibility that a definition might consist of only one ultimate differentia (see, e.g., 643b17–23). The issue in *De Partibus Animalium* is not whether the genus and differentiae constitute a plurality but whether a single ultimate differentia can express something's entire essence. There Aristotle insists that the definition needs to include a plurality of differentiae because he thinks that a single *series* of differentiae derived by bifurcate division will not express the essence of an animal. The differentiae in a definition must come from several different series but they must each be the ultimate differentia in their series, and they each include implicitly all the other differentiae in the series.

These observations do not, however, remove all qualms about the consistency of Z 12 and *De Partibus Animalium*. Z 12 presumes that the definition and thus the thing defined will be one, and it advances proper differentiation as a means of insuring this unity. If, though, a definition must include a plurality of ultimate differentiae, proper differentiation would not seem sufficient to insure the unity of the definition, and the reasoning of Z 12 (or perhaps my interpretation of it) is undermined. This latter conclusion can be avoided by insisting on two points. First, proper differentiation must apply to every series of differentiae that falls under a genus. Each ultimate differentia must be proper to the genus under which it falls; thus, even if several ultimate differentiae divide a genus, each of them should implicitly include that genus. In this way, Z 12's account remains intact, except that it is not precisely an account of the unity of definition but an account of the unity of a single series of differentiae and their genus. Second, if the motivation for the analysis of Z 12 is valid, then a definition with a plurality of ultimate differentiae would still need to be one. We would just need to account for its unity in a different way. The doctrine of proper differentiation cannot account for the unity of a plurality of ultimate differentiae. Later in the first book of the *De Partibus Animalium,* Aristotle claims that each bodily part exercises a function subordinate to that of the whole body (A 5, 645b14–20). Since an ultimate differentia expresses a bodily part, this is an assertion of unity.

Indeed, it seems to draw on a doctrine we will see in *Metaphysics* H 6: the unity of the composite lies in its function. The problem of how a plurality of ultimate differentiae could form a unity is one that Aristotle should have dealt with in *Metaphysics* Z-H. Without it, his discussion of the unity of form or essence remains incomplete.

Can this unity of the essence be reconciled with Aristotle's denial in his biology that a single differentia expresses the entire definition? This seeming contradiction may simply reflect a difference of emphasis in the two disciplines: whereas metaphysics shows how the parts can somehow constitute a single *ousia,* biology aims to know the character of the different parts. Metaphysics considers in virtue of what something is, and in practice this comes to considering why it is one. Biology is concerned with all the essential attributes and properties of the thing. Though the latter discipline can acknowledge the subordination of the parts to the whole (as, e.g., at 645b14–20), its grasp of the essence of the thing remains incomplete until all the parts are known. Even though the biology discounts the possibility of defining an animal species with only one ultimate differentia, the idea that all the species' characters are linked together and depend on a form is a central tenet of Aristotle's biological method. His project of showing the dependence of the attributes of animals upon their essential natures (*De Part. An.* A 1, 642a31–b4) only makes sense if they each have a single essential nature. A biological investigation differs from a metaphysical one in its concern with all the differentiae and attributes of a nature, but it is not thereby inconsistent with metaphysics. It has recently become popular to look to Aristotle's biology for help in understanding his metaphysics.[126] The difference in perspective between these two disciplines suggests that we need to exercise caution before moving between them.

On the other hand, the doctrine of proper differentiation that serves to resolve the problem of Z 12 has striking consequences that Aristotle seems aware of in his biology. First, it requires that any ultimate differentia fall under only a single genus, or more precisely that the same differentia divide two genera only if one of them includes the other. The reason is obvious. The ultimate proper differentia by itself can express the definition because it implicitly contains its genus and the other proper differentiae. If it fell under two distinct genera, it would implicitly contain both of them; and a complete definition of the species would include two distinct genera (cf. *De Part. An.* A 3, 643a9–12). If it were necessary to state the genus in addition to the differentia, Aristotle would not be able to account for the unity of a definition by showing that it contains only a single constituent. A differentia that fell under distinct genera would face the same sort of unity problems that proper differentiation is introduced to resolve.

Another consequence of proper differentiation is that apparently identical differentiae of genera that are not included in each other can be, at most, analogous. Suppose, for example, that footed differentiated not only mammal but also reptile and bird. It would implicitly contain all three generic characters and so fail to be a unity. Aristotle is aware of this difficulty. It forces him to insist that despite appearances, human two-footedness is distinct from bird two-footedness (*De Part. An.* A 3, 643a3–4). This expedient seems artificial, but modern evolutionary theory countenances similar distinctions; for example, that between the human thumb and the panda's thumb.

Z 12 accounts for the unity of form by means of proper differentiation. There is no mention here of the unity of the physical composite. Since the latter is treated in H 6, there ought to be no question of these chapters' being a doublet. In Z 12 the genus is a kind of matter for the ultimate differentia, but it is an intelligible matter (cf. H 6, 1045a36; Z 10, 1036a9–12; Z 11, 1037a4–5). In H 6 Aristotle considers the unity of form and physical matter; and, as we will see, he advances a different doctrine to explain it.

How does Aristotle justify proper differentiation? Neither *Metaphysics* Z 12 nor the two other passages that mention the doctrine (*De Part. An.* A 2–3; *Topics* Z 6, 143a30–32) directly support it. Aristotle's reason for accepting the doctrine lies in the considerations about unity that constitute Z 12. If form is to be, it must be one. How can it be one if its formula consists of genus and differentia? It can be one if the ultimate differentia implicitly contains the other differentiae and the genus. For in this case the formula consists simply of the ultimate differentia, and there is no longer reason to doubt the unity of the form. Since form must be one, and since proper differentiation seems to be the only way to make it one, proper differentiation must hold. Such an argument is not conclusive, for it fails to exclude other explanations of a form's unity. Yet, without alternative explanations, we are left with proper differentiation. In effect, Aristotle argues for proper differentiation by showing that it will solve the *aporia* of the unity of form.

How, though, does Aristotle know that form must be one? Is this not exactly what he is supposed to be showing here according to my interpretation? Aristotle does need to show that form is one in order to identify it as primary *ousia*. However, he cannot demonstrate the unity of form with a syllogism. To do so he would need to know the essence or form of form—something that is as yet unclear. What he does instead is to proceed negatively: he removes reasons for thinking that form is many.

The entire treatment of essence in Z 4–12 consists of arguments removing various reasons to think that form or essence is many. Aristotle shows that essence can be one if it does not include various things that would make it a plurality. We began in Z 4–5 with composites of *ousia* and attributes. By examining their formulae, we saw that a composite of this sort is a kind of plurality. *Ousia* can be one only insofar as it is distinct from and does not include the accidental and *per se* attributes that inhere in it. Similarly, in Z 7–9 it became apparent that the generated composite is a plurality of form and matter. To preserve the unity of *ousia,* Aristotle denies that the physical matter belongs to *ousia. Ousia* is simply the form. In Z 10–11 we saw that the unity of this form is threatened by the plurality of material parts that seem to be present in the formula of the form. Again, Aristotle preserves the unity of *ousia* by excluding material parts from form. Finally, Z 12 disposes of the threat to the unity of form posed by its formal parts. By identifying form with what seems to be one of its parts, Aristotle again preserves the unity of form. In short, Z 4–12 show that form can meet the criterion of *ousia* only if it does not include accidents, accidental composites, *per se* attributes, the physical matter of individuals, the parts of the physical matter, or the generic matter. In the process of showing how form can be one, Aristotle also refines our notion of form. (Z 11 identifies form as the motion of a sensible composite, a description that Aristotle develops in book H.)

We can view the entire discussion in Z 4–12 as an account of how a particular composite like Socrates can be an *ousia.* The difficulty is that while an *ousia* is one, Socrates seems to be a plurality in a variety of ways. First, he consists of a substrate and a variety of accidental attributes. Z 4 argues that the accidental attributes do not belong to his *ousia.* Then, he also has *per se* attributes. Z 5 excludes these from his *ousia.* Third, Socrates seems to be a plurality of form and physical matter, the matter for generation. Z 7–9 argue that physical matter does not belong to his *ousia.* Then again, Socrates' form may still seem to be a plurality because it seems to include parts of the matter in which the form is always found, such as flesh and bones. But this matter must also be excluded from form, as Z 10–11 argue. Finally, Z 12 removes the threat to the unity of the form posed by the existence of parts of the form. Socrates has a genus and an ultimate differentia, but he is not many because his ultimate differentia implicitly includes his other differentiae and his genus. Despite appearances, form is one, and Socrates' form is his *ousia.* The plurality of his parts does not preclude his essence from being one because his essence does not include these parts. Again, the entire discussion of Z 4–12 removes all apparent obstacles to the unity of essence.

Still, none of this shows that essence must be one. Aristotle assumes throughout this complex analysis that *ousia* is one, and he explains how to delimit essence so that it can meet this criterion. His aim is to show that form *can* meet the criterion of unity. Should Aristotle not argue instead that form *does* meet the criterion of unity? After all, Z 4–12 belong to his examination of the four candidates for *ousia.* To insist that form must be defined in such a way that it meets the unity criterion of *ousia* is, it would seem, to beg the question. Although Aristotle's reasoning is not deductive, this criticism is unjustified. First, the character of form is particularly problematic. Aristotle rejects the Platonic view of form; he should give some support for his own view. Indeed, to justify a view of form should be an important part of metaphysics. If my interpretation of Z 4–12 is correct, these chapters do justify some aspects of Aristotle's view. That they do so by, in effect, assuming that form should possess the unity of *ousia* should not disturb us. For—and this is the main point to bear in mind—the other candidates for *ousia* fare quite poorly. A necessary part of the argument that form or essence is primary is that all the other candidates for primary *ousia* fail to be one in the necessary ways. It is because the account in Z 4–12 of how form can be one seems to be the only possible account of how any of the candidates for *ousia* can be one that we ought to accept it. Something must be *ousia*, Aristotle assumes. Everything else but essence inevitably lacks the requisite unity. Essence could be one only if the doctrine of proper differentiation and all of the other doctrines advanced in Z 4–12 obtain. Hence, these doctrines do obtain and essence is one. With this conclusion the issue that has been before us since Z 4 is resolved: essence or form is primary *ousia*. It still remains to show that the two other candidates for *ousia*, genus and universal, are unsuccessful, a task to which Aristotle now turns.

2.9 Z 13–16: THE UNIVERSAL

Even though Z 3–12 have shown that the material substrate is not primary *ousia* and that essence or form can meet the criteria for primary *ousia*, a thorough treatment of *ousia* requires that Aristotle consider the other two candidates proposed in Z 3 (1028b34–36), universal and genus. Further, in showing that these candidates cannot meet the criteria for primary *ousia*, Aristotle will bolster his case for form and for the restrictions on form that allow it to be one. Treatment of these candidates is also appropriate because some of the characteristics that Aristotle ascribed to form earlier are also characteristics of the universal (e.g., he claimed that the formula is of the essence [5, 1031a11–14] and that the formula is of the universal [10, 1035b33–1036a2]). The discussion of universal and genus will help to distinguish them from essence and thus to refine further our notion of essence. It is generally acknowledged that Aristotle treats both genus and universal together in Z 13–16, even though he refers only to the universal as the subject of this section (1038b1–3).[127] There is no doubt that the aim of this section is to deny that what is said universally is *ousia* (16, 1041a3–5).

One of the problems is just what Aristotle includes under the term "universal" and thus what he denies is *ousia*. In discussing Z 3's list of candidates for *ousia*, I argued that this term includes species, genera, and nongeneric universals like one and being, and that when it is used together with "genus," it refers to nongeneric universals. The intervening discussion of essence and substrate equates or nearly equates essence or form (τὸ εἶδος) and universal (e.g., 1035b33–1036a1).[128] How can Aristotle make this equation while also denying that a universal can be an *ousia?* How, moreover, can he assert that two composites share the same form, as he does in Z 7-9, if the form is not universal? As I have said earlier, these are classic issues of Aristotelian scholarship. I mention them here because one approach to them is to refine the meaning of "universal." It is argued that species do not belong among the universals that Z 13-16 deny are *ousiai,* and, accordingly, that this section denies only that *some* universals—generic universals—are *ousiai.*[129] The basis for this position is a supposed distinction between universal and what is said universally; it is supposed to be only the latter that Z 13-16 deny are *ousia.* This distinction has been criticized by many.[130] Aristotle does not appear to be aware of any such distinction in Z 13. An additional drawback is that the lists of candidates for *ousia* in Z 3 and at the beginning of Z 13 include the universal but not what is said universally. It is highly implausible to suppose that Z 13 goes on to consider, not that candidate whose need to be treated it announces (1038b6-8), but a different candidate that does not appear on any list of candidates. An alternative approach to the classic problem draws on the traditional distinction between two senses of εἶδος: form and species. The species is a universal and not *ousia*; the form is not a universal but is *ousia.*[131] More needs to be said about this alternative, and I shall defend something like it in the fourth chapter. However, it seems to me a mistake to come to Z 13-16 with this issue uppermost in mind. Like other arguments that we have seen, those of Z 13-16 draw on the characteristics of what is under discussion. Aristotle shows that nothing possessing the characteristics possessed by universals can be an *ousia.* Once we understand which characteristics prevent universals from being *ousiai,* it will be a relatively easy task to determine which things Aristotle understands as universals here. Accordingly, we should direct our attention to Aristotle's arguments and to the assumptions that these arguments make about *ousiai.*

What are the pertinent characteristics of universals? As we might expect by now, the unity of the universal plays a central role in the arguments of Z 13-16. So far, we have seen Aristotle use the assumption that *ousia* is one to exclude candidates for *ousia* and to refine our understanding of the essence that is *ousia.* Since unity is a criterion of *ousia,* universals would surely seem to be *ousiai,* for the universal is *defined* by its unity: it is a "one over many" (1040b26-29; Δ 26, 1023b30-32; *De Intp.* 7, 17a39-40; cf. *Met.* I 1, 1052a34-36). Let me suggest that it is precisely because a universal is one that, as Aristotle declares at the beginning of Z 13, it "seems to some to be a principle and a cause most of all" (1036b6-8). This connection between the universal's being a principle and its being one also comes out in book B. There Aristotle claims that genera seem to be principles because they are the constituents of definitions (3, 998b4-8). But why are constituents principles? Because, as we have seen, they are more one than what is composed of them. Later in book B, Aristotle states that "one is the form of a principle"

(999a1–2; also M 8, 1084b13–20). On this basis he argues that the least universal genus is more of a principle because it is more indivisible and thus more one (999a1–6). The types of unity ascribed to the universal in these two passages from book B differ, but both make universals principles because of their unity.

The unity that makes a universal a principle should also make it *ousia*. Why, then, does Aristotle deny that it is *ousia*? Either universals fail to meet other criteria of *ousiai* or they are not one in the way that *ousia* is one. In this section I shall argue for the latter: Aristotle's arguments against universals being *ousiai* show that universals lack the type of unity required by *ousia*.

This failure is hardly predictable from what we have seen earlier in Z. The unity that Aristotle ascribes to essence in Z 8 is unity in species (1033b31–32; 1034a8), that is, unity in formula (Δ 6, 1016b31–33). Further, the discussion of essence from a logical perspective (Z 4–6) presumes that the essence of an *ousia* is one in formula; only so could Aristotle point to formulae that contain or fail to contain additions as grounds for denying that that of which they are formulae are *ousiai*. Most universals are also one in formula (see I 1, 1052a29–36); the exceptions are the *summa* genera and nongeneric universals (Δ 6, 1016b31–1017a2). Since unity in formula is common to essence and to universal, Aristotle cannot use it to distinguish them. On the other hand, just because Aristotle has thus far used a character common to both in order to characterize the essence, it is now necessary for him to inquire into their differences. If there is some truth to my analysis of Z 4–12 in terms of unity, then the treatment of Z 13–16 is rhetorically necessary. Aristotle needs to consider whether the forms he has been describing are *also* universals, the position held by Platonists. Twice during Z 13–16 Aristotle identifies *ousia* and essence (1038b14–15, b16–17). The question is whether universals ought to be admitted into this equation.

Since universals and essences are each one in formula, if they do differ in unity, it must be by a different sort of unity. The pertinent unity is numeric unity, and this section will argue that an important reason that the universal is not a form or essence is that it lacks the numeric unity possessed by essence. Since this numeric unity is also a requirement of *ousiai*, essences are and universals are not *ousiai*. How can essence be numerically one? Does not Aristotle explicitly deny numeric unity of form in Z 8 when he asserts that essence is one in species but not one in number (1033b31–32)? The reason that form is not numerically one there, we may recall, is that what is numerically one has a single matter (Z 8, 1034a7–8; Δ 6, 1016b31–32). This is the type of numeric unity possessed by a composite *ousia*. If essence is numerically one, it must be so in some other way. Is there some other type of numeric unity that essence could possess? Earlier I said that there is, but the difficulties in finding it and in making sense of this text are formidable. Let us now turn to Aristotle's arguments.

2.9.1 Z 13, 1038b9–16: Arguments 1 and 2

Aristotle's first argument runs as follows:

The *ousia* of each thing is what is proper to it and does not belong to another, but the universal is common. It belongs to many by nature. Of which will it be the *ousia?* Either of all or of none. But it is not possible for it to be the *ousia* of all, and if it is the *ousia* of one, the others will also be this [one thing?, universal?], for things whose *ousia* and essence are one are themselves one [ὧν γὰρ μία ἡ οὐσία καὶ τὸ τί ην εἶναι ἕν, καὶ αὐτὰ ἕν] (1038b9–15).

The universal clearly runs into some problems with its unity, but of what sort are they? The text admits of different interpretations. By nature, a universal belongs to many things. On the assumption that it is the *ousia* of these things, will it be the *ousia* (1) of all or (2) of one? According to Ross, the text dismisses the first alternative because the *ousia* of each thing is proper to it, and then argues that were the second alternative true, that is, were the universal the *ousia* of one thing only, this thing would be identical to all the others because things with the same *ousia* are one.[132] According to Harold Cherniss, Aristotle first shows that the second alternative reduces to the first (the others would also be this *universal*), and then dismisses the first alternative in the last line of the argument: a universal cannot be the *ousia* of all the things that fall under it because, though the universal is one, the things that fall under it are not one.[133] While Ross's interpretation is possible, Cherniss's is more plausible because he puts the force of the argument on the refutation of the Platonic claim that one universal is the *ousia* of many things, rather than on the refutation of the obviously mistaken claim that the universal is the *ousia* of only one thing.[134] Further, the argument Cherniss sees in this passage is close to what we find elsewhere; in a parallel passage at B 4, 999b20–22, Aristotle uses a claim similar to the last line of the present passage to refute the supposition that the *ousia* of a group of things, such as all men, is one.

However we interpret this argument, its crucial step lies in the last line. It is because universals somehow fail to meet the requirement of unity that they are not *ousiai*. But what is this requirement? "Things whose *ousia* and essence is one are themselves one." The first point to notice is that it is not obvious that universals fail to meet this requirement. Let us suppose, for the moment, that the universal animal is the *ousia* of a group of animals. All of these animals are one in formula.[135] The (presumed) *ousia* and essence of all animals is one (universal) and they are one (in formula): things whose essence and *ousia* is one in formula are one in formula. Thus, if the unity mentioned in the requirement is unity in formula, there is no obstacle to most universals being *ousiai*. But Aristotle uses the requirement to *exclude* universals. It can have this function only if the unity in the second part of the requirement is numeric unity: when Aristotle speaks of things whose *ousia* is one themselves being one, the second "one," the unity of the things, must be unity in number.

What about the other *one* in the requirement, the *one* in its first part? What kind of unity pertains to the essence and the *ousia?* When Aristotle speaks of the essence and the *ousia* as one, does he mean that the essence and *ousia* of many things is the same, or does he intend to ascribe unity to the essence and *ousia?* As a whole the requirement stated in 1038b14–15 is implicitly conditional; it can only be effective *against* universals if they do meet the first part. Thus, if the essence of things is a universal, it should be true that they are "things whose essence is one" and false that these things are "themselves one." Just how is the presumed essence, that is, the universal, one? The easiest answer is that it is one in formula. Then, if the universal were the essence of many things, it would be true that their essence is one, and the requirement would say: when many things have an *ousia* that is the same in formula, these things are all numerically one. Since the things which fall under the universal are numerically many, the universal would fail to satisfy the requirement.

So understood, the requirement resembles a principle we saw at work in Z 4–5, the principle that only what is one has an essence and a definition. There, though, Aristotle shows that a formula is a plurality and infers that that of which it is the formula is not one. Here, he would be claiming, on this understanding of the requirement, that where the formula is one, that of which it is the formula is numerically one. It is implausible to take the two ones in the requirement differently. Even if we do, does unity in formula guarantee numeric unity in the thing? There is some reason to think the answer is no. Although what is one in number is also one in formula, not everything that is one in formula is also one in number (Δ 6, 1016b31–36). If A and B can both be one in formula but not one in number, is it not implausible to think that A's being one in formula would entail B's being one in number, even if A and B are, by virtue of Z 6, one and the same? Why should the unity in formula of an *ousia* imply that the things of which it is an *ousia* will be *numerically* one? Is there anything in the character of *ousiai* that would indicate that each is one in *formula* while that of which it is *ousia* must all be one in *number?* At most the unity in formula of an *ousia* would imply that its instances are one in formula; but, as we saw, there would be no difficulty with that.

Again, it seems necessary to interpret the unity in the requirement as numeric unity: when the *ousia* and essence of things are numerically one, that of which they are the *ousia* must also be numerically one. But, as I mentioned, for the requirement to work against universals, they must satisfy the first part of it, they must be numerically one. How can a universal be numerically one? It is clearly not numerically one in the sense that Aristotle describes at Δ 6, 1016b31–33 because it has no sensible matter and its intelligible matter, if it has any, does not individuate it. The universal is one in number in the sense that it can be distinguished from other universals. For example, we speak of horse as one species and human being as another, and we count both together as two. Aristotle may have this weak sense of numeric unity in mind. If so, then the point of the argument is that if the universal were an *ousia*, it would be the *ousia* of its instances, and many things would have a single *ousia*. That is, the *ousia* would be numerically one because it is a single entity, the particular universal under which the things fall. In this case the presumed *ousia* is one, but the things of which it is the *ousia* are many. This violates the requirement; hence, universals cannot be *ousiai*. This interpretation fits well with Aristotle's formulation of the argument, and it is plausible so long as the requirement is correct. However, it does not make the requirement itself very plausible: why should this weak numeric unity of the *ousia* imply a much stronger unity in the thing? Does the *ousia*'s being distinguishable from other things entail that that of which it is the *ousia* is a self-subsistent entity?

It seems to me that the argument is somewhat more plausible if Aristotle's ascription of numeric unity to the universal were simply a concomitant to the assumption that it is *ousia*. Then the argument should be understood as follows: Suppose that universal is *ousia*; then it must be numerically one because an *ousia* is numerically one. But when the *ousia* is numerically one, so is that of which it is the *ousia*. So all of the things which fall under it should be numerically one; but they are not, a contradiction. Therefore, the initial assumption is wrong: universals are not *ousiai*. This interpretation of the argument is very similar to the preceding, weak numeric unity interpretation. The key idea in both is the same, that the universal is a single entity and thus a numeric unity. Deciding between them turns on the question of whether this is Aristotle's view or a view he assumes in order to refute. The decision is not entirely clear-cut because in a way the universal is numerically one and in a way it is not. I doubt that the weak numeric unity it has would do for this argument. The argument does not require that the universal be one in number but that we suppose it to be such.

If this interpretation is correct, the argument assumes that *ousia* is numerically one. In saying that the *ousia* is one, Aristotle is saying both that many things would share a single entity as their *ousia* if universals were *ousiai,* and also that the *ousia* itself possesses numeric unity. When an *ousia* is numerically one, the thing(s) of which it is the *ousia* is (are) numerically one.

That the unity here is numeric is confirmed by another text where virtually the same claim functions in much the same way as 1038b14–15. At Z 16, 1040b17 Aristotle declares, "The *ousia* of one thing is one, and things whose *ousia* is one in number are one in number." The argument here is parallel to the one under consideration. In fact, this claim of Z 16 is even stronger than the requirement expressed at 1038b14–15, for in Z 16, in the first clause of the quoted line, Aristotle asserts the unity of *ousia* categorically, whereas the requirement expressed in the earlier text is merely hypothetical. Given the parallel between the two clauses of the claim made in Z 16, when Aristotle states the first, "The *ousia* of one thing is one," he must have in mind unity in number.

What is significant and surprising here is the assumption that an *ousia* is one in number. What justifies this assumption? Since it occurs in the discussion of Platonic universals, it might be thought to be a statement of a Platonic principle (cf. B 6, 1002b12–32, esp. b30–32). Could Aristotle perhaps assume the numeric unity of *ousia* in order to show the absurdity to which the Platonists are committed in also maintaining that universals are *ousiai*?[136] Elsewhere he does argue that Platonists are wrong to make principles both one in number and universal (M 8, 1084b13–32), but this cannot be his point here. For the conclusion that Aristotle draws from this argument is not that the universals advanced by the Platonists cannot be *ousiai* but that nothing said universally can be *ousia* and, in Z 16, that neither one nor being can be the *ousia* of things. Moreover, the numeric unity of *ousia* follows from the requirement: since the thing is numerically one, its *ousia* should also be numerically one.

What, then, justifies the requirement? Ross does not discuss its justification. Owens thinks that the reason things with the same *ousia* are all one is that *ousia* is the cause of unity in the individual.[137] This interpretation is unlikely because it requires reading the result of Z 17 (1041b11–28) back into the text of Z 13. However, even if Owens is mistaken about the origin of the requirement of 1038b14–15, his view has the virtue of giving it a good sense in Aristotle's philosophy. It shows that Aristotle has some ground for holding it independently of its application to universals. This is significant because we need to be sure about the truth of the principle before we can legitimately apply it to universals.

It seems to me that the justification for the requirement lies in the identity between thing and essence established in Z 6 (see also 10, 1035b33–1036a2, a16–20).[138] Whatever belongs to a thing should also belong to its essence (or *ousia*) and *vice versa*. If, then, the thing is one, its essence and *ousia* should also be one, and if essence is one, the thing should be one. Moreover, the type of unity that belongs to the essence should also belong to the thing. The principle enunciated in 1038b14–15 follows immediately. Indeed, there is no need even to go through this process of reasoning. As we saw, Z 6 justifies the claim that thing and essence are one by arguing that each is one and that together they are not many. It is obvious that thing and essence are each one in the same way. Moreover, it is obvious that thing and essence each have some sort of numeric unity because the thing here is primary, it is not predicated of anything else.

Recognizing the requirement as a consequence of Z 6 provides the key to understanding why it excludes universals but not Aristotle's form. The question is, what are the things whose essence is one and that are themselves one? The usual answer is that these things are composite individuals, though it has also been suggested that they are species. As long as we are talking about universals, composite individuals or species have to be the things because universals are each, by definition, a one over many, as Aristotle reminds us here (1038b11–12). Were the universal an *ousia,* it would have to be the *ousia* of all the things of which it is predicated. Many things would have an essence that is one, that is, a single essence, but *not* themselves be one—a violation of the requirement and of Z 6's conclusion that thing and essence are one. The requirement applies to essence differently, though. Here, the "thing" should mean exactly what it did in Z 6, form. Form is a thing whose essence is one, and, as we saw in Z 4–5, form must itself be one to have an essence. Because essence is proper to the form, form easily satisfies Aristotle's requirement.

What, though, about the composite individuals? Does Aristotle not think that form is their *ousia?* Should not they be able to satisfy the requirement? In the strict sense the essence is the *ousia* of the form; as we saw earlier, the composite is known through this essence, but a part of it remains unknowable. Socrates' essence is his *ousia,* but only in a derivative way. Of course, more needs to be said about how its essence makes the composite an *ousia,* a task to which Aristotle turns in book H. Since the composite is numerically one, it is possible for it to be the thing in the requirement; the composite and its essence are both numerically one. Since, though, they have different kinds of numeric unity, the composite is not properly the thing mentioned in the requirement.

This interpretation of 1038b14–15 requires that we be able to take the ὤν both collectively and distributively, so that the passage would say: "When the *ousia* and essence of each thing is one, the thing is one." Again, support for this interpretation lies in the parallel passage at 16, 1040b17. Since the one in the latter passage is numeric unity, and since the first part of this latter passage attributes unity to the *ousia* of some individual,[139] its ὤν must also admit of being taken distributively. In neither 1040b17 nor 1038b14–15 does taking ὤν distributively imply that there are forms of individuals. For the thing that is one and whose essence is one is not the composite but the form.

In sum, the first argument against universals being *ousiai* relies on the earlier identity of *ousia* or essence with the thing. Were universals to be *ousiai* and essences, they would need to satisfy this identity, an impossibility. It is in virtue of this argument that Aristotle is entitled to assert that the *ousia* of each thing is proper to it and does not belong to another, a claim that appears at the beginning of the passage under discussion (1038b9–11). If this were certain from the start, the argument just discussed would be unnecessary, and the putatively Platonic view that the universal is *ousia* could be rejected right away. Instead, this claim (1038b9–11) expresses the conclusion of the argument, a frequent occurrence in the *Metaphysics*.[140]

Just as the first argument shows that *ousiai* are proper rather than common, the next argument points out another character of *ousiai* that universals lack:

> Further *ousia* is said in respect of no substrate, but the universal is always said in respect of some substrate (1038b15–16).

In other words, the problem with universals is that they are not ultimate substrates. They are always said of something else. How do we know that *ousiai* are substrates? Aristotle showed this in Z 6 when he argued that things which are primary are one with their essences (1031b13–14). It is substrates that are primary, and the formal substrate or form is one with its essence. Since the universal is not a substrate, it cannot be essence, and thus it cannot be *ousia*. Insofar as the universal is predicated of something else it is always added to something and so, by the reasoning used earlier, is not itself one. In contrast, to imply that *ousia* must be primary is to imply that it must be one.

This argument is closely connected with the first argument. Both draw on the identity of thing and essence argued in Z 6. As I explained, the first argument presupposes this identity in its requirement of unity, and the second presupposes it in its insistence that *ousia* be primary. Also the second relies on a characteristic of universals enunciated in the first, that the universal is said of many (1038b11–12). Both arguments show that the universal lacks characteristics of essence, a conclusion assumed in the next set of arguments (see 1038b16–17).

2.9.2 Z 13, 1038b16–1039a23: Arguments 3–6

The four arguments that constitute the rest of chapter 13 aim at refuting the Platonic and Academic notion that universals are the constituents of things. This is a position that was broached in book B (998a21–b14), and it derives its plausibility from the genus' being one. In book N Aristotle considers Academic attempts to make one and the indefinite dyad the elements of all things (1, 1087a29–1088b13). Here he limits himself to the narrower question of whether universals might have some claim to be called *ousiai* if they were elements of individuals.

2.9.2.1 Argument Three: 1038b16–23

The first of these arguments (1038b16–23) begins with the supposition that universals are present in essences in the way that animal is present in man and horse (1038b16–18). In other words, it begins by supposing that universals are constituent parts of essences. The text offers no justification for this supposition. It is clear, though, that being a constituent of essence would support the claim of the universal to be an *ousia*. Why? If the preceding analysis of book Z is correct, essence is an *ousia* because it is one. If the universal were a constituent part of essence, it would be more one and thus more of an *ousia*.

Aristotle rejects the supposition that the universal is a part of the essence because it results, he claims, in the same consequence as before (1038b22). However, what this consequence is and what argument leads to it are unclear from the terse, ambiguous, and disputed text of 1038b18–23. Assuming that the universal is a part of the essence, Aristotle reasons,

> It is clear, then, that there is some formula of it. But it makes no differ-
> ence if there is no formula of all things that are contained in the *ousia;*
> for none the less this will be the *ousia* of something, as man [is the
> *ousia*] of the man to which it belongs. So that the same will follow
> again, for it will be the *ousia* (like animal) of that form in which it
> properly belongs.[141]

The key claim here is that even if the universal were a part of an essence it would still be the *ousia* of something, apparently, of the part of the thing to which it belongs. The text asserts that this follows obviously if the universal has a formula and apparently less obviously if it does not have a formula (1038b18–20).[142] This makes sense in light of Z 4–5 and 10–11, for there Aristotle uses unity in formula to mark off *ousiai*. If the universal has a formula, it would seem to fulfill Z 4–5 and 10–11's criterion for being an *ousia,* provided, of course, that its formula is one. If the universal is a part of the essence and if there is a formula of the essence, there should be a formula of the universal, and it thus meets a criterion for *ousia.* But suppose the universal has no formula. It is still *one* element of the essence. Just as the essence belongs to the thing (or form), an element of the essence should belong to a part of the thing. Thus, the universal should be the essence or *ousia* of that part of the thing (or of the form) to which it belongs. In short, whether or not the universal has a formula, it is more one than the essence of which it is a part, and thus it should be the *ousia* of a part of the thing or form.

If, though, the universal is an *ousia* in this way, then, Aristotle concludes, we have the same problem as before (1038b22). Why? Because the universal is the *ousia* of each thing in which it is present. Since a universal like animal is present as a part of many essences, the unity requirement of 1038b14–15 again works against universals. The forms of which a universal would be the *ousia* are many rather than one. In short, the problem once again is that while the *ousia* is proper (ἴδιος) to that of which it is the *ousia* (1038b9–10), were the universal a part of an essence it would be proper to many forms (cf. b22–23).[143] Moreover, since the universal is not identical with the form of which it is supposed to be the essence, it will belong to it, a violation of the stipulation that the *ousia* is primary. Hence, even if the universal were a constituent of essence it could still not be *ousia*.

This reconstruction of the argument goes beyond the text, but it has the virtue of drawing upon the assumptions that Aristotle uses in the two preceding arguments, both of which involve unity. Its ability to tie these three arguments together is a point in its favor.

Aristotle's argument is clearly directed against a Platonic view of *ousia*, but not necessarily against a view held by any particular Platonist. Since the genus is part of the definition of an essence, it seems to be a constituent of the essence and, as such, more one than it. From what we learn later in chapter 13, a universal could not be present in an essence except potentially, but Aristotle does not use this here. The point of the present argument is that even if a universal were present in an essence, it would still be common to many and thus not an *ousia*. Whereas the earlier arguments of Z 13 were mainly directed against the lower genera or species, the present argument shows that higher genera cannot be *ousiai* either for the same reasons.

2.9.2.2 Argument Four: 1038b23–29

If, though, the universals are not *ousiai*, as this last argument shows, and if they are still constituents of essences, then non-*ousiai* will be prior to *ousiai*. The next argument (1038b23–29), the fourth in Z 13, draws this absurdity and leaves us to infer that universals are not constituents of essence.

The problem here is that the argument seems to assume what we would expect it to prove—that universals are not *ousiai* but attributes—and to conclude the opposite of what it should be assuming—that the universals are the constituents of essence (1038b16–18). Would the argument not vanish if the universals were constituents of essence and also *ousiai*, as the Platonists presumably maintain?[144] The assumption that universals are constituents of essence was made at 1038b16–18 as a way in which universals might possibly be *ousiai*. In this context, the present argument makes more sense if it assumes not that a universal is not an *ousia*, but that it is not a this. Earlier in book Z, Aristotle had spoken of the Platonic form as a such and contrasted it with a composite individual, a this (8, 1033b19–26); and he makes the same contrast between composites and universals elsewhere (*Cat.* 5, 3b10–21). Only a this, he notes in the passage from Z 8, can exist apart (παρά); universals cannot be prior, he claims here in Z 13, because they are attributes that are not separate (χωριστά) (1038b27–29). The point here is that a universal lacks a character that we know characterizes *ousia*: it is not a this (cf. 1037b27). We also know from Z 4–12 that essence meets the requirements for *ousia*. If essence is composed of universals, then qualities or non-thises are prior to essence. Hence, universals are not constituents of essences nor can they be *ousiai* as constituents.

Though there is no mention of unity here, the idea that the parts of essence are prior to the whole essence presupposes the priority of unity to plurality, as we saw in the discussion of Z 10–11. The absurdity that results from supposing universals to be parts of essence is that they should be thises because they are prior but they cannot be thises. The thisness that the argument claims universals lack is either identical with numeric unity, as I proposed earlier, or closely connected with it. The connection will be apparent once we look at the next two arguments.

2.9.2.3 Argument Five: 1038b29–30

The next two arguments are more interesting from the perspective of unity. The first runs as follows:

> Further, an *ousia* will be present in Socrates; so that it will be an *ousia* of two things (1038b29–30).

Like the preceding arguments, this passage assumes that universals like animal ("the constituents of formulae"—1038b31–32) are *ousiai*. But Socrates is also an *ousia*. Somehow it follows that there are two *ousiai* where there should be one. How does it follow and what are the two *ousiai* Aristotle has in mind here?

According to Ross, the problem here is that animal will be the *ousia* of two things, itself and Socrates.[145] He does not explain what is wrong with animal being the *ousia* of two things. Clearly, this would violate the unity condition of 1038b14–15. But this deficiency is easily remediable: someone could just say that Socrates is an *ousia* in a different way from animal. Indeed, Aristotle himself thinks that a composite and an essence are *ousiai* in different ways. So if Ross's interpretation is correct, the argument does not have much force. Alternatively, Pseudo-Alexander takes the argument to be that if animal is *ousia*, there will be two *ousiai* in Socrates.[146] This interpretation makes the argument stronger, and it is supported by an alternative text in some manuscripts.[147]

The latter interpretation of the fifth argument also has the advantage of making it fit well with the preceding argument. The fourth argument assumes that the universal is a kind of quality and draws the absurd consequence that an *ousia*, essence, would be composed of non-*ousiai*. Suppose we insist, as the fifth argument does, that the universal is an *ousia*. The consequence is no better: a composite *ousia* like Socrates would then be a plurality of *ousiai*. Or to put both arguments more perspicuously, either the universal is not one and not a this, in which case it cannot be a constituent of what is one or a this; or the universal is one, in which case that of which it is a constituent is a plurality. So understood, the fourth and fifth arguments work together. They constitute a dilemma. The only way out is to deny that universals are constituents of *ousiai*. But the reason that we assumed they were constituents of *ousiai* is that it seemed to be the only way to explain how they could be *ousiai*. Consequently, we must conclude that universals cannot be *ousiai*.

Interestingly, Aristotle infers from this argument that no universal can exist apart or separately from *ousiai* (1038b30–34). How does this follow? All we can say from the text is that Aristotle begins from the claim that "man and what is said in this way are *ousiai*" (b30–31) and that he takes the universals to be constituents of the formulae (b31–32). As in Z 10–11, we would expect a part of the formula to be prior to the whole formula. However, the two preceding arguments (four and five) show that the universal cannot be prior to the formula of the whole because this latter formula expresses a this while the universal is only a quality and because the unity of the whole would be destroyed if the universal were one. Since the universal is not and cannot become one, it follows that it cannot exist apart from *ousiai*.

Questions have been raised about which man Aristotle intends to call *ousia* in 1038b30–31.[148] Considering the fifth argument, I think "man" here is most likely the composite man, and that Aristotle means to deny that the universal can exist apart from composites. But all that Aristotle really requires to show that universals cannot be separate is the unity of *ousia,* for if *ousia* is one, a part of it would lack unity and so could not exist separately. As if to confirm this interpretation, Aristotle notes in an addendum, "if the foregoing is not so," that is, presumably, if the universals were separate, "many consequences would follow and also the third man" (1039a2–3). Aristotle cannot generate a *third* man paradox without assuming that there are at least two distinct men, each of which is one. He must assume that if the universal were separate, it would be one. The composite man and universal man would be two distinct unities, and there would need to be a third man in respect of which they are each man. Here, as earlier, separateness and unity go hand in hand.

2.9.2.4 Argument Six: 1039a3-8

Chapter 13's final argument against universals being *ousiai* is the most profound:

> It is impossible for any *ousia* to be composed of *ousiai* that are present as actualities. For what is two in actuality in this way is never one in actuality, but if something is two potentially, it will be one. . . . So that

if *ousia* is one, it will not be composed of *ousiai* which are present in it in this way (1039a3–8).

The problem is that if the universals were *ousiai* and if they were present in individuals (as Aristotle has assumed since 1038b16) as actually existing constituents, the individuals could not be one. This passage states explicitly what I have argued is assumed earlier: *ousia* is one, and the existence of parts of *ousia* would imply that *ousia* is a plurality. Further, it is the *numeric* unity of *ousia* that the existence of parts would call into question: something that is actually one is one in number. Aristotle's specification here that the parts be present in actuality is not different from what was assumed earlier, but this new formulation indicates the solution. Were the parts of Socrates actualities, he would be many. As long as these parts are merely potentialities, Socrates can be one. The universals are, in some sense, parts of Socrates. Insofar as they are merely potentialities, they do not prevent Socrates from being one. We can infer that universals are potentialities. Since an *ousia* is one, universals can be constituents of individuals only because they exist in individuals potentially.

This argument excludes any plurality of actualities. Since we know from previous arguments that attributes do not belong to a thing's *ousia,* the only parts of an *ousia* that we need to worry about in this argument are the parts that might themselves be *ousiai*. [149] The argument excludes universals existing as actual *ousiai* that are parts of some other *ousia*. Thus, this argument closely resembles the fifth argument.

One result of Z 13's arguments is a new *aporia:* since universals are not *ousiai,* and since *ousiai* are not composed of actual *ousiai,* all *ousiai* will be incomposite and will thus lack definitions; but we have been assuming that *ousiai* have definitions most of all (1039a14–20; cf. 5, 1031a11–14). Why is an incomposite indefinable? There seem to be two distinct ideas here. First, since the formula is of the universal, and since the *ousia* is neither universal nor contains a universal, it does not admit of a formula. At best, the formula could express a potentiality; the *ousia* is something that is one in actuality. The second idea here is that anything that is incomposite cannot be defined. Why does being one make something indefinable? Aristotle's point is not that definition requires many terms (why could it not have one term?), but that what is incomposite or one must be fully actual and thus not definable with an expression that signifies a potentiality. Thus, the two ideas are really the same.

Earlier, we saw one reason that Socrates has no definition (his matter—10, 1036a2–6). The argument here implies that he has no definition because of his form: he is an incomposite actuality. But this is not Aristotle's final word on the question. Z 13 concludes with the words:

. . . or in some way there will be a definition and in another way not.
But this issue will be more clear from what is said later (1039a21–23).

The text to which this passage refers is Z 15, and I shall return to this issue when I discuss that chapter (2.9.4).

All the arguments of Z 13 wrestle with the problem of how a universal can be the *ousia* of something else. By and large, the obstacle is that the unity of *ousia* or of that of which it is the *ousia* could not be retained. Either all the things of which the universal would be the *ousia* would need to be one, or each of these things would need to be many. The first three arguments draw on the idea that the universal is said of other things; these things, a plurality of substrates, are not one. The last three arguments assume that a composite individual is one. The universal lacks the unity and thisness required of a part of an *ousia*; but if the universal were one of its parts, the whole could not retain the unity it needs to be an *ousia*. Since Aristotle insists that there are composite *ousiai*, and that an *ousia* must be one, the universal cannot be an *ousia*. That the universal is a predicate and a constituent is a familiar Platonic notion or, perhaps better, a familiar Aristotelian interpretation of Plato. Having argued against the universal being either, Aristotle turns in the next chapter to what amounts to arguing against the universal being both.

2.9.3 Z 14

The first sentence of Z 14 asserts that the preceding analysis shows the consequences that follow for those who "say the ideas are separate *ousiai* and who make the form out of the genus and the differentiae" (1039a24–26). No doubt, the people that Aristotle has in mind here are Platonists, and his complaint is that they make the forms both separate and composed of other separate forms (1039a24–26, a30–33).[150] Just as the final argument of Z 13 shows the absurdity of trying to include one *ousia* as a constituent of another, the present chapter presents the problems that result from including one Platonic form in another. If the argument of Z 14 followed the former argument precisely, we would expect Aristotle to point out that a form could not be one in actuality if its constituent were one in actuality. However, there is no reason to think that Platonists think of form or *ousia* as an actuality. To show the internal inconsistency of the Platonic view of form, Aristotle must take another tack.

He poses the issue that occupies the entire chapter as a dilemma:

> For if there are forms, and animal is in man and horse, then animal is either [1] one and the same in number or [2] different (1039a26–28).

In other words, the problem is whether the animal that is a constituent of man is one and the same with the animal that is a constituent of horse. There is no question that the animal in both is one in formula (1039a28–30); the question is whether it is one in number. The chapter argues against both possible answers: the animal in both can be neither one in number nor different in number. It concludes that forms of the sort posited by the Platonists cannot exist (1039b17–19). There are two brief arguments against a form like animal being numerically one in its instances. The first points to an absurd consequence. Aristotle asks, if animal is numerically one,[151] "how will that which exists in separate beings be one, and why will this animal not be apart from itself?" (1039a33–b2). It seems impossible for something to be one if it exists in a plurality of separate things. The connection between separation and unity is apparent: the separate existence of kinds of animals seems antithetical to animal being numerically one in each. An apparently equivalent formulation (one that we also find at *Parmenides* 131b) is that if animal were in many separate animals (i.e., species of animal), it would be apart from itself.

A second argument (1039b2–6) against animal being numerically one in its instances draws on the contrary differentiae of a genus. If animal were numerically one in horse and man, then one and the same being would be both two-footed and many-footed; thus, contrary characters would belong to one being, a violation of the principle of non-contradiction (1039b2–3). It makes no difference whether animal partakes of these differentiae, is mixed with them, or is in contact with them; contraries would somehow belong to one nature (b4–6). Aristotle could also have added that the violation of non-contradiction cannot be avoided by specifying the time or respect in which two-footed and many-footed belong, for these latter are both parts of the essence and belong *per se*. They both belong always and in the same respect.[152] Hence, the animal in various animals is not numerically one.

The arguments against the other horn of the dilemma are more difficult. They begin from the assumption that animal is numerically different in each instance and go on to draw absurd consequences. First, it follows that there would be an indefinite number of things whose *ousia* is animal because man is constituted from animal "not accidentally" (1039b7–9). What is the argument that the text presupposes? The point is that because animal is part of the *ousia* of man and part of the *ousiai* of the other things in which it is present, the things whose *ousia* is animal are indefinite. Aristotle assumes that an indefinite number of animals is absurd and thus dismisses the initial assumption. Why is it absurd for the things whose *ousia* is animal to be indefinite? Ross claims that this would contradict Aristotle's earlier stipulation that things whose *ousia* is one are themselves one (1038b14–15).[153] An apparent difficulty with this interpretation is why we should think that the indefinite number of animals all have one *ousia*. The assumption that governs this horn of the dilemma is that the animal in each differs (1039b7). Why, then, should we suppose that the *ousia* of each is the same, namely, animal? First, it is clear that Aristotle makes this assumption, for he speaks of the "things whose *ousia* is animal." The reason that animal is the *ousia* of the various animals is that they are one in formula, and their formula expresses their *ousia*. The point is that even though animal is numerically different in each animal (by assumption), they each contain animal in their formulae "not accidentally," and it is the same animal in each essential formula. Accordingly, the absurdity here is that, as Ross realizes, there would be many different things with the same *ousia:* the *ousia* of horses, men, and dogs is animal.

Whereas the preceding argument points to the plurality of animals, the next two arguments show that animal itself will be many if the form of animal is numerically distinct in species. The first of these (the second argument under this horn of the dilemma) claims that because the animal in each thing is an *ousia*, the animal itself will be many (1039b9–10).[154] Why is the animal in each an *ousia?* Aristotle explains that man is not said in respect of something other than animal; "if it were, man would be composed of it [this other], and it [the other] would be the genus of man" (b10–11). In other words, because man is said in respect of animal, animal must be (or be part of) its *ousia*. But, we are assuming that the animal in man differs from the animal in horse and other species. It follows that the *ousia* of each differs. But the *ousia* of each is animal itself. Hence, animal itself must be many.

The third argument is difficult and has been variously construed. It begins with the claim that all the constituents of man are ideas (1039b11–12). From this Aristotle infers that the idea of something will not be the *ousia* of something else (1039b12–13). It follows, he claims, that animal itself will be each of the constituents of animals (1039b13–14). This latter implies the conclusion of the preceding argument: once again, animal itself will be many.[155] As I understand this argument, Aristotle reasons that since man is composed of ideas, each of these ideas has a claim to be the *ousia* of man; he has been assuming that each idea is an *ousia* (1039a25), and it is not the *ousia* of something else. But, as the preceding argument shows (1039b9–10), animal itself is the *ousia* of man. Consequently, animal itself will be each of the constituents of man, and indeed each of the constituents of any animal. It follows again that animal itself is many.

This argument is difficult to understand because the moves seem so implausible, but they follow from the Platonic assumption, announced at the beginning of the chapter, that each idea is an *ousia*. Assuming that there is one *ousia* for each thing and that the *ousia* of a man is the animal itself, then the latter will be a plurality. Animal itself is each of the ideas of which man or any other animal is composed.

Like the third argument, the fourth is also terse and confusing:

> Further, from what will this come, and how will it be from animal itself? Or how is it possible for the animal whose *ousia* is this itself to be apart from the animal itself? (1039b14–16).[156]

The "this" here is apparently a particular species of animal, like man. The problem is how such a species of animal could come from animal itself (1039b26) if animal itself is numerically distinct in each species (1039b7).[157] Aristotle's point is, I take it, that since animal differs in each species, the animal in a particular species cannot be identified with animal itself; and yet animal itself is supposed to be a constituent of the species. How can the species come from animal itself: what could be added to the latter to make the former? Equivalently, what could the animal in a particular species have that would enable it to differ from animal itself? If the genus animal is numerically distinct in its various species, as Aristotle now assumes, then one genus is not a constituent of the many species. The genus would have to be numerically one in the species in order to be a constituent in the way that the Platonists think it is. Hence, the initial assumption, that animal differs numerically in the various species of animal, is mistaken.

These four arguments show the consequences of the initial assumption. The discussion of the second horn of the dilemma concludes with the claim that even worse consequences result if sensibles are considered (1039b16–17), an indication that the plurality of animals under discussion has been a plurality of species.

The entire chapter concludes by denying the existence of Platonic forms (1039b17–19). As we have seen, the assumption that animal is numerically one in its instances leads to absurdities and so does the assumption that animal is numerically distinct in its instances. The initial characterization of animal must have been mistaken. Forms such as animal cannot be both composed of other forms and also themselves separate *ousiai*. Such a form would have to be both one in formula and one in number, but there are arguments against supposing that it is or is not one in number.

By this point it should go without saying that considering the unity of a form in a plurality amounts to considering the unity of the form *simpliciter*. Form can only be one in a plurality if it is one by itself. The form that has one formula in its many instances is itself one in formula, and the form that is numerically one and the same in many instances is itself numerically one. It follows that the problem here is not just whether the Platonic form is or is not numerically the same in its many instances, but whether it is itself numerically one. Later in the *Metaphysics,* Aristotle accuses the Platonists of making the forms both universal and individual (M 9, 1086a32–34). In the terms that we find in Z 14 this amounts to saying that the form is one in formula and also one in number (cf. B 4, 999b33–1000a1). But this assertion expresses only the first horn of the dilemma.

If the Platonists assert only the first horn, why does Aristotle go on to consider the second horn at all? The second horn is problematic because it supposes in effect that form is one in formula but not one in number, that is, that form is universal but not particular. How could any Platonist hold that form is numerically distinct in its instances if this amounts to denying the numeric unity of form? Aristotle argues against the assumption that form is numerically distinct simply by showing that it does lead to the position that a form like animal itself is many. He takes it as obvious that the numeric plurality of form would be absurd. Why? Because form must be one, an assumption that Aristotle and the Platonists share. To refute those Platonists who say that the animal in man and horse differs in number, Aristotle shows that they unwittingly deny the numeric unity of animal. The second horn might be addressed to Platonists who advance mathematical forms (cf. B 6, 1002b17-25). They do not deny the numeric unity of form intentionally; they simply emphasize the form's unity in formula. Aristotle's point in Z 14 is that form must be or not be one in number in its instances. The Platonist needs to choose which, but either choice leads to absurdities. The standard Platonic position is that form is one in number (or individual), but in arguing against both alternatives Z 14 shows that there are difficulties however Platonic forms are conceived. The problems are insurmountable as long as the Platonists insist that one form is composed of others and that all forms are separate *ousiai*.

Surveying the terse and complex arguments of Z 14, we can now see the extent to which they depend on unity. Aristotle assumes that the Platonic forms are one in formula and argues against their being either one in number or many in number. Either a form like animal is one in number in all species, in which case one thing will have contrary predicates and be in many different things at the same time, *or* the form animal will be many in number in different species, in which case animal itself, an *ousia,* will be many. The problem is how to preserve the unity of form given the Platonic characterization of it. Because preservation of unity is impossible, Z 14 concludes that forms of the sort posited by Platonists cannot exist.

2.9.4 Z 15

Z 15 consists of two parts. Its first part argues that individuals are indefinable and unknowable (1039b27-1040b7). Since the basis for this conclusion is that individuals have matter, the argument may seem, at first glance, to be only marginally relevant to the main theme of Z 13-16, universals. However, this discussion of indefinability introduces the main theme of the chapter (1040b8-27), the argument that because Platonic forms are separate individuals, they too are indefinable.

We can connect this latter result with the earlier arguments that explicitly involve unity simply by remembering Aristotle's claim that there is no difference between saying one in number and individual (B 4, 999b33-34). In effect, Z 15 argues that because the Platonic forms are numerically one, they are indefinable. Instead, definition is of the universal. Viewing Z 15 in terms of unity, we can see immediately that it continues along the lines of the preceding chapter. In Z 14 Aristotle had dismissed claims that form is both one in formula and one in number. What he argues now is, in effect, that if we insist on the numeric unity of form, that is, if we insist that it is an individual, it loses its universality or unity in formula.

The text of the main argument begins from the supposition that form is separate and an individual (1040a8–9). A definition would be a verbal formula, but words are "common to all" and thus must apply to other things as well. Hence, a definition would belong to many rather than to one.[158] To avoid this conclusion it might be suggested that although one word considered apart from the others applies to many things, together all the words in a definition may belong to only one thing (1040a14–15). As Ross recognizes, this response is a good one, but it will not do for the Platonist.[159] The problem is that, as we saw in the discussion of Z 14, a Platonic form like animal is composed of other forms. Even if the conjunction of two-footed and animal defines man, the conjunction does not apply to man uniquely; it also applies to each of the constituents, animal and two-footed (1040a15–17). Why does the conjunction apply to each? Aristotle explains that each is a distinct eternal being that is part of the composite and prior to it. If the conjunction applies to the genus it should apply to the differentia as well (1040a17–21). Hence, even the conjunction of terms in a definition would not define a single form.

It is important to distinguish this argument for the unknowability of Platonic form from what Plato himself gives at *Theaetetus* 202d–203b. Plato suggests that things are known through their elements and that forms are indivisible elements. It follows that forms cannot be known. Later in the dialogue, Plato rejects this conception of form. In the argument before us, Aristotle makes exactly the opposite assumption about the Platonic form. He assumes that it is composed of constituent forms. The reason that it is indefinable is that terms which apply to it will also apply to its constituents.

If a form is numerically one and also contains parts, it could not be defined or known. If, as the Platonists assume, a form can be defined by universal formulae, it cannot be numerically one. Either way, the conclusion that we are left to infer is that the forms as they are understood by the Platonists cannot exist.[160]

Sensible individuals lack definitions because, containing matter, they are generated and destroyed. Since eternal individuals, such as the sun and moon, resemble the forms in not being generated or destroyed, we might suppose that they have definitions, a view apparently ascribed to the Platonists. However, they too lack definitions, Aristotle claims. He probably has Z 4 in mind when he says that attempts to define them err in "adding" characteristics which could just as well be "subtracted" without the thing being altered (1040a29–32). This is a mistake because sun and the other eternal sensibles are each *ousiai* (1040a32–33). If my earlier analysis is correct, Aristotle mentions that sun is an *ousia* in order to say that it is one and thus cannot be defined by an addition.[161] In the context of Z 15, a more important reason that eternal sensible *ousiai* lack definitions is that they are subject to the same argument as Platonic forms: a sensible individual can no more be defined with terms that apply universally than can an individual form. Attempts to define eternal sensibles like the sun and the moon err in giving them a formula common to many (1040a33–b1; cf. *Theaetetus* 208d). Not that there need be other things with their attributes; it is enough that there could be other things with their attributes (1040a34–35). It seems, then, that individuals like Socrates could not be defined even if they had no matter. Definition is of the universal. Something that is numerically one is not knowable except as an instance of a universal.

⸀Does it follow from these arguments that Aristotle's own form is also unknowable, as was suggested at the end of Z 13? It is generally supposed that Aristotle's form is not one in number. Were this so, the arguments of Z 15 would pose no threat to it. If Aristotle's forms are one in number, as I have argued, these arguments seem to imply that they too are unknowable. A closer look shows that this is not so. The arguments that Aristotle levels against Platonic forms assume that each such form contains constituents and that words which characterize the forms will also characterize the constituents. An Aristotelian form contains no such actual constituents. Nothing prevents it from being defined by words that express its unique function and that apply only to it. The argument against having knowledge of eternal sensibles also fails to exclude knowledge of Aristotelian form. The eternal sensible is unknowable because what we grasp is its form and this same form could exist in another matter. The Aristotelian form contains no material parts and it is grasped insofar as it exists apart from matter; it is separate in formula.

Z 15 seems to show that individuals cannot be known, but what it really shows is that what is one in number but still composed of actual constituents and what is one in number because it has a single matter cannot be known. The arguments do not apply to something which is numerically one in a different way. It is clear from these arguments that if Aristotelian form is to be knowable, it must be numerically one in some other way.

2.9.5 Z 16, 1040b5–16

Though indefinable, the sun and the moon are *ousiai* (1040a32–33). In contrast, most of the other entries on Z 2's list of what seem to be *ousiai* (1028b8–13) are not. The opening lines of Z 16 contend that the parts of animals are not *ousiai* because they are not separate, and the material elements like earth, air, and fire are not *ousiai* because they lack unity (1040b5–9). All these non-*ousiai* are mere potentialities. As we saw in Z 10–11, a hand that is separated from a body is only equivocally called a hand because it is no longer able to function (1036b30–32, 1035b23–25). The material elements are also potentialities; they exist as mere heaps until some unity is made out of them (1040b8–10).

In these claims from the opening of Z 16, Aristotle equates existing as an actuality with being one, just as he did in Z 13 (1039a3–8). This equation allows him to treat a difficult case: the parts of some animals continue to live even after the animal has been "divided" (1040b13–14). Does this show that the parts exist as many unities and actualities? No, for when the animal is one and continuous, its parts can exist only as potentialities unless the animal is a freak (1040b14–16). As a thing that exists in actuality, the animal must be one; its parts are non-*ousiai* even if they have the potential to become *ousiai* when separated.

The text speaks of matter being built up and made into a unity (1040b9–10) and of animals being divided into parts (b13–14). Matter and parts, the constituents of *ousiai,* have a peculiar mode of existence. As we saw earlier in book Z, the animal comes to be from matter. But when the animal has come to be, the matter no longer exists as matter; it has become a part of the animal. At the division or death of the animal, the parts cease to exist as parts; they become matter or, sometimes, a different animal. Material elements and parts of animals can never come to be *ousiai* without becoming something other than what they are. The reason is that in themselves they are never one.

What kind of unity is required of an *ousia?* This passage refers to an animal as "one and continuous by nature" (1040b14–15). Here the unity that marks something as an *ousia* is apparently continuity (Δ 6, 1015b36–1016a17; I 1, 1052a19–21). This raises obvious problems about what the text rejects as *ousiai.* Is not a severed arm also continuous? Is not a rock also continuous? In a way they are. However, when we look closely at the characterization of unity by continuity that Aristotle gives in Δ 6, we see that severed arms and rocks are not continuous in the most proper way. Δ 6 defines continuity through motion: something whose motion is indivisible in time is continuous, and something whose motion is indivisible by nature is more continuous than something whose motion is indivisible by art (1016a4–6). Accordingly, a sensible individual is one by continuity in a way that its parts or its matter is not. Because it is more one, the sensible individual has a greater claim to be an *ousia* than either part or matter has.

In this discussion Aristotle assumes that what is properly one by continuity is also an actuality. This association is significant because continuity is defined by motion, and motion is a kind of actuality. (I shall have more to say about this when I discuss book H.) Since continuity belongs to what has matter or to what has been abstracted from matter, such as mathematicals, the *ousiai* that Aristotle has in mind at the beginning of Z 16 are composites. Nevertheless, it is possible that something else could be an actuality by possessing a unity other than continuity. The section under discussion does not exclude this; it only insists that an *ousia* be separate and one in actuality. It remains open whether something other than a sensible composite can be one in actuality and separate. It would need to possess another type of numeric unity.

Why does Aristotle include a discussion of parts and of matter in the midst of a treatment of universals? I propose the following answer. The two preceding chapters criticize Platonic forms by showing the difficulties that arise from the kinds of unity such forms are said to possess. The mistake of the Platonists is to think *ousiai* that exist separately can come from other separately existing *ousiai* and can retain those other *ousiai* as parts. The present passage indicates how Aristotle avoids this error.[162] The parts of *ousiai* are not *ousiai* in themselves but mere potentialities; *ousiai* do not come from other *ousiai* but from matter. If Platonic forms were parts, they would be potentialities. In effect, the discussion of the difficulties with Platonic forms and the way to avoid them removes an obstacle to the unity of the *ousia* and thus to its existence.

2.9.6 Z 16, 1040b16–1041a5

In the final portion of his discussion of universals (1040b16–1041a5), Aristotle continues to argue against Platonism. He has already rejected Platonic attempts to characterize forms as one in number and one in species. Now he also argues that the one itself (for Platonists, the essence of forms—A 7, 988b4–6) cannot be *ousia*. This argument relies on an assumption that we saw in the first argument of Z 13.[163]

> Since one is said just as being, and the *ousia* of one thing is one, and things whose *ousia* is one in number are one in number, it is clear that neither one nor being can be the *ousia* of things (1040b16–19).

The argument is clearly aimed at nongeneric universals, being and one. On what ground does Aristotle deny that these latter are *ousiai*? Let us suppose that the one were an *ousia*. Then, by the principle asserted here, the things of which the one is the *ousia* would themselves be one in number.[164] If the one were an *ousia*, it would be the *ousia* of all things. Then the *ousia* of all things would be one in number, namely, the single entity, the one; and all things would be numerically one. *Reductio ad absurdum*. Hence, the one is not an *ousia*. Nor is being an *ousia* because being is said in the same way as one.

This argument uses two different ones: the one itself, which it rejects as *ousia,* and the numeric unity that the one itself would bring to its instances if it were an *ousia.* There is no ambiguity, but it is important to see that though one itself may or may not include numeric unity in its essence (Aristotle does not decide here), Aristotle treats it as a numeric unity. The one itself is numerically one in the sense that it is a single entity (or it would be a single entity if the Platonists were right). If it were the *ousia* of all things, then there would be just (numerically) one *ousia,* one itself. Likewise, if being were the *ousia* of all things, then their *ousia* is one in number, and they too must be one in number. Being is one in number in the sense that it is a single entity. The argument works equally well against either being or one.

The text goes on to apply this result to the essence of principle and the essence of cause (1040b19–22). They, too, cannot be *ousiai* because they are universals. Why, though, should Aristotle be interested in this possibility? In other passages he also compares principle and cause with one and being (Γ 2, 1003b22–25; I 1, 1052b5–16). The similarity, I suggest, is that both pairs are characteristics of other things that are (incorrectly) treated as if they were entities. Just as the Platonists apparently went from using one as a character of form to speaking of the one itself, so too someone could (and perhaps did) attempt to make principle or cause an entity. The latter attempt would fail for the same reasons as the former, and it is even less well grounded.[165]

The text continues with what appear to be more reasons for denying that one and being are *ousiai.* First, Aristotle claims that nothing that is common can be an *ousia; ousia* belongs to nothing except that which has it, that of which it is the *ousia* (1040b23–24). In other words, the *ousia* of a composite is not something else apart from it but something that belongs to it.[166] Presumably, we are to notice that one and being are common and infer that they are not *ousiai.* Further, Aristotle asserts that "the one cannot be in many places at once, but something common is in many places at once" (1040b25–26). From this he infers that no universal exists separately apart from particulars (1040b26–27).

How is this conclusion derived? It is often thought to follow from the preceding claims that no *ousia* is common.[167] But then the argument would assume what it should be proving, not at all what we would expect from the ἔτι at 1040b25 or from the claim at b27–29, which suggests that universals cannot be *ousiai* because they are not separate. Instead, the first step toward understanding the argument is to notice that Aristotle's use of "the one" here is surprising. From the previous arguments we would expect it to refer to the Platonic one, the one itself,[168] but the stated conclusion of the argument (1040b26–27) and the contrast that this passage makes between the one and what is common make this unlikely; the Platonic one is probably common. Moreover, to get the conclusion Aristotle draws here we need to follow Ross in taking the one as one in number or individual.[169] If all this is correct, the argument stated in the text goes as follows. Something which is numerically one and individual is not in many places at once, but a universal belongs to many in common at once. Hence, a universal is not separate from individuals. We still need to add an implicit premise. The reason that something common is not separate is that it is not one in number. Aristotle must be assuming that only what is one in number is separate. Only what is numerically one is a self-subsistent entity; universals are common. Hence, they cannot exist separately apart from what is numerically one. Since separate existence (or numeric unity) is a criterion of *ousia,* it follows that no universal is *ousia.*

These conclusions, that universals cannot be separate and thus cannot be *ousiai,* support Z 16's final dismissal of Platonic forms. Aristotle claims that the Platonists are right to separate the forms, but mistaken to say that a "one over many" is a form (1040b27–30). The reason the Platonists make the "one over many" a form is that they are unable to say what the incorruptible *ousiai* are apart from the particulars and sensibles. They make their forms the "same in species" as the corruptibles so that they can know the corruptibles by knowing the forms, but they do so merely by adding an "itself" to the sensible thing (1040b30–34).

My analysis suggests a way of interpreting these claims. Aristotle concedes that the Platonists were right to make form separate. They were right because they wanted to make their form *ousia,* and *ousia* is separate. If my interpretation of the preceding argument is correct, this amounts to saying that the Platonists were right to insist that form be numerically one. The problem is that they tried to give their forms another sort of unity, that of the "one over many." (Why else would Aristotle refer to the universal here as a "one over many" unless he wished to emphasize that the Platonists did ascribe a kind of unity to form?) But this type of unity is incompatible with being separate. What the Platonists end up doing is not at all what they intend to do. They take a universal and treat it as if it were separate. In reality, they are doing nothing more than taking a species of sensibles and adding the term "itself" to it. They begin with a form that is one in species or one in formula and treat it as though it were also numerically one as a separate individual. The forms, as the Platonists conceive them, cannot have both characteristics required of *ousiai.*

So understood, the argument of Z 16 fits well with Z 15. The latter argues that if the forms are separate individuals, that is, one in number, they cannot be defined or known. Z 16 assumes that each form is a universal (a "one over many"), and shows that it cannot be separate or one in number.

Are there any separately existing *ousiai?* They would have to be one in number, and we know from Z 15 that they could not contain matter if they are to be knowable and definable. At the end of Z 16 (1040b34–1041a3),

Aristotle insists that there are grounds for asserting the existence of such *ousiai*, but this remains to be shown.

2.9.7 Species and Genus

As I mentioned at the beginning of this section (2.9), one position that has been argued recently in an effort to save Aristotle from the apparent inconsistency of both maintaining and denying that εἴδη are *ousiai* is that Z 13–16 deny not that all universals are *ousiai*, but only that genera are *ousiai*. Species, on the other hand, are thought to escape these arguments. Having examined this text, we are now in a position to ask whether species are subject to the arguments against universals.

The arguments in Z 13–16 are of three sorts. In one, Aristotle draws on the identity between a thing and its *ousia*. If the *ousia* is one, then so is the thing of which it is the *ousia*, and *vice versa*. In another, he rejects universals as *ousiai* because they are predicates. The third sort points out the problem of supposing that one *ousia* is composed of another *ousia*. It might be thought that the species are not subject to the third argument because Aristotle denies that genera are *ousiai* and because a species consists of a single ultimate differentia that implicitly contains all its genera. But Aristotle also maintains that composite *ousiai* are substances. Since form or species is a constituent of the composite, one *ousia* would be composed of another if, as Michael J. Woods maintains, species and form cannot be distinguished. Thus, species are subject to the third argument. The most interesting part of Woods's interpretation is his denial that species are predicates on the ground that we need species to pick out individuals and they need to be picked out before we can apply predicates to them.[170] If this were right, species would escape from the second argument. But it is hard to see how Woods's point could be reconciled with the epistemology Aristotle presents in *Posterior Analytics* B 19. There he describes how we extract universals from sense perception, a process of which lower animals are incapable. The universal is a "one besides the many which is one in all ones" (100a7–8), and this is true even of the lowest universal, the species (100a15–16). *Metaphysics* A 1 endorses this epistemology, and Aristotle consistently defines the universal as a one over many. There might be something to Woods's argument if the species were the only way to pick out a thing, but Socrates can be identified by paleness, sitting, or other sensible attributes. There is no evidence that Aristotle has any hesitation about predicating species of individual instances. So the species cannot escape the second argument either. Once we accept a species' being a "one over many," we can see that the first argument also applies to it. Let us suppose that a species like human being is the *ousia* of all human beings. Then there is a single entity, the species, that is the *ousia* of many, a violation of the principle that where the *ousia* is one, that of which it is the *ousia* must also be one (1040b17-19; 1038b14-15). A universal would be numerically one in the sense that it can be distinguished from other universals, and so the things of which it would be the *ousia*, the individual human beings, would all have to be one as well. As I said earlier, this argument does not assume that the universal is one in number, but that it would need to be one in number if it were an *ousia*. Aristotle's argument applies equally to all universals. Even if there were textual evidence to distinguish species from other universals here, and there is not, the logic of Aristotle's arguments would exclude species.[171]

Since species (εἴδη) belong among the universals that Z 13-16 argue are not *ousiai*, it is necessary to follow tradition and distinguish them from the forms (also called εἴδη) that Aristotle regards as primary *ousiai*.[172] Whereas species are predicates, forms are constituents and essences. Even after this distinction problems remain. What sort of an entity is form? Aristotle's arguments against universals help to delimit the nature form must have. It must not be composed of constituent forms, it must not be a predicate, and it must be numerically one and one with its essence. As we have seen, all of these are unity conditions. Form could meet them all if it were first numerically one; for it would then lack parts, be self-subsistent and not a predicate, and be capable of being one with its essence. The last condition also requires that form be one in formula. That form must satisfy all these conditions emerges from the present section. So understood, Z 13-16 contribute to clarifying the conditions for form. The problem now is what sort of thing form must be in order to be one in both ways.

This is a problem that the Platonists are unable to solve, and the present section shows why. The Platonists make the forms separate when they are not (1040b26-28), they maintain that some forms are constituents of others (1039a24-26), and they think that *ousiai* contain constituents that exist in actuality (1039a3-8). Their mistake lies in thinking that the forms are universals and also separate. Universals cannot be separate because they are predicates; they depend on something else. As Aristotle says later, universals are not one in actuality; they are merely potentialities (Θ 8, 1050b34-1051a2). If his own form is to avoid these problems, it must be one in actuality. How, though, does ascribing this character to form enable it to avoid the problems? This remains to be explored.

2.10 Z 17: *OUSIA* AS CAUSE

Aristotle's dismissal of universals as *ousiai* in Z 13-16 completes his discussion of the four candidates for *ousia*. Z 17 makes a new start. Here he tries to determine the nature of *ousia* by assuming that "*ousia* is a principle and a cause" (1041a9-10) and finding the entity that could have such a function.

Has Aristotle argued earlier that *ousia* is a cause? The idea that *ousia* is a principle and cause is expressed in book A (3, 983a26–29).[173] In his treatment of *ousia* in book Δ, Aristotle characterizes *ousia* as the cause of being (8, 1017b14–16). We can also see evidence of this view of *ousia* in book Z: in chapter 13 Aristotle notes that universals are thought to be *ousiai* because they seem to be causes and principles (1038b6–8).[174] So Aristotle does not express a new idea when he claims in Z 17 that *ousia* is a cause. But we can still ask, how do we know that *ousia* is really a cause? No Aristotelian text aims to prove that it is a cause, but I think that Z 1 provides the basis for Z 17's approach. As we saw, in that chapter Aristotle argues that other things are beings through (διά) *ousia* (1028a25–31). This is tantamount to saying that *ousia* is the cause of being in non-*ousiai*. Further, Z 1 claims that *ousia* is prior to other beings in knowledge and in all other ways (1028a31–33). Since we know a thing when we know its first cause (A 3, 983a25–26) and since the other beings are known through *ousia,* it should be their cause. Analogously, any priority of *ousia* to other beings should imply that *ousia* is a cause and principle. For insofar as *ousia* is prior, the others depend upon it, and that upon which the others depend is their cause.[175] Accordingly, Z 1 provides a basis to think that *ousia* is the cause of other beings. However, when Aristotle calls *ousia* a cause in Z 17, he does not refer only to the relation of *ousia* to non-*ousiai*; he means also that the *ousia* of a particular composite *ousia* is the cause of being in that particular *ousia*. Again, this is supported by Z 1's claim that *ousia* is the primary and simple being (1028a30–31). Insofar as it is primary, *ousia* should be the source of being to all beings, including composite *ousiai*.

The same conclusion is implicit in the rest of book Z's inquiry into *ousia*. As we saw, Aristotle aims to find primary *ousia*. (All the candidates have some claim to be called *ousia*. Aristotle seeks the one with the best credentials; this is the form—cf. 7, 1032b1–2.) Insofar as form is primary *ousia*, the other *ousiai* depend upon it, and it is the cause of their being *ousiai*. But insofar as they are *ousiai*, they are beings. Thus, primary *ousia* is the cause of being even in secondary *ousiai*. For all these reasons, Z 17 is justified in calling *ousia* a cause.

What does it mean to investigate *ousia* as a cause? Just what does it mean to say that *ousia* is a cause of being? What sort of cause could it be? A substantial portion of Z 17 is devoted to answering these questions. An important task of Z 17 is to determine how to investigate *ousia* as a cause.

The first point that Aristotle makes is that an inquiry into a cause always seeks to know why something belongs to something else (1041a10–11), a point familiar from the *Posterior Analytics* (cf. B 1, 89b29–35). Here he supports this claim with an example: to inquire into the cause of the musical man being a musical man is to ask why the man is musical and not possessed of another character (1041a11–14). The problem is to understand how *ousia* could be the cause of something's possessing some character. Aristotle considers the suggestion that we might be seeking why each thing is itself, and he rejects it (1041a14–20). His reasoning is terse; I reconstruct it as follows. In order to inquire into a "why" question, the that (τὸ ὅτι) or the is (τὸ εἶναι) must already be clear (1041a15). (Again, this is a point made in the *Posterior Analytics,* and even the example used here, the eclipse of the moon, also appears there [B 1, 89b29–31; 2, 89b37–90a1].) Accordingly, in order to inquire *why* each thing is itself, we must already know *that* each thing is itself.[176] But once we know that each thing is itself, there is nothing more to be said about why it is itself. In a "why" question we seek "one formula and one cause for all" (1041a17), but there is no formula or cause of each thing's being itself, unless it is that each thing is indivisible in respect of itself (a18–19). This, though, is just the essence of the one (τὸ ἑνὶ εἶναι). It is common to all, but a "shortcut" (σύντομον).

If the "why" question is understood as the question, "why is something itself?" there is no way to give a significant answer. We could say that this man is a man because man is one and that that is what it is to be one. But this would tell us nothing about why *man* is. Because it is an answer to every "why" question, it answers none.

It is significant that the only way to answer the question "why is something itself?" is to refer to the one. Here being is taken to lie in a thing's being itself, and the position Aristotle rejects is that unity is the cause of being.[177] The last lines of the text (1041a18–20) just described make this clear. The only thing that could be the cause of each thing's being itself is indivisibility because, besides being, only this is common to all. But indivisibility is (apparently) the essence of unity (I 1, 1052b16), and this essence is simply a "shortcut."

What is wrong with an essence that is a shortcut? On what ground does Aristotle reject unity as a cause? Finally, what does Aristotle's rejection of unity as the cause of being have to do with the "that" and "why" questions which Aristotle makes so much of here? All these questions need to be answered; I begin with the last. The text claims that to pose a "why" question, we need to begin by assuming a that: we need to assume that being belongs to the thing (1041a15). But whatever is is also one (Γ 2, 1003b22–32; I 2, 1054a13). Thus, once we know *that* something is, we know immediately that it is one. To go on to ask the "why" question is, Aristotle assumes here, to seek some unity in virtue of which each thing is itself. But we already know this unity once we know that the thing is. To ask the "why" question is superfluous. Aristotle is punning, I think, when he says that to seek why something is itself is to seek nothing (οὐδέν = οὐδ᾽ ἕν), that is, no one (1041a14–15; cf. 1041b3–4). Such an inquiry seeks nothing that would not already be clear before the inquiry could be undertaken. In knowing that something is, we already know why it is if knowing why amounts to grasping that unity in respect of which it is.

Does knowing why amount to grasping this unity, the essence of one? The Eleatics think so or, at least, Aristotle thinks they do. A hint of why Aristotle rejects this view may lie in another interpretation of the pun I mentioned earlier. The one which all things share, indivisibility, is not only immediately apparent, it is "no one" or nothing (cf. 1041a14–15) in the sense that there is no thing which is indivisibility. Later, Aristotle distinguishes the essence of one from the things that are one; the essence of one is merely a formula (I 1, 1052b5–7, b16–19). It belongs to everything because of each thing's nature. It is not a cause; it is not even a thing. Another reason that the essence of unity cannot be a cause is that, if it were, all things would be the same. This universal unity is not the cause of being; it goes hand in hand with being. Both are caused.

From all this it follows that the essence of one cannot be the cause that is *ousia*. There must have been something wrong with trying to conceive of *ousia* as the cause of why each thing is itself. Aristotle proposes instead a different understanding of what it is that *ousia* should cause. What needs to be explained, he contends, is why something belongs to something else (1041a23–25). When, for example, we ask, "why does it thunder?" we really mean to ask, "why is there noise in the clouds?" (1041a24–25). To ask "what is the cause of the house?" is to ask "why are boards and bricks a house?" (1041a26–27). To find the cause of a being we first need to analyze it into a form that belongs to a matter.

Aristotle seems to assume here that each being is really a kind of plurality: each consists of something which belongs to something else. Yet this is obviously not true; for, as he says later in the chapter, there is no inquiry into what is simple (1041b9–11). So not everything will admit the analysis that he proposes. Why should we think that this type of analysis is possible often or that it is unique? The text contains no argument supporting it. Let me suggest that support for the analysis lies in Aristotle's earlier treatment of the candidates for *ousia,* especially essence. Recall that in Z 4 he defined "primary" as something which does not contain one thing said of something else (Z 4, 1030a3–11; cf. 6, 1031b13–14). If *ousia* belongs only to what is primary, then everything else should fail to be primary: everything else should contain one thing said of something else. Thus, the analysis proposed in Z 17 preserves the distinction between what is one and simple and what is many that Aristotle uses earlier to locate *ousia.*[178] He regards each non-*ousia* as many and each *ousia* as one. Since *ousia* is the cause of being in the other beings, it should cause something to belong to something else. Conversely, if we can find what causes something to belong to something else, this must be *ousia.*

Two points about Aristotle's procedure here should be noted. First, what is caused is a unity from a plurality, something's belonging to something else, and the ultimate cause of this unity must have more unity than the unity it causes. If the cause of something's belonging to something else were the same sort of plurality made into a unity, some other thing's belonging to still another thing, then we would need to seek a cause for its unity, and so on. The ultimate cause of why one thing belongs to another must be one in a stronger way. This, the middle term, is what Aristotle identifies as *ousia*. *Ousia* is the cause of a plurality's being one. Second, although Aristotle speaks of composites here in much the terms he uses in Z 4–5, he is not primarily concerned with composites of attributes and *ousiai* but with composites of form and matter, that is, with composite *ousiai*. This amounts to a refinement of the distinction between *ousia* and non-*ousia* based on unity and plurality that he makes in Z 4–5. Primary *ousia* is one; but secondary *ousiai,* such as composites of form and matter, are pluralities like non-*ousiai*. This refinement is consistent with the earlier distinction, and it is familiar from Z 7–11.

Aristotle identifies the composition of form and matter with the being of the thing. That is to say, the unification of its constituents is the being of the composite. Hence, Aristotle aims to find *ousia* by locating the cause of being or, equivalently, the cause of unity in a composite. Aristotle indicates his concern lies in finding the cause of being (αἴτιον . . . τοῦ εἶναι) at least twice in the chapter (1041a31–2; 1041b28; and 1041b5 if the manuscripts can be trusted). That Aristotle treats why questions by analyzing what appears to be one into something that belongs to something else has often been noted,[179] but that this analysis is undertaken to find the cause of being has not.[180]

There are several types of causes. Aristotle notes that any of them could be given in response to a "why" question (1041a28–b2). He mentions, in particular, the final and the efficient causes; and, if the manuscripts are correct, he identifies the cause with the essence.[181] Even if the manuscript reading is wrong, there is no doubt that Aristotle regards the formal cause as an equally justified answer to a "why" question. For he goes on to maintain that the cause of a matter's possessing a form is just the form or essence that it possesses (1041b5–6). The rest of Z 17 is, I maintain, devoted to showing that this is so and that form is thus the cause of being.

After mentioning the need to seek the cause (1041a27–32), Aristotle continues with what seems at first like a recapitulation of claims he made before:

> And the thing sought is overlooked most of all when it is among what are not said in respect of each other; for example, what is [τί ἐστι] man? is sought through what is said simply without distinguishing that these [things] are this (1041a32–b2).

What is interesting and problematic about this assertion is the appearance of a "what is it" question.[182] There is no reason to find it disturbing, for the *Posterior Analytics* maintains that "what is it" and "why" questions are always the same (B 2, 90a14–15). But it is an interesting formulation because

we also know from the *Posterior Analytics* that a "what is it" question presupposes an affirmative answer to an "is it" question (89b37–90a1), and the
latter is a question about being (90a9–11). We can ask what man is only if we
already know that man is, and when we ask what man is, we seek the cause
of his being. The point of the quoted passage is that we can find this cause if
we analyze the thing in question into something that belongs to something
else. So this passage confirms the interpretation I have advanced. Aristotle
assumes that a being consists of something complex, a plurality that has been
unified, and the cause of being is the cause of the plurality's unity. Analysis
of being is supposed to be the first step.[183]

That Aristotle intends to apply his point about the analysis to the particular
case of being is clearly indicated by what follows in the text:

> Since it is necessary that being [τὸ εἶναι] hold and belong, it should
> clearly be asked, why the matter is [something?]; for example, why are
> these [materials] a house? Because the essence of a house belongs. And
> this is a man, or this body having this [form]. So the cause of the matter
> is sought (this is the form) by which it is something; this is the *ousia*
> (1041b4–9).

The observation that Aristotle begins from and aims to account for is that
being belongs to each thing. Since the thing consists of something (namely,
form) that belongs to something else (matter), it has being when its form
belongs to its matter. Consequently, the question about the cause of a particular thing amounts to a question about why a form belongs to a matter. The
answer to this latter question is that the form belongs because of itself, that
is, because of what it is, the essence of the thing. For this reason, the form or
essence is *ousia,* the cause of being.

There are two textual problems that tend to obscure the proper analysis of
the passage quoted in the preceding paragraph. According to the manuscripts, the first question in the above passage asks why the matter is. Most
editors accept Christ's addition of τί, understanding this question to ask,
"Why is the matter something?"[184] There is no doubt that the question is
answered by using the latter formulation (see 1041b8). Even the illustration
of the question that follows ("Why is something a house?"—b5–6) seems to
be an instance of the "why is matter something" question. And the mention
of being in the first part of the sentence could easily have misled scribes to
think the question ought to be why matter is. So there are good grounds to
accept the emendation. On the other hand, the point at issue here is, in a way,
the being of the matter (as part of the composite—Aristotle's usage is loose),
and his point is that this question needs to be posed as a question about why
the matter is something. A question about being is just a question about why
something belongs to something else. Thus, the manuscript reading could be

retained. Either way the sense of the passage is the same. A second, similar textual problem is whether "this is the form" at 1041b8 is simply a marginal note that worked its way into the text. Again, the answer is that it makes no difference. If the phrase is retained, the sentence should be rendered as either: (a) "therefore, what is sought is the cause of the matter by which it is something, and this is the form"; or (b) "therefore, what is sought is the cause of the matter, and this is the form by which it is something." Ross accepts what amounts to (a) on the ground that Aristotle would not refer to the cause of the matter.[185] But we just saw what appears to be a reference to the cause of matter at 1041b5, that is, to the cause of matter's being. It makes sense for Aristotle to speak of the cause of matter; form is the cause of the being of matter just because for matter to be matter is for it to be a part of a composite and form is the cause of the composite. At 1041b4–5 Aristotle points out that being belongs to a thing and asks, apparently, why matter has being. To answer this question he applies the analysis of being that we saw earlier: the cause of matter's being is that form belongs to matter. So we can seek the cause of being by seeking the cause of form's belonging to matter. The cause of form's belonging or, at any rate, *a* cause of form's belonging to matter is just the form itself. A reason matter has a form is that matter is, in a way, what it is to be the form; the essence belongs to the matter. As Aristotle puts it, the cause of these bricks and stones being a house is that the essence of house belongs to them (1041b5–6). Since form is essence, the cause of matter being is the form that makes it what it is—exactly what the manuscripts seems to say at 1041b7–8 on the (b) reading of the passage. However, since Aristotle equates the cause of being and the cause of being something here, it makes no difference to the doctrine he advances whether we adopt the (a) reading, or indeed whether we excise the phrase, "this is the form." His discussion here leaves no doubt that form is the cause of being. The (b) reading allows us to make sense of the passage's structure and, as I shall argue shortly, it is consistent with what follows, but my interpretation does not depend on it. In sum, neither of these two textual problems poses an obstacle to my interpretation of 1041b4–9.

Although it should now be clear that Aristotle advances form or essence as the cause of being in this passage, he has not yet presented arguments for this position. A nice feature of my interpretation of this passage is that it enables us to understand the rest of Z 17 as just such an argument. Conversely, the context of the latter half of Z 17 lends support to my interpretation of 1041b4–9.

The key to understanding the connection between the latter passage and the rest of Z 17 lies in the convertibility of being and one. In 1041b4–9 Aristotle seeks the cause of being; the second half of Z 17 considers the cause of unity. We know from elsewhere in the *Metaphysics* that whatever is is one (Γ 2, 1003b22–32; I 2, 1054a13). But we do not even have to rely on other statements of convertibility here; for implicit in the analysis of the question about being into a question about form's belonging to matter is the assumption that for something to be is for its form to belong to its matter, that is, for its form and matter to constitute a unity. Indeed, this connection of the being of something with its unity is tantamount to the convertibility of being and one that Aristotle proclaims in Γ 2.

Despite this close connection between unity and being, it is still not obvious that Aristotle's discussion of the cause of unity in the second half of Z 17 contributes to the investigation of the cause of being that had been his concern up to this point. As he conceives of an inquiry into the cause of being, it asks why a particular form belongs to a matter. This is a question about unity, but the issue of the last half of Z 17 is why the material constituents are one, an apparently different unity question.

Aristotle begins his discussion of this latter question by considering the composite. This is one, he claims, not like a heap but like a syllable (1041b11–12). A syllable cannot be the same as its constituent parts, nor can flesh be simply fire and earth because even when the former are destroyed or dissolved, the latter elements remain (1041b12–16; cf. 10, 1035a17–21). It follows that the composite contains something else besides its elements (1041b17–19). What could it be? Suppose that this something were either (1) an element or (2) a composite of elements (b19–20). In the first case the same argument would apply: when the composite is destroyed, this element would remain along with the other elements; the composite would still not be identical with its elements; and there would need to be still another thing present with the elements, and so on *ad infinitum* (b20–22). Let us then suppose that the something else in the composite is itself a composite of elements (case 2). This would, in turn, consist of either (a) one element or (b) many elements. The former is just case 1; it is impossible, as we saw. Likewise, (b) is also impossible because if the something else had many elements, it would be like the syllable and flesh, and the original argument would apply (b22–25). Since the assumption that the other thing in the composite besides the elements is itself either an element or a composite of elements leads to absurdities, we should conclude that the assumption is mistaken. The other thing in the composite which makes it different from a heap of elements cannot itself be an element or a composite of elements.

Although the argument shows that something besides an element must be the cause of the composite's *unity,* Aristotle concludes with the assertion that something besides an element must be the cause of the composite's *being* (1041b25–28). Given the convertibility of being and one, this is not surprising, except that, as I said, the unity which the argument shows is the unity of elements, whereas being lies in form's being present with matter. Does an argument showing the unity of elements support an inference about the unity of form and matter?

Before we examined the details of the argument, the answer to this question would not have been obvious; but once we see what Aristotle argues, we can also see why Aristotle can move back and forth between the two types of unity. The argument I have just presented shows that there must be some other thing besides the material constituents which is the source of their unity. This principle which makes them something more than a heap must be the form. Hence, the unity of the elements is also the unity of form and matter. In showing the cause of the former, Aristotle shows the cause of the latter. But the cause of the former unity is the form, and the latter unity—the unity of form and matter—is or is convertible with being. Consequently, form is the cause of being. Since, moreover, Aristotle assumes that the cause of being is *ousia,* form is *ousia.*

So understood, Aristotle's analysis of being and inquiry into its cause in Z 17 are consistent and coherent. He advances form as the cause of unity among the elements in order to show that form causes the unity of form and matter and thus that form is the cause of being. The key to understanding the argument lies in the role of unity. Nevertheless, as is typical of the argumentation we have seen throughout book Z, the conclusion of this argument makes no mention of the unities upon which it depends.

Several objections and loose ends remain. First, Aristotle does not identify the cause of the elements' unity as form or essence, as we would expect. All that we have in the text is an argument that the cause cannot be matter and a cryptic remark that the *ousia* of things that have an *ousia* is the nature (φύ-σις) which is not an element but a principle (1041b30–31). Still, there is no doubt that the cause of unity and being in the composite is its form. What else besides form is a part of the composite but not an element? What Aristotle calls elements here is what he calls matter at 1041b5 and b8 (cf. 1041a26–27).[186] Moreover, the *De Anima* advances similar arguments to show that soul is not a material element of a living thing (A 5, 410b10–12 ff., esp. 411b5–14). Also, we already know from earlier in book Z that the matter persists when it is separated from the form of a composite (Z 10, 1035a17–21), an indication that the elements are matter and that form is not an element. In short, even though Aristotle does not say so, the cause of being and unity in the composite which his argument shows to be distinct from matter must be form. This argument therefore supports the claim made or only suggested (if the editors' excisions are correct) earlier in Z 17 (1041b4–9) that essence or form is the cause of being in a composite. Essence is the answer to both the "what is it" question and the "why" question (see 1041b1). It is *ousia.*

My interpretation has the advantage of lending support to the otherwise peculiar text found in the manuscripts at 1041b4–9, a text I defended earlier on different grounds. As I said, what is odd about this text is that Aristotle seems to inquire into the being of matter (1041b5) and to advance a cause of matter (b7–8). Both are consistent with the rest of the chapter, as I have interpreted it. Aristotle goes on to argue that the unity of the material elements is caused by a nonmaterial principle, form. Sticks and stones are the matter of a house when they are united into a house, and the form of the house is what makes them one and makes them be matter. Thus, the cause of the being of the composite is also the cause of the unification and being of the matter, exactly the interpretation I advanced earlier. Z 17 shows that the reason that the house is, the reason that the boards and bricks are a house, the reason that the boards and bricks are one, and the reason that the boards and bricks have being as matter, that is, exist as something more than just boards and bricks, is the same: the form or essence of the house. So even though it seems odd to speak of the cause of matter's being, the text of the manuscripts is precisely what we would expect to find given what follows.

To understand Aristotle's account of form as the cause of unity and being we need to recognize the questions he has not yet answered. Z 17 regards the form as the cause of the presence of form in matter. It says nothing about what it means to say that a plurality of materials are one or how the apparent duality of form and matter can itself be one. In locating the cause of the unity of matter, Aristotle has opened the question about the unity of form and matter. The composite must be more than the mere conjunction of form and matter, for such a conjunction would be merely a heap. How can form and matter be one?

A first start on the problem of how the composite is one is to consider the kind of unity it has. Of the various ones that Aristotle describes in Δ 6 and I 1, which is the one that form brings to the material elements? What sort of unity does form cause in a composite? It is obvious that form is the cause of the composite's being one in formula because the formula of the composite is the formula of its form, as Z 10–11 showed. But this is not the unity that is at issue in Z 17. Instead, this chapter concerns a unity that belongs to material constituents. What type of unity is this? From examples like flesh and house, it seems that the unity that Aristotle has in mind here is continuity (Δ 6, 1015b35–1016a17; I 1, 1052a19–21). The boards and bricks form a house when they are placed together in the right way; their relative positions are the difference between a heap of material and a house. According to the argument of Z 17, form causes unity in the sense of continuity. Just how it does so remains to be explained. A house and flesh are continuous in accordance with the characterization of continuity given in the *Metaphysics*; they are capable of moving together (Δ 6, 1016a5–6; 1052a20–21). (A house, though, is not continuous by nature, the highest type of continuity.) A composite like a syllable is also continuous, but not because its parts move together. It is continuous according to the terms of Aristotle's more frequent characterization (*Phys.* E 3, 227a10–12; *Cat.* 6, 5a1–2), for the letters in a syllable share common limits. However continuity is understood, it is a kind of numeric unity. Something that is continuous has one matter and is thereby numerically one (Δ 6, 1016b31–33). Accordingly, in arguing that form is the cause of unity, Aristotle shows that form is the source of numeric unity in a composite. Thus, both the composite's unity in formula and its unity in number are due to form.

Since form is the cause of both types of unity, it should possess them itself in a higher degree than the composite does (α 1, 993b24–26). Thus, form is one in number, a conclusion we reached earlier in this section and in other sections on quite different grounds. When we compare this conclusion with the preceding conclusion that the composite is numerically one, an obvious problem emerges: how can a part of the composite be one and also the cause of the unity of the whole composite? If form is one, then the composite should be a plurality; if the composite is one, form should be merely a potential part. To be sure, form and composite are one in different ways, but this by itself does not solve the problem. For both are one in number. In rejecting universals as *ousiai*, Aristotle argues that were they *ousiai*, a composite like Socrates could not be an *ousia* because it would be many (1038b30–34). Presumably, form can be *ousia* without preventing Socrates from also being an *ousia*. Z 17's argument that form is the cause of unity in the composite does not show how this can be so. Because form is the cause of unity in a composite, form is also the cause of its being an *ousia*. But how can the composite be an *ousia* if its part is also an *ousia*? How can it be one if it contains as a part something that is one? Part of the answer to these questions is that form is not an element of the composite, but more needs to be said about the relation of form and composite. Quite appropriately, the composite is the theme of book H.

Surveying Z 17 as a whole, we can now see that the method Aristotle successfully pursues to locate *ousia* as form is just the opposite of the method that he proposes and rejects near the outset of the chapter. The latter aimed to find the unity that causes being. The successful method recognizes that the unity associated with being is not the cause but what is caused, for a thing has being when it is one. As we saw, Aristotle begins by analyzing being as the presence of form in a matter, that is, as the unity of form and matter. He then argues that form is the cause of the unity of the material elements. Since it is the presence of form that makes matter one, form is also the cause of the unity of form and matter and, thus, the cause of being. Since the cause of being is *ousia*, form is *ousia*. This last conclusion, left implicit here, is just what we saw earlier in book Z, but Z 17 adds a new dimension to our understanding of form. To cause unity in the composite, form must be one itself and more one than the composite. But form is not only one; it is also the cause of unity in the composite. How both form and composite can be numerically one is a problem that remains to be resolved.

2.11 BOOK H 1–5: THE COMPOSITE

Most commentators regard book H as a haphazardly connected appendix to book Z that pursues the same theme.[187] In contrast, I shall argue here that book H completes the inquiry into categorial *ousia* by investigating two candidates for *ousia* that book Z quickly dismissed. These are the matter and the composite. Both were mentioned as kinds of substrates (1029a2–5) and set aside (a30–32) in Z 3. Book H takes them up again. Most of the book consists of an examination of the composite,[188] and this examination further refines our understanding of form. By drawing upon the preceding discussion and continuing to focus attention on the role of unity, I shall show that book H is a reasonably coherent sequel to book Z.

2.11.1 H 1

The first sentence of book H announces the need to "reckon up" the results of the preceding discussion and to tie them together to attain the end (1042a3–4). Much of the rest of the first chapter (a4–24) consists of a summary of the results of book Z. Toward its end Aristotle turns his attention in a different direction, one that is presumably calculated to lead us toward the "end" of the inquiry into categorial being:

> And let us now consider the *ousiai* that are agreed upon. These are the sensible *ousiai,* and all sensible *ousiai* have matter (1042a24–26).

What this passage calls "sensible *ousiai*" are obviously composites. A reference to the "agreed upon" *ousiai* earlier in H 1 calls them the "natural" *ousiai* and mentions as examples, the simple bodies, plants, animals, the heavens, and the parts of the last three (1042a7–11). The latter passage repeats Z 2's list of things to which *ousia* "seems to belong most clearly" (1028b8–13).[189] While the bulk of book Z concentrates on the list of *ousiai* in Z 3, book H examines the first list.

Why does Aristotle retain the parts of animals and the simple bodies on the list? Has he not already excluded them as *ousiai* in Z 16? A parallel question could be raised about Aristotle's remarks immediately after the passage quoted above. He claims that the substrate is *ousia* and that "substrate" is said in three ways: matter, form, and composite (1042a26–31). This distinction repeats what appears in Z 3 (1029a2–3).[190] But has not Aristotle already argued that two of these three substrates are not *ousiai?* Must we conclude that the two books are inconsistent and perhaps written at different times?

Such a conclusion is not at all justified. In Z 3 Aristotle argues that form is "prior to and more of a being than" matter and the composite (1029a5–6;

a29–30). The latter are set aside only because form is primary. Book H returns to these lesser *ousiai*. Though unstated, the reasons are easy to see. First, having shown in Z 17 that form is the cause of being and unity in the composite, Aristotle must now explain how. Second, having found the primary entry from Z 3's list of *ousiai*, Aristotle should now use it to assess and account for the entries on the other list of *ousiai*, the list of Z 2. These latter "agreed upon" *ousiai* have some claim to be called *ousiai*, even if they are not primary. An understanding of the primary *ousia* should be able to explain why all the other *ousiai* are *ousiai*, including those like parts of animals and composites that we know are not primary or even properly *ousiai*. Even though we do not find discussions of all of these secondary *ousiai* in book H, it is still appropriate for Aristotle to include them all in a list of *ousiai*.

A qualm about matter may remain. Z 3 maintains that it lacks all determination and is neither a this nor separate. It would seem not to be *ousia* in any way. But Z 3 makes these claims about a matter that has all determination stripped away. What we learn from Z 3 is that matter by itself is not self-subsistent; the material substrate depends on form. This lesson is apparent in H 1's description of it: "By matter I mean what is not a this in actuality but potentially a this" (1042a27–28). Here Aristotle explains matter in terms of a this, form (1042a28–29). Thus, the matter under consideration in H 1 is not the completely undetermined matter that Z 3 dismisses.

This characterization of matter in terms of form or this is significant because Aristotle defines the third type of substrate as the composite of the other two (1042a29–30). Thus, the three substrates are: (1) what is potentially a this, (2) the this, and (3) the composite of the first two. All three are understood in terms of the this. On what ground does Aristotle assert that all three substrates are *ousiai* (1042a26)? Let me suggest that the reason is that the this is an *ousia*, as we already know from book Z. The others are called *ousia* derivatively. Much of book H is devoted to showing the basis for calling the other substrates, matter and composite, *ousiai*.

2.11.1.1 1042a32–b8: Matter

H 1 concludes with a brief discussion of matter. These remarks begin with the claim, "that matter is *ousia* is clear" (1042a32). The reason this is clear, Aristotle explains, is that matter is the substrate "for all opposite changes" (a32–34). Why is this a justification? The usual view is that this text asserts that matter is *ousia* because, as Aristotle says in the *Categories* (4a10–11), *ousia* is a substrate for opposites.[191] However, on this interpretation, his mentioning generation and destruction—changes in respect of *ousia*—at 1042b1–3 becomes puzzling: how can he support the claim that matter is *ousia* by speaking of the matter as underlying changes in *ousiai*? How could an *ousia* be the substrate of an *ousia*? If matter underlies *ousia*, it is not an *ousia*. This problem vanishes and the passage makes more sense in its context if we emphasize the "all" in 1042a32. Then, matter is an *ousia* because it is a substrate for *all* changes, not only accidental changes but also changes in *ousia*. Aristotle illustrates the claim that matter is the substrate of change by first pointing out a different matter for each type of accidental change (1042a34–b1). In the same way (ὁμοίως), he continues, there is a substrate for changes in respect of *ousia,* changes like generation and corruption (1042b1–2). In one sense, the substrate underlies as a this; in another, in respect of a privation (b2–3).

Why, then, is matter *ousia?* Throughout book Z Aristotle assumes that what is a this is clearly an *ousia* (e.g., Z 12, 1037b27). As we just saw, matter underlies as a this or in respect of a privation. If it underlies as a this, it is an *ousia.* The cases when matter underlies in respect of a privation are cases of change in *ousia.* Here the matter is potentially a this, as Aristotle described it earlier in H 1; matter is *ousia* because it is capable of becoming a this (1042a26–28). Properly, it is only potentially an *ousia;* but, in virtue of this capacity, matter deserved to be called *ousia.* Just as the acorn is, in a way, an oak, matter is, in a way, *ousia.*

On the foregoing interpretation, the treatment of matter in 1042a32–b8 aims to justify the claim that matter is *ousia,* and this latter claim in turn both explains and supports the earlier assertions that the substrate is *ousia* (1042a26) and that matter is substrate (a26–27).[192] Aristotle reiterates the result of this final section in the opening sentence of H 2, where he claims that the *ousia* which is matter and substrate is potentially (1042b9). Thus, two statements of the conclusion (1042a26–28; b9–10) sandwich the argument, 1042a32–b8.

An advantage of this interpretation is that it ties together the entire final section of H 1 (1042a26–b8). The whole passage aims to show that matter is an *ousia* through form. The interpretation also accounts for other details of the text. The final lines of H 1 maintain that the other changes "follow" generation, but that the latter does not follow all of them (1042b3–5). That is, a matter capable of substantial change is also capable of other kinds of changes, but matter capable of local motion is not necessarily capable of generation or destruction (1042b5–6). Why does Aristotle emphasize the primacy of change in *ousia?* If such changes are primary, then the matter for them is also primary. I think his point is that even though the matter for *ousia* resembles the other kinds of matter, it is primary. Such matter has the best claim to be called *ousia.* Because what is properly an essence is primary, the matter for it is also primary.

This type of primacy is double-edged. In H 2 Aristotle speaks of composites of attributes and *ousiai* as themselves *ousiai* "by analogy" (1043a4–5). It follows that matters for local, qualitative, and quantitative change could also be called *ousiai* insofar as they are potentially these composites. If wood in a certain position is an *ousia* of some sort, then before undergoing the local motion that brings it into this position, the wood is potentially this particular *ousia*. As a potentiality for an *ousia,* the wood could be called *ousia* on the same ground that the matter for changes in *ousia* is called *ousia*. Matter for changes in *ousia* and matter for other kinds of changes are all *ousiai* as potentialities. Aristotle does not bring this out in H 1. Indeed, his characterization of the substrate as what is potentially a this (1042a27–28) applies only to the matter for change in *ousia*. However, his distinction of kinds of material substrates in this chapter amounts to a distinction of various types of *ousiai*. All the various kinds of matter thus have some basis to be called *ousiai* because each is potentially some sort of form, but the matter for the this has the best claim to be called *ousia*.

This discussion of matter has no direct connection with unity, but it does dovetail nicely with Aristotle's discussion of a type of unity in Δ 6. There he maintains that continuity is a unity that belongs to things whose (local) motion is indivisible *per se* in respect of time (1016a5–6). H 1 tells us that something with a particular kind of motion has a particular kind of matter for that motion. It follows that something which is continuous should have a particular kind of matter which is the substrate for the thing's motion. Moreover, to say that something is continuous is to say that its matter is capable of moving in a way that is indivisible in time, that is, that it is capable of changing in place all at once. Continuity is, then, a unity of the matter that belongs to it in virtue of its motion. As we will see in the next subsection, the relation between matter and continuity is not unique.

In sum, the brief account of matter at the end of H 1 aims to show why it is an *ousia*. The material substrate is called *ousia* because it is either a this or potentially a this. We would expect this to be followed by a treatment showing that the other substrate mentioned in 1042b26–31, the composite, is also an *ousia,* and this is what we find.

2.11.2 H 2: *Actuality and Accidental Composites*

The first sentence of H 2 announces that since *ousia* as matter is agreed upon, "it remains in respect of the *ousia* which is the actuality of sensibles to say what is it [τίς ἐστιν]" (1042b9–11). Clearly, Aristotle intends to continue the investigation of substrate that he began in the preceding chapter with a discussion of matter. Having answered the "what is it" question about matter, he now turns to the "what is it" question about another substrate. The discussion should be governed by the distinction between three kinds of substrate in 1042a26–30. Although this passage does not mention actuality as a kind of substrate, it says of matter that "though not a this in actuality, it is potentially a this" (1042a27–28). The actuality under discussion in H 2 should thus be what is a this in actuality, that is, form. But one type of form has already been discussed at length in book Z. What we find here in H 2 is a treatment of a different type of form, the form of an accidental composite, along with the composite to which it belongs. He calls the former differentiae, and he maintains that they are the actualities of the composites.

Although the opening lines of H 2 assume that form is actuality, they provide no argument for this equation. We have seen indications in book Z that form or *ousia* is actuality (10, 1035b16–18; 11, 1036b30–32; 13, 1039a3–7), but there were no arguments there either. Since this identification is obviously important, we must look carefully in this discussion and throughout book H for considerations that might support it.

2.11.2.1 Differentiae: 1042b11–31

H 2's discussion of *ousia* as actuality begins with some criticism of Democritus (1042b11–12). According to Aristotle, Democritus thinks that the "underlying body, the matter" is one and the same, but that it can differ in three ways, by shape, by position, and by order (b11–15). Aristotle insists that there are many more differentiae of the matter (b15) and proceeds to mention some:

> Some things are said [to be] by a composition of matter, such as things which [are said to be] by blending, like honey water; others [are said to be] by a binding, such as a bundle; others by glue, such as a book; others by nails, such as a casket; others by many of these; others by position such as the threshold and the lintel (for these differ by the way they are placed); others by time, such as dinner and breakfast; others by place, such as the winds; others by affections of the sensibles, such as hardness and softness, density and rarity, dryness and wetness—some by some of these, others by all of these, and, in general, some by excess and some by defect (1042b15–25).

One reason that Aristotle is able to distinguish so many kinds of differentiae is that, unlike Democritus, he also distinguishes between the various types of matter. What he has really given here is a list of composites. Earlier, I called composites of *ousiai* and instances of other categorial genera "accidental composites" (see Z 4, 1029b22–27). The list here also includes artifacts and what we can call "natural composites," such as the north wind and ice (cf. H 4, 1044b9–10). I shall refer to them all as "composites" or, in order to distinguish them from the composite natures discussed in Z 17, as "accidental composites." Many differentiae mentioned here are other beings that belong to matter (such as a binding or a time). All the differentiae are specific for particular types of matter; thus, a meal eaten in the morning is breakfast, but a meal eaten in the afternoon or evening (if it is good sized) is dinner. But these times do not differentiate matters such as wood or wind. One group of differentiae in the above list is of special significance for a study of unity. Binding, glue, and nails, are Aristotle's standard examples of causes of continuity. They are even mentioned as causing unity in the same composites (Δ 6, 1016a1; I 1, 1052a19–20, a23–25; *Phys.* E 3, 227a15–17).

From this discussion of differentiae Aristotle draws a conclusion about being:

> So that it is clear that being [τὸ ἐστι] is said in as many ways [as there are differentiae]. For a threshold exists because it lies thus, and to be [in this case] signifies its lying this way; and in the case of ice to be [signifies] being compacted so (1042b25–28).[193]

A small but significant difference between this and the preceding discussion of differentiae is that Aristotle now describes the differentia with a verb: position (1042b19) has become "lying thus." The text continues by referring to differentiae that were called "composition," "blend," and "binding" (δεσμῷ) (1042b16–17) as "being mixed," "being blended," and "being bound" (1042b29–30).[194] This change in terminology is easy to understand from the context. The difference between a threshold and a doorpost is the position of the wood. Thus, position differentiates the two. But the wood is a threshold just when it is lying in such and such a position. The differentia is a kind of being; significantly, it is a being that differs from what it differentiates. It differentiates just when something possesses it. But when something possesses the binding, the thing is bound; when something has a particular position, the thing lies in such and such a way. In short, it is entirely appropriate to designate a differentia with a verb, for the differentiae are functions. Furthermore, insofar as the differentia is a function of some matter, it is appropriately called an actuality of that matter. The wood is potentially a threshold; when it lies in such and such a position, its potentiality is realized, and it becomes an actual threshold. It is the actuality, that is, the function that is the differentia, that makes the wood into a threshold. As Aristotle said earlier and perhaps suggests here (1042b31), the hand is a hand only when it functions as such (Z 11, 1036b30–32). Thus, it is the differentia, the function that the matter has, which makes the matter what it is.

With this discussion, we can see why "it is clear that being is said in as many ways [as there are differentiae]." A composite exists when a particular kind of matter possesses a differentia of a certain sort, that is, when that matter has the function which the differentia signifies: ice exists when the water is frozen, the honey-water when the honey and water are mixed; and both composites cease to exist as such when the function ceases (1042b36–1043a1). Since to be for each of these is (for something) to have a particular differentia, there are as many kinds of being are there are differentiae.

The foregoing interpretation would be straightforward but for the problem of how Aristotle could be identifying the being of the composite with its differentia (1042b26–28). The latter is (or is included in) the essence of the thing and the thing's being surely differs from its essence. Pseudo-Alexander[195] and later editors[196] have tried to avoid the apparent identification of being and essence by placing "ice" in the dative and adding a dative "threshold" at 1042b27. Then "the being for ice" (τὸ κρυστάλλῳ εἶναι), the essence of ice, could be properly identified with the differentia. This avoids the problem at hand only by introducing a new difficulty, for Aristotle would then be describing the essences of ice and of threshold in order to justify his claim about the different ways of being. A more radical approach to the problem is taken by G. E. L. Owen. He retains the text of the manuscripts but understands Aristotle to be advocating not an equation of essence and being, but the paraphrase of "exists" with other predicates: "ice exists" becomes "ice is solidified in such and such a way."[197] There are textual reasons to doubt that this is Aristotle's position. Most importantly, throughout H 2 it is the matter that takes on the differentia. Being compacted in a particular way characterizes ice; it does not differentiate it from other ice. Being compacted in a particular way *does* differentiate some water from other, noncompacted water.[198] Aristotle is not advocating paraphrasing the predicate "existent" with some other predicate. He is analyzing the being of something into the inherence of something else in some matter.

As this analysis suggests, Aristotle's discussion in H 2 closely resembles Z 17.[199] Likewise, the difficulties in the manuscripts of H 2 at this point resemble those that we saw in Z 17,[200] except that whereas there Aristotle speaks of the cause of the being of the matter when we would expect him to mention the being of the composite, here he speaks of the being of the composite when we might think he means to discuss the form.[201] It seems to me that, properly understood, the text of the manuscripts in H 2 should stand. First, it is easy to see why there are as many ways of being as there are differentiae: matter always exists in one form or another. (Even the heap of wood has the form of the wood.) The form implicitly contains a matter: it makes no sense to speak of being compacted, for example, without recognizing that something is compacted. Consequently, the kinds of being are just the kinds of differentiae. Another way of putting the point is to say that there are just as many beings as there are kinds of things.[202] The differentiae are the actualities which make each thing be what it is. So, once again, there should be as many beings are there are differentiae, and the being of each thing lies in the function that is its differentia.

2.11.2.2 Composites: 1042b31–1043a28

Aristotle's justification for the claim that there are as many beings as differentiae (1042b26–31) leads to a discussion of the role of the differentia in the composite. It begins in 1042b31 and extends, I think, throughout the rest of book H.[203] Since the treatment of the composite is prefigured by the three-fold distinction of substrates in 1042a26–30, this latter passage is the key to the organization of the book.

The first point Aristotle argues in this discussion of the composite is that the differentia is the principle or cause of being in the composite (1042b32–33; 1042a2–4). The argument begins from a list of examples of composites that exist when they have the function associated with their differentiae and do not when they lack this function. Aristotle continues:

> It is clear from these [examples] that, since *ousia* is the cause of each thing, we must seek in these [differentiae] what is the cause of the being of each of these things (1043a2–4).

The apparent premise that *ousia* is the cause of being is actually superfluous for the conclusion. That the differentia is the cause of being follows immediately from the examples. What the premise about *ousia* does do, however, is remind us of the result of Z 17 and suggest an analogy. Since the differentia is the cause of being in the composite, and since the *ousia* of a nature is the cause of being in it, the differentia is, in a way, the *ousia* of the composite. The text explains the analogy clearly:

> None of these [differentiae] is an *ousia,* nor even a *per se* attribute.[204] Nevertheless, it is analogous in each. And as the actuality is predicated of matter in *ousiai,* also in other definitions [actuality is predicated of matter] most of all (1043a4–7).

A differentia stands to an accidental composite just as form stands to a nature: both cause composites to be.[205]

This analogy is hardly new. Z 17 also uses it, but in the opposite way: there Aristotle uses the example of the house to infer that form is the cause of being in a nature (1041a26–28, b5–6). H 2 draws on this latter conclusion to find the cause of composites. Just as form is the cause of being in a composite *ousia* because the *ousia* exists when form is present in a matter, so too the differentia is the cause of being in an accidental composite because the composite exists when the differentia is present in its matter. Both discussions regard the cause as something immaterial. H 2 does, though, contain something new: it views the cause of being in both composite *ousiai* and accidental composites as an actuality (1043a5–7). This addition is significant. We have seen its consequences throughout H 2. It is because the differentiae are actualities that Aristotle speaks of them as "being compacted," or "lying in such and such a position." The differentia is a kind of function the matter undergoes.

Does identifying the differentia as an actuality contribute anything to the inquiry into categorial being? Considering Aristotle's usual reticence about what progress the parts of his inquiry make toward its end, we should not be surprised that the text contains no explicit answer to this question. However, we can get some insight into the significance of this identification, and a motive for it, if we consider the differentia as the cause of unity along the lines of Z 17. One of the problems of H 2 is that Aristotle claims that the differentia causes the composite to be and also constitutes the being of the composite. The wood is a threshold because it lies in a particular position and, for it, to be is just to lie in such a position. How can the differentia have both roles? In the discussion that follows, I shall suggest that the differentia can be both cause and essence just because it is a kind of actuality or function and that the way to understand this is to consider the problem in terms of unity. An added attraction of this interpretation is that it will enable us eventually to answer problems about unity that emerged in Z 17 and also to understand the rest of book H.

In Z 17 Aristotle argued that form is the cause of being in a nature by showing that it is the cause of unity. Analogously, the differentia is not only the cause of the composite's being but also the cause of its unity. Just as the question of the being of a nature is tantamount to a question about its unity (i.e., whether a form belongs to a matter), the question about the being of the accidental composite is tantamount to a question about its unity (i.e., whether the differentia belongs to the matter). In Z 17 Aristotle argued only that the cause of unity must be something that is not material and then identified this cause as form. H 2's further identification of form as actuality enables us to explain how it can cause unity.

How does form cause unity? The first point to notice is that, as I mentioned earlier, some of Aristotle's examples of differentiae—glue, nails, and binding—are also his standard examples of the causes of one type of unity, continuity. It is not quite accurate to say that the binding makes the sticks into a bundle. The binding need not do anything to the sticks unless it is wrapped around them. Or to make this point in the terms of Z 17, a material constituent of a bundle, such as its binding, cannot be the cause of unity because there must be something else, something nonmaterial, the form, which unites the binding with the other material constituents. What is this cause? The answer is quite simple, it is the function of being bound. The cause of the sticks being a bundle is their being bound. Not the binding, but the function it has makes the sticks into a unity. How does this function cause unity? It causes the sticks to be continuous. As I mentioned earlier, in the *Metaphysics* things are continuous if they have a motion which is indivisible in time (Δ 6,

1016a5–6). Being bound makes the sticks continuous because as a bundle they can all move together.

This function that causes unity is also, Aristotle claims, what it is for a composite like a bundle to be. How can the being of the composite be identified with its differentia? Again, focusing on unity enables us to answer this question. As I said, something is continuous if it can move all at once. Now, a function or actuality is, in a way, a kind of motion.[206] To have the function of being bound is thus to be moving all at once, that is, to be moving in the motion of being bound, if we can call this a motion. Insofar as the sticks possess the function of being bound, they are one because they can move together; and the motion that they thus acquire is just the motion of being bound. Insofar as the sticks are possessed of the function of being bound, they are, in a way, continuous. But the very motion which they have insofar as they are continuous is just the motion or function that is their nature. Likewise, the cause of the pages being one book is their being glued together in a particular way; the pages are one because, in virtue of the glue, they are all able to move together. But the function of being a book is just the motion or function they have when they do move together, the motion of being glued. In short, the motion through which each composite is defined is just the motion in respect of which it is continuous. So the function that is the source of unity is just what the thing does insofar as it is one.

At first glance, the preceding analysis seems quite implausible. A major problem is that it fails to make the important distinction between being glued and the motion that the glued thing has, between being bound and the motion that the sticks can have while they are bound. The former is the cause of unity; the latter is perhaps the essence, form, or actuality of the thing. Another problem is that being bound or glued still seems to be a state rather than a function, even if each is designated by a verb. In fact, both of these problems can be resolved with a distinction that appears in the *De Anima,* a distinction that would need to be introduced into this discussion in any case. The actuality of a composite has two senses (B 1, 412a21–28). An active functioning, such as the act of knowing, is called a second actuality in the *De Anima.* The first actuality, in contrast, is a potentiality that can be actualized further, such as knowledge that is not in use. A first actuality is potentially a second actuality, and is thus both potential and actual. Aristotle defines the soul as a first actuality (412a27–28), and it is easy to see that this is the sort of actuality he must have in mind in H 2. The composites discussed here have being so long as they are *able* to function; they do not cease to be when they cease to function. A house exists when the boards, bricks and so forth become continuous in such a way that they *can* be a shelter for goods and living things (1043a16–17). This potential is realized when the house is actually serving as a shelter, but the house does not cease to be a house when it is empty because it does not lose its capacity to shelter and it is a house because of this capacity.

With this, let us look again at the two problems. Is there a distinction between being glued and functioning like a book? Of course there is, but the former is the potentiality for the latter. Being glued in a particular way is the first actuality of functioning in the way a book functions. The pages function as a book when someone picks them up, turns the pages, and reads. But being read does not define the book. The pages become a book when they acquire the capacity to be read in this way; and being glued, their first actuality, is this capacity. Likewise, the pages are continuous not because they do move in the way that a book does (the second actuality), but because they can so move, and this capacity they have insofar as they are glued together. Hence, the actuality that defines the composite and the actuality that makes it continuous are the same, the first actuality. So far from ignoring the distinction between being glued and the motion of the glued thing, my interpretation depends upon it. Thus, the first problem vanishes.

As for the second problem, is being bound or glued a state rather than a function? In respect of the active functioning of the thing that is bound or glued, just being bound or glued seem like states. But in respect of the matter that is bound or glued, each is a kind of function. As I said, being glued and being bound are each first actualities. That is, they are functions that amount to capacities for other, more active functions. The sticks are engaging in the function of being bound when the binding is around them. Thus, both problems are easily dismissed.

With this distinction between first and second actuality, I need to refine slightly my analysis of how actuality causes unity. The cause of unity in a composite is a first actuality. The sticks are continuous just because they have the capacity to function (or to move) together, because they have the capacity for a second actuality. What gives them this capacity? Their being bound, of course. When the sticks are bound they are able to move together in the way that a bundle moves. The cause of their continuity is the cause of their capacity for moving together in a particular way. But having the capacity for this particular motion is just what it is to be a bundle. Being bound is the cause of the sticks' unity because it enables them to be together, and being bound is just what they are because they take their identity from their capacity for particular motions. Being bound is able to be both the cause of unity and the nature of the bundle because it is a first actuality, and both the continuity of the thing and its nature lie in its *capacity* for a particular kind of function, a second actuality.

Thus far, I have concentrated on those differentiae which are also causes of continuity. Some of the other differentiae mentioned in H 2 do not cause continuity; for example, the affections of sensibles: hardness, softness, dryness, and wetness (1042b21–24). These other differentiae do, however, cause unity in a parallel way. Water becomes ice by being compacted. Like being glued, being compacted seems to be a state rather than a function. But it, too, must be a first actuality because, in being compacted, water acquires the

potential for quite different kinds of motion; it acquires the potential to behave as ice does. In other words, what makes water into ice is just the
function of being compacted, a function that is itself potentially the activity
of ice. Without this function water is not one; it is just a heap (Z 16, 1040b8–
10). The function of being compacted is at once the cause of unity and what
it is for ice to be. Even though the differentiae are most readily understood as
causes of continuity, virtually the same analysis holds for all. The composite
is one just when all its parts have the capacity to function together, and the
capacity for this function is just what it is.

From the perspective of modern science, this account of the causes of ice
and of a book has nearly nothing to say to us. The reason is not that it relies
too heavily on language or that it fails to treat being compacted and being
glued as states, but that it fails to explain the mechanism of the compaction or
the action of the glue. Aristotle's concern is not to find a mechanism but to
answer the metaphysical question of how a plurality of material constituents
can be one, a problem that modern scientists and philosophers of science do
not generally consider. The latter may feel more comfortable with the approach of Democritus. He makes the matter *one* and then speaks of its differentiae (1042b12–15); for him, the question of the unity of differentia and
matter apparently remains unanswered. Nor is he very concerned about this
omission, so far as we can tell. Why should he be? The account of the unity
of the composite implicit in our text adds nothing to our understanding of any
particular composite. Aristotle's concerns in this text are metaphysical rather
than scientific.

The foregoing account goes beyond what is in the text, but it ties together
various points made in H 2 and also explains the significance of the identification of form as actuality. In addition, it fits well with the discussion of
matter at the end of H 1. There, matter is described as a potentiality for
motion. This potentiality is realized when the matter actually moves. H 2
describes a kind of intermediate realization of matter's potentiality for motion. The actuality that belongs to matter in the composite as its differentia is,
in effect, a kind of motion or function that partially realizes the matter's
potentiality. Matter for local motion, for example, is made into a composite
when it is glued or nailed together. Being glued or nailed is a partial realization of matter's potency. Insofar as the matter is glued together, it can move
all at once in characteristic ways and thus actively fulfill its potential for local
motion. Analogously, all the differentiae are realizations of a matter's potential for motion, and the composites formed by them are, in turn, potential for
further actualizations.

It is clear from the descriptions of the composites in H 2 that the actualities
of different matters differ (1043a11–12). Since different sorts of matter can
be actualized in different ways, a particular differentia can belong only to a
certain type or types of matter. This makes it possible to define composites in

either of three ways. We can define a composite with its differentia, with its matter, or, thirdly, with both differentia and matter (1043a14–18). Although Aristotle does not say so explicitly, the best definitions of composites specify both form and matter. The reason is that some differentiae could belong to different matters and the same matter might admit of different differentiae. Stones and boards may, in some way, define a house, but many other things can be formed with them. Likewise, calm can belong to both water and air (1043a22–26).[207] Including both form and matter in a definition of a composite avoids ambiguity.

How, though, can matter be included in a definition? Earlier, Aristotle claimed that it is unknowable; indeed, he also denied that composites are definable (10, 1036a2–9). Can this be consistent with H 2? As I explained earlier (2.7.3), in saying that matter is unknowable *per se,* Aristotle denies that matter can be known as matter. We can know it insofar as it is potentially something else, or insofar as it itself has a form. When Aristotle speaks of stones and boards as the matter for the house in H 2, he is giving the form that the matter possesses. The formula of the matter is formula of the matter's form. Aristotle also spoke earlier of a universal composite composed of "this formula and this matter taken universally" (10, 1035b29–30). The definition of the composite described at the end of H 2 is such a universal composite. It includes the matter taken universally, and it includes the formula of the form or differentia. Not only is the expression for matter a universal formula; the expression for the form is also a universal formula. Though the differentia is properly an actuality or function, its formula and definition is a kind of universal.

2.11.3 H 3: Definitions of Accidental Composites

H 3 continues the discussion of accidental composites, but it is difficult, at first glance, to see that is has any organization. The final lines of the chapter (1044a11–14) purport to offer a summary of the chapter, but what they mention, the generation and destruction of composite *ousiai* and their being led back to numbers, are parts of the chapter that are usually thought to be peripheral.[208] What I want to show in this subsection is the significance for the treatment of *ousia* of Aristotle's remarks on the similarity of numbers and the definitions of composites. To do so, I need to tie together some of the remarks made in H 3. Since the connections are not explicit in the text, I shall reconstruct them. The same sort of considerations about unity that have played an important role thus far enable us to make good sense of the organization of H 3, a further indication that its author is concerned with problems about unity.

The chapter begins by noting that it is unclear sometimes whether a word like "house" signifies a composite or an actuality (1043a29–36). Coming immediately after Aristotle's claim that a composite can be defined in *three* ways (1043a26–28; cf. a14–19), this statement is surprising. We would expect the word "house" to have threefold ambiguity; it should also be able to signify the matter. Does Aristotle perhaps omit matter here because it *is* always clear when "house" signifies matter? Not at all, for the chapter goes on to maintain (drawing on the arguments of Z 17) that a definition containing only matter would be inadequate; the *ousia* must be something that is not a material element (1043b4–14). Even definitions that include the differentia would be inadequate if they treated it merely as a material element. A formula consisting of the differentia and the genus as two distinct constituents effectively "subtracts" the form or *ousia,* the cause of being (1043b10–14).

Along with excluding definitions that consist only of material constituents, Aristotle denies that the distinction between actuality and composite is really important for his inquiry into sensible *ousiai* (1043a37–b1). The reason he gives is that "the essence belongs to form and actuality" (1043b1–2); and this claim is supported, in turn, by the observations that the soul and its essence are identical and that man and the essence of man are not identical, unless the soul is called man (1043b2–4). So in a way the composite and the form are identical, though in a way they are not (b4). What exactly is Aristotle's reasoning here? The main argument is that it makes no difference to the inquiry into sensible *ousia* whether we consider the form or the composite because in a way they are the same. Why are they the same? Here Aristotle reminds us of the conclusion of Z 6, the identity of essence and form, by saying that essence belongs to form. Does this show the identity of the composite and the form? It does if the essence here is the essence *of the composite.* The essence of the composite man is its form, the soul. We know already that the essence is the *ousia* of the thing. Thus, it makes no difference whether we consider the composite or the form because the essence or *ousia* is the same in either case. The essence of the composite is just the actuality of its matter (1043a35–36; b1–2).[209]

Ironically, despite the putative unimportance to our inquiry of the distinction between actuality and composite, the rest of H 3 is devoted to spelling out the relation of form and matter in the composite. The first part (1043b4–14) of this discussion explains that the *ousia* of a composite is not a constituent of it nor itself composed of constituents. Rather, the *ousia* is the cause of being in the composite (b13–14). Of course, the *ousia* here is the form or the actuality of the matter, what H 2 calls the differentia. The text does not justify the assertion that it is not a constituent or composed of constituents, but it does not need to, for this is obviously the result of Z 17 applied to accidental composites. *Ousia* is neither an element nor composed of elements because it is the cause of the composite's unity.

The next sentence (1043b14–16) in the text asserts that form is either eternal or never in the processes of coming to be or being destroyed. Aristotle goes on to remind us (b16–18) that this result was established earlier, no doubt a reference to Z 8 (1033b3–10). As I noted earlier, most editors take 1043b14 as the beginning of a long parenthesis, despite the apparent reference to it in the chapter summary that concludes H 3. Yet ἀνάγκη δή, with which this passage begins, suggests that an inference follows.[210] It is easy to see how the claim that form is unchanging is a consequence of what precedes. If form is not composed of elements, it has no parts and is one. As I explained in the discussion of Z 8, what is one is unchanging. The insight expressed in 1043b14–16 is that form can be unchanging in either of two ways: (1) by being eternal or (2) by not admitting the process of generation or the process of destruction. In the latter case, form does not change because it never becomes something else, though it could, of course, cease to be. Thus, form does not need to be eternal to be one; it can be one so long as it is never in the process of change.

Is the form of a composite unchanging because it is eternal, or is it unchanging because it is never in the process of changing? Aristotle does not pose the question in these terms, but what he does ask is equivalent. Immediately after the reference to Z 8, he mentions the question whether the *ousiai* of destructible things are separate (b18–19). Separate *ousiai* would be eternal. If the *ousiai* are not separate, they are unchanging in the second way, unchanging in the sense that they are never in the process of change. The question implicit in the text is, are the *ousiai* separate and eternal? Aristotle answers,

Whether the *ousiai* of destructible things are separate is, as yet, unclear; except that in some cases it is clear that the *ousia* cannot be separate: in cases of things that are unable to be apart from the particulars, such as a house or a tool (1043b20–21).

Is it clear that a house cannot exist apart from a particular house? The text does not elaborate. A reason to think that the house is separate is that, as we saw, it is possible to give the formula of the house without mentioning the matter; we can say that it is a kind of covering (1043a32–33). That is to say, the form of the house is "separate in formula" (cf. 1042a28–29). But how could the function of covering exist without the matter that performs this function? In the case of a house or a tool, it is clear that the function or actuality that is the form does not exist apart from the matter whose actuality it is. Since these forms cannot exist apart, they must be unchanging, not as eternal or separate, but in the sense that they are never in the process of coming to be or the process of being destroyed. Because they have no parts, these forms are one; but they are not one in the way that Platonic forms are one. They are unities that exist in matter as the actuality of the matter.

At this point (b23–25), Aristotle notes that the *aporia* of Antisthenes and other ignoramuses is pertinent. They apparently objected to the definitions of simples. Rightly, Aristotle thinks.[211] We cannot define composite *ousiai* with simples; our definitions are always composites of form and matter (1043b28–32). In short, only one of the three possible definitions of composites is truly appropriate, the one that includes form and matter.

If, though, the definitions contain form and matter, do they not make the very mistake that Aristotle criticized in 1043b10–14, the mistake of supposing that a syllable, for example, consists of the letter and the synthesis? No, for the form is not something that exists apart from the composite or even in the composite as a separate constituent. It is the actuality of a matter. The analogy between numbers and the definitions of composites which constitutes the final section of the chapter (1043b32–1044a11) clarifies the relation. Before we look at it, it is important to see why it is appropriate. If the definition of a composite necessarily contains a term for the form and a term for the matter, then the definition is some sort of plurality. However, it is not just a plurality of constituents, but a plurality that is somehow made into a unity by its form. In the latter respect the definition is very much like a number, it is a plurality that is somehow one.

The aim of Aristotle's discussion of the analogy between number and definition is to expound the unity of each. He begins by pointing out that "since the *ousiai* are somehow numbers, they are so in this way, not as some say, pluralities of units" (1043b33–34). Neither these *ousiai* nor the definitions that define them are numbers in the sense of being a plurality of units. That numbers are pluralities of units is a Platonic view; that definitions are analogous pluralities is the view excluded in 1043b10–14. Rather, definitions and *ousiai* are numbers in the sense that Aristotle understands numbers, pluralities that are made one by some differentia (1044a3–6; cf. M 8, 1083a1–4). The first point of analogy is that (1) there must be something by which a definition is made one just as there is something by which units are made into one number. Besides this point, H 3 mentions three other similarities between numbers and definitions: (2) both definitions and numbers are divisible into indivisibles; (3) subtracting a part of either alters the whole; and (4) just as number does not admit of the more or the less, neither does *ousia* in respect of form, although the *ousia* with the matter might. (The latter is the composite; but definition is of the *ousia* in respect of form, even if the definition somehow includes matter. So the last point of comparison is that, like number, the definition does not admit of the more and the less even though the composite might.)

The reference to indivisible constituents of definitions in the second point of analogy (1043b35) suggests the primary elements mentioned by Antisthenes (b30). The reference to subtraction in the third point reminds us of what Aristotle accused the Platonists of (b12–13). Thus, the analogy between numbers and definitions with which H 3 ends draws on the analysis contained in the rest of chapter. The point of the entire chapter has been that the definition of a composite is some sort of plurality of form and matter that is not merely two constituents but a unity. It is a plurality that has been made into one, just as the number 5 is a plurality of units that is one number. What this chapter tells us about this unity is that it is unlike that of the point or unit; it is rather the unity of an actuality or nature (1044a7–9).

This interpretation fills in the gaps in the text, and it has the advantage of uniting Aristotle's seemingly scattered remarks in H 3 into a coherent and cogent treatment of the definition of the composite *ousia,* a treatment that has the effect of excluding two of the three definitions of composites that Aristotle offers at the end of H 2. A definition that included only matter would be like the definitions of Antisthenes; a definition that included only form would subtract that in which the form must be present, the matter of which it is the function. The definition that includes both in a unity caused by form, just the sort of definition numbers have, is the best definition.

Whatever its merits, this analysis of the text may seem to be at odds with my overall interpretation of Z-H. All along, I have pointed to the assumption that *ousia* is one. It now seems that an *ousia* and its definition are each necessarily many. In fact, though, this result is just grist for my mill, for the *ousiai* that have been before us since H 2 are composites. Most of these composites are not properly *ousiai;* they are not even attributes of *ousiai* (1043a4).[212] They are accidental composites that are only analogous to *ousiai* (1043a4–5). In the middle of H 3, Aristotle suggests that only natures or things "put together by nature" are *ousiai* (1043b21–22). The analogy at the end of the chapter between definitions and numbers applies to the definitions of both accidental composites and individual composite natures, for both are pluralities that are somehow made into unities. The analogy should hold most of all for those composites that are most one. These are the composite natures, just those composites that Aristotle also says are most properly *ousiai.*

On what basis does Aristotle deny that artifacts like house are properly called *ousiai* (b21–22)? He does not offer an argument; but, because this claim immediately follows his denial that their forms can exist apart (b19–21), it is tempting to think that artifacts fail to be *ousiai* because of this lack of apartness. However, it scarcely seems legitimate to deny that composites are *ousiai* because their *forms* are not separate. Aristotle probably has another, unstated reason for denying that artifacts are *ousiai.* Further, Aristotle does not ask about separation to exclude artifacts; it is relevant to the larger concerns of the chapter. If forms are separate, they can be defined without including matter, and not the composite definition but the definition that consists only of the differentia would be the best. Since the forms of artifacts do not exist apart, they do not admit of definitions that contain only differentiae. But this result may not be entirely relevant to the question whether *ousiai* admit of such definitions because artifacts are probably not *ousiai.* This is, I think, Aristotle's reasoning in 1043b18–23.

What is his unstated argument against artifacts being *ousiai?* An objection to them that fits well with the rest of the chapter is that artifacts are pluralities. An *ousia* is one, and its form is the cause of its unity. Although flesh and arms are parts of a human being, they function together in the composite individual; indeed, they have no function apart from the composite nature (Z 10, 1035b23–25). In contrast, the wood that is made into a house retains all its functions as wood even when it is in the house. So the house has at least two functions or actualities, that of its matter, the wood, and that of the house. Since an *ousia* is one and an artifact is many, an artifact cannot be an *ousia.*

A reason to think that this is the argument Aristotle has in mind is that it uses the assumption about the unity of *ousia* that has played such an important role in book Z and in this chapter of H. As we saw, H 3 makes a point of denying that a definition consists of the matter and the form if both are treated as mere constituents. Instead, the form must be the actuality of the matter; it must be the cause of its being and, thus, of its unity. Aristotle uses artifacts to illustrate this point, and the forms of artifacts do cause unity. Nevertheless, they are less one than composite natures. They, more than natures, are like a Platonic plurality of units. Natural forms can confer a greater degree of unity. H 3 treats both accidental composites such as artifacts and composite natures, and both are pluralities made into unities by their forms. But the latter have a greater right to be called *ousiai* because they are more one.

The definitions of composites that Aristotle compares to numbers are what Aristotle terms in Z 4, formulae "by addition." Such a formula fails to express only what is most properly *ousia,* the form. It somehow includes the matter. Conversely, a formula without matter would fail to add what necessarily belongs to the composite. In H 3 Aristotle also criticizes definitions that treat form and matter as joint constituents on the ground that they subtract something, namely, the form (1043b9–10).[213] This remark and much of the rest of the discussion in the chapter makes very good sense if Aristotle is treating his subject in terms of unity.

Just how is the plurality of constituents in the definition of a composite made into a unity? Can the genuine composite *ousiai* be defined without addition? These questions remain unanswered at the end of H 3. To answer them we will need to look still more carefully at the definitions of composite *ousiai.* This is the task of H 6; but, for reasons that will be clear shortly, before Aristotle undertakes it, he examines the matter of composites.

2.11.4 H 4–5: Proper Matter

Like the preceding portions of book H, chapters 4–5 contain no explicit indication of their relation to the rest of the book. Since they are sandwiched between H 3's comparison of the unity of numbers and of composites (1043b32–1044a11) and H 6's continuation of the treatment of unity, they should have some bearing on this theme if they make any sense in their present position. Although it is often overlooked, the topic treated by these chapters, proper matter, plays an important role in H 6 (1045a17–19). The discussion of matter in H 4–5 prepares the way for the account of the composite's unity presented in H 6.

H 4 begins with the claim that even if all things come from the same primary matter, there is a matter proper (οἰκεία) to each thing (1044a15–18). While fire and earth belong to the matter of a man, the proper matter is that which is nearest (ἐγγύτατα) to the composite and peculiar (ἴδιον) to it (1044b1–3).

Is there a proper matter of *each* thing, as Aristotle claims? I think that he intends the seemingly scattered topics of H 4–5 to answer unstated objections to this claim. His answers also make clear the limits of its applicability.

The first two of these objections are problems about the one and the many, to judge from what I take to be the responses to them in the text. The first passage goes as follows:

> There are many matters of the same thing whenever one is from another; for example, phlegm is from the fat and the sweet if the fat is from the sweet; and phlegm is from bile by dissolution of the bile into its first matter. For one thing is from another in two ways, either because one is before the other on a path, or because one is dissolved into its [constituent] principle (1044a20–25).

This answers an unstated objection to the existence of a proper matter. The objection is, how can there be proper matter if one thing can come from many different things? Aristotle's answer is twofold. First, when there are many different matters of one thing, they must be sequentially ordered. Though the sweet and the fat both seem to be the proper matter of the phlegm, only the fat is its proper matter, and the fat comes from the sweet. Second, sometimes when something comes from another, the thing it comes from is not its matter at all. Even though phlegm comes from bile, the latter is not its matter; for the phlegm comes when the bile is divided into its matter.[214] In short, even though there sometimes seem to be many matters, closer inspection shows that a single thing has a single proximate matter.

The text that follows considers the converse of the preceding, cases in which one matter is the proper matter of several things:

> It is possible for different things to come from one matter by the moving cause; for example, from wood comes a chest and a bed. But sometimes the matter of different things must be different; for example, a saw could

not come from wood, nor is this in the power of the moving cause. For
it will not make a saw from wool or wood. But if it is possible to make
the same thing from different material, it is clear that the art, that is,
the moving principle, is the same; for if the matter and the mover were
different, what has come to be would also differ (1044a25–32).

Why does Aristotle refer to the role of the efficient cause at this point? Let
me suggest that this passage, like the preceding one, answers unstated objections to the doctrine that there is a single proper matter. Here an objection is,
how can something have a matter proper to it when its matter could also be
the matter of many other things? How, for example, can wood be the proper
matter of a bed if it is the matter for the chest as well? Aristotle's response is
that the same matter is made into different things by different efficient
causes. That is to say, the art of carpentry by which a bed is made differs
from the art of carpentry by which a chest is made. Though the matter is the
same, the efficient causes differ.

Does Aristotle mean to say that the art of bedmaking differs from the art of
chestmaking or that these are distinct branches of the same art? Apparently
the former.[215] But whatever his answer to this question, Aristotle's point
seems to be that since any particular matter becomes a composite by some
particular efficient cause, there is no reason that wood cannot be the proper
matter of both the bed and the chest. Any particular composite will still have
come to be from one matter.

Another objection to the existence of proper matter that is implicit here is
that the same composite could have come from several distinct matters. This
closely resembles the first objection except that here Aristotle has artifacts in
mind. Can wood be the proper matter of a chest if the chest could also have
come to be from metal or some other material? Aristotle responds by stress-
ing the efficient cause. The efficient cause, the art of carpentry, would be the
same in formula whenever the same sort of chest were produced. If the
matters and the efficient causes differ, then what comes to be must also
differ, Aristotle insists. Presumably, if the matters are the same and the
efficient causes are the same, the things generated must also be the same.

Do these latter observations answer the objection to there being a proper
matter if the same thing can come to be from different matters? Not yet, but
what they show is Aristotle's concern with the questions of when a composite
will uniquely determine the matter from which it can come and, conversely,
when knowing the matter will enable us also to know the composite it will
become. If there were a single matter for each composite, then these unique-
ness conditions would obtain, and some matter would be proper to each
composite. However, in the examples from the text now under consideration,
the composite does not entirely determine its matter. The form of the composite determines the matter only to a certain extent: you cannot make a saw

from wood or wool. Something besides matter or form has a hand in determining what form a matter takes on: Aristotle emphasizes that what a matter comes to be depends on the "art" (τέχνη) applied to it (1044a31). Obviously, the cases in which different matters can take on one form or the same matter different forms are cases of artifacts. Since, as we already know, artifacts are not properly *ousiai,* their lack of proper matter is not an argument against the claim that material *ousiai* always have a proper matter, the claim Aristotle makes at the beginning of the chapter (1044a15–18). Conversely, a reason to dismiss whatever claims artifacts have to be *ousiai* is just that they lack a proper matter.

But how do we know that natural *ousiai* avoid these problems? Can a nature perhaps come from different matters? As we contemplate the possibility of silicon chips manifesting human intelligence, this question is pertinent and interesting. Aristotle, though, just assumes that there is a fundamental difference between artifacts and natures. He discusses the causes of a nature in 1044a32–b2. In a nature like a human being, the formal and final causes are identical (1044a36–b1). We know further that both of these are the same in species as the efficient cause (e.g., *Phys.* B 7, 198a24–26). A nature is the efficient cause of another matter's coming to possess the same nature. Further, Aristotle maintains that the matter of human beings is the menstrual fluid. Since such matter comes from something with a nature in more or less the same way, and since the efficient cause is the same, natural generation is always the same. For natures, then, there is no reason to think that the composite can be generated from more than one matter. In a nature, the form does determine the character of its matter, and the latter is proper to the form. Thus, Aristotle's response to some of the objections to the existence of proper matter is that those objections pertain only to artifacts.

As we have seen, this analysis requires a good deal of interpretation. The explicit aim of 1044a32–b2 is to emphasize the need to state all four causes. It seems at first that Aristotle merely chooses a nature to illustrate the point. But just before mentioning the cause of sensible and eternal *ousiai,* Aristotle indicates that the preceding discussion has concerned "physical and generable *ousiai*" (1044b3). So the example of a nature at 1044a32–b2 has not been arbitrary. Indeed, it seems to me that Aristotle stresses the need to know all four causes precisely because only by knowing the causes can we distinguish artifacts from natures (cf. *Phys.* B 1–2; e.g., 192b27–33), and only natures have proper matter. All natures that are the same have the same material and efficient causes. Thus, for any nature, there is one matter proper to it, one matter from which it comes. This is the matter "nearest" to the form (1044b1–3), in contrast with its ultimate matter, such as, perhaps, fire or earth.

By this point it should be clear that the matter proper to the form of a composite nature is one. A matter is proper to a form if there is a unique, one matter/one form relation; and, if my analysis of H 4 is correct up to this point, this chapter removes objections to the existence of such a relation in composite *ousiai*. In what way is this proper matter one? Can Aristotle mean to say that each composite comes to be from a single stuff? Phlegm may come to be from one nature, the fat, but can there be just one matter of something as complex as a dog or a human being? Later in H 4, Aristotle does speak of the first (matter) which experiences sleep and suggests it may be the heart or something else (1044a16–17), and this resembles the suggestion in Z 10 that the heart or the brain is "that in which the formula and *ousia* is first" (1035b25–27). Passages like these suggest that the proper matter is a single organ. On the other hand, Aristotle has thus far spoken of the proper matter not as the matter which persists in the composite but as the matter out of which the composite comes to be. As I said, he suggests that the proper matter of a human being is the menstrual fluid (1044a34–35), an example where the matter is also numerically one. So Aristotle speaks of proper matter as numerically one in kind; the proper matter is a single type of constituent that takes on a form. Nevertheless, nothing that he says in this chapter commits him to this view; proper matter could just as well be numerically many in kind but one generically. An automobile, for example, is made from many different sorts of matter, yet it makes sense to say that it has a single proper matter because it is always made from these same materials in much the same way—though, of course, speaking about the proper matter of artifacts leaves us open to the objections raised earlier. The unity that Aristotle requires of proper matter is not the numeric unity of an individual nature but the unity that belongs to a group of things that together always take on the same form.

H 4's final objections against proper matter begin from the distinction between things that have such matter and things like the heavenly bodies that are eternal (1044b3–6). The implicit objection here is that the latter do not seem to have any proper matter because they do not come to be. Aristotle seems to concede the objection. Eternal things either have no matter at all or they have matter only for local motion (1044b6–7; cf. H 1, 1042a32–35). How can any sensible *ousia*, whether eternal or generated, lack matter? The text goes on to explain that things that are by nature but are not *ousiai*, what I earlier called natural composites, also lack matter; instead, the substrates for attributes in these composites are *ousiai* (1044b8–9). The eclipse, for example, does not have a matter; it is something that happens to an eternal substrate *ousia*, the moon (b9–11). Aristotle's denial that the eclipse has a matter is surprising; for in H 2 he had no hesitation in referring to the matter of natural composites like calm air and ice (1043a23–28), and a substrate *ousia* does come to possess a differentia. Neither water nor any other substrate of a natural composite mentioned in H 2 is properly an *ousia*, but there is a sense in which an *ousia* is the matter for generation of a natural composite. Moreover, the *ousia* in a natural composite is the material cause. This is just Aristotle's point here: even though the eclipse does not really have a matter, the *ousia* which experiences it, the moon, is its material cause. That his concern is the material cause is apparent from the remark that follows the discussion of the eclipse: "In the case of sleep it is unclear what the first thing which has this attribute is" (1044b15–16). In other words, what is the material cause of sleep? In one way, it seems to be the animal; in another, the heart or some other organ (b16–17).

Ostensibly, the aim of this discussion of natural composites is to emphasize the need to find all four causes when we inquire. What makes this point more than pedestrian is the apparent lack of matter is cases like an eclipse and, perhaps, sleep. This apparent lack of matter is also an objection to the doctrine of proper matter. I think Aristotle's discussion here aims to answer this objection. First, he can concede that eternal *ousiai* may lack matter because that would still not call into question the doctrine that the matter of a composite is proper to it. Further, even though there may not be matter, strictly speaking, in a natural composite, there is still a proximate material cause. The latter is, or plays the role of, proper matter in natural composites. To understand the composite we must grasp it and the agency by which it acquires its form (b18–20).

There are other things which do lack proper matter and material cause. At the beginning of H 5, Aristotle mentions things which are neither generated nor destroyed but are not eternal (1044b21–22; cf. 3, 1043b14–16). Examples include points, lines, and other mathematicals, and, more interestingly, forms like white (b22–23). White, Aristotle explains, does not come to be; some other thing comes to be white (b23–24). White is or is not without having come to be through a process. Nor does it come to be from black: it is, rather, the white (or pale) man that comes to be from the dark man (b24–28). It follows that not everything that is contrary comes from each other (b24–25; see *Phys.* Γ 5, 205a6–7 and Λ 7) and that white and other forms that do not change have no matter (b28–29).

This second conclusion allows us to place these remarks in the context of H 4's discussion of proper matter. First, the forms that Aristotle considers here are forms of attributes, for *ousiai* do not come to be from contraries. Forms of white, of other qualities, and of other attributes that have contraries, and forms of mathematicals have no matter. Consequently, such forms pose no difficulties for the doctrine of proper matter (1044a15–18). The doctrine applies only to things that have matter, composite *ousiai*. Attributes are not proper to any matter because they can be present in many different matters.

A more substantial difficulty lies in the fact that some matter can become either of two opposites; water, for example, can become wine or vinegar. It seems again that one matter can become two different composites. Moreover, since vinegar can come from water or from wine, one thing again appears to come from two different matters (1044b29–36). Aristotle gives us no reasons for raising these particular *aporiai,* but they closely resemble the points he makes at 1044a20–27. The difference is that here the two forms are contraries and one apparent matter is a contrary. Why is the apparent existence of many forms from one matter or many matters from one form an *aporia* in H 5? The obvious answer, indeed, the only answer, is that either would violate the principle that one matter is proper to one form. That such a violation generates an *aporia* in H 5 supports my claim that Aristotle mentions the similar apparent violations in H 4 as obstacles that need to be overcome to assert the doctrine of proper matter.

Aristotle removes the *aporiai* of H 5 by noting that one of the two things a matter can become is a nature through the possession of a form and the other is the contrary to this nature and results from the privation of the form (1044b32–34). The latter is generated only accidentally (1044b36–1045a1). Although it is possible for both contraries to come from each other, before vinegar becomes wine, it must pass into their common matter, water (1025a3–6). Thus, the form must be distinguished from its privation as well as from its matter. The point is that even if we include the privation in our account, as we must if it is to be complete, it remains true that one matter is proper to one form.

If the foregoing interpretation is correct, Aristotle's seemingly scattered remarks in H 4–5 aim to bolster the doctrine of proper matter by removing objections to it. There is one matter proper to one form.

For the most part, the matter under discussion in this section is the matter for generation, the matter out of which the composite comes to be (cf. H 1, 1042b1–3). Only once does Aristotle mention another matter here, the matter for the local motion of eternal sensible *ousiai* (1044b6–7). The omission is surprising because most of his examples are accidental composites. Yet, on reflection, it becomes clear that Aristotle does not really omit other types of matter. A bed comes to be when wood acquires a particular shape, and sleep when an animal or, perhaps, a heart comes to possess an attribute. While the wood or the heart are matter out of which the composites comes, matter for generation, the generation is not absolute but qualified (cf. *Phys.* A 7, 190a31–33). So wood and heart are more properly matter for a quality than matter for a generation.

The matter for absolute generation is more troublesome. In the *Physics,* Aristotle insists that matter persists through change (190a9–13), and he refers to the seed as the matter for plants and animals (b3–5).[216] Apparently, the seed somehow persists in the composite as its matter. How, though, is this to be reconciled with his suggestion that the first matter for sleep and perhaps for the animal is an organ like the heart? For an artifact, the matter from which it is generated and the matter which persists in the composite are the same. For composite *ousiai,* these two matters do not seem to be the same because the matter of the composite, the organs, does not exist except in composites.

None of this casts any doubts on the central conclusion of H 4–5, the doctrine that one matter for generation is proper to one form. But it suggests the question whether the matter in the composite is also proper to its form. This latter question should be raised along with another question, what is the significance of proper matter for the inquiry into *ousia?* To answer this latter we need to turn to H 6.

2.12 H 6: THE UNITY OF THE COMPOSITE

The final chapter of book H begins by raising a question that H 3 suggested while comparing numbers and definitions: what causes a definition or a number to be one? (1045a7–8; cf. 1044a2–6). The subsequent discussion ignores numbers and focuses on explaining the unity of definitions. This topic is usually thought to be peripheral to the main concerns of Z–H; but if the foregoing analysis is correct, it is central, and the treatment of it in this chapter is the capstone of Z–H.[217]

2.12.1 1045a7–33: Problem and Solution

H 6's question about the unity of definition is the same, at least in formulation, as that raised in Z 12; and, as I mentioned earlier, the two chapters are often taken to be a "doublet."[218] Both chapters do share the assumption that the definition will be one if it is the definition of one thing (Z 12, 1037b25–26; H 6, 1045a12–14). But just this similarity shows their difference, for the thing whose unity is at issue in Z 12 is the form, whereas the thing whose unity H 6 must explain is the composite. The composite *should* be under consideration in the latter because it has been before us since H 2, and the chapter's opening description of the problem leaves no doubt that this is the case. There Aristotle argues that all things which have parts and do not exist as a heap have a cause of unity "since even among bodies the cause of unity for some is contact, for others it is stickiness or some other such quality" (1045a8–12). Since these are causes of continuity, and the examples are continuous by art, though not by nature, the unity here must be continuity (Δ 6, 1015b36–1016a9; cf. I 1, 1052a19–20, a23–24). The argument is that since even artifacts have a cause of unity, *a fortiori* a composite nature must also have a cause of unity. Since even what is merely in contact or what is just stuck together has a cause, things with even more unity must surely have a cause.[219] From this argument it is clear that the cause of unity in the thing will be the cause of its continuity. Were the thing here a form, it would make no sense to mention causes of continuity as possible causes of its unity; continuity belongs to what has matter. Again, the thing here must be the composite, and the issue is how the formula of a composite, especially the formula of a composite *ousia,* can be one.

As I mentioned, Aristotle assumes that the formula will be one if the composite of which it is a formula is one: "The definition is one formula not by being conjoined like the *Iliad* but by being the formula of something one" (1045a12–14; cf. Z 4, 1030b8–10). Hence, to show that the formula is one Aristotle needs to show that the composite is one.

Why, then, is the composite one? This question is, I maintain, the topic of the remainder of H 6. But at least two obstacles stand in the way of accepting this interpretation: first, why is not Aristotle's account of the cause of a composite's unity complete when he refers to the causes of continuity, "contact, stickiness, or some other quality" (1045a12–14); second, why does Aristotle continue to pose the problem in the same terms as he used in Z 12, as when he asks, "What is it which makes man one, and why is he one but not many, such as animal and two-footed?" (1045a14–15). In regard to the first problem, the reason that reference to the cause of continuity in a composite does not suffice to explain the composite's unity is that, as I suggested earlier, it leaves open the problem of the unity of this cause and the material which it causes to be continuous. Contact may be the cause of the continuity of two pieces of wood, but what is the cause of the unity of the contact and the pieces of wood? In Z 17 Aristotle argues that the cause of unity in a composite must be something different from the material elements (1041b11–28). Without this conclusion, any attempt to account for the unity of elements would face a vicious regress of causes. If there were a cause of the unity of the elements that were itself an element, we would also need a second cause to account for the unity of this cause with the other elements, and still another cause to account for the unity of the second cause with everything else, and so on *ad infinitum.* But even if Aristotle avoids this regress by identifying the cause of unity as a principle distinct from matter, he still faces the problem of accounting for the unity of this principle and the material elements it unites. In respect of what is the principle and the matter one? If they are one in virtue of something else, it will be necessary to ask in respect of what are principle, matter, and the something else one, and so on. Thus, knowing that the cause of unity is a principle or even that it is form does not, by itself, explain why the composite is not a plurality of form and matter.

That this latter is the point at issue in H 6 is apparent from Aristotle's formulation of the problem as the question of the unity of sphere and bronze in a bronze sphere: "so that the thing sought is the cause of the bronze and the sphere being one" (1045a27–28). Sphere is the form that causes the matter, the bronze, to be what it is. As we have seen, a complete definition of an artifact like bronze sphere would include distinct expressions for both bronze and sphere (2, 1043a22–26). Likewise, a complete definition of man ought, it would seem, to include distinct expressions signifying the physical matter and the form. But such definitions would each contain a plurality of constituents. Thus, the plurality of the definition stems from the plurality of matter and form in the composite. If Aristotle can explain how the composite is one, he will also explain the unity of its definition and so attain the goal of this chapter.

If, though, the unity of the composite is at issue in H 6, then why does this chapter continue to pose the problem of unity in the same terms that Aristotle uses to formulate the question of Z 12? It is puzzling, at least for my interpretation, that Aristotle goes on in H 6 to treat the problem of the unity of the composite as if it were tantamount to problem of how a genus and a differentia could be one. As in Z 12, he asks here how animal and two-footed can be one (1045a14–15). Does he assume that the genus is the physical matter, a position defended by Richard Rorty and others?[220] H 6's discussion of the unity of animal and two-footed implies nothing of the kind; and, despite similarities with the formulation of the problem of Z 12, it addresses a different issue. Z 12 considers definitions derived from *diairesis* (1037b28–29); H 6 examines definitions constructed by adding a form to a matter (H 2, 1043a26–28)[221] or, as he puts it here, by giving a form of two-footed and a form of animal (1045a14–17). Aristotle considers two-footed animal as the definition of the composite man because, like other investigations, H 6 formulates the issues in terms that Aristotle thinks his predecessors used or should have used. Here he wants to show that the problem of the unity of a composite could not be solved if there were separate forms of animal and two-footedness, "as some say" (1045a14–17). For if there were such forms, "men would not be by participation in man nor in one [form] but in two [forms], animal and two-footed, and in general man would not be one but many, animal and two-footed" (1045a17–20). Aristotle's use of the plural "men" in this passage shows that his chief concern is the unity of the particulars. His contentions are that Platonic forms cannot account for the unity of a particular like man because the latter is what it is by partaking of two forms and that even the form man would be unable to make a particular one because it would itself consist of two forms. The accuracy of Aristotle's interpretation of Plato need not concern us here. The salient point is that in H 6 the problem of the unity of animal and two-footed is not a problem about the unity of form, as it was in Z 12, but a problem about the unity of the composite. In H 6 the question of the unity of animal and two-footed is just one way, a Platonic way, of examining the problem of the unity of the composite. Significantly, H 6 identifies the problem of the unity of animal and two-footed in man with that of the unity of bronze and sphere in the bronze sphere (1045a25-26). Both pairs (animal and two-footed, bronze and sphere) represent apparent obstacles to the unity of a composite *ousia*.

Ross sees H 6 quite differently. He thinks that the issue here is the same as in Z 12, the unity of the genus and the differentia, and he maintains that 1045a25-26 uses the "more familiar" unity of form and sensible matter to illustrate the unity of differentia (form) and intelligible matter.[222] This interpretation is obviously inconsistent with the discussion of continuity with which H 6 opens, which indicates that the unity to be explained is continuity, a unity that cannot belong to differentia and genus. Further, Aristotle does not claim that the *aporia* about the unity of a bronze sphere illustrates the *aporia* about the unity of genus and differentia, as Ross would have it. As already noted, Aristotle *identifies* the two *aporiai* (1045a25-26), for in H 6 the former is also an *aporia* about the unity of a composite, not about the unity of differentia and intelligible matter. He resolved the latter problem in Z 12.

The opposite sort of mistake is to try to read H 6's problem of the unity of form and physical matter back into Z 12. It would be an error to try to defend Rorty's position by arguing that Aristotle's identification of the *aporia* about the unity of the bronze sphere and the *aporia* about the unity of man indicates an identity of genus and physical matter. As I just said, Aristotle considers the plurality of animal and two-footed to be a possible obstacle to the unity of man because of his interpretation of Plato. Rorty points to the actual existence of freaks like mules that exhibit characteristics of a genus rather than a single species to support his claim that there are things that belong to no species in a way that matter without form is a heap.[223] This example does not prove his point: would we say, for example, that the wood and bricks that are the matter of the house are the same as its genus, buildings, just because they are both determined by form in some sense? Nor is there any basis for thinking that Aristotle regards animal as the physical matter of man.[224]

The analysis I have advanced is likely to disconcert those commentators who are convinced that Aristotle solves problems about unity simply by recognizing that the constituents of the composite or the constituents of the essence are form and matter. They assume that the unity of form and matter is obvious. This is Ross's error. He thinks that to account for the unity of genus and ultimate differentia it suffices to say that they are matter and form.[225] Earlier (2.8), I argued at some length that Z 12's account of this unity also requires an additional doctrine, the doctrine of proper differentiation. Here, in H 6, Aristotle proposes to explain a composite's unity by identifying form as actuality and matter as potentiality.

> If, as we say, the one is matter and the other form, *and* the former is potentially and the latter actually, the thing sought no longer seems to be an *aporia* (1045a23-25; cf. a30-33).

Like Z 12, this chapter supplies an additional reason for thinking that a form and a matter constitute a unity. Here it is the potentiality/actuality doctrine.

Before looking at how an actuality and a potentiality constitute a unity, let us consider what may have led commentators to the conclusion that form and matter are obviously one. One source may be a passage from the *De Anima:*

> Therefore, it is unnecessary to inquire whether soul and body are one, just as it is unnecessary to ask whether wax and its shape are one or, in general, whether the matter of something and that of which it is the matter are one. For one and being are each said in many ways but the most proper instance of both is actuality (B 1, 412b6–9).

Commentators often suppose that the relation of soul and body or of form and matter is simply the solution to the problem of unity.[226] The passage does counsel us against further inquiry into the unity question, but its plain sense is that we need not inquire further because form is actuality, and in maintaining this, it relies, I suggest, on *Metaphysics* H 6. The reason that it is unnecessary to inquire further into why soul and body are one is that, as H 6 shows, form is actuality. In any case, the above passage does not assert that nothing need be said about why form and matter are one, but that the doctrine of actuality renders the problem moot. That the *Metaphysics* does not regard form and matter as obviously one is clear from Aristotle's complaint that other philosophers are unable to account for the unity of matter and form and of soul and body (Λ 10, 1075b34–37; cf. H 6, 1045b7–17). Although a complete solution to the problem would require a discussion of the unmoved movers, the actuality doctrine expounded in book H does the lion's share of the work (H 3, 1044a7–9).

Even though the problem of the unity of the form is distinct from the problem of the unity of the composite, the identification of form as actuality which solves the latter problem has implications for the former as well. According to Z 12, the ultimate differentia is the form or essence, and it is this that H 6 identifies as actuality. The genus which Z 12 treats as implicit in the differentia can now be recognized as a kind of potentiality for this actuality. This move allows Aristotle to avoid a problem that beset the Platonic forms. The problem, described in Z 14, is whether the same genus in two different species is the same or different. Because Plato insists that the genus must be one, there are arguments against both alternatives. If the genus is a potentiality, the problem vanishes. It can then exist in each of the species without either being apart from itself or being made many. The genus is merely a potency for a more specific determination. This type of potentiality, important though it is for avoiding the criticisms that Aristotle brings against the Platonic forms, differs from the potentiality possessed by the physical matter. The latter is potentially an actual individual. Again, there is no basis for identifying genus and physical matter.

2.12.2 1045a33–b17: Form without Matter

A distinction between intelligible and sensible matter appears in H 6:

> Of matter, some is intelligible and some is sensible, and in formulae one part is matter and another part actuality, for example, the circle is a plane figure. Those things which have no matter, whether intelligible or sensible, are each immediately something one [ὅπερ ἕν τι], as they are each some being [ὅπερ ὄν τι], the this, the quality, the quantity— therefore, neither being nor one is present in their definitions; and the essence is immediately something one [ἕν τι] and some being [ὄν τι]— therefore, there is not any other cause of unity for any of these except the cause of its being something. For each is immediately some being and something one, not because it is in the genus of being or unity or as being separate from individuals (1045a33–b7).

What are the things that have no matter and are thus immediately one? Most commentators take this passage to be a discussion of intelligible matter. Since a genus is the matter of a differentia, a *summum* genus lacks matter. According to Ross, the present passage asserts the unity of each *summum* genus;[227] each is immediately one by its own nature. Support for Ross's interpretation lies in the list of categorial genera (1045b1–2) that Aristotle gives just after the claim that what lacks all matter is one. Apparently, it is these categorial genera that lack matter.

Ross's interpretation poses no difficulty for my analysis of the rest of the chapter. Still, it is worth looking more closely at a passage likely to remain difficult on any interpretation. There are good grounds to question Ross. On his account, the passage lacks connection with the chapter's principal theme, actuality. Whereas the rest of H 6 explains how actuality is the source of unity, the present passage would, if Ross were right, ascribe unity to what lacks actuality, the *summum* genus. This result is absurd. Aristotle treats *summa* genera as potencies; he chides Plato for positing them as first princi- ples because they are mere potencies. Aristotle's *summum* genus does not exist separately but is always actualized by a differentia. It has none of the characteristics of what Aristotle does recognize as a unity without matter (Λ 8, 1074a35–37). Moreover, it is only because genera are not unities that Aristotle can explain the unity of genus and differentia by showing that the genus is matter. Ross cannot be correct.

Could it be, though, that the present passage ascribes a different sort of unity to the *summum* genus? This might save Ross's interpretation. What kind of unity could the *summum* genus possess? Of the different types of unity that

Aristotle distinguishes in Δ 6 and I 1, only "one by generic substrate" (Δ 6, 1016a24–32) could apply to a *summum* genus. Something is one in this way if it is one instance of a genus; for example, man is one animal. The genus itself could also be called one in this way because it is the matter for differentiae. Does 1045a36–b1 assert that what lacks all intelligible or sensible matter (a *summum* genus) is one because it is the substrate for differentiae? It would be paradoxical and perverse for Aristotle to assert that what has no matter is one because it *is* matter. Further, the unity of generic matter is inconsistent with the solutions to both unity problems. As I said, it is only because matter is *not* one that form and matter do not constitute a plurality. In short, the passage cannot be about the *summa* genera.

How, then, are we to understand it? From the claim that what lacks all matter is immediately one and a being, Aristotle infers, "therefore, neither being nor one is present in their definitions" (1045b2–3). The *Metaphysics* contains another argument for the same conclusion: since neither "one man" nor "man is" adds anything to "man," one and being must already be contained in the *ousia* of man. Hence, the *ousia* of each thing is immediately one and a being (Γ 2, 1003b22–33; I 2, 1054a13–17). The consequence of this argument is that being and one need not be added to a definition, though Aristotle does not say so explicitly. Why does H 6 not simply refer to this argument? How does this chapter use the idea of what lacks matter to arrive at the same conclusion? There may well be a lacuna in the text we possess, but let me suggest that when Aristotle refers to what lacks all matter at 1045a36 he has in mind something similar to what he means when he speaks of what lacks matter at 1045b23, the closing line of this chapter. The latter passage refers to the pure actualities. Each of these is immediately one and immediately a being because it lacks anything to make it many and because actuality is a kind of being (Δ 7, 1017a35–b1). When Aristotle speaks of what lacks intelligible or sensible matter at 1045a36, I think he intends to refer to the essences or forms of sensibles. Insofar as each of these can be distinguished from its matter, it is an actuality. Moreover, actualities can belong not only to *ousia* but to other categories as well (Θ 10, 1051a34–b1; Δ 7, 1017b1–6, cf. H 2, 1043a4–27), and this is what I think Aristotle intends to indicate by beginning to list the categories in 1045b1–2. This list simply explicates his claim that an essence is immediately a being: each essence is immediately an instance of a category. In short, I propose that when Aristotle refers to what has no matter at 1045a36, he is speaking of forms or essences (falling under all categories—cf. H 5, 1044b22–23) in contrast with the matter of these forms.

Support for my interpretation lies in Aristotle's inferences that being and one are not contained in definitions and that essence is immediately one and a being (1045a36–b3). Aristotle draws these inferences about what has no matter. Then he goes on to assert that *essence* is immediately one and a being

(1045b3-4). The things without matter should be essences. In other words, given that Aristotle goes on to say about essences in this passage just what he maintains about what lacks matter, the things which lack matter should not be *summa* genera but essences. We know from the earlier discussions in book Z that essence does not contain matter; Z 10-12 argue that neither sensible nor intelligible matter belongs to form, though form contains its genera implicitly and sometimes does not exist except in a sensible matter. Moreover, Aristotle's claims about what has no matter are immediately true of essence if it is an actuality. Then, essence is immediately one and a being, and its formula does not contain these latter terms. An additional benefit of this interpretation is that it explains and justifies the conclusion Aristotle drew in Γ 2, 1003b32-33. In contrast, Ross is forced to resort to the unlikely expedient of treating the claims made in 1045b2-4 as if they were about *summa* genera alone. They apply to all forms.

Further support lies in Aristotle's remarks, immediately after the quoted passage, that other thinkers resorted to participation, communion, and (even) composition and binding to solve "this *aporia*," namely, the problem of unity (1045b7-12). Those who spoke of participation faced still more difficulties: what is it? and, what is its cause? (b8-9). The difficulties Aristotle has in mind here stem, I think, from a version of the third man. To account for unity by referring to participation is insufficient because we still need to account for participation. If participation has a distinct cause, then we need to account for the unity of this cause with the thing that partakes, and so on. The other accounts of unity suffer from the same difficulty, for their unity also requires explanation. This is what I think Aristotle means to indicate when he asserts, "the same argument applies in all cases" (1045b12). The reason, he explains in a discussion reminiscent of passages in H 2 and 3 (1042a25-31, b7-11; 1043b4-14), is that:

> To be healthy will be a communion, binding, or synthesis of a soul and health, and to be in the case of a bronze triangle [will be] a synthesis of bronze and triangle, and to be in the case of white will be a synthesis of surface and whiteness. The reason is that they seek a unifying formula and a differentia of actuality and potentiality (1045b12-16).

The mistake is to think that the source of unity in such composites lies in the synthesis, the binding, or the communion. This is a mistake for the same reason that it is a mistake to speak of participation: each of these supposed causes of unity seems to be itself caused by something else.[228] The "reason" that Aristotle mentions in the last sentence of the quotation is the reason that these thinkers take synthesis, communion, etc. to be constituents of the composite: they seek a cause of unity over and above the form and the matter. In contrast, Aristotle's own cause of unity, form, does not require something else to cause its unity. Why not? Because form by itself is immediately one (cf. 1045b23). Unless he assumes the immediate unity of his own form, his criticism of other accounts of unity in 1045b7–17 makes no sense. The immediate unity of form is just the point of 1045a33–b4 I have been arguing.

My interpretation of this text would be on firmer ground if the text were clearer about the role of the categories at 1045b2–3 and if there were explicit evidence that the essence mentioned at 1045b3 is what lacks intelligible and sensible matter at 1045a36 and is the essence of sensibles. Accordingly, nothing in my subsequent discussion of H 6 will rely upon it. What I shall say is compatible with more traditional interpretations of 1045a33–b4. Nevertheless, the interpretation that I have presented here has the advantage of allowing the passage to fit very well into the context of H 6. It emphasizes the importance of actuality, the central theme of this chapter; and it enables us to see the chapter as following a coherent sequence of topics. At 1045a29–33 Aristotle resolves the problem of the unity of the composite by identifying form as actuality and matter as potentiality. Then, 1045a33–b4 focuses on the actuality: it is immediately a being and immediately one. The subsequent lines of H 6 (1045b4–17) go on to claim that neither participation nor any other additional thing can account for unity in the composite.[229] The sequence is precisely what we would expect. To explain the unity of the composite, Aristotle identifies its constituents as actuality and potentiality. Then he shows that the actuality by itself is immediately one. If, then, potentiality and actuality are one, the problem of the unity of the composite is solved without recourse to participation or any of the other doctrines that other philosophers introduce to solve it.

2.12.3 1045b17–23: Justification and Interpretation of the Solution

On what basis does Aristotle identify form as actuality and matter as potentiality? Typically, Aristotle's justification for it lies only in its ability to resolve the *aporia* addressed in the chapter.

> It is clear that if they proceed to define and to give formulae as they are accustomed, it is impossible to explain and solve the *aporia*. But if, as we say, the one is matter and the other form, *and* the former is potentially and the latter is in actuality, the thing sought no longer seems to be an *aporia* (1045a20–25).

In other words, it is possible to explain the unity of the composite by recognizing form as actuality and matter as potentiality. We know that there must be some cause of this unity (1045a10–12); and, as we saw, none of the other proposed causes works (1045b7–17). Since the identification of form as actuality and matter as potentiality seems to be the only way to account for the unity of the composite, it must be true. No other argument is given to support this identification. (As we saw earlier [2.8], the same type of reasoning lies behind Z 12's introduction of the doctrine of proper differentiation.)

All that remains is to explain how the identification accounts for the unity of the composite. How does identifying form as actuality and matter as potentiality solve the problem? Has Aristotle not simply substituted one duality for another? Are actuality and potentiality more obviously one than form and matter? Given the significance of the identification of form as actuality, it is surprising how little Aristotle says here about why actuality and potentiality are one. Midway through the chapter he raises the question of why the bronze and the sphere are one (1045a27–28). He answers it by pointing to the identity of actuality and potentiality (a29–31) and then asserts, "Nothing else is the cause of what is potentially a sphere being actually a sphere, except this is the essence of each" (a31–33). After the lengthy interlude (1045a33–b17), which, as I just maintained, shows the immediate unity of form, Aristotle takes up the problem of the unity of the composite at the end of the chapter:

> It is just as has been said: the proximate [ἐσχάτη] matter and the form are one and the same, [the former] is potentially and the latter is in actuality; so that it is the same to seek the cause of unity and the cause of being one.²³⁰ For each thing is one, and the potential and actual are somehow one (1045b17–21).

Proximate matter here should be what H 4–5 call "proper [οἰκεία] matter" and the matter that is "nearest" to the composite and peculiar (ἴδιον) to it (1044b1–3). As we saw, H 4–5 emphasize that a particular kind of matter is peculiar to a particular form. H 6 goes a step further. It identifies the proper matter with the form to which it is proper: the form is actuality and its proper matter is a potentiality for it (1045a31–33).

What exactly does Aristotle mean by the proximate matter? In H 4–5 the proper matter is the matter out of which something comes to be. Although there are one or two references in H 6 to the generation of the composite from matter by an efficient cause (1045a30–31, b21–22), this chapter's main concern is not the matter for generation and its unity with form, but the matter that persists in the composite and its unity with form. When Aristotle asks about the cause of unity in a man, he is not primarily concerned with why the soul is one with menstrual fluid (1044a34–35), but with why the soul is one with a body (e.g., 1045b11–12). The matter pertinent here is not the matter for generation (as in Z 7–9) but the material substrate that was also discussed in Z 10–11. It is proximate to the form in the sense that it is "nearest to the form" (H 4, 1044b1–3), not nearest as the first matter for generation but as the first matter in which the form is present (cf. Θ 7, 1049a34–36), for example, the heart, the brain, flesh, or other organs (Z 10,

1035b25-27; cf. H 4, 1044b15-20). This distinction between two types of matter is obscured in H 6 by Aristotle's use of artifacts as illustrations. In a bronze sphere, the matter for generation is the same as the matter which receives the form (cf. Z 7, 1033a19-22). Is Aristotle so taken with his examples that he neglects to observe that these matters differ in natures? Perhaps. The arguments in H 4-5 for the existence of proper matter apply most of all to matter for generation in natures and natural composites. H 6 needs to assume that there is a single proper material substrate for each form before its equation of form and matter makes sense; but H 4-5 provide little explicit basis for thinking that *this* sort of matter is proper. As we saw, Aristotle speaks of an *ousia* as the substrate that receives the form of the eclipse (1044b8-11), and he suggests that the heart may receive the attribute of sleep (b15-17). Both are substrates that persist when they receive the form, but for both the reception of the form is merely a qualified generation. Having noted Aristotle's failure to show in H 4-5 that the matter that receives the form in a composite *ousia* is also proper matter, I must acknowledge that there are no real obstacles to extending the notion of proper matter so as to include this type of matter. Perhaps Aristotle introduces examples like eclipse and sleep in H 4 just to extend the notion of proper matter in the way that H 6 requires. In any case, the characteristic feature of proper matter, namely, its being determined by the form, belongs to both the matter for generation and the matter that persists in the composite. So even if H 6 does not distinguish the different types of matter, its claim about the unity of form and ultimate matter remains unaffected.

Ironically, it is just because the matter for generation in an artifact is the same as its material substrate that the artifact fails to be properly an *ousia*. As I said earlier, because the matter of an artifact retains its own nature, the artifact is a kind of plurality. Furthermore, for artifacts and probably for natural composites, that is, when the matter for generation and the material substrate are the same, the matter is not proper to the form. For, as we saw when discussing H 4-5, an artifact can often be made from different matters. It follows that the unity of form and proper matter propounded by H 6 holds less well for artifacts than for *ousiai*. The text of H 6 does not, however, distinguish between *ousiai* and artifacts; it uses the latter to illustrate the former. Both are one for the same reason; the artifact is just less one than the nature.

This observation brings us back to the question raised earlier, why are form and proximate matter one? How does their identification as actuality and potentiality account for their unity? Why are actuality and potentiality one? We have seen the pertinent texts of H 6. The chapter gives us little with which to answer these questions. To understand why actuality and potentiality are one, we need to reconstruct Aristotle's reasoning.[231] Fortunately, we can draw on the analysis of H 2. There, too, Aristotle identifies form as actuality. What is new in H 6 is his identification of matter as potentiality and his emphasis on the proximate matter. This latter is always the matter for a particular form; it is always a potentiality for a particular actuality. Since Z 12 explains the unity of form by showing that the ultimate differentia implicitly contains generic matter, we might expect H 6 to explain the unity of actuality by showing that an actuality implicitly contains its potentiality. Aristotle does assert that a potentiality depends upon and is known through an actuality (Θ 8, 1049b12–17; 1050a4), but this comes later. His approach here is not to locate the unity in one of the elements but to identify the two elements. Because this identity exists only between form and proximate matter, attempts to see an analogy between H 6 and Z 12 break down. The first physical matter is probably earth, fire, and so forth (H 4, 1044a17–18); it is not this matter that H 6 claims is one with form. In contrast, the matter that Z 12 includes in the differentia is the *first* genus and all subsequent genera. Whereas Z 12 includes all the generic matter in the ultimate differentia, H 6 includes only the proximate physical matter in the form. This difference shows that the matter considered in each chapter differs and thus that the two chapters should not be equated. More important for the question before us, the difference shows that the reason genus and differentia are one will not be the reason that form and matter are one, for if they were, form and *all* matter would be one. We must look elsewhere for an account of the unity of actuality and potentiality.

Let us return, then, to the passage from the end of H 6 quoted above (1045b17–21). Here Aristotle claims that to seek "the cause of unity" is like seeking "the cause of being one" (1045b19–20). Just what does Aristotle mean by "the cause of unity" and by "the cause of being one"? If the one is *like* the other, they should also be different (I 3, 1054b6–11). In what way do they differ? Although the apparatus does not contain alternative readings, it is possible that the original text at 1045b20 mentioned the "cause of being" and that "one" was added to the manuscripts early on. In this case, Aristotle's point here would resemble what he said in Z 17, that the cause of unity is also the cause of being. However, if this were the point, we would expect some manuscript evidence, and there is none. Besides, this reading works less well with the rest of the chapter than the interpretation I shall now propose. Let us then assume that the manuscript readings are correct.

Aristotle uses the expression "cause of being one" early in H 6; the announced aim of the chapter is to find the cause of a definition's being one (1045a8), and he compares this cause to stickiness and contact, causes of a composite's being one (a11). Thus, initially Aristotle aims to find some cause that makes the constituents of the definition be one. Midway through the chapter he concludes that "the thing sought is the cause of the sphere and the bronze being one" (1045a27–28). In drawing this conclusion, Aristotle is rejecting the Platonic approach to the problem of unity, the approach that seeks the cause of unity in something else (1045a14–15; a17–20). Likewise, it is the Platonists and others who seek a "one-making formula and differentia" (1045b16–17) that he rejects when he identifies the cause of unity and the cause of being one. Thus, if the cause of unity differs in meaning from the cause of being one, then the difference is that the former is a cause that unifies constituents, the sort of cause that Aristotle argues in Z 17 cannot be a material element, whereas the latter is the cause of everything in the composite's being one. In saying that they are alike, Aristotle is saying that the cause of unity in the composite is neither communion, synthesis, participation (b13), nor any other thing which exists apart from the composite (b6–7). The cause of unity lies in the composite: the cause of the constituents' being one is form, as we know from Z 17. What causes form and matter to be one? The cause is similar: form is in actuality and matter is potentially, and "what is potentially and in actuality are somehow one" (1045b20–21). Just as form causes unity among the constituents, it causes itself and matter to be one insofar as it is the actuality of the matter. Because form or essence is immediately one (1045b3–4), each composite is also one (b5–6, b20).

The alternative interpretations of this passage (b17–21) make little sense. Ross, for example, thinks that Aristotle says here that seeking the cause of the unity of actuality and potentiality or of form and matter is like seeking the cause of being one, and that the latter is an absurd question.[232] As I said, Aristotle's central and persistent question in H 6 is the cause of being one, and he contends that the only way to account for the composite's being one is to recognize that the composite consists of form and matter and that form is actuality and matter potentiality (1045a23–33). So Ross thinks the central issue is obviously absurd and that it serves to illustrate the similar absurdity of an inquiry into the unity of actuality and potentiality. This confuses the problem with its solution. If anything, the obvious unity of actuality and potentiality or form and matter should be like the general question about the cause of something's being one. This interpretation, the converse of Ross's, is more plausible than his. But the problem with it is why the cause of form and matter's being one is only "like" the cause of something's being one. Earlier, Aristotle equated them: we can find the cause of something's being one by recognizing one part as form or actuality and another part as matter or potentiality (1045a27–31). So pointing to a resemblance between these questions is too weak, and pointless once their identity has already been asserted. It is more likely that Aristotle assumes this identity in inferring the likeness of the cause of unity to the cause of being one from the unity of actuality and potentiality. The cause of the composite's being one is the cause of the unity of form and matter, but these latter are one, somehow, because they are actuality and potentiality. All this shows that the cause of being one lies in the composite. If this is so, then the cause of unity must also lie in the composite. So the question about the cause of unity must resemble the question about the composite's being one, that is, the question why form and matter are one.

This interpretation makes the chapter cogent, but it does not answer either question. How does form cause unity? Why are actuality and potentiality one? The identifications of the constituents of the composite as form or actuality and as matter or potentiality is clearly significant, but the text does not explain precisely how they solve the problem.

Earlier, in discussing H 2, I explained why actuality is the cause of unity. The matter is one just when it possesses a form or actuality. That is, it is one just when it can act together. The paradigm consists of cases like two sticks that can move together because they are bound or water that becomes one by being compacted. As I said, actuality here consists of what the *De Anima* (B 1, 412a24) calls first actuality: the sticks are one when they have the capacity to move together, and water is one when it acquires the capacity to behave in the way that ice behaves.

To this doctrine, H 6 adds that the matter and its form are one because the matter is a potency for the form. Even though the chapter gives an artifact, the bronze sphere, as an example (1045a28–33), the identification of form and matter is, at best, weak for artifacts. To put the problem raised earlier in terms of actuality, the bronze may be potentially a sphere, but it is potentially other things as well. The definition of bronze does not include its capacity to be formed into a sphere (cf. Θ 8, 1049b12–15). The glue makes the sticks one, and the sticks are potentially glued, but this latter is merely incidental to being a stick.

The situation is quite different for composite *ousiai,* natures. Our organs cease to be properly organs when they are separated from us. A hand which is cut off can no longer perform its function and is thus called a hand only equivocally (Z 10, 1035b23–25); it is only a hand when it has the potential to act as a hand does, and this occurs only when form or soul is present (11, 1036b30–32). Like accidental composites, composite *ousiai* are one because their material constituents can act together. But the material constituents of composite *ousiai* are defined in terms of the work that they do, their function in the whole. In the strict sense, it is inappropriate to speak of these material constituents as "possessing" a form, for they have no existence apart from their form. In composite *ousiai,* the matter is just the potency for the function that characterizes the *ousia.*

Again, these functions are themselves potentialities for other functions, second actualities. Let us, following Aristotle's standard example, suppose that the function that characterizes us is the capacity for walking on two feet. In order to have this function we need a matter of a certain type. Obviously, we need two feet, and each foot must have a structure that enables it both to support weight and to move. We also need a heart to send blood to the foot, and we need lungs, brain, and so forth. In short, we could not engage in our characteristic activity (our second actuality) unless our matter had the structure that it has. But insofar as it is so structured, our matter is, in a way, identical to our form: both form and matter are potentially our second actuality. Proper matter is not earth or air; it is a matter that is already structured. In virtue of this structure it has the capacity for certain functions. But what is form other than the capacity for those same functions? Our proximate matter is thus virtually the same as our form. The identity holds because the proximate matter is so structured that it is capable of performing those characteristically human functions whose capacity to perform is our nature or form. Our capacity to walk lies primarily in the structure of our legs. References to man as a two-footed animal do not merely point to material constituents, two feet; they indicate the function of having a capacity for walking in a particular way (see *H. A.* A 4, 489a26–29). Precisely the same reasoning applies to all natures.

Two-footed animal is not the best characterization of man, but it has the advantage of deflecting attention from questions about disembodied reason. The latter may be an exception that is peculiar to human beings. In general, the natures of plants and animals consist of the potency for the active functioning of their organs, and these active functions are characteristic of a species just because of the peculiar structures of the organs of the species' instances. The definitions of composite *ousiai* include matter in the sense that they refer to these organs and to their capacity for being exercised (cf. E 1, 1025b30–1026a6). They do not include matter that has a different nature, as the complete definition of an artifact or a natural composite would (H 2, 1043a16–26). This notion of form or soul as the structure of the organ in virtue of which it has the capacity to perform its characteristic functions demystifies life: except to explain the first cause there is no need to refer to anything beyond the functions and the organs that perform those functions. Aristotle has little to say here about what those functions and organs actually are. His concern here is mainly to show how to account for form and matter being one; he devotes his biological works to describing functions and organs.

With this analysis, we can see that the composite nature is one because it is a single actuality, but it is an actuality that is necessarily the functioning of some matter. The formula of this composite is one because it need only include the actuality. Because this actuality is a first actuality, it is virtually identical with the organs that have the particular function, and it is the latter that are often mentioned in definitions. Once we recognize the peculiar character of the actualities of sensible natures, we can see that the mention of organs in a definition is not at odds with Aristotle's insistence in Z 10–11 that material parts not belong to the form or formula. There he excluded the matter in which the form exists (e.g., 1035b25–26; 1036b3–4). The subsequent analysis enables us to see that organs like the heart and brain are not simply substrates but, in a way, the (first) actualities that define the nature. Ironically, while much of book Z argues for excluding matter from the *ousia*, H 6 shows that the unity of the composite requires the virtual identification of form or essence with some matter, the proper matter.

One difficulty remains. The unity of the composite requires that the form or actuality of the composite be one. This actuality is, I maintain, just the capacity of a matter to function, and it is virtually identical to the organ that has the capacity. How can the actuality of anything be one if the thing has many organs? Although he insists that *ousia* must be one throughout Z–H, Aristotle does not address this question here or elsewhere in the *Metaphysics*.

Still, the problem is important, for it is precisely on this point that Z–H seems to be at odds with Aristotle's biological works. In *De Partibus Animalium*, for example, he rejects bifurcate division because it produces only one differentia (A 3, 643b13–17, 643b28–644a10). He insists that we need to recognize not only the ultimate differentia but all the differentiae in a single series, and that a definition needs to include differentiae of other genera as well. In other words, a definition of a species should include many organs. Can all of this be reconciled with Z 12 and H 6? Despite appearances, there is no inconsistency here. *De Partibus Animalium* argues against the possibility of defining an animal by one ultimate differentia or by a single series of differentiae on the ground that the animal is more than just the one attribute indicated by the ultimate differentia and more than all the attributes in a single series. Man, for example, is more than just cleft-footed because this character is combined with a series of other differentiae and because man has other characteristics (643b28–644a10). This is obvious, and the *Metaphysics* does not deny it. The point of Z 12 is that a genus and series of differentiae are implicitly contained in the ultimate differentia because in order for something to have this ultimate differentia, it would need to possess those other characteristics as well. *De Partibus Animalium* also assumes that the differentiae in a series are implicitly contained in the last (2, 642b7–9; 3, 643b17–23), but it counsels us to remember that the whole series is important to differentiate other genera. Likewise, when H 6 claims that form and matter are one as potency and act, it does not say that matter performs only a single function. This would be contrary to earlier claims about the hand that exists as such only when it can function. In explaining the unity of form and matter, I suggested that if the proper function of human beings is to walk on two feet, we need other organs, such as a heart, lungs, and brain, in order to perform this function. In saying that the form or actuality of a human being or other composite *ousia* is one, Aristotle need only mean that the functions of our other organs are subordinate to one organ. He makes exactly this point at *De Partibus Animalium* A 5, 645b14–20. The *Metaphysics* emphasizes the unity of the form and the composite in order to show that it is an *ousia*, but the single function to which the others are subordinate obviously does not suffice for a science concerned with knowledge of what those functions are. Unfortunately, the problem of a plurality of organs is not addressed in the *Metaphysics,* but there is some evidence that Aristotle does think one function primary: he speaks of "that which is supreme and in which the form is contained primarily" and he suggests that this might be the heart or the brain (Z 10, 1035b25–27; cf. H 4, 1044b15–20). The subordination of a plurality of organs to a single one could also be the key to reconciling the discussion of the differentiae of a single genus in Z 12 with the emphasis on a plurality of genera in *De Partibus Animalium.* The other genera are somehow potentialities for a primary genus. It is not surprising that such a solution is not advanced in Z 12, for actuality and potentiality do not play a prominent role in the argumentation of book Z. Unfortunately, though, Aristotle does not return to this problem of a plurality of genera in book H.

H 6 does not consider all aspects of the problem of the unity of the composite and even what it does consider is terse and undeveloped. It is clear, however, that Aristotle supports the identification of form as actuality and matter as potentiality on the ground that it alone explains how a composite can be one. From these remarks and also from other claims in Z–H and the *De Anima,* I have reconstructed an account of how actuality is the cause of unity in a composite and how it is virtually identical with the matter that is a potency for it. This account does not appear in our text explicitly, but that should not be an argument against it. No account appears in our text. Some reconstruction is necessary if we are to make any sense of the claims made here. Aside from its ability to account for the text, the advantage of my analysis is that it ties together several other texts in a coherent and consistent way. Moreover, if my analysis is right, H 6 is rightly placed at the conclusion of the inquiry into categorial being. In showing that form is the cause of unity in the composite and that form and matter are one, this chapter shows form to be both the *ousia* of the composite and the cause of the composite's being an *ousia.* Significantly, to establish that form is *ousia* Aristotle shows that form is able to solve problems of unity. *Ousia* is the cause of unity in a composite, and the composite is one despite its containing *ousia* as a kind of part. H 6 shows that these specifications can be fulfilled if *ousia* or form is actuality and matter the potentiality for this actuality. Conversely, the identification of form as actuality is supported just by its capacity to resolve problems about unity. The characterizations of *ousia* as form, essence, and now actuality all emerge as determinations that allow it to be one and to cause unity.

2.13 Z–H: ONE AND CATEGORIAL BEING

Z–H's treatment of categorial being is the most densely argued and difficult portion of the work. In order to keep the issues and the results before us, this section will briefly summarize the strategy of these two books. I shall return to some of the more substantial problems after discussing book Θ.

The overall results of the argumentation of Z–H are: *ousia* is primary being, form is primary *ousia,* and form is essence and actuality. Aristotle's method of reasoning often relies upon the assumption that *ousia* is one. There are other criteria for *ousia* at work in Z–H, but they are usually assimilated to unity. Separateness, for example, is treated here as a consequence of being numerically one. To determine whether something is an *ousia* Aristotle determines whether it is one. To show that something is not an *ousia* or, better, not most properly an *ousia,* he shows that it is not one. The characteristics that he ascribes to primary *ousia* are those that enable it to be one and to be the cause of unity in composite *ousiai.* Accordingly, the whole treatment of categorial being amounts to series of one/many problems. Aristotle shows how *ousia* can be one when it seems, in various ways, to be many.

Let me briefly recount the broad outlines of the argument we have seen. Aristotle's first move (Z 1) is the reduction of the consideration of categorial being to the consideration of *ousia* on the ground that *ousia* is primary. *Ousia* is primary because it is more one than other beings. It is the single nature in respect of which the others are called beings and thus the nature of all beings. The bulk of book Z examines four candidates for *ousia:* substrate, essence, universal, and genus. The first of these is further divided into three: matter, form, and composite. The material substrate seems to be *ousia* because insofar as it underlies everything else, everything else is a kind of plurality, and it is a unity. But when everything predicated of the material substrate is subtracted, what remains is not something one but an indeterminate nothing. Two of the other candidates for *ousia* are also rejected because they are not one in the pertinent ways. Genera and other universals are each a "one over many," and this unity makes them seem good candidates for *ousia.* However, they are not numerically one in way that an *ousia* must be because they are predicated of many individuals: they cannot be the *ousia* of these many things because things whose *ousiai* are numerically one are themselves numerically one. Were they *ousiai,* they would be numerically one and so would that of which they are predicated, an absurdity. Further, if universals were numerically one, what is composed of them, for example, the species, would be many, also absurd.

Essence or formal substrate is Aristotle's most successful candidate for *ousia,* and a large portion of Z–H examines it. While the other candidates seem to be one but turn out on closer examination not to be, essence seems to be many but turns out to be one. Typically, Aristotle's concern in his discussion of essence is how it could be one, that is, what needs to be true of essence if it is to be one. The first reason that essence seems to lack unity is that the formulae of many things fail to be unities. These formulae should each express a thing's essence, but they do not because they are not formulae of what is one. In particular, the formulae of accidents, accidental composites, *per se* attributes, and *per se* composites all fail to be formulae of something one because they either add or fail to add something. The only things whose formulae do not add or fail to add are *ousiai*. Consequently, it is only formulae of *ousiai* that are definitions and express essences. The obstacles to essence being one can thus be removed if we limit essence to *ousia*. Since only the essence of an *ousia* would be one, only an *ousia* has an essence. Other beings have essences in a lesser sense by addition and subtraction.

To avoid the possibility of there being an infinite plurality of essences and the possibility of something which has being failing to be knowable (and thus one in the way that what is known is one), Aristotle identifies the essence with another candidate for *ousia,* the formal substrate. Essence and form are not many but one and the same. Thus, the thing, form, not only has an essence, it is essence. Essence must be form if it is to be *ousia* and if *ousia* is to be one.

Another apparent obstacle to the unity of essence is that it is present in things that are generated and destroyed, and things of this sort must have parts. Aristotle's response is that form is ungenerated. What is generated is the composite, and generation occurs when a preexisting form comes to be present in a matter. Although the composite has a plurality of parts, the form need not. Form can be one despite being present in a changing composite so long as the form does not contain the matter in which it comes to be present.

Still another apparent obstacle to the unity of essence is that material constituents are sometimes contained in a definition. If the definition has many components, the essence that it defines is a plurality. To this, Aristotle's response is that definitions that include material constituents are definitions of composites; the definition of a form or essence does not include material constituents. Again, Aristotle insures that form is one by excluding matter from it.

The final obstacle to the unity of essence also arises from an apparent plurality in its formula. Since the definition of a form consists of genus and differentia, the form or essence seems to be many. To avoid this inference, Aristotle introduces the doctrine of proper differentiation. The formula of the form can be expressed as the ultimate differentia of a genus because this differentia implicitly includes an entire series of differentiae and also the first genus. Despite appearances, the definition and thus the form it defines are one, the ultimate differentia.

All the obstacles to the unity of essence are overcome by limiting essence and excluding things that make it many. This process of peeling away matter for generation, material parts, accidents, and so forth both delimits essence and defines it. By showing what essence must be to be one, Aristotle shows what its nature is. Moreover, while he excludes other things from essence, he also shows their dependency on essence. Attributes and composites, for example, can be defined through a kind of addition to essence. Essence is not only primary being; it is the source of being to the others.

Ostensibly, Aristotle's investigation of the candidates for *ousia* centers on the issue of which is most properly *ousia*. But, as we have seen, Aristotle tackles this question by considering which is most one and how it is that essence can be one. Formulating the problem of *ousia* as a question about unity shows us at once the affinity of Z-H with Platonic claims about unity. According to Plato, because the sensibles change, they are pluralities; only form existing apart from sensibles can be one (*Phaedo* 80b). Z-H seek something which is one among the sensibles. Of the candidates for *ousia*, only essence can be one, and it can be one only if it is limited to form in contrast with matter, accidents, and so forth. Since Plato regards the existence of a unity among sensibles as impossible, Aristotle's first task is to show that and how it is possible. In showing the unity of what is primary, Aristotle accepts the Platonic delineation of the requirements for primary being, at least he accepts what he thinks are these requirements. However, Aristotle also argues that Plato's own account of the primary beings and the way they cause unity in sensibles (through participation) is impossible; so too are materialistic accounts of unity. Because all attempts to account for unity seem to be unsuccessful, Aristotle's explanation of how essence can be one amounts to an explanation of how it must be one. In the absence of possible alternatives, Aristotle need only show the possibility of essence's being one to demonstrate its necessity.

Several of the doctrines that appear in Z 3-16 are justified because (while they are consistent with other doctrines) they help to explain how essence can be one. Proper differentiation is an example. But the treatment of *ousia* in these chapters is only a first step. Since the form exists in sensibles, Aristotle needs to explain how. This, too, is a problem about unity; indeed, it is several unity problems. First, as the primary being, *ousia* is the cause of being in a composite, and this means, as we saw, that it must cause the composite to be one. The idea that one thing causes unity in other things seems incoherent because it remains necessary to find still another thing that causes the cause and the other things to be one. Aristotle avoids this difficulty by insisting that the *ousia* be something whose character differs from those things that it unites. Another, similar problem is how the *ousia*, the form, can cause a composite to be one if it is itself one and a part of the composite. If the form of the composite is one, the whole composite should be many. If, on the other hand, the whole composite is one, then form should be a mere part and thus not one. Considered only in terms of unity, the problem seems insoluble. (And this way of treating the problem resembles the Academic attempts to avoid Parmenides' conclusion that all is one by showing that all things are composed of being [or one] and something else, such as the indefinite dyad—a formulation that Aristotle calls archaic [N 2, 1088b35-1089a6].) The key to solving problems about unity lies in the idea that form is actuality and that the matter in which it exists is a potentiality for a particular actuality. Insofar as it is an actuality, form can be both the cause of unity in the composite and the essence of the composite. Both form and composite are one, and thus *ousiai,* but in different ways. Form or essence is one in that it is a single actuality. The composite is one because its matter is unified by the form: it is one in the sense that it is continuous. The continuity of material constituents is just their capacity to move or function together. The material constituents are continuous when they can function together, and this unity is caused by form. How? The form is the first actuality of the matter; it is just the capacity of the matter for further actuality. Insofar as the form is present in the matter, the matter has the capacity for a particular function. But it is just the having of such a capacity that is the continuity of the matter. Thus, the form causes the matter to be continuous because possession of the form *is* just what it is for the matter to be continuous. In this way, that is, as the actuality of a matter, form is both the cause of unity in the composite and the essence of the composite.

This explains how the form causes the composite to be numerically one; it causes the matter to be continuous. What about the other problem? How can the composite be one if it contains form and matter, and form is one? As we saw, Aristotle identifies this problem with the problem about the cause of unity. The answer to both lies in the character of the form. As the actuality of the matter, the form is, Aristotle maintains in H 6, virtually identical with the matter that is a potency for the form. In accidental composites such as artifacts, the form—or what Aristotle (using the result of Z 12) terms the differentia—exists as something that is distinct from the matter. In natures, though, the matter has a peculiar structure in respect of the presence of form. The matter that Aristotle identifies with form is the last matter, structured matter, such as organs. In virtue of its structure, it has the capacity to act and the latter capacity is just its form. Thus, form and matter are, in this way, the same; and the composite is, consequently, one.

Form and composite are each *ousia* because they are one, but they are one in different ways. Form is one in number just to the extent that it is separate from matter; and because it can be defined without matter, it is "separate in formula" and, thus, one in formula. The composite is one because it is continuous, and it is made continuous by the presence of form. Form is a first actuality, a capacity for further motion or activity. Matter possessed of this actuality is continuous, for this is just the definition of continuity in the *Metaphysics.* Form is the cause of unity because unity is defined as the capacity to move together; and form is, insofar as it is an actuality, a kind of motion. At the same time, form is the structure of the matter that enables it to function in a characteristic way. In this latter respect, form is one with the matter that receives it because the matter only has the potential for this characteristic function by virtue of the presence of form; that is to say, it is its structure that enables the matter to be matter. Consequently, the formula of the composite is the formula of the form, and the composite is one in formula.

This account of the unity of the composite and of the way form causes unity in it shows how form exists in sensibles and, thus, shows the possibility of *ousia* existing in sensibles. To be sure, it is a peculiar mode of existence; just how it should be understood is a problem to which I shall return after examining Aristotle discussion of actuality. It is important to realize that Aristotle can account for the unity of the composite only by identifying form as actuality. Unity, an idea that is fundamental for other Greek thinkers, depends upon actuality. The treatment of essence in Z–H begins with definitions and formulae; these are prior to us because they are the way that we know an essence. We have seen that this treatment relies heavily on the assumption that *ousia* is one. (Since Aristotle regards unity as the principle of knowledge [B 4, 999a27–28], it is hardly surprising that he would seek to know *ousia* as a unity.) To explain how *ousia* can be one, Aristotle identifies essence as form and ultimately as actuality. This progression follows the order that we would expect from a passage that appears in the manuscripts at the beginning of the treatment of essence in Z 4 (1029b7–13). Though one is prior and more knowable to us, actuality is prior in nature. Z–H shows that *ousia* must be actuality because only so can it be one. Ultimately, the study of categorial being leads us to actuality as its first cause. It is thus appropriate for the next book of the *Metaphysics* to consider the third way of being, actuality.

Chapter 3

Book Θ: Actuality and Truth

Book Θ continues the investigation of the ways of being begun in E 2. The first nine chapters examine actuality and potentiality. Since the discussion of categorial being in books Z–H leads to the identification of primary being as actuality, it is entirely appropriate for Aristotle to turn to this type of being next. The final chapter of book Θ examines the fourth way of being, truth. Neither discussion contains the dense argumentation that we saw in Z–H. Nor does either rely on unity to the extent that Z–H do. Problems about unity still play some role in Aristotle's discussions, but here they are reflected in structure and doctrine. Accordingly, my analysis of book Θ can be much briefer than my treatment of the two preceding books.

3.1 Θ 1–5: POTENTIALITY

The first five chapters examine various things that are said to be potentialities. These are potentialities for motions (cf. 6, 1048a25–26), in contrast to the more important potentialities for actualities that Aristotle discusses along with the latter in Θ 6–9.[1] For our purposes, the interesting feature of potentialities for motion is that they come in pairs. In each case, an important concern is whether and when the pair can be identified.

3.1.1 Θ 1: The Potencies of Doing and Suffering

Although he acknowledges it is "not the most useful for what we now seek," Aristotle begins in the first chapter with a discussion of what he calls the primary potency (1045b34–1046a1). This first potency to which the others are related is the principle of change in another or *qua* other (1046a10–11; Δ 12, 1019b35–1020a5).[2] In Δ 12, from which the present discussion begins (1046a4–6), Aristotle mentions two examples of this potency: the art of building insofar as it exists in the builder rather than what is built and the art of medicine insofar as it exists in the doctor rather than the patient *qua* patient (1019a15–18). So this primary kind of potency is a potency to act on another (1046a11–12). Related to this potency is the potency to suffer change initiated by another (1046a12–13; 1019a19–20; 1020a2–4). Aristotle also mentions, in nearly the same breath, the potency not to be made worse or to be affected by something else (1046a13–15). The latter is really an *impotency*, and the passage describes different types of incapacities parallel to the two different potencies, the potential to do (or to act) and to suffer (1046a13–15; 1019a26–32; 1020a4). Further, he mentions the potential to do and to suffer well (1046a16–19; 1019a23–26).[3]

In short, the potential to act on another provides the basis for defining other potentialities. This potential to act is primary, though Aristotle ties it closely to the potential to be acted upon. It is tempting to think that the potential to act on another is primary because without it there would be no potential to be acted upon, but the converse is also true: without the potential to be acted upon, there would also be no potential to act on another. Rather, the potential to act is primary because the others are defined in terms of it: "In all these definitions the formula of the primary potency is present" (1046a15–16).

Aristotle's chief concern in discussing these potentialities is to raise the question whether the potencies of doing and of suffering are one (1046a19–29). On one hand, they are the same, "for something is potential [δυνατόν] both by itself having the potency of suffering and by another [having the potency of suffering] by it" (a19–21). In other words, we are speaking of the same potentiality whether we speak of a thing being able to be acted upon by another or the other thing's having the capacity to act on the first.[4] The capacity to build a house is, in a way, the capacity of the boards and bricks to be built into a house. On the other hand, the two potencies must differ because the potential to act is in one thing and the potential to be acted upon is in another (a22–28).

In Z 7 (1032a32–b14) Aristotle argued that the form in the agent is the same as the form realized in the patient; now he claims that the potency for the motion that realizes the form is, in a way, the same in both agent and patient. However, there the form or essence of the agent and of the thing made are one. Are the potencies to act and to suffer also one in form or essence? If they are, then how could the potency to act be primary? The primacy of the potency to act is, we saw earlier in this subsection, based on the priority of its formula. But if the potency to suffer has the same essence, it should have the same formula as well. Aristotle does seem to regard the two potencies as one or nearly one in essence and formula (cf. 1046a9–16); they should have the same formula because the actuality of both is the same, and both share the formula of the actuality. Though the potencies are many in number, they are apparently one in formula.[5] Perhaps, though, Aristotle does not think their unity in formula undercuts the primacy of the potential to act because the principle of something's being acted upon lies in its matter (a23–24) and the principle of acting lies in the composite agent and stems from its form. The potential to act is prior because form is prior; its formula is prior because the formula is properly the formula of the form.

Since the potentials to act and be acted upon are numerically distinct,

Aristotle infers that insofar as something is organically united (συμπέφυκε), it cannot be acted upon by itself, "for it is one and not other" (1046a29-30). The text makes no attempt to assess the significance of this conclusion; this task falls to us. Elsewhere Aristotle describes organic unity as the highest type of continuity (Δ 4, 1014b22-26; *Phys.* E 3, 227a13-27; *Met.* K 12, 1069a5-12; cf. I 1, 1052a19-25). Although there are some difficult cases— cases in which the parts have the potential for independent existence and are thus one by nature but not organically one (Z 16, 1040b13-15)—organic unity is, in general, the unity of an *ousia*. It is the unity caused by form. Thus, the conclusion Aristotle draws here is that an *ousia* cannot act upon itself, at least insofar as it is an *ousia*. This qualification is important. Of course, I can act on myself in some sense; I can stand up or sit at will. Likewise, the doctor can cure himself. But he does not act *qua* being cured, nor is he cured *qua* being a doctor; neither can I act on myself *qua ousia* (cf. 1019a16-18). I cannot, for example, alter my nature. The potency at issue here is a principle of change by another or *qua* other (1046a10-11). Thus, the potentials to act and to suffer are a pair that always exist in distinct individuals or an individual with distinct parts. (Even their privations can require a plurality, for the interesting privations arise when something which should by nature have a potency is deprived of it by something else [1046a31-36].) Because these potencies require a plurality, and because *ousia* is one, they cannot belong to *ousia* at least insofar as it is *ousia*. *Ousia* cannot be a potency to act or to suffer. As we saw, Aristotle prefaces his remarks on potency with the disclaimer that the primary potency he is about to describe is not "the most useful for what we now seek" (1045b35-1046a1). What we now seek is to grasp primary being, *ousia*.[6] Thus, the potencies to act and to suffer are not useful for grasping *ousia*, for they do not pertain to *ousia* insofar as it is *ousia*. According to my interpretation, the analysis Aristotle provides of the potencies to act and to suffer and his inference that what is an organic unity cannot act on itself help show why these potencies are not very important for inquiry into *ousia*.

3.1.2 Θ 2: Rational and Nonrational Potencies

The second chapter of book Θ introduces a second pair of potentialities, rational and nonrational potentialities (1046b1-2). The former are principles present in what has no soul, and the latter principles present in what does have soul (1046a36-b1). From these claims Aristotle concludes that arts and "productive sciences" are also potentialities because they are principles of change in another or *qua* some other (b2-3). Obviously, arts fall under the rational potencies.

Aristotle distinguishes the two potentialities by noting that the *same* rational potentiality is a potentiality for contraries, while for nonrational potencies there is "one [potency] of one [effect]" (1046b4-6). The reason that a

rational potency can be realized in two ways is that it is possessed by someone who knows a formula, and the same formula belongs to both contraries,
though not in the same way, for one contrary is a thing and the other its
privation (b7–12). Hence, the same formula would belong to a rational potency, to the positive effect it can produce, and to the privation of that positive effect. The doctor can bring about health and disease because the
formula of both is present in his soul. Both are "encompassed by one formula" (b24). In contrast, the other potency is nonrational because it is
"without formula" (b22–23).

Compare these results with what emerged from the preceding discussion,
the conclusion that the formula that belongs to the potency to act also belongs
to the potency to be acted upon. First, the present discussion enriches this
duality by dividing the potency to act into rational and nonrational potencies.
Then, this section expands the scope of the formula for rational potencies. A
rational potency can be realized in two ways, and the potencies for both
realizations, as well as the potency to be acted upon, all have the same
formula. At first glance, it seems that a nonrational potency should be excluded from the equation because Aristotle says it is without formula. But it
too is a potency to act; so the results of Θ 1 should apply to it. Also, in Z 7–9
Aristotle argues that the formula in the agent and the formula in the patient
are the same, even in cases of chance. So the nonrational potencies are not
entirely without formulae. They might be better described as not subject to
choice. For rational potencies, the formula includes potencies for two contrary realizations, the realizations, and the potencies for coming to be those
realizations. For nonrational potencies, the formula includes only one potency, its realization, and the agent.

Do rational and nonrational potencies realize themselves in different actualities, or can they be potencies for the same actuality? Aristotle does not
address this question in Θ 2, but his examples here suggest that they can be
potencies for the same actuality. His example of a rational potency is knowledge of medicine (1046b6–7); and his nonrational potencies are, the wholesome, heat-making, and cold-making potencies (b18–19).

> The wholesome makes health alone, the heat-making potency heat, and
> the cold-making potency cold; but someone with knowledge can produce
> both (1046b18–20).

Both what? Both contrary effects, but the passage mentions *three* apparently
different effects. Can someone with knowledge produce both heat and cold or
both health and illness? We could take the second portion of the quotation as
a general claim about rational potencies, as is usually done, but there is no
need to do so; for these two pairs of contraries are identical or, at least,
closely related. Recall that in Z 7 Aristotle describes the doctor as healing a

patient with heat, and he notes that accidental contact with hot things can produce the same effect (1032b21–26). So the wholesome and heat-making potencies are the same, and knowledge of medicine is *both* a heat making potency (i.e., a wholesome potency) and a cold-making potency (an unwholesome potency). Hence, rational and nonrational potencies can realize themselves in the same actuality, a conclusion that is clear from Z 7 anyway. It follows further that a rational potency, and two contrary nonrational potencies, and the two contrary actualizations all have the same formula.

Aristotle emphasizes the ability of a single formula to encompass diverse potentialities, but the more the formula includes, the less it tells us about the process of becoming. The entire complex process of a potentiality's realizing itself escapes scrutiny, at least as far as its formula is concerned, because the same formula applies to virtually all the moments within this process. Thus, it is only the actuality whose formula can be known. Potentiality and becoming are known only through their relation to this actuality.

Both rational and nonrational potencies produce an effect in something else. So despite their single formula, their existence requires a plurality of things. Again, their plurality excludes them from being *ousiai*.

3.1.3 Θ 3–4: Potentiality and Actuality

In Θ 3–4 Aristotle examines and rejects the Megarian position that "something is potentially only when it acts, and when it does not act, it is not potentially" (1046b29–30).[7] In other words, the Megarians "make potentiality and actuality the same" (1047a19–20): they make them one. Initially, their view seems both silly and only marginally relevant to Aristotle's inquiry into potentiality. However, the result of the two preceding chapters is that a variety of potentialities have one formula, a formula that they share with an actuality. Thus, actuality and potentiality *are* one—one in formula. Hence, Aristotle's own view resembles the Megarian view. It is just this similarity that makes the discussion of the Megarians relevant and that makes it important for Aristotle to distinguish his own view from theirs. The difference is that while Aristotle thinks actuality and potentiality are one in formula, the Megarians think they are one in number. It is numerical sameness that he must have in mind when he accuses them of making actuality and potentiality the same.

The consequences of the Megarian position are easy to see. Nothing which is not in actuality could come to be actual; nothing that is actual could cease to be actual. In short, there could be no motion or becoming (1047a14). Interestingly, Aristotle claims that actuality seems to be motion (1047a32). Though Aristotle does not draw any inferences from this point, it should follow that, in identifying potentiality with actuality, the Megarians deny actuality.

The Megarians err in ascribing too much unity to actuality and potentiality. We can only speculate on their motives, but I think it is significant that the consequence of their position is the loss of motion. The Megarians apparently focused on the logical unity of actuality and potentiality, their unity in formula. They appear to have pressed the results of logic despite the disagreement of these results with physics. Actuality and potentiality must be numerically many if there is to be motion.

In what sense does Aristotle make them numerically many? He characterizes something as potential if it can be but is not, or if it is but can come not to be (1047a20–22). (Also, what is potential can become actual without any contradictions [a24–25].) Thus, something numerically one is both an actuality and a potentiality, but it is a potentiality for *not* being what it is, and it is the actuality of a potentiality different from the one that it has. A particular actuality and the potentiality for it are numerically distinct in that they belong to distinct things or to the same thing at different times.

One point that emerges from the discussion of the Megarians is that actuality and potentiality are present in each of the categories (1047a18–24). This is a significant conjoining of categorial being and actuality/potentiality. In each category, being is a particular actuality and non-being a potentiality. At the end of chapter three, Aristotle explains that although non-beings are never in motion or actuality, some are potentialities (1047b1–2). What about the non-beings that are not potentialities? They are impossibilities: at the beginning of Θ 4, Aristotle insists that potential beings need to be distinguished from impossibilities (1047b6–14). What is potentially can come to be actual or not come to be actual; what is impossible cannot come to be actual.

The potentialities under consideration here do not coexist with their actualities; they are destroyed as they are actualized. Nothing here indicates that all potentialities are of this sort. Some potentialities, such as those first actualities that Aristotle identifies with form, are not destroyed when they are realized. Those that are destroyed are potentialities for motion. The numeric difference between these latter potentialities and their actualities shows again that they cannot define *ousia,* nor can the motions whose definitions depends on them define *ousia.*

Θ 4 introduces another pair of potentialities. These are things whose being is potential and dependent. Aristotle argues that if B's existence necessarily follows from A's, and if A is possible, B must be possible (1047b14–16). The text gives us no hint of what this contributes to the overall analysis of Θ. Unlike the other pairs of potentialities, the potentiality of A and B in this argument is not a potentiality for some other effect, but a potentiality for being. There are some things whose being depends on others. This argument shows that in such things the possibility of one depends on the possibility of the other. Again, since this possibility is shared by a pair, it cannot character-ize *ousia*.

3.1.4 Θ 5: Natural and Nonnatural Potencies

The fifth chapter of Θ introduces still another distinction between poten-cies. It begins with some remarks on their acquisition. Potentialities come from nature, from habit, or from instruction; whereas the first belong to a thing by virtue of its capacity to be affected, the other two require a previous activity in the thing (1047b31–35). Potentialities from nature are nonrational potencies; the other two are or include rational potencies (1048a2–5). Because, for the former, one potency has one effect, the thing with the poten-tial to act will act whenever it is brought into contact with what has the potential to be affected. With rational potencies, two contrary effects can result. So some other principle, choice or desire, must determine the effect (1048a5–16).

This discussion synthesizes the distinctions made in the preceding chapters of Θ with a new distinction, that between natural and nonnatural potencies. The latter consist of what are usually called moral and intellectual virtues. Aristotle speaks of rational potencies as instances of nonnatural potencies, but he does not say whether they are the only instances. Whether moral virtues, which are acquired by habit, are also rational potencies is not ad-dressed here. Aristotle treats them like rational potencies because he takes them as capable of two contrary effects. Unlike the rational and nonrational potencies discussed in Θ 2, the natural and nonnatural potencies of Θ 5 are defined by the way they are acquired and they way that they come to be realized.

The text of Θ 5 does not refer to the argument of the preceding chapter, and commentators do not notice any connection. However, potentialities ac-quired from habit or instruction are examples of potentialities connected with other potentialities, the pair discussed in Θ 4. Because the exercise of knowl-edge and virtue is possible, and because this exercise is the cause of the existence of these in our souls, the potentialities for further exercise acquired by habit and by instruction must exist. (Of course, they differ greatly in degree.) In contrast, natural potentialities are merely capacities to be af-fected; they are not the result of other capacities. But they do cause effects in others, and to this extent there is a connection between the natural potency and the potency for its effect in something else. Since one (natural) potential-ity has one effect, this connection between potentialities is necessary (1048a5–7). Aristotle's insistence that the time, manner, and other conditions be present in the definition of the potency (1047b35–1048a2), an otherwise puzzling stipulation, enables him to describe potencies as necessary and not contingent upon external conditions. Likewise, a nonnatural potency has an effect on something else, and it too becomes necessary if its conditions are incorporated into its definition. Here, though, we must include not only time, manner, etc., but also desire and will, for without these, the potency could have two effects.

Why should Aristotle try to show that potentialities have an element of necessity? Although Aristotle endorses contingency and points to the disastrous consequences of its denial (by the Megarians), he locates it within the realm of what occurs necessarily. All potentialities are defined by reference to the actualities for which they are potentialities.[8]

Aside from synthesizing the earlier results about potentiality, Θ 5 continues to describe potentialities in pairs. The potentialities under consideration are those by which one thing acts upon or moves another. Aristotle terms them potentialities for motion (1, 1046a1–4; 6, 1048a25–26): their actualization is a motion. As he says at one point, "actuality seems to be motion most of all" (1047a32). His discussion points out various aspects of the process of realization, the potency in the agent, the potency in what is acted upon, the difference between rational and nonrational agents, the difference between potentiality and actuality, the difference between natural and nonnatural potencies. Through all of this, potentiality remains a capacity for one thing to affect another thing or one part of a thing to affect another part. Potentialities of this sort presuppose a numerical plurality. Likewise, the motion that is realized must also involve a plurality. As we saw, a single formula applies to the actuality and to various types of potencies. In the discussion of Z–H we also saw that *ousia* must be both one in number and one in formula. Hence, the potentialities' unity in formula is insufficient to characterize *ousia*. Consequently, the conclusion of Θ 1–5 is just the remark that Aristotle makes near the beginning, that these types of potentiality are not very important for what is sought (1045b36–1046a1). Discussion of them merely prepares the way for a treatment of another potentiality, one that is what is sought (6, 1048a27–30). That is, the discussion of potentialities for motion shows that they do not pertain to *ousia*. It plays roughly the role of the examinations of unsuccessful candidates for *ousia* in book Z: in seeing why potentialities for motion fail to be primary in this schema of beings, we see what makes the other potentiality prior and ultimately what actuality requires in order for it to be primary being. It requires not only unity in formula but also numeric unity.

3.2 Θ 6–9: ACTUALITY

In Θ 6 Aristotle turns to actuality, the second term in the actuality/potentiality schema. Although it also appears in the preceding treatment of potentialities for motion, he now defines it without motion. Ironically, though, this definition consists of an analogy with the actuality that is motion, that is, the actuality that we saw earlier in Θ.

> Just as someone who is building is to someone who can build, as waking is to sleeping, as someone seeing is to someone with closed eyes, as that which has been shaped from matter is to the matter, and that which has been completely fashioned to what can be fashioned—let actuality be marked off by one part of this difference and the potential by the other. . . . Some [things are called actualities] as motion is in respect to potentiality; and others are [so-called] as *ousia* is to some matter (1048a37–b9).

Building and being awake are motions whose potentialities Aristotle discussed in Θ 1–5. His interest here lies in the other three actualities. Among them is the actuality that book H identifies with form.

Since Aristotle defines actuality through this analogy with motion, and since it and the potentiality for it differ from motion and the potentiality for motion, the analogy calls for a distinction between motion and actuality. This Aristotle provides in 1048b18–35, a corrupt passage that is absent from the best manuscripts. Most editors nevertheless include it here and H. Bonitz's emendations are widely accepted. According to this text, motions are incomplete because the thing in motion lacks the end of the motion. In contrast, an actuality is complete; its end belongs to it. As an illustration and a verbal test, Aristotle notes that for an actuality, the act and its end are the same: to think and to have thought, to live well and to have lived well, to see and to have seen. Unlike motions, actualities are timeless in the sense that their definitions need not include time.[9]

For the present discussion, what is especially interesting about this description of actuality is that it shows why each actuality is one. Potentialities for motion are described in pairs, and they all involve an agent that acts on something else. The potential to act and the potential to be acted upon are one in formula but many in number, as we saw. Consequently, the end of the motion is something distinct from the motion, for it lies in something other than the thing that does the moving. In contrast, an actuality is complete: since an actuality is identical with its end, nothing need lie outside of it. Because seeing and having seen occur together (1048b33–34), there is never a point in seeing when its end has not been attained. Though a motion has a plurality of parts—a beginning, middle, and an end—an actuality has no such parts. Thus, a motion is inherently many; an actuality is one or, at least, more one than a motion.

Whereas Θ 6 explains the nature of actuality, Θ 7 returns to potentiality, not the potentialities discussed in Θ 1–5, but potentialities that are matter for the actualities examined in Θ 6. The question here is, when does something exist potentially and when not? (1048b37; 1049b2–3). Aristotle's answer is that the potential is that which would become actual either through the choice of an agent (in the case of artifacts) or through itself (in the case of natures) if nothing else interferes (1048a5–16). Such a potential is the matter for generation, and Aristotle insists that it be the last matter before the form. It might seem that this stipulation is unnecessary, for both the first and the last matter can come to be a thing; for example, both earth and bronze can become a statue. However, matter other than the last requires additional principles of change: the earth must become bronze before it becomes a statue (1049a16–17; a21–22). Only what can become the thing with a single principle of change, that is, only the last matter, is properly or simply a potentiality.

Simple potentiality here resembles proper matter in H 4–5. It is first conceived as the matter for generation. But, as in H 6, the matter that seems to be Aristotle's primary concern is the matter that receives the form, the material substrate of the composite. Through the first half of Θ 7 (1049a1–18) Aristotle speaks of the matter for generation and of the efficient cause of this coming to be. Here his examples of matter include the seed, the potentially healthy person, and the matter that becomes a house. In the second half of the chapter, Aristotle's matter is the material substrate of the composite (1049a18–b2, esp. a27–30). The transition is not marked in the text, and it is disturbing here because a main point in the second half of the chapter seems to be the persistence of matter in the composite. Aristotle points out that a composite is called by its last matter; but, used in this way, the name of the matter takes on a suffix. A casket is not called wood but wooden, and wood is not earth but earthen (1049a19–27; cf. Z 7, 1033a5–23). This use of the matter to refer to the composite marks the persistence of matter in the composite. As a part of the composite, the wood takes on a new form, but it preserves, to some extent, its character in the composite. For this reason we speak of the composite not as wood but as wooden.

There is no difficulty in applying these remarks to artifacts. As I said earlier, the matter for generation of an artifact persists unchanged in the artifact as its material substrate. This continuing duality of form and matter in artifacts is, I proposed, the reason that they are not properly *ousiai*. How can Aristotle's remarks on matter apply to natures? We call a casket wooden, but we do not call a man by his matter for generation, the seed or the menstrual fluid, except perhaps as an insult. Do these matters for generation persist in the composite? I raised this issue earlier (2.11.4), and I suggested that they must in some sense; but whatever sort of persistence this is, it is not reflected by our calling human beings with these terms. There are, though, passages where Aristotle speaks of being fleshy or brainy (*H. A.* I 11, 493a1). Thus, the linguistic test for the presence of matter that Aristotle proposes in Θ 7 applies to the material substrate but not to the matter for generation. However, the material substrate of a nature, its organs, differs from the material substrate of an artifact in that the organs cannot exist apart from the composite (cf. Z 10, 1035b23-25). The form and matter of a nature are more closely connected than the form and matter of an artifact, but Θ 7 does not pursue this line of thought.

Although Aristotle does distinguish artifacts from natures (by their efficient causes) (1049a11-14), he does not apply this distinction to his assertions about the material substrate. Most of his examples in this portion of the chapter are artifacts. Is he misled by his examples? We could accuse Aristotle of error if he identified the matter for generation and the matter in the composite, but he neither asserts nor supposes their identity in Θ 7. The issue is when does something exists potentially (1048b37; 1049b2-3), and Aristotle supplies two distinct types of answers. Both insist that something exists potentially when it is the last matter before the actuality, either the last matter that comes to be the thing (1049a13-18) or the ultimate matter of which the this is predicated (a34-36). The former is what H 4-5 call the proper and proximate matter, and the latter is called ultimate matter also in H 6 (1045b18).

As part of his discussion of substrate, Aristotle compares the substrate of which the form is said with the substrate of which the accidents are predicated (1049a27-34). The former is the prime matter; the latter seems to be the composite. This matter of which the this is said and the attributes which are said of the composite are both indeterminate and receive their determination from the this (1049b1-2). Since Aristotle mentions the material and composite substrates here, we expect him to mention the third substrate, formal substrate (Z 3, 1029a1-5). He does speak of the this which is said of matter, the form; he just does not call form a substrate here. It is easy to see why. As I said, the problem in this chapter is to explain when something is in potentiality. The material substrate is potentially the form it acquires, and the composite has a potency for accidental attributes, but the formal substrate has no potentiality: the attributes which belong to form are necessary and eternal. So formal substrate is not directly relevant to this issue, except as what causes matter to be actualized.

This discussion of potentiality in a composite contrasts sharply with the treatment of potentiality in Θ 1-5. Instead of emphasizing that there are a plurality of potentialities, Θ 7 treats the potentiality within a single composite. Without mentioning the unity of the last matter and the form, it shows the close affinity between a form and the potency for it. Barring external impediments, a potency for generation will be realized. When it is, the matter of the composite, indeterminate in itself, will be determined in accordance with the form or the this. Since the matter of the composite is not a this (a27-29; a34-36), it does not make the composite into a plurality. The this or form through which the potentiality is defined is actuality; it is an actuality that is not a motion.

The rest of the discussion of actuality in Θ 8–9 characterizes the priority of actuality to potency. In a passage reminiscent of Z 1 (1028a32–33), Aristotle claims that "actuality is prior to all such potencies both in formula and in *ousia;* and it is prior in time in one way, and not in another way" (1049b10–12). The entire chapter consists of arguments for these types of priority. These arguments make few overt references to unity. But, like those of Z, some of the arguments rely on the idea that to show priority is to show unity. The argument for priority in formula (1049b12–17), for example, resembles what we saw in Z (1, 1028a34–36). Aristotle argues that actuality is prior in formula because a (primary) potency is defined in terms of the act it is a potency for: the potency possessed by a builder is the potential to build. In other words, actuality is prior in formula because it is a part of any definition of a potentiality: it is prior because it is more one. Although Aristotle does not refer to the unity of the formula of an actuality, his argument presupposes that the part is more one than the whole.

Actuality is prior in time in the sense that whenever a potentiality comes to be actual, there must have existed previously some other actuality that is one in species with the actuality that comes to be. The actuality that is prior is not one in number with the actuality that comes to be (1049b18–19). An individual man, grain, or act of seeing comes to be an actuality from previously existing potentialities, matter, seed, and the capacity to see (1049b19–23). But these latter, in turn, are generated from preexisting actualities (1049b23–26).[10] Hence, actuality is prior in time.

This argument scarcely seems valid. The issue here is a well-worn conundrum: which came first, the chicken or the egg? Aristotle answers, the chicken because without a chicken there can be no egg. The obvious rejoinder is that without an egg there can be no chicken. Could Aristotle be making such a simple-minded mistake? Could he not make an equally good case for the temporal priority of potentiality? Indeed, in Z 7 and 8, a text to which the present discussion refers (1049b27–29), Aristotle argues that *both* the form and the matter must exist prior to the composite's coming to be. Can this conclusion possibly be consistent with the position he takes here? Z 7–8 speak of a different sort of matter. There matter includes all material substrata, and Aristotle preserves the unity of form by excluding this matter from it. The matter under consideration here is the last matter of generation, the matter that comes to receive form. In Θ 7 Aristotle proposes, as an example of this matter, the seed, but he insists that it is not any seed that is a potentiality, but only one that is in another and changes (1049a14–16). That is to say, the seed becomes a potentiality only through the action of agents, the parents. Thus, before any potentiality can come to be actual, the potentiality must itself come to be, and this latter process requires a preexistent actuality. If we think of the problem of the chicken and the egg solely in temporal terms, neither seems to be prior. But in calling the chicken temporally prior,

Aristotle need not suppose that there was a time when there were only chickens and no eggs. It seems to me that Aristotle's argument for the temporal priority of the chicken depends on identifying a step that is the logical beginning of the process. The process of becoming begins with the agency of the actuality, for this agency is what makes something into a potentiality. This logical beginning is also its temporal beginning. Hence, actuality is temporally prior to potentiality.

Actuality is also prior to potentiality in *ousia,* and much of Θ 8 explains why (1050a4–1051a2). Aristotle argues that since actuality is posterior in the generation of an individual, and since what is posterior in generation is prior in form and *ousia,* actuality is prior in *ousia* (1050a4–7). Because the potential becomes actual when it acquires the form, the form or actuality is posterior in generation and prior in *ousia.* He also argues that since all motion proceeds toward an end, and since actuality is that end, potentiality is also for the end (1050a7–14). Again, it follows that actuality is prior in *ousia.*

While illustrating the principle that motion proceeds toward an end (a10–14), Aristotle mentions an unexpected example; he claims that the art of housebuilding is for the sake of housebuilding (a11–12). Housebuilding is usually an example of a motion rather than an actuality. Here, though, it is an actuality in contrast with the art of housebuilding. The claim that motion is an actuality is not unusual. The *Physics* defines motion as a kind of actuality (Γ 2, 202a7–8). Further, earlier in book Θ Aristotle defines actuality through an analogy with motion (6, 1048a37–b9, quoted above). As we saw, the latter passage goes on to distinguish actuality and motion.

This same vacillation on the status of motion is apparent in another argument that actuality is prior in *ousia* (1050a15–b4). Aristotle begins with the claim, "Matter is potentially because it might go into the form; and when it is in actuality, it is in the form" (a15–16). The same always holds, he maintains, even when the end is a motion (a16–17). Why mention motion here? As usual, Aristotle does not explain his strategy, and the sequence of the argument is not obvious. It seems to me that motion serves here as a handy illustration. When its form is motion, it is clear that when the matter "goes into the form," when, that is, the matter comes to be in motion, the motion is in the matter. The act of building, for example, is in the things that are being built, and "in general, motion is in what is moved" (a28–29; a31–34). By analogy, an actuality is in the agent (a35–b2). That is, when a matter is in act, then the actuality is present in the matter. This actuality is the form of the matter; and, because it makes the matter what it is, the actuality is the *ousia* (b2–3). Consequently, actuality is prior in *ousia* to the potentiality (b3–4). Actuality is prior to potentiality in *ousia* just because it is the *ousia* of the potentiality.

Although the foregoing argument uses motion to make a point about actuality, it also distinguishes motion from actuality. A motion produces some other thing apart from the motion; the result of housebuilding is the house. In contrast, an actuality like seeing, thinking, or living produces nothing apart from itself: it is identical with its function (1050a34–b2). Even though the motion is more obviously present in the matter, the actuality is more *properly* present in it. For the *ousia* of the matter is its actuality, not its motion.

Although Aristotle does not mention unity here, actualities are unities in a way that motions are not: motions presuppose a distinction between the activity and the product, but an actuality is its own product. Since *ousiai* are each one, they cannot be motions. So construed, this discussion, like the preceding chapters of book Θ, parallels the remarks in Z–H that remove reasons for thinking that *ousia* is a plurality. Here Aristotle avoids plurality in *ousia* by restricting it to actuality in contrast with motion. Moreover, because the product of a motion is its end, actualities are also distinguished from motions by having their ends within themselves. Or to put this point in terms more pertinent to Aristotelian science, the formal and final cause of an actuality are the same.[11] Again, actualities are more one than motions and things in motion.

The assumption here that actualities are forms which are present in matter reflects the results of Z–H, particularly the last chapter of H. Though H 6 uses the unity of the composite to identify form as actuality, it presupposes that form by itself is one, as we saw. In Θ 8 Aristotle concentrates on the form itself. If my analysis is correct, Aristotle shows, in at least one argument, that actuality is more one than potentiality in order to show that it is prior to it. Since actuality is more one because it is form, Θ 8 not only draws on Z–H, it also extends the latter's characterization of form and essence.

As I said, there is no explicit reference to unity in this discussion, but once we suppose that Aristotle's aim here is to show the unity of *ousia*, his treatment of eternal actualities (1050b4–28) makes sense. Since potentialities are always potentialities for two contraries, what is eternal has no potentiality (b6–8). Lacking potentiality, they are pure actualities. They are thus more one than those actualities which exist in matter. Since unity is a criterion of *ousia*, these pure actualities are more *ousia* than actualities that exist in matter. Accordingly, they are prior in *ousia*. If actualities are prior in *ousia* because they are *ousiai*, then pure actualities are still more prior because they are even more properly *ousiai*. Even though there is no mention of unity here, the priority of actuality to potentiality and the priority of pure actuality to actualities that are in matter reflect their greater unity.

The argument in Θ 9 that actuality is better and more honorable than the good potency also seems to point implicitly to the unity of actuality. It runs as follows: A potency is always potentially both contraries (1051a5–6). So the potential for good is always also a potential for bad. Since two contraries cannot belong together, contrary actualities cannot belong together. But the potencies for both contraries can be present together (1051a10–12). One of the contraries is good,[12] and the potential for it is both good and bad or neither (a13–15). The good actuality is then better than this potentiality, and this potentiality is, in turn, better than the bad actuality (a15–16). From this Aristotle infers that the bad does not exist apart from things and that nothing that is eternal is bad (a17–21).

Stated more simply, the first part of the argument is that a potentiality for good is also a potentiality for bad, and insofar as it is a mixture of both, it is less good than that which it is a potential for. This argument seems unnecessarily long-winded. If we already know that a particular actuality is good, as Aristotle assumes we do, then it is obvious that what is only potentially this actuality, what is not yet this actuality, is less good than it. Why, then, does Aristotle bother to describe potentiality in terms of the contraries? He uses this description to infer that the bad actuality is less good than the potentiality. If the potentiality is some sort of mixture of good and bad, as Aristotle seems to think, it is better than what is simply bad.

From the latter point Aristotle somehow infers that the bad does not exist apart from things. How does the final conclusion follow? The reason that bad lies in things is not that it fails to be an actuality. For the text under consideration speaks of two contrary actualities (1051a11–13), doubtless good and bad actualities; also, Aristotle argues that the actually bad is worse than the potentially bad. The reason that bad does not exist apart is that it is posterior. As posterior to the good and to the potential, the bad depends upon them. To be apart from them the bad would have to be independent. However, this idea, that the bad depends on the potential, seems to be at odds with the result of Θ 8 that the actual is prior to the potential; for, as I just said, the bad is an actuality.[13] An example of good and bad actualities are wine and vinegar, and the potentiality for both is water (H 5, 1044b31–1045a6). According to Θ 8, the actualities wine and vinegar are prior to water; according to the argument of Θ 9, the wine is prior to the water, and water and wine are prior to vinegar. In H 5 Aristotle claimed that water is matter for each in different ways. It is the matter for the wine in respect of form and the matter for the water in respect of privation (1044b31–34). Wine and vinegar are both prior to water as actualities. If, though, the vinegar is a privation, it is posterior to the water which is closer to the form of wine. In short, the claims that actuality is prior to potentiality and that the bad actuality depends on the potential for bad are not necessarily inconsistent. We need simply to distinguish the different ways that actualities and potentialities are prior.

So construed, the argument of Θ 9 is intelligible and pertinent both to the study of actuality and to the treatment of the unmoved movers in book Λ. There is no need to bring in considerations about unity. Yet, when we reflect on the argument, we can easily view it in terms of unity. As a sort of mixture of the contrary actualities, a potentiality is a kind of plurality. Its constituents are the good and the bad actualities. They should both be prior to potentiality because the latter is composed of them. However, we can see that there is a hierarchy of goods: the good actuality, the potentiality, and the bad actuality. Since the last of these depends on the others, it is less one than they are. It cannot be apart from them. So it cannot be in things that are truly one; namely, what is eternal. (It is a kind of privation, like vinegar.) On the contrary, the good actuality is "better and more noble" than the potentiality: it is more one. Even though there is no explicit reference to unity in this argument, the argument serves to remove a reason for doubting the unity of actuality. It is only the good actuality that is better than potentiality. Actuality is one, provided we limit the scope of actuality to the good actualities. Indeed, this is what we find Aristotle doing in book Λ.[14] It is the good actuality that is the pure actuality of Θ 8.

In sum, unity and the problems associated with it play no explicit role in book Θ's treatment of potentiality and actuality. Aristotle shows that many potentialities, those that are potentialities for motion, involve pluralities. But he does not follow this up by explicitly emphasizing the unity inherent in actualities. Nevertheless, as we have seen, the text is easily interpreted as removing reasons to doubt the unity of actuality. The particular points that Aristotle includes in his treatment of actuality make more sense if he intends to show that actuality, in contrast with potentiality, is one. Perhaps the reason that Aristotle does not make this motivation clear is that he has already used unity arguments in books Z–H to show that form is actuality. The assumption that *ousia* is one, an assumption that is central to Z–H, is justified and refined by the analysis of actuality in book Θ. This analysis shows that an actuality should be one and that an eternal actuality is even more one than an actuality that is present in matter. Not all actualities are one, though. Motions are actualities, as are attributes of an *ousia*. The actualities that are one are just those that are forms and *ousiai*. The primary instance of categorial being is also the primary instance of the actuality/potentiality schema.

3.3 E 4, Θ 10: TRUTH

After the treatment of accidental being (E 2–3), categorial being (Z–H), and actuality (Θ 1–9), all that remains to complete the discussion of the ways of being is a treatment of the true and the false. A brief discussion of them appears in E 4, but Aristotle takes them up again at greater length in Θ 10.[15]

As the opening lines of E 4 make clear, what is true is, and what is false is not (1027b18–19; Δ 7, 1017a31–32). They both involve combination and division, Aristotle claims (b19); and his description of how clearly invokes unity.

Truth is an affirmation in regard to what is combined and a denial in regard to what is separated, and falsity is the opposite of this partition.

> How it is possible to think the "together" and the "apart" is a different discourse. I mean [to think] the "together" and the "apart" not successively but so that [the thoughts] become one (1027b20–25).

The problem is how two thoughts can be made one by being brought together and, what is even more puzzling, how they can be made one by being kept separate. This is not a problem that Aristotle addresses here. It belongs not to metaphysics but to another discourse, and the reason is, apparently, that truth and falsity lie not in things but in thought (b25–27). A thought is true if it unites what is united in the thing or if it separates what is separated in the thing. Apparently, truth is a correspondence of unity or plurality in thought with unity or plurality in things.

E 4 dismisses this sort of being as a proper object of metaphysics. Because the combination and the division are in thought rather than in things, Aristotle declares that this sort of being differs from the being which is primary (1027b29–31). The cause of truth is an attribute of thought that concerns the "remaining genus of being but does not make clear whether there is some nature of being beyond" (1027b33–1028a3). In other words, truth does not really introduce a new type of being; it concerns the combination and separation of thoughts about the other beings.

On the other hand, E 4 also postpones the consideration of being and non-being in the sense of truth and falsity (1027b28–29); and Aristotle's reason, though less clear here, is apparently the same as the reason he dismisses this consideration; namely, that truth is not in things (1027b25–28). How can Aristotle dismiss *and* postpone the treatment of truth, and do both for the same reason? Are not these two texts contradictory?[16] Not necessarily. Aristotle dismisses only the truth that is an attribute of thought. If there is another kind of truth, or even another aspect of truth, it should be investigated further. Immediately before announcing the need to investigate truth later, Aristotle does speak of a truth that is not in thought, that of the simples and the essences (τὰ τί ἐστιν) (1027b27–28). So when he says in the next sentence that "this way of being" (τὸ οὕτως ὄν) needs further investigation, he apparently means, not truth in general or truth in thought, but truth in the way that simples are true.[17] As long as there are two sorts of truth, rather than two views of truth, there need be no inconsistency in both dismissing and postponing truth. Truth in thought is not a proper subject for metaphysics; the other truth is, but its investigation is postponed.

What exactly is this other truth? As I said, E 4 suggests that it belongs to simples. Θ 10 does, in fact, treat the simples, and their truth lies not in thought (διάνοια) but in the intellect (νοεῖν—1052a1). So the truth that is postponed could be the truth of the simples. But Θ 10 does not treat only this type of truth; and there is another, better explanation of which truth is postponed. Although Aristotle is almost always cited as an exponent of a correspondence theory of truth, there are texts where he speaks of another type of truth, a truth that is not in thought but in things.[18] I propose that this objective truth is the subject of Θ 10 and that it is what Aristotle postpones in E 4. Is there any evidence for objective truth in Θ 10? We need to examine the chapter carefully.

Θ 10 begins with the paradoxical claim that being and non-being are said in one way as the categories, in another way as actuality and potentiality and in a third way, τὸ κυριώτατα ὂν ἀληθὲς ἢ ψεῦδος (1051a34–b2). The most natural translation would be, "and [in a third way] the most primary being is [said as] truth or falsity." How could truth possibly be the most primary being? We have just seen that E 4 specifically denies that it is the most primary: because truth is in thought and not things, it is a "being other than primary being" (1027a29–31).[19] But E 4 also dismisses truth in thought. If, as I propose, there is a different sort of truth, such as a truth in things, Aristotle might not be inconsistent in calling it the "most primary being." It is this other sort of truth which is, I suggest, the subject of Θ 10. The opening sentence does not mean that truth is more primary than the other ways of being, categorial being and actuality, but that the truth under discussion here is more primary than the truth that E 4 dismissed, truth in thought.

Some support for my interpretation lies in Aristotle's assertion, immediately after calling truth the most proper being:

> This [most proper being] is, for things, being united or being separated (1051b2–3).[20]

This truth is not most properly an attribute of thought but something that belongs to things. Aristotle does go on to describe truth in terms similar to what we saw in E 4, as a correspondence of unity or separation (plurality) between belief and thing (1051b3–5), but here he emphasizes the causal role of the thing:

> You are not white because we believe truly that you are white, but it is because you are white that we who say this speak truly (1051b6–9).

Truth in thought is caused by things.

Θ 10 does not ascribe truth to things in quite the terms that Aristotle could have used nor, for my interpretation, should have used. But it does what amounts to the same thing: it ascribes being, the being that signifies truth, to things. He must have this type of being in mind when he says,

> To be is to be combined and to be one, and not to be is not to be combined but to be many (1051a11–13).

Being here belongs to things that are combined, things that are one. Is it possible that this being might not be truth? Could it be another type of being, such as, actuality or categorial being? Accidental composites are also combined into a unity; in Z–H Aristotle treats their unity as a categorial being. Might he mean this type of being here? No. The unity of an accidental composite, treated in Z 4, allows accidental composites, like white man, to have definitions and essences of a sort. These composites are peculiar natures that lack the unity requisite to be *ousiai* and yet have sufficient unity to be treated sometimes like an *ousia*. Knowing the quasi-essence of such a nature tells us nearly nothing about the particular composite before us. In contrast, the unity Aristotle ascribes to things in Θ 10 consists of the conjunction of particular individuals. If the "is" signifies categorial being, to say "the white man is" or "the man is white" is to say that the composite white man has an essence. If being is truth, the same assertions mean that white and man are actually combined in some particular composite. Categorial being belongs to an essence; truth belongs to particulars. Further, it is possible to say, "the man is not white" if "is" is truth. We cannot make this claim with the categorial "is" unless we have in mind primary and secondary being, a distinction quite different from true/false.

If this is correct, being as true is the being that belongs to individuals. Later philosophers called it "existence." Because Aristotelian science is of the universal, this type of being does not admit of knowledge. Aristotle does little more than describe it. Moreover, since Aristotle applies being as truth to particulars that are always combined and not-being as falsity to particulars that are never combined, it is easy to miss the distinction between categorial being and being as truth; for what is always combined is always true, and what is never combined is not only false but without an essence. What is never combined lacks both types of being. Elsewhere, Aristotle declares that the "false as a thing" is something that cannot be put together and thus is not (Δ 29, 1024b17–21). Hence, truth and falsity, as ways of being, belong not merely to thoughts but to things, to particular things.

To claim that Aristotle espouses an objective truth is so contrary to received opinion that it is worth citing another passage where he also asserts this view. In α 1 Aristotle says:

> So that what is more true is always the cause of truth in what is posterior. Therefore, the principles of eternal beings must be always the most true, for they are not sometimes true, nor is there some cause of being for these, but they are the cause for the others. So that as each stands in respect of being, so it stands also in respect of truth (993b26–31).[21]

There is no question that the principles of what is eternal, the principles that this text declares to be most true, are not mere thoughts. They are things. So the passage claims that the eternal things are (or should be) most true. They are most true because they cause truth in others. By the same reasoning, the things that are combined are more true because they cause truth in beliefs. But this seems patently false, for separation in things can also cause truth in belief. If, for example, Socrates is not white, and if I believe this of him, my belief is true. According to the quoted passage, "what is more true is the cause of truth"; since the separation of the things causes my belief to be true, things that are separated should be more true, contradicting the previous conclusion. So the claim made in α 1 does not seem to apply here. However, the difficulty is an instance of the problem of non-being: how can we think true thoughts about what is not? Aristotle's answer is that non-being depends upon or is related to *ousia* (Γ 2, 1003b5–10; Z 4, 1030a25–27). Applied to the issue at hand, this claim means that there would not be a separation of things unless they were each one or unless at least one were one. So even true claims about what is separated presuppose some truth in things, truth (or unity) in the individuals that are separated. Later, I shall argue that truth in thought depends on truth in *ousia*. With this we can see that, though it needs refinement, the claim of α 1 that the cause of truth is more true holds even for truths in thought.[22]

There is no need for me to dwell further on the question of whether Aristotle recognizes an objective truth. For my purposes here, it suffices to accept that things somehow cause truth in thought and that Aristotle characterizes this causal relation through unity. Both points are clear.

Aristotle's treatment of truth in Θ 10 contains two parts. First, he examines truth in regard to composites (1051b9–17) and then truth in respect of incomposites (1051b17–33). He begins the former by distinguishing things that are always combined, things that are always separated, and still other things that can be both (1051b9–11). The text continues with the passage, quoted earlier, that to be is to be combined into a unity and not to be is to be many (1051a11–13). From these claims Aristotle infers:

In regard to those things that can be both, the same belief or the same statement becomes true and false. In regard to what cannot be otherwise, [beliefs and statements] do not become sometimes true and sometimes false, but the same are always true or always false (1051b15–17).

This inference does not follow immediately from what precedes it. What does follow immediately is that some things always are, others cannot be, and still others may or may not be. The inference just quoted concerns statements and beliefs about these three classes of things. A belief or statement can become false if the thing that it is about alters. So beliefs or statements about things that sometimes are and sometimes are not are sometimes true and sometimes false, but statements and beliefs about what always is or always is not never change their truth value.[23] Consequently, the truth or being of the statement and the belief depend on the truth or being of the thing. The latter truth and being are unity; the former are sameness. So, as I said, a true statement need not be about a true thing; a statement is true if its unity or plurality is the same as that of the thing.

By this point the claim that to be is to be combined into a unity should be familiar. As I mentioned, we saw something similar in the treatment of categorial being; for example, in Z 17 and H 2. There, though, Aristotle's concern is the character of the combination; he argues that form is the cause of unity and the nature of the composite. Θ 10 does not use unity to consider the nature of the composite; it scarcely considers the nature of the composite. Rather, Aristotle's concern here is only the fact of combination, whether or not the elements are combined, for on this depends the being of the composite and the truth of statements and beliefs about it. He mentions two examples of composites: (1) "the white wood" and (2) "the incommensurable" with "the diagonal" (1051b20–21).[24] The combination of the first pair is merely possible; the combination of the second pair is either necessary or impossible, depending upon the relative lengths of the sides. The unity possessed by these elements, if they are combined, is only the unity of their conjunction, a numeric unity. There is no suggestion here that white and wood share a nature or essence, nor that incommensurable and diagonal are a single nature. The composite has being when its elements are conjoined, and assertions about it are the case when the unity or plurality they ascribe to it is one and the same as the unity or plurality in the thing. Thus, being in the sense of true belongs to composites and to statements by virtue of their unity.

The discussion of incomposites which occupies the rest of Θ 10 begins by pointing to the difference between composites and incomposites (1051b17–23). Obviously, Aristotle cannot explain the latter in terms of combination and separation, for incomposites have no parts. Instead, he defines truth in respect of the incomposites in terms of contact: "contact [τὸ θιγεῖν] and assertion are truth . . . and to be ignorant is not to have contact" (1051b23–35). Or, as he puts it later in the chapter, "truth is to grasp these things with the intellect [τὸ νοεῖν], and there is neither falsity nor error, but ignorance" (1052a1–2). We can only be in error about the incomposites accidentally (1051b25–28).[25]

Aristotle's point is that we cannot be mistaken about things that are incomposite. We can fail to grasp an incomposite, but if we do grasp it, there is no room to be mistaken. The faculty by which we grasp the truth in incomposites is the intellect (nous). Although Aristotle does not characterize this faculty, it seems to differ from the faculty by which we grasp truth in composites, thought (dianoia) (see E 4, 1027b25–28). Thought can be mistaken; the intellect cannot be.[26]

According to this account, the truth pertinent to incomposites lies in their character. It is because they are one that the mere grasp of them constitutes having the truth about them. Without parts, they cannot be known partially. They must be grasped with a single act of the intellect, not by composition or division. Moreover, because the incomposites are one, they cannot change and thus falsify our grasp of them. Aristotle describes them as actualities that neither become nor perish (1051b28–30). As we saw in the discussion of Z 7–8, something that is one cannot be in the process of coming to be or the process of ceasing to be. It either is or is not, all at once.

A question often raised about Θ 10 is, what does Aristotle include among incomposites? The usual answer is that they are the eternal actualities of Θ 8.[27] A motive for this view is that other actualities seem to admit of partial knowledge; for example, we can know the genus of a particular animal without knowing its species. But this is inadequate, for knowing that a thing falls under a genus does not amount to partial knowledge of a form or species but knowledge of how to apply a species to individuals. The one aspect of our knowledge of incomposites that Aristotle admits can be partial is the knowledge of how to apply them, but such knowledge is accidental and causes accidental errors, as we saw. Besides, we need to know what the form is before we can decide whether something is an instance of it. But, it may still be objected, can we not know a genus, without knowing any of its species? This would be partial knowledge. It would also be merely potential knowledge; a different sort of knowledge from actual knowledge of actual things (M 10, 1087a15–18). Further, Aristotle maintains that our knowledge begins from particulars and proceeds to what is more universal (*An. Po.* B 19, 100a15–b3). So we know the species and the form before the more universal genus. Again, knowledge of the genus is not partial knowledge of a species; it is posterior to knowledge of a species.

The preceding discussion undermines the motive for identifying the incomposites as the eternal actualities. These incomposites should be the forms or essences of any *ousiai*. For in Θ 10 Aristotle describes incomposites in the same terms he uses to describe sensible *ousiai* in Z–H. Thinking about the incomposites, he denies here that there is error about the "what it is" (1051b25–26), and he calls the incomposite "a being [ὅπερ εἶναι τι] and an actuality" (1051b30–31). The text of Θ 10 justifies neither of these claims explicitly, but if my analysis of Z–Θ 9 is correct, it is easy to see how Aristotle arrives at them. We have seen a lengthy argument that, despite appearances, essence or form is one. Essence is thus an incomposite. From the end of book H and from book Θ, we know that this essence is an actuality. While a non-*ousia* has an essence or a "what it is" in a way, it is *ousiai* that properly have essences. Thus, it is *ousiai* that are properly incomposites, all *ousiai* including the sensible *ousiai*. As we have seen, what is one need not be eternal; it must come to be or cease to be without being in the process of coming to be or ceasing to be (cf. H 3, 1043b14–16), a condition met by all *ousiai*.

After the elaborate efforts to come to know *ousiai* that constitute the central books, Aristotle declares that knowledge of *ousiai* requires only grasping an incomposite with an act of the intellect. He is not talking about an *a priori* intuition; still less is he speaking about an empirical procedure. The modern dichotomy between *a priori* and empirical knowledge does not exhaust the alternatives. Rather, recalling the mode of argumentation in Z–H, we can see that someone acquires knowledge of *ousia* by excluding alternative interpretations. Moreover, the discussion of *ousia* in these books shows it to be one and thus, given Θ 10, to be something that is grasped by the intellect.

Apparent pluralities such as the genus and differentia of a species have been avoided by the careful characterization of what *ousia* must be if it is to be one. Since a genus and its differentia are not many but one (the ultimate differentia), they can be grasped by a single act of the intellect. Attributes and composites are pluralities and, thus, known differently.

If, though, sensible *ousiai* qualify as incomposites, the pure actualities mentioned in Θ 8 should qualify also. Although Aristotle does not say so here, it is clear that they are more properly incomposite than sensible *ousiai*. Without matter, they are more one.[28] In sum, the answer to the question of what Aristotle understands to be the incomposites is that they are just the essences or actualities that he has been considering throughout Z–H–Θ.

This conclusion has interesting and important consequences. Earlier in this section, I distinguished the categorial being possessed by composites from their being as truth. It should be clear that we cannot make a corresponding distinction for incomposites. For the latter, their essence or *ousia* is their existence as particulars, their truth. Each exists simply by being what it is, an essence. That even a sensible *ousia* exists as a particular by virtue of its nature is scarcely consistent with medieval treatments of essence and existence, especially that of Thomas Aquinas. Insofar as Aristotle has any concept of what later came to be called existence, it is his being as truth. His identification of this and essence does not undermine the primacy of the unmoved mover, for sensible essences still depend on it. What the identification does is to avoid the need for a creator god. I shall have more to say about the identification of these two types of being in the next chapter.

The final lines of Θ 10 explain when an incomposite will not be subject to error. In the process, they indicate the kind of unity possessed by an incomposite. Aristotle begins by claiming that if the triangle is unchanging, it cannot acquire an attribute at one time and lose it at another (1052a4–7). However, we could be mistaken about whether an attribute belongs to it because the attribute might belong to some triangles but not to all triangles;

we might, for example, mistakenly suppose that the attribute of being prime belongs to no even number (1058a8-9). But there is a circumstance where we need not worry about error:

> This [type of error] would not happen to things that are one in number.[29]
> For such things will not be supposed to be and not to be something,
> but will be true or false because they always stand in the same way
> (1052a8-11).

That is, we could be mistaken about what is merely one in species because something might be true of some individuals but not true of others; but we cannot make the same sort of mistake about what is one in number. Incomposites must be both one in formula and one in number.

This result fits perfectly with the results of books Z-H. As we saw, in his discussion of categorial being, Aristotle maintains that *ousia* is both one in number and one in species. Now it turns out that incomposites have the same sort of unity—further support for my earlier identification of the incomposites as *ousiai*.

Let us not, though, be hasty. According to the usual view, the final lines of book Θ do not discuss form and essence but individual instances of a species: the way to avoid error is not to ascribe attributes to classes but to individuals.[30] This interpretation makes no sense at all. It is as if someone were to suggest that we could avoid error by speaking of Socrates instead of human being because some attributes may belong to some instances of the human being but not to others. Can we not be just as mistaken about whether those same attributes belong to Socrates? Even worse, this is inconsistent with Aristotle's view that the individual composite is unknowable (Z 15, 1039b27-30). Aristotle surely does not wish to say that attributes that belong to Socrates or any other composite individual belong to it "in this way always." Indeed, it is absurd to say that Socrates is an incomposite: throughout the central books, Aristotle uses Socrates and other instances of species as examples of composites. Socrates is not a primary *ousia* because he consists of form and matter. Although he is one in number and one in species, he is not an incomposite at all. So if Aristotle's position is at all cogent, he must intend to ascribe a different sort of numeric and specific unity to incomposites.

It might be suggested instead that in this passage the incomposites are the ultimate species. They are obviously one in species; they could be said to be numerically one in the sense that each can be distinguished from the others as an individual species. This looks tempting, and it seems consistent with Aristotle's concluding remarks. Since some triangles have attributes that others do not, the way to avoid error is to fasten not on triangle, but on a particular kind of triangle, the equilateral triangle, the isosceles triangle, or whatever. Then, though triangle is both scalene and equiangular, there would be no reason to think that an ultimate species like equilateral triangle is scalene and equiangular. So our grasp of an ultimate species seems incorrigible. Moreover, the problem of coming to know incomposites resembles Aristotle's concern in the final chapter of the *Posterior Analytics,* and there he discusses the way we acquire knowledge of species from individuals. Yet, however tempting it may be to think so, Aristotle cannot have the ultimate species in mind as the incomposite. A species is one in form (or formula), and the last species is most one in this way (cf. B 3, 999a2–6). However, as we saw in discussing Z 13–16, neither a species nor any other universal is one in number. If an incomposite must be one in number, it cannot be the species. Further, a universal such as a species is a potentiality (its actuality is an individual—Θ 8, 1050b34–1051a2; M 10, 1087a16–18). In contrast, the incomposite is an actuality. But is Aristotle, perhaps, mistaken in insisting on the numeric unity of the incomposite? Will not the ultimate species do as the object of an incorrigible grasp of the intellect? No. A species is a predicate; even the ultimate species depends upon something else. As we saw, what is always said of another contains an addition; it is a plurality. Of course, this is a central reason why Aristotle denies that any species is *ousia.* The species is not properly an incomposite. Its plurality is also the source of errors similar to those Aristotle mentions at the end of Θ. Because some equilateral triangles are wooden, someone might mistakenly say that equilateral triangles are wooden; for the species is a predicate.

In contrast, someone who thinks the essence of the triangle is or includes wood has simply failed to grasp the essence. He can only have in mind some other nature. Because form or essence is numerically one, it is not subject to the same type of mistakes as the universal. Because it is one in species, it is not subject to the mistakes we could make about a particular individual (such as thinking the individual is alive when she is not). Thus, insofar as essence is one in both ways, we cannot be mistaken about it. The thing that is both one in species and one in number must, then, be essence. To the extent that it is one, it has no attributes. Whatever characteristics it may seem to have, belong to its nature. To conclude, the incomposite about which we cannot be mistaken must be essence or form because essence is one in species and one in number.

This conclusion supports further my earlier arguments that the incomposites in Θ 10 are the essences or forms that Aristotle examined through most of book Z. Both essence and incomposite must be one in the same ways, one in number and one in species. We have seen that essence is *ousia,* form, and actuality. Θ 10 adds to this that the essence is an incomposite that is grasped through the intellect. Not only its results but also its method is consistent

Chapter 4

Being, One and *Ousia* in the Central Books

4.1 CONVERGENCE

Aristotle's treatment of truth in Θ 10 completes the examination of the ways "being" is said that he began in E 2. As we have seen, each of the *per se* ways of being consists of a schema of beings. The longest and the most difficult discussion concerns being as the categories, but Aristotle also treats being as actuality and potentiality and being as truth and falsity. The really significant result that emerges from the central books is the convergence of these ways of being: *ousia* or form is primary in each schema. The primary categorial being is *ousia,* and the primary *ousia* is form or essence. Likewise, Aristotle argues that actuality is prior to potentiality, and he equates actuality with form. In the schema of truth, incomposites are prior to everything that results from combinations or separations, including truth and falsity in statements and beliefs. These incomposites are forms or essences of *ousiai,* and they are objectively true. Hence, form is primary in each of the three *per se* schemata. Aristotle indicates the primacy of form in each schema by identifying it as, respectively, essence, actuality, and incomposite. These are not, of course, equal in extension; formal substrate, essence (in the narrow sense), and incomposite are restricted to the genus of *ousia;* actuality is not. But the actualities in *ousia* are clearly prior to those in other genera. Hence, the primary instances of all three schemata lie in the genus of *ousia.* The three schemata converge in the sense that their intersection includes the beings that are primary in all the schemata.

The fourth way of being, accidental being, is not treated as a schema. Since, as Aristotle argues, it cannot be known, it does not properly belong to the science of metaphysics. Nevertheless, Aristotle enjoins us in E 3 to seek the causes of accidents. His treatment of the *per se* ways of being shows that accidents depend upon the genus of *ousia* because an accident is always an accident of some *ousia.* Hence, *ousia* and, more properly, form, is a cause of *all* beings.

Most commentators treat Aristotle's claim that being is *pros hen* as an assertion about the relation of *ousia* and the other categories. It is obvious, however, that all beings must be related to *ousia* if being is to be *pros hen.* The central books show that such a relation does obtain. Not only are the other categories related to *ousia,* but also potentiality, falsity, and even accidental beings are related to *ousia,* just what Aristotle had indicated in book Γ (2, 1003b5–10; cf. E 2, 1026b21), where his list of beings obviously includes items from all the ways of being.

More importantly, the central books use the *pros hen* relation to explain the nature of being. Each schema of *per se* beings consists of *ousia* and beings that are related to it. These other beings are what they are by virtue of their relation to *ousia.* In the process of showing the primacy of *ousia* in each schema, Aristotle also shows how *ousia* causes the other beings to have the natures that they possess. In this way, the central book's inquiry into the nature of primary being is also an inquiry into how the primary being causes being in other things.[1]

The subject of inquiry and the conclusion can be stated without referring to unity, but the arguments that justify the conclusion rely on unity. The reasons that essence or actuality is primary in each *per se* schema of being are that it is more of a unity than the other beings in each schema and that it causes unity in the other beings. In the schema of categorial being, form or essence is more one than attributes and accidental and *per se* composites, all of which possess whatever unity they have by the addition and subtraction of *ousia;* and form is a cause of unity in these and in composite *ousiai.* Similarly, an actuality is indivisible or one in formula. A potentiality is a potentiality for a particular actuality, and it is defined by the formula of that actuality. So whatever unity a potentiality has, it owes to the unity of its actuality. The schema of the true/false is difficult, but we saw in the preceding chapter that truth in things lies in their unity and that falsity lies in their plurality and consequent non-being. What is most true are the incomposite essences, the *ousiai,* that we grasp by "contact," and these and entities that depend upon them serve as constituents of composite truths. Even falsity depends upon unity because plurality consists of many elements, each of which (or some of which) are one. Thus, essence is most true because it is most one, and it is the material cause of truth and falsity in other things. Since truth in beliefs and formulae is also a kind of sameness (or oneness) with the thing and falsity a kind of otherness, unity is also, indirectly, the cause of these. Thus, for each schema of being, form causes unity in the other beings in the schema. Because whatever is one also is (e.g., Γ 2, 1003b22–24; I 2, 1054a13); insofar as form causes unity, it also causes being. Accordingly, Aristotle can show that form is primary being by showing that it is more one, and he can show how it is the source of being in other beings by showing how it causes them to be one. Unity functions as a key tool of inquiry, even though it does not appear as part of the conclusion.

While recognizing this convergence of primary beings, we should also realize that the schemata of being differ in important respects. The schema of the categories divides all beings into genera, and there is a different essence and "what it is" in each of the categories (Z 4, 1030a21–25, a28–32). Actuality and potentiality cut across categorial lines: there are actualities and potentialities in all the categories (Δ 7, 1017a35–b2; Θ 10, 1051a34–b1). The incomposites known by contact with intellect are properly instances of *ousia,* and composites consist of an individual *ousia* and particular essential or inessential attributes. As we saw, the accidental beings are simply pluralities of other beings. They are accidental because they lack unity. Thus, the four ways of being amount to different ways of slicing the same pie. Though we always deal with the same things, Aristotle's account shows different ways to group these beings so as to bring out pertinent similarities. The intersection of the primary beings in each of the three *per se* schemata consists of the essences and actualities that are in the genus of *ousia.* This is what I have been arguing in this section: form is primary in all three schemata. However, it is primary in different ways in relation to the other beings in each schema. Furthermore, there are indications in the central books that these other beings as well as form depend on a principle that is still higher, the *ousia* that has no matter (H 6, 1045b21–23) and is pure actuality (1050b19). Because it exists apart from matter, such an actuality is more one than any of the beings examined in the central books. It is, Aristotle says, "simply one" (1045b23). Since unity is a key criterion of *ousia,* something that is one in the highest way ought to be an *ousia* in the highest way. The central books do not, of course, draw this inference, but they certainly suggest it, and they lay the foundation for the treatment of first principles that appears in book Λ. Neither the latter nor the central books refer to each other, but considering the central books in terms of unity enables us to begin to see their connection.

My discussion of the central books has ranged over the details of many complex and controversial texts. Doubts about my interpretations of particular arguments may well remain. However, taken together, these interpretations provide overwhelming support for my contention that in the central books Aristotle uses unity to resolve problems about being and *ousia.* All that remains in this discussion of the central books is to pull together the conclusions of these arguments, to show how they resolve some *aporiai,* and to present Aristotle's doctrine of *ousia.* As we should expect by now, the way to achieve all these ends is to examine the unity of *ousia.* Before we can do that, however, we must turn to what has become the key point of contention among scholars concerned with the central books.

4.2 FORM, UNIVERSAL, AND INDIVIDUAL

The classic question about the central books is how to reconcile the apparently contrary demands that Aristotle places on *ousia.*[2] Essence is clearly the most successful of Aristotle's candidates for primary *ousia*. Essence is form, and many particular individuals apparently share the same form (Z 8, 1034a5-8; I 9, 1058b5-9). Yet, Aristotle also argues, in Z 13-16, that no universal is *ousia*. How can essence be common to many if it is not universal? To pose the problem differently, since *ousia* is not universal, it should be individual; but since many individuals share one essence, *ousia* should be universal. How can *ousia* be both? Because an essence cannot be both, Aristotle's account seems hopelessly inconsistent.

The question of essence's universality or individuality is not one that Aristotle specifically addresses in the central books, but it is hard to see how he could have overlooked it. He does include a similar question among book B's *aporiai*. The last of these asks whether principles are universal or individual, and he argues that absurd consequences result whether they are universal or nonuniversal (B 6, 1003a5-13). Since Aristotle thinks this *aporia* can be resolved—he advances a solution in M 10—it would surely be unlikely if the parallel problem in the central books were insurmountable.

Accordingly, the idea that Aristotle's position on essence or form is inconsistent ought to be a last resort, something to turn to if all else fails. Though some interpreters do maintain that the demands on form made by the central books are inconsistent,[3] most attempt to save him from contradiction. Three approaches have been defended: (1) each composite has its own unique form, so that form is individual; (2) generic universals cannot be *ousiai* but species-forms can be, so that form is a universal; (3) form is neither universal nor individual.

Each of these positions has troublesome passages to deal with. First, some, such as Rogers Albritton, who are sympathetic to the first position and think that Aristotle endorses it elsewhere doubt that there is conclusive evidence for it in the central books.[4] Others argue that there is firm evidence for the position in book Z, and the position has recently become popular.[5] Support for it seems to lie in Aristotle's arguments against universals being *ousiai*, but its proponents need to explain away Aristotle's remarks that many composites share the same form and that matter individuates. On the other hand, those who maintain that form is universal accept these latter remarks at their face value and reinterpret Aristotle's apparent denial that a universal can be *ousia*. Michael Woods argues that Aristotle intends to deny only that *generic* universals are *ousiai,* and that Aristotle identifies *ousia* with the lowest universal, the species.[6] The third approach to the problem, the denial that form is either universal or individual, a position advanced by Joseph Owens,[7] is tough to square with Aristotle's positive remarks on form, and besides most commentators have dismissed as nonsensical the notion that anything could be neither universal nor individual. Thus, all who would find a consistent doctrine in the central books must interpret some texts in less than obvious ways. The issue is not whether to interpret, but when and how:

which texts should we take at their face value and which should we understand differently?

Even apart from the necessity for interpretation, none of these alternatives is very plausible. The preceding analysis of the central books shows why, but the reasons might easily be obscured by the analytic detail. Accordingly, I shall present and tie together pertinent portions of my earlier treatment. What evidence supports each of the apparently contrary requirements for form? Establishing the evidence for both sides of the dilemma is the first step of an account and justification of still another solution to the problem of form.

4.2.1 Universal Form

Let me begin with the requirement that form be universal. Why should form be universal? What is the mistake of those who maintain that it is individual? Early in his discussion of essence, at Z 4, 1030a11–13, Aristotle says, "essence belongs to nothing which is not a species of a genus." The reason is that only a species is "not said by something's being said of something else"; it is "primary" (1030a7–11). When he repeats this result later in the same chapter, he substitutes one for primary and *ousia* for species (1030b4–10). Thus, essence belongs to *ousia* because it is one. In the same breath he speaks of an essence in a lesser sense that belongs to other beings because they too are one, though one in a lesser way. So *ousia*, that is, a species of *ousia*, most properly has an essence. In Z 6 Aristotle argues that the thing and its essence are the same. It follows that *ousia* not only *has* an essence; it *is* its essence. But the *ousia*, the thing with an essence, is the species. So the species is essence. Since the species is a universal, the essence should also be universal. In short, because only a species has an essence, and because the thing and its essence are one, the essence is the species, a universal.

From this argument it is clear that not all species have essences. Accidents, accidental composites (like white man), *per se* attributes and *per se* composites (like snub nose) lack essences in the proper sense because they contain additions. Their plurality is reflected in their formulae which, for just this reason, fail to be definitions. Only species of *ousiai* have essences because they alone are unities, and their formulae do not contain additions. In what way are they one? At the very least, they are "one in formula" because their formulae are not divisible into parts that signify the same thing (Δ 6, 1016a32–36). Aristotle uses this type of unity to define one in species (1016b31–33); thus, *ousiai* are each one in species. Under the heading "one in species" Aristotle includes not only species but also a particular instance of a species, an individual composite *ousia*. The species human being is one in species; so is Socrates. But Socrates is not a primary *ousia* because in Z 3

Aristotle denies that composite individuals are primary *ousiai* on the ground that they are composed of form and matter (1029a29–32 with 1029a5–7). So if we ask whether there is anything besides the species that is one in species and could be *ousia,* the answer seems to be no. Proponents of individual forms would try to avoid this answer by claiming that their forms also belong under the heading "one in species," so that there are nonuniversal *ousiai.* But in what sense would an individual form be one in species (= one in formula)? Presumably, it would be one in species in the same way that the composite Socrates is one in species, by having a single formula. But this formula would also be the formula of other individual forms. Aristotle's insistence that *ousia* be one in formula amounts to the insistence that *ousia* be knowable, but grasping the formula of an individual form would not constitute knowledge of that form any more than it would constitute knowledge of the other forms that share the formula. The only way an individual form could conceivably be known is by adding something to this universal, but then the individual form has a formula by addition and fails to be *ousia.* On this reasoning, individual forms, if they exist, could not be *ousiai.* Apparently, if an *ousia* is to be one in species or one in formula, it must *be* the species. Again, *ousia* should be a universal.

Another argument for the universality of essence or form appears in Z 7–8. There Aristotle describes the generation of a composite individual as a form's coming to be present in a matter, and he asks whether the form is generated in the generation of the composite. Suppose that form were generated. It would then consist of its own elements and another form, and it would come to be when those elements acquired that other form. But we would then have to ask the same question about the elements and this other form, are they generated? If either is generated, it must come from still another form and matter, and we can raise the same question about them. To avoid an infinite regress, some form and some matter must be ungenerated.

If form is not generated along with the composite, we need to ask how it comes to be present in the composite. Aristotle maintains that it is passed from the agent to the composite: "man generates man" (1033b32). It follows that Socrates' form and that of his son are the same. Perhaps, it might be objected, the forms here are the same in species but not numerically the same. Then there could be individual forms. But this will not do, for we would then need to explain where the form of Socrates' son comes from. Is it generated? That was excluded by the previous argument, the conclusion of which is repeated elsewhere (Z 15, 1039b21–34; H 3; 1043b17–18). Also, since form is indivisible (1034a8), it cannot be generated. Is form ungenerated because it comes to be without being in the process of generation?[8] This would undermine Aristotle's naturalistic account of generation, for it would remain a mystery how the form could come to be and come to be present in the composite. How could there be a natural cause of a form's coming to be if form comes to be through no process of becoming? Obviously, no biological mechanisms could produce a form that has come to be without any process; so, unique forms cannot come from biology. (Accidents are and are not without being in the process of coming to be or ceasing to be [E 3, 1027a29–30], but their causes are not natural.) Nor does Aristotle believe that a form exists somewhere in a repository of souls before birth. The only source of a form is a parent, the father. How could the father cause his offspring to possess a unique and ungenerated form? Obviously not through reproduction because then form *would* come to be through a process. Something with its own unique and ungenerated form could never be the source of some *other* ungenerated form. Since the parent does cause its offspring, the offspring must share the form of the parent. Merely being *in* the same species will not do; the form in both cases must *be* the species. It cannot be anything peculiar to the individual.

Another argument for the same conclusion begins with Aristotle's claim that the human form we share is indivisible (ἄτομον) (Z 8, 1034a8). It cannot be further divided into individual forms or species (cf. B 3, 999a4–5; I 9, 1058b5–10). As Aristotle puts it elsewhere, man is not the genus of individual men (B 3, 999a5–6). Socrates and Callias differ through their matter, not their species (1033b31–32; 1034a5–8; cf. Λ 8, 1074a31–34). If they had unique individual forms, they would differ in form. Again, form is the species, a universal.

There is also some support for universal forms in Z 10, though the text is a bit ambiguous. Aristotle denies that man and horse and other universals are *ousiai* (1035b27–30). They are composites of formula and "matter as universal." These composites—Ross calls them "materiate universals"[9]—cannot be Aristotle's usual universals because the passage goes on to distinguish parts of form or essence from parts of the composite and to insist that there is a formula of only a part of the composite, the form (1035b31–1036a1). Since he declares in virtually the same breath that the formula is of the universal, the form must be universal. It is not the materiate universal's universality that prevents it from being *ousia*, but its plurality, its consisting of a universal form and a universal matter—just the theme of Z 10, I argued earlier. *Ousia* is a part of this composite, the universal form.

Still another reason to think that essence is universal is the account Aristotle gives of its unity in Z 12. At issue there is how that whose formula is a definition can be one (1037b11–12). The chapter shows that a formula can consist of a single constituent, the ultimate differentia, because the latter implicitly contains all the other differentiae and the genus. "The definition is some one formula and of an *ousia,* so that it is the formula of something one; for *ousia* is something one and a this" (1037b25–27). Since the formula is one, the *ousia* it defines is one. But the formula that is one is the formula of the species; so, again, *ousia* or form must be the species, a universal.

Further, as I said, individual forms would be unknowable (cf. Z 15, 1040a8–22), for we know when we grasp a formula and the formula is of the universal (Z 10, 1035b34–1036a1). It is because knowing something consists of grasping its formula that Aristotle declares knowledge to be of the universal (B 6, 1003a13–15; Z 10, 1036a8; M 10, 1086b20–22). He insists that essence is knowable (Z 6, 1031b6–7; 5, 1031a11–14; 13, 1039a14–22). Hence, essence or form cannot be individual. Since the formula of an essence would inevitably be universal, no essence that was unique to an individual could be known.[10]

In M 10 Aristotle qualifies his claim that knowledge is of the universal: only potential knowledge is of the universal. Does this discussion offer a way to skirt the preceding argument against individual forms? M 10 distinguishes between the knowledge of universals, a knowledge that is itself universal and indeterminate and thus merely potential, and actual knowledge, the knowledge of an actuality, a this (1087a15–21). Actual knowledge is always the knowledge of something, but the object of potential knowledge, the universal, does not exist as a single distinct entity. Knowledge of a universal remains potential until we identify some individual thing as an instance of it. However, actual knowledge of this individual does not include additional content, for we know the actual thing when we have its formula and this formula is of the universal. Apparently, knowledge is actual only because there is some particular individual to which we ascribe this formula. If all this is correct, M 10 does not allow for individual forms; it provides another reason to reject them. For if there were individual forms, we could know them only through universal formulae, and each formula could apply to several different forms. However, as long as we used the same formula to know these different forms, the features that distinguished one individual form from another would remain unknown. If Socrates' form and Callias' form are both known through the formula of human being, then whatever makes Socrates' form unique is unknown. Could his form be the same as Callias'? Then his form would not be individual. But, perhaps, his form is formally the same but numerically different. This will not work either, for how could forms differ numerically? They have no matter, the usual source of numeric unity, and formally they are, it has been conceded, the same. In short, because actual knowledge adds no new content to potential knowledge, even if an individual form could be the object of actual knowledge, it would remain essentially unknown. Aristotle accepts an unknowable matter in a composite because it does not alter the form or render it or the composite unknowable (Z 10, 1036a8–9). An unknowable form, though, would mean that *ousia* is unknowable, an intolerable consequence. Again, forms must be universal.

The clearest evidence for individual forms is often thought to lie in Aristotle's distinction between "your form" and "my form" in book Λ (5, 1071a20–29).[11] It should be obvious that merely speaking of "my form" or "your form" does not show that they differ. What Aristotle claims in this passage is that your form, matter, and mover differ from mine, though they are the same universally. That *all* these principles differ does not imply that they *each* differ. But my position entails not only that forms of different people need not differ, but that they *could not* differ. Why, I may be asked, would Aristotle mention form here if it could not differ in different people? One answer to this objection is that Aristotle's point here is that the causes of distinct individuals can differ, and he makes this point simply by enumerating all the causes in the way he had done earlier in the chapter: form, matter, and mover. In a parallel discussion in I 3, Aristotle offers the sameness of you with yourself as an example of sameness in formula and number (1054a32–b1), and of the corresponding type of otherness he writes, "things are also other unless both the matter and the formula are one; therefore, you and your neighbor are other" (1054b16–17). Two people are other because they do not have one form *and* one matter. This type of otherness is not characterized by a difference of form and a difference in matter but by a difference of either form or matter, and it is this type of otherness that Aristotle must have in mind in book Λ, for the example there is the same, you and your neighbor. Hence, the passage from book Λ does not prove the existence of individual forms.

On the other hand, there is a way that Aristotle could sanction individual forms even while insisting that form is universal. Just as white man has an "essence" (Z 4, 1030b12–13), Socrates could also have an essence; it would be a secondary essence. Since Socrates is a composite of form and matter, his essence should be a composite of the essence of man, that is, the universal form, matter (taken universally), and the essences of whatever attributes happen to belong to this composite (Z 10, 1035b27–1036a8; I 9, 1058b10–11). Such a form would be unique to Socrates and individual, but it would not be a primary *ousia*. Since this form includes matter, it seems unlikely that Aristotle has it in mind in book Λ when he mentions "your form" and "your matter."[12]

From all these arguments it seems to follow that form or essence is universal. However, if we look closely at what Aristotle has really argued, what we find is only that essence must be one in formula. Species seems to be *ousia* because, without attributes and without material or formal parts, it contains no additions and is thus one in formula. Species also seems to be *ousia* because it is a principle of generation that is indivisible yet common to parent and offspring; it is common because both parent and offspring share one formula, and it is indivisible because that formula is indivisible. In both types of argument, species seems to be *ousia* because it can meet the demand that Aristotle places on *ousia*, to be one in formula. But nothing in the text would exclude something else from being *ousia* if it too could meet this demand in the relevant way.

At one point (Z 4, 1030a11–12) Aristotle does declare that the species alone has an essence, a claim that is tantamount to declaring it to be *ousia*, as we saw. (Aristotle leaves no doubt that he means the species in this passage, and not the form—another translation of τὸ εἶδος [*to eidos*]—because he speaks here of the "*eidos* of a genus.") Nevertheless, Aristotle often uses his terms loosely. "Species of a genus" here may refer only to what is one in formula (cf. 1016b31–33). In any case, his arguments do not show that essence is the universal species. They show only that essence or whatever is *ousia* must be one in formula.

4.2.2 Individual Form

Let us now turn to the other requirement. Why should form be individual? One passage that may seem to provide evidence for this is Aristotle's equation of thing (ἕκαστον) and essence in Z 6. If "thing" here referred to the composite (καθ᾽ ἕκαστον), essence would be individual. But the equation would also be unintelligible because the composite contains matter besides form. Fortunately, we need not worry about this difficult consequence, for the thing equated with essence cannot be the composite. The equation holds only for things that are "*per se* and primary" (cf. 1031b13–14, 1030a7–11), and the composite lacks these characters. What, then, are the things equated with essence? From the description of primary in Z 6, only substrates are primary. Since, as we know from Z 3, the material and composite substrates depend on form, only the formal substrate could be primary and *per se*. Hence, only the formal substrate, the form, is one and the same with its essence. Z 6's identity of essence and thing is an identity of essence and form: it is a qualified identity of two candidates for *ousia* (Z 3, 1028b33–36; 1029a2–3).

This doctrine explains a puzzling argument in Z 13 that nothing said universally is *ousia*. The argument's key premise is, "things [ὦν] whose *ousia* and essence are one are themselves one" (1038b14–15). The reason that this argument excludes universals is that, by definition, they are common to many things (1038b11–12). If a universal were the *ousia* of these things, they would have one *ousia,* and they should all be one. Clearly, no "one over many" could meet this requirement for *ousia*. The problem with Aristotle's argument is that it seems equally effective against his own essence: since many things share the same essence, their essence and *ousia* would be one while they are many. Since Socrates and Callias have the same essence, their essence and *ousia* is one, and they too should be one, an absurdity. Is Aristotle caught in his own trap? No, the argument does not exclude essence because the thing whose *ousia* is essence is not the same as the things whose *ousia* would be the universal. Universals belong to composites like Socrates and Callias. If universals were *ousiai,* they would be the *ousiai* of these composites. Since a universal is, by definition, a "one over many," it could never be the *ousia* of one thing, as 1038b14–15 requires. Let us suppose instead that the thing here is the form, the thing Aristotle discusses in Z 6. Applied to this thing, the requirement of 1038b14–15 insists that whenever form is one, its essence is one. We know that this requirement is met because, as Z 6 argues, form and essence are one and the same; whenever the form is one, the essence must be as well. Moreover, Aristotle argues in Z 6 that the thing (form) and its essence are one and the same by showing that they are each one. In short, the requirement excludes universals but not Aristotle's own essences because the "things" of which each is, or would be, the *ousia* differ. The requirement applies very differently in the two cases.

If this interpretation is correct, Z 6 not only explains the key premise; it justifies this premise. Moreover, since it is only things that are primary that are one and the same with their essences, and since this type of identity is presumed by the key premise, this premise must also be limited to what is primary. It asserts only that things that are primary and one have essences that are one. Consequently, the premise does not commit Aristotle to thinking that since Socrates is one, his essence is one. Socrates, a composite of form and matter, is not primary. Form is primary, and it and its essence are one.

In what sense are they one? Aristotle's statement of the requirement later in a similar argument (Z 16, 1040b17) shows that the unity of both must be numeric, a point that we could infer from Z 13 anyway. This is very odd, to say the least, for it means that the universal would need to be one in number before the requirement could exclude it. How could the universal be one in number? Aristotle's point here is not that universals *are* numerically one but that they would *need to be* numerically one to be *ousiai*. Were a universal, such as being, the *ousia* of its instances, many things would have an *ousia* that is (numerically) one, namely, being. *If* it were an *ousia,* being would be an entity that is numerically one, but this would imply a false consequence (1040b16–19). If this interpretation is correct, Aristotle's argument against universals excludes all of them, even the species (*pace* Woods and Albritton). In contrast, form is able to be numerically one without contradiction. It can thus meet the requirement that generates this argument, that *ousia* be numerically one or individual. On this interpretation, the argument dismisses universals because they are not properly one.

To sustain this conclusion, I need to reject alternative accounts of why the argument does not apply to Aristotle's essence. According to one possible account, essence escapes from the argument because the crucial premise makes a claim about things whose essence and *ousia* are one, but Aristotle's essence is either not one or not one in the pertinent way. Were essence one, that of which it is the essence would have to be one; since, on this interpretation, essence is not one (or not one in the pertinent way), there is no obstacle to its being the essence of many things. This interpretation is unlikely. As we have seen, Aristotle continues to assume that essence is one throughout the central books. Could essence fail to be one in the pertinent way? The pertinent type of unity here is numeric, and there is plenty of evidence that each Aristotelian essence is one in number. First, since form or essence causes numeric unity in the composite, it must be more numerically one than the composite (cf. α 1, 993b24–26). (This remains true even though the numeric unity of the essence differs from the numeric unity of the composite, continuity.) Also, when Aristotle claims that the formula of an *ousia* is a definition because it is the formula of something one (Z 4, 1030a6–16; b4–13), he must mean that the *ousia* is *numerically* one. Otherwise, the claim would be trivial: it would amount to saying that the formula of an *ousia* is one because the *ousia* is one in formula. The reason that the formula is one is that the thing or essence of which it is the formula does not contain additions and is, thus, one in number. Likewise, Aristotle's identity of essence and formal substrate in Z 6 presupposes their numeric unity, for he argues that were they different, the result would be an impossible numeric plurality (1032a2–4). Further, Aristotle argues that if universals were actual *ousiai*, then *ousiai* would be composed of *ousiai*. This is impossible because "what is two in this way in actuality is never one in actuality" (1039a4–5). Apparently, an *ousia*, that is, an essence, must be one in actuality; it must be numerically one. Since essence must be numerically one, the key premise in the first argument of Z 13 must apply to it. Consequently, it is a mistake to try to skirt this argument by declaring that essence lacks numeric unity.

Since essence is numerically one, the premise tells us that that thing of which it is the essence is also numerically one. So essence cannot be a universal. It must, then, be individual.[13] Moreover, the foregoing arguments showing that essence is numerically one also show that essence is individual because to be one in number is to be individual (B 4, 999b33–34).

Another approach to exempting Aristotle's forms from the first argument of Z 13, that of Michael Woods, is to say that the argument is spoken by the Platonist.[14] Woods's Platonist aims to argue against the position that *ousia* is universal, a position that Woods thinks is Aristotle's, by showing the absurdity to which it leads. However, he is unsuccessful, for Aristotle responds by showing that the argument excludes only what is "said universally," higher universals, but does not affect other universals among which, according to Woods, is the lowest species, *ousia*.

As explained earlier, this is an unlikely reading. Aristotle rarely presents his opponents' arguments in such detail. The text contains no indication that the Platonist is speaking, the argument is not one he would likely make, and no subsequent text answers it. Further, Woods needs to show that Aristotle's essence, the species on his view, escapes from this argument against universals and from those brought later in the chapter. One of these arguments poses particular difficulties for his view. In a voice no one doubts is his own, Aristotle denies that one actual *ousia* can be the constituent of another (1039a3–8). It follows that animal and other genera cannot be *ousiai*, for they are constituents of species—no problem for Woods. What, though, about the species itself? To identify essence as species Woods needs to collapse the distinction between species and form, a seemingly plausible move because the term for both is the same and because Aristotle never distinguishes them explicitly. Form or, if Woods is right, species is part of a composite. But how can an entity that is defined as a predicate (1038b11–12; *De Int.* 7, 17a38–b1) also be present in a composite? Also, how can the species be *ousia* if the composite of which it is a part is also *ousia?* Aristotle faces a problem similar to the latter on my interpretation, but he has the resources to answer it; he makes form the actuality of the composite. Woods strips him of this response by making the species *ousia.*[15]

Woods would, I suppose, dismiss this problem as bogus because, he thinks, the composite cannot be distinguished from its species. He points to a special logical relation between species and instance: the species defines and demarcates its instance so that it is impossible to "distinguish men independently of their possession of the form."[16] This will not do, for Aristotle does distinguish the composite from its form, or from its species, if you will (in Z 3, 1029a29–32); the composite consists of its species (or form) and matter. Moreover, even granting Woods's special logical relation, we would be pressed to imagine how Aristotle's claims about essence could hold of the species. Could species and proximate matter be one? Could the matter be a potentiality for the species? Could species cause the composite's material constituents to be continuous and function together? These are functions of form. All this implies that the traditional distinction between species and form is well founded.[17]

Still another problem with Woods's view is the lack of textual support for his distinction between universals and what is predicated universally.[18] As I said, universals are defined as predicates. Aristotle also speaks of species as predicates (Θ 7, 1049a34–36; Δ 9, 1018a3–4).[19] (A remark against universals predicated of sensibles being *ousiai* is probably also directed against species [1039b16–17].) So it is a mistake to say, as Woods does, that species are universals but are not predicated universally. Finally, in Z 16 Aristotle seems to dismiss all universals (1040b25–27; cf. Z 13, 1038b9–11); and when he summarizes the results of this section, he denies that *any* universal is *ousia* (H 1, 1042a21–22; I 2, 1053b16–17). So much for Woods's notion that species are universals that are *ousiai*.

For all these reasons Woods's interpretation of the first argument must be mistaken. So we cannot avoid the application of this argument to Aristotle's essence by putting it in the mouth of the Platonist. There seems to be no other way to avoid this application besides the course I proposed at the beginning of this subsection, recognizing that Aristotle's own form is individual. Moreover, while excluding alternative interpretations, I have advanced additional arguments for form's being individual.

Aristotle's other arguments against universals also show that form or essence should be individual. My remarks here can be brief. Most of these arguments against universals turn on two characters: (1) universals are predicated of substrates and (2) they are composed of other universals. Since universals are predicated of substrates they must be defined through addition; in some sense, they are many. If universals were *ousiai*, some *ousiai* would be composed of other *ousiai*. What would be wrong with this? Aristotle explains that were the universal to have a plurality of actual constituents, it would not be one in number (1039a4–6). Again, he assumes that *ousia* is one in number; it is a self-subsistent individual.

Though all these arguments support the view that essence is individual, what they really show is that essence or form must be one in number. The universal seemed to be *ousia* most of all (1038b2–7) because it is one, but it lacks the pertinent type of unity. Assuming that it is numerically one, as the Platonists do and as we must if it is to be *ousia*, generates an absurd consequence. Hence, universals lack the numeric unity required of *ousiai*.

Just what type of numeric unity is required of *ousiai*? It is not the numeric unity possessed by a composite. Socrates' matter makes him one in number (Δ 6, 1016b31–33). Essence is the other component of a composite. In book Λ Aristotle speaks of an essence without matter (the first unmoved mover) as numerically one and of matter as what makes a species many (8, 1074a31–37).[20] An unmoved mover has no matter because it is an actuality. But he also takes the essences that exist with matter in composites to be actualities. Insofar as these essences can be separated from matter, they too are numerically one (H 6, 1045a36–b7), I argued earlier. They are not simply one, as an unmoved mover is (cf. H 6, 1045b23), but somehow one and, of course, somehow not one.

4.2.3 Form as neither Universal nor Individual

Thus far, I have argued that form or essence is universal because it is one in formula and that it is individual because it is numerically one. Since it would seem that nothing can be both universal and individual, it is possible that form is neither. This is the third alternative that I mentioned at the beginning of this section.

This alternative requires that we distinguish between two usages of the Greek term *eidos* (τὸ εἶδος), as I did earlier.[21] How else can we understand Aristotle's simultaneous endorsement and rejection of *eidos* as *ousia*? One *eidos*, the species, he dismisses. The other, form, is essence and *ousia*. Aristotle also equates the latter with shape (ἡ μορφή) (Z 8, 1033b5–6) and uses "shape" for "form" throughout book H (e.g., 1042a29; 1043a26, a28; 1045a23, a29, b18). Apparently, form is not universal nor, as we saw in the preceding subsection, is it individual in the way that a composite is.

A motive for this third interpretation is that it alone seems consistent with Aristotle's notion that form causes the composite individual to be one and to be what it is. How could the cause of unity in an individual be something that is itself an individual and a part of the thing whose unity it causes? If a part of the composite is one, the whole would lack unity. Nor could a universal cause the composite individual to be one, for how could a predicate signifying a common property unify matter? How could something which is not itself an actuality cause the individual to be actual? (The cause of the actual book is not the universal glue but an actual glue that makes an actual bond.) Insofar as it causes unity and actuality in the composite, essence can, it seems, be neither universal nor individual.

Despite its merits, most writers have dismissed this interpretation as nonsensical.[22] A reason may be that they have tended to approach the *Metaphysics* from the perspective of contemporary logic, which recognizes only two sorts of entities, predicates and the individuals that receive them (respectively, F's or P's, and x's or a's). These correspond to Aristotle's universals and individuals.

The claim that some entities are neither universal nor individual should no longer seem surprising. First, contemporary physics does, I submit, sanction such entities because it understands elementary particles as probability distributions or ensembles of possible configurations or states. Their ontological status bothered Einstein, but they have been widely accepted because there are powerful arguments for them. Significantly, to deal with such entities logic requires special modifications.

More to the point, Aristotle recognizes entities lacking the unities that are the hallmarks of individuality and universality. In Z 16 he denies that simple bodies, like water and earth, or parts of plants or animals are each one and a this (1040b5-10; Θ 7, 1049a26-27). Without such unity, they are not individuals (cf. B 4, 999b33-34). Nor are they universals. Metaphysically, they are neither. I say "metaphysically" here because we do treat these things as individuals most of the time. Although only an individual, an *ousia,* is properly the subject of a predication, we do make simple bodies and parts subjects of predications: warm water, pretty flower, and broken leg. Logic often allows us to treat them as individuals even if they are not properly individuals from a metaphysical viewpoint. But if we press this logical usage, we find paradox. "Mass terms" like water do not admit of plurals so that combining some water with other water yields only water.[23] Since legs and flowers cannot retain their nature apart from the animals and plants of which they are parts, their attributes belong, somehow, to the *ousiai* of which they are parts. This could generate fallacies of composition: If the flowers are pretty, must the plant be pretty? If the leg is broken, must the man be broken? Obviously, these are not devastating problems, but just how does Aristotle block them? I think he avoids them by denying that parts and elements are properly individuals. In so doing, he limits the scope of logic. The proper task of Aristotelian logic is the demonstration of necessary properties of species.

As nonsensical, and perhaps even repulsive, as this may seem to philosophers influenced by the work of Russell, Quine, and Kripke, there are textual grounds to think that Aristotle does limit logic's scope. But I shall not pursue them here. My motives for mentioning the limited applicability of logic are to show that something can be treated as an individual or a universal without being either and to explain why Aristotle can deny that parts and simple bodies are either universal or individual. None of this shows that Aristotle's essences are neither individual nor universal. My point is just that it is not nonsensical to ascribe this position to Aristotle, even though it entails giving up some current views on logic.

So the third alternative is possible, but is it true? There are good reasons to reject it. Although the requirement that form cause numeric unity in the composite seems, I argued earlier, to support the third alternative, when considered closely, the requirement works against it. For if form is the cause of unity, it should itself be most one, by the principle that the cause of a character should possess that character in the highest degree (α 1, 993b24–26). And insofar as form is most one, it should be an individual.

Further, the third alternative is inconsistent with Aristotle's characterizations of form in the central books. Initially, it seems as though he argues against essence being either individual or universal. But as we look more closely at the arguments, we see that they concern not universality or individuality but corresponding types of unity. Aristotle does not argue that form lacks both ones but that it *is* one in both ways. He equates individual and one in number and suggests a parallel equation between one in formula and universal (B 4, 999b33–1000a1), and he refers to both form (Z 6, 1031b6–7; 1031b20–21) and universal (B 4, 999a28–29; Z 10, 1036a8; I 1, 1052a29–b1) as the principle of knowledge. It follows that essence or form should be both individual and universal. This is a fourth alternative.

4.2.4 Universal and Individual

How can anything be both universal and individual? These are usually taken to be contrary. As usually understood, they are. A universal is a one over many, and an individual (καθ' ἕκαστον) is one of the many. Nothing can be both. However, both terms also have extended senses. Aristotle calls first philosophy "universal" because it is primary (E 1, 1026a29–31), and this is not the universality of a predicate. On occasion, he applies "individual" to the species (e.g., *An. Po.* B 13, 97b28–31), no doubt an extended usage.

Let me propose that Aristotle's identifications of individual with one in number and universal with one in formula (B 4, 999b33–1000a1; cf. 999b24–31) also extend usual usages. Usually, Aristotle reserves the term "individual" for a composite *ousia*, something that is one because it has a single matter (Δ 6, 1016b31–33). As I noted earlier, an unmoved mover is also numerically one, but on different grounds: it is one because it has no matter (Λ 8, 1074a31–37). If anything that is numerically one is, in some sense, individual, then even an unmoved mover is individual. Analogously, an unmoved mover resembles a species in being one in formula (1074a34–37). If not only a species but anything that is one in formula can be called universal, then an unmoved mover is also universal. So an unmoved mover is an example of something that is both individual and universal in their extended senses. I think that Aristotle must also have an extended sense of universal in mind when he declares in Z 4 that only the species of a genus has an essence, for he argues not that species in the usual sense has an essence but that what is one in formula has an essence.[24] These extended usages differ in an important respect from the more common narrow usages. Usually, universal and individual refer to entities, respectively, to predicates or sensible composites. In their extended usages, universal and individual refer not to kinds but to characteristics. Accordingly, these extended usages open the possibility that something might be both universal and individual. Nothing could fall under two contrary kinds; but the same thing might have both characteristics if the characteristics are ways of being one.

When proponents of the third account deny that essence is either universal or individual, they use these terms in their narrow senses: essence is neither universal nor individual because it is neither a sensible composite nor a predicate. It is a different type of entity. Advocating the fourth account, I agree that form belongs to neither of these kinds, but form has characteristics of both because it is one in formula and one in number. This is often the way that Aristotle speaks of form in the central books. He shows that form is *ousia* by showing that it has both types of unity. Though form is neither universal nor individual in their narrow senses, it is both in their extended senses.

In short, resolving the classic problem about the central books hinges on recognizing the types of unity possessed by form. The apparent inconsistency in form's being both universal and individual vanishes as soon as we understand claims about form in terms of unity.

Evidence for this solution lies in its ability to reconcile Aristotle's claims about categorial being. The problematic assertions in the central books include: Z 4's ascription of essence only to species, Z 6's identification of thing and essence, Z 13's assumption that things whose essence and *ousia* is one are themselves one, Z 17's conclusion that form is the cause of unity in the material constituents of a composite, and H 6's identification of form and proximate matter. The first of these implies that form is universal; the others are easier to reconcile with individual forms. According to my interpretation, essence belongs to form because form is one in number and one in formula. Z 6 shows that form not only has an essence; it is its essence. This identity (or unity) of form and its essence motivates Z 13's claim that things whose essence is one are one. For if thing and essence are identical, essence must be one when thing is one. Since the thing, form, is one, so is its essence. In contrast, universals cannot be the *ousiai,* because the things to which they belong, composites, are many. Z 17 and H 6 concern the relation of form and the composite. Only a form that is itself one in number could cause numeric unity in the composite. Only if form is itself one in number can form and what is potentially this form, its proximate matter, be one. The central books insist that *ousia* be one and the cause of unity in the composite. Aristotle argues that form or essence is *ousia* because it, and it alone, is one and the cause of unity. The central books also insist that *ousia* be knowable and the cause of generation. Again, form is *ousia* because it can be both, and it can be both because it is one in formula. Numeric unity is required for form to be a principle of being; unity in formula for it to be a principle of becoming and a principle of knowledge.

These observations remove apparent inconsistencies and obstacles to a plausible account of sensible *ousia,* but they do not say much about the nature of the entity that has both types of unity. Just what type of entity is the Aristotelian form? Part of Aristotle's case against Plato (e.g., in Z 14) is that form cannot be both one in number and one in species. We still need to explain how he can ascribe both unities to his own forms. These issues hinge on the character of form, and I shall soon propose that Aristotle's identification of it as actuality resolves them. This discussion will be easier if we first look at other problems involving unity.

4.3 THE CENTRAL BOOKS AND THE *APORIAI*

That the central books do not directly address the *aporiai* presented in book B is well known.[25] Early in book Z Aristotle lists a series of questions that ought to be investigated, and one of these resembles the eighth *aporia.*[26] Yet, rather than answer these questions directly, Aristotle proceeds to "sketch what *ousia* is" (1028b31–32). The sketch bears directly on problems raised in a central group of *aporiai,* the sixth through the ninth (B 1, 995b27–996a2; 3–4, 998a20–1000a4). These *aporiai* all arise, at least partially, I maintain, from problems in the unity of principles. Each shows that a principle should possess two apparently contrary types of unity. I propose that, in showing that form is one in number and in formula, the central books break the deadlock of these *aporiai*. If this is right, my treatment of unity in the central books fits well with the *aporiai* of book B.

Let me begin with the sixth *aporia*, are the principles the genera or the constituents into which each thing is divided? (995b27-29; 998a20-b14). The former are constituents of the formula and the latter constituents of the composite. A motive for thinking that each is a principle is that each is one (cf. Δ 3, 1014b6-9). The problem is that each is one in a different way. A constituent of a formula is one in formula, and a constituent of a thing is one in number. The central books loose the fetters that generate this *aporia* by showing that a principle can have both kinds of unity. Form is both one in number and one in formula.

The next *aporia* asks whether the principles are the highest genera or the lowest genera (995b29-31; 998b14-999a23). A lowest genus is indivisible in species and thus more one (999a1-6). But a highest genus seems to have the advantage of being "apart" and "separate" from the individuals (999a17-23). The *aporia* arises because these two characteristics that principles should have seem to lie in distinct things. It could be broken by finding something with both characteristics, and this is just what the central books do. Because it is one in formula, form is indivisible in species. For the same reason, form is also "separate in formula" (H 1, 1042a28-29). The latter is not the absolute separation book B envisions, but the central books block objections by showing that no genus could be separate and that no genus is *ousia*. If neither a highest genus nor any other genus could be more separate than form, separation is not a reason to think that genus is more of a principle than form. So, once we recognize that indivisibility and separateness can belong to a single principle, the *aporia* vanishes.

The "most difficult and most necessary" *aporia*, the eighth, asks whether there is some principle apart from the individuals (995b31-36; 999a24-b24). The reason that there should be something apart is that without "something one and the same" which belongs universally, there will be no knowledge (999a26-29). That is to say, the principle needs to be apart because one is the principle of knowledge and only something that exists apart can be one. But it seems impossible for genera to exist apart (999a29-32); and even if they could and were *ousiai*, since everything whose *ousia* is one is one, everything falling under such a genus would be one, an absurdity (999b20-23; cf. Z 13, 1038b14-15; 16, 1040b17). Again, the problem here centers on the unity of the principle. And once again, it is resolved by showing that form satisfies both unity demands. Like the universal, form is a principle of knowledge because it is one; it is one in formula and, thus, separate in formula. But, in contrast with the universal, form is not a "one over many."

It is an individual; it is one in number. As such, form has no difficulty in meeting the requirement that thing and *ousia* each be one: insofar as it is one, it can be the thing whose *ousia,* essence, is one. Nevertheless, form exists with matter in a composite. Though form is, in one sense, the *ousia* of the composite, the composite is not a primary *ousia* and there is no reason to think that all composites with the form should be one. Thus, in virtue of its unity, form has the degree of separation necessary for it to be a principle of knowledge; but, also by virtue of its unity, form can be the principle of many composites without making them one. Since a principle, form, can be a principle of knowledge without being (completely) separate, the *aporia* is resolved.

The ninth *aporia* asks whether the principles are one in number or one in species. The problem here is that if the principles are one in number, it does not seem that there will be anything else besides individuals (999b31–34). But if the principles are universal, how will there be any individuals? (999b25–26). The source of the difficulty is that nothing seems to be one in both ways. However, as we have seen, the central books show that form is both one in number and one in species, though, to be sure, not in the way that this *aporia* envisions. The principle, form, is numerically one, but not in such a way that it cannot exist somehow in many composites. Form does not preclude the existence of individual composites; form is what enables composites to exist. Nor does form preclude the existence of universals. Because of form, many individuals do share common characteristics.

In sum, the central books' account of the unity of *ousia* breaks the bonds of *aporiai* 6–9 by showing that something is able to possess seemingly contrary types of unity. The Platonic forms are thought by their proponents to possess these types of unity (e.g., 998b9–11; cf. Z 14); but, as Aristotle never tires of showing, they are impossible. Why is Plato unable to advance principles that are both one in number and one in formula? How does Aristotle avoid the difficulties upon which Platonic forms founder? The central mistake of Plato is to advance as principles separated universals (Z 16, 1040b27–30). Insofar as they exist separately, they are individual. So the Platonic forms are both universal and individual, in the narrow sense of these terms. From Aristotle's criticism of Plato on this score, most commentators infer that his own forms do not have both characters. This does not follow. Aristotle does not object to anything being both universal and particular, but to Plato's account. The vigor of his arguments against Platonism masks the similarity of his own position to Plato's. He avoids *aporia* not by changing the requirements for principles, but by finding a principle capable of meeting these difficult requirements, the imminent or indwelling form (Z 11, 1037a29). For the latter to be a principle, Aristotle needs to reinterpret the requirements. Forms are separate, numerically one, and universal, but these characteristics are now understood more broadly than in book B.

The puzzles of book B are antinomies. Were they to remain unresolved, we would be forced to conclude that no nature could exist. Hence, the *aporiai* of book B must be resolved.[27] The account of form advanced in the central books must be right, Aristotle thinks, because it, and apparently it alone, can avoid these antinomies. The success of the central books in avoiding them is an argument for the doctrine it advances.

This is not to say that Aristotle's forms are not puzzling. Quite the contrary, he insists that the investigation of being is perennially puzzling (1028b2–4). But the puzzles inherent in that account differ from those in book B. The latter block thought; they must be resolved. The puzzles of the central books persist even after Aristotle advances the doctrine of form. What are these puzzles and why do they persist? More importantly, what can we finally say about *ousia* after the central books?

4.4 THE NATURE OF *OUSIA*

The preceding discussions of the classic problem and of the *aporiai* remove difficulties, but only in a formal way. *Ousia* can meet the apparently contrary demands Aristotle places on it because these demands turn on unity, because *ousia* is form, and because form is one in number and in formula. In confronting the unity demands that *ousia* must satisfy, Aristotle leads us to the nature of form. The really crucial question is what sort of entity form must be if it is to have both sorts of unity. This question is particularly pressing because Aristotle needs to show that his own forms will not succumb to those criticisms he brings against Plato's forms, forms that Plato intends, Aristotle supposes, to be one in both ways.

Aristotle's ascription of seemingly contrary characteristics to form reflects neither confusion nor shift in doctrine; it is the first step of his aporetic method. The next step is to expound the nature of form in such a way that the apparently contrary requirements can be met. My claim is that Aristotle's identification of form as actuality, an identification that, though mentioned at various points in books Z–H is emphasized in H 2, argued in H 6, and explored in the following book, shows how form can meet the unity requirements and is itself further justified by its enabling form to meet these requirements. Although (as I suggested in my discussion of Z 4, 1029b3–12) unity is prior to us because we know form first through its unity, form's actuality is "prior in nature." Form's actuality is prior because it, and only it, can account for the various ways form is one. Even though the bulk of the central books, especially the lengthy treatment of categorial being, examines unity problems, by showing that the resolution of these questions depends on actuality, they show the preeminence of actuality. Unity gives way to actuality.

Let me first explain how actuality causes both types of unity. Actuality causes numeric unity in the composite because it causes continuity. In Z 17 Aristotle argues that the cause of unity in a composite cannot be a material constituent (Z 17, 1041b11–28); it must be form (1041a26–b11).[28] Just how form causes the material elements to be one is indicated in H 2–3 by Aristotle's characterization of form as actuality. The material constituents are one because, by virtue of the presence of form, they can act together, and the capacity to act or function together is just what it is to be continuous. This raises a new unity problem, one that he addresses at the end of book H, how can form and matter together be one? The matter that is one with form is the proximate matter, a matter that is a potentiality for that particular form. Because this matter exists as matter only insofar as it has the capacity to function (a finger severed from a body is not a real finger—Z 10, 1035b24–25), and because the form is just the capacity to so function, the two are virtually identical. In other words, the form is just the capacity of bits of matter to work together, a capacity matter has by its shape, its position—in a word, by its form. Proximate matter acquires a form by being organized or united in such a way that it can work together; but the matter exists as such only in the composite because only there can it function, and the matter's being able to function together is its form.[29] The proximate matter of living things consists of their organs. Though it can be distinguished from form by its plurality, this matter is identified with form because form is, or depends upon, all the organs working together or having a single function. So form and matter are one if form is one. Form can be one because Aristotle has, in book Z, excluded from it everything whose presence might make it many: accidents, *per se* attributes, matter for change, and generic matter. Without these components, form can be a single characteristic function. In short, form is one because it is the single characteristic function or actuality of matter that makes the matter be what it is. In book Θ we learn that form is an incomposite actuality known by "contact" (10, 1051b24–30). On both counts, form is numerically one insofar as it is an actuality.

Form is also one in formula because it is an actuality. In order that the formula of the form be one, Aristotle, in Z 12, identifies it with the formula of the ultimate differentia; but this differentia is an actuality, as we learn in H 2. So the formula expresses an actuality. Though a single entity can have many functions, one must be primary. Because an actuality is complete and indivisible, the formula that expresses the primary actuality cannot be divided into another formula that also expresses it, precisely the criterion for unity in formula given in Δ 6 (1016a32–35). Hence, insofar as form is an actuality, it has a single formula.

Thus, actuality is the source of form's numeric unity and its unity in formula. So these two types of unity are not contrary. Indeed, they are closely related. Since form is an actuality, it contains no parts. Thus, it is numerically one and its formula is indivisible.

All this concerns the relation of actuality and unity. What can we say of actuality itself? What can we know of form not as it is for us but as it is in nature?

The term "actuality" (ἐνέργεια, ἐντελέχεια) refers to the function (ἔργον) in virtue of which an entity is what it is. To say that the form or essence of a human being, for example, is our actuality is to say that we are what we are by virtue of our human functioning. This actuality is our soul, and Aristotle conceives of soul as an activity. His pure actualities, the unmoved movers, consist entirely of their function (Θ 8, 1050b16–17; Λ 6, 1071b19–22). They are complete; their ends lie within themselves. He contrasts them with motions, processes whose ends lie outside of themselves (Θ 6, 1048b18–35). Other actualities, such as, the human soul and the essences of sensible *ousiai,* occupy an intermediate position. They too are complete and contain their ends within themselves, but they retain a close connection with matter. They cannot exist apart from matter, and they come to be present in and pass out of matter. Aristotle also refers to them as motions (E 1, 1026a1–2; Z 11, 1036b28–30), and he suggests that they are potentialities (Θ 8, 1050b11–13). These seemingly contrary characterizations can be reconciled by comparing his standard definition of human being in the *Metaphysics* and his account of soul in *De Anima* B. In the *Metaphysics'* central books, Aristotle is never more than tentative about what we are, but his exemplary definition is "two-footed animal." Walking on two feet seems to be that peculiarly human function that distinguishes us from other *ousiai* and somehow accounts for the other things we do. But we do not cease to be human when we sit. It is not walking that really defines us, but being able to walk. As Aristotle puts it in the *De Anima,* our soul is a first actuality (B 1, 412a21–b1). It is at once the actuality of the matter and a potentiality for further activity, the actual walking. Since we have the capacity to walk by having legs, our first actuality is an organ, and our form is virtually identical with its proper matter, as I just explained. Thus, "two-footed animal" expresses an actuality, the properly human capacity to walk on two feet. In general, the actuality of a sensible *ousia* is a capacity to function that is a peculiar organ. This is a lesser actuality than that of the unmoved mover because it contains potentiality within itself, but more of an actuality than matter.

Of course, the capacity to walk on two feet is not our proper function, but it serves the purposes of the *Metaphysics* well because it allows Aristotle to skirt those difficult questions about disembodied souls that his more considered view of human functioning would not and because it shows the close connection between actualities of sensibles and matter. With the possible exception of human beings, the (second) actuality of a sensible *ousia* is a function that we would expect Aristotle to regard as motion. We would ordinarily think of walking on two feet as a motion. In calling it an actuality, Aristotle takes it to contain its own end. If it were our actuality, we would not walk for some other goal; we would walk because that is just what we are, beings that walk. For Aristotle, the end of human living lies in nothing more mysterious than living as a human being, that is, using our human organs. Other animals are also defined by behaviors peculiar to them and, thus, by the organs that enable them to engage in those behaviors. The capacity of these organs to function is neither matter nor motion, Aristotle insists, but an actuality that is its own end. And the same holds for every form of life. I have chosen Wittgenstein's phrase "form of life" intentionally because I think it captures the individuality of form rather than its collective nature (though Wittgenstein's meaning may be no less controversial than Aristotle's). Form is not *a* universal; it is not (properly) shared by or predicated of a plurality. It is a particular kind of entity, an actuality. This entity is a particular function, a function which is also a capacity and which is its own end.

Although we have a properly metaphysical understanding of form when we grasp it as a first actuality, this conception of form does not, by itself, account for the relation of that single entity to a plurality of composites. Ironically, this relation, at the core of the classic problem at issue here, lies outside of the scope of metaphysics, as Aristotle delimits the discipline. Nevertheless, by reflecting on the character of actuality, we can easily see Aristotle's full solution to the classic problem.

As we saw, actualities of sensible *ousiai* cannot be separated from matter because they are, in a way, the functioning of matter. This association with matter has a variety of consequences. Matter inevitably wears down; each sensible composite must decay and die. To sustain itself, each nature must reproduce. We saw earlier that form is not created in the generation of a composite. Instead, generation must consist of a form's coming to be present in a matter; the processes of growth and development occur as form continues to manifest itself in the matter. Because these processes do not alter form, they are motions that, in some sense, lie outside the nature of form: form is what it is independently of how it came to be present in matter and of the processes by which it ceases to be present because its own end lies in its function not its reproduction. Thus, the central books divorce form from the physical processes through which it comes to be present and ceases to be present in matter because these processes lie outside of the actuality that is form. However, these processes are obviously determined by form. Birth, development, and the other motions undergone by each *ousia* follow characteristic patterns that are set by the form that comes to be realized or passes away through them. In the *Physics* Aristotle places these motions under the heading of what is "by nature" or "according to nature" (B 3, 194b17–22; 8, 198b23–27 with 199a5–6; 198b24–25 with b34–35).[30] They are essential attributes of natures, inevitable concomitants of form's existing in matter.

If, though, reproduction, birth, and development are necessary consequences of the nature of form, then so too is the plurality of composite individuals that must result. Because forms of sensibles must exist with matter, they are inevitably involved in processes of generation and destruction. To sustain itself, each form must reproduce, and the result is many instances of the same nature. That is to say, form individuates itself. Individuation is a physical process that is a kind of *per se* attribute of the form that is individuated; it results from the nature of form. Because form exists in matter, it must exist in many matters. The particular plurality of instances is accidental to the form; what is essential is that it must exist in some plurality of composites.

The traditional view is that matter individuates form.[31] On the other hand, texts where Aristotle says that form is the principle that makes something what it is point to form as the principle of individuation.[32] From what we have seen, both accounts are too limited. First, form, as actuality, is the source of unity in the composite and thus a cause of the composite's being an individual. But the individual composite requires matter as well, and it is matter that distinguishes one composite from another. Hence, what is usually called the problem of individuation is two problems: (1) What is the principle that makes the composite what it is, the principle of its identity? and (2) What is the principle that makes it different from other composites? The answers to these questions are, respectively, form and matter. This, though, is merely the logical dimension of the problem. Individuation is primarily a problem of physics.[33] The problem is to explain the coming to be of individual composites. The solution lies in the character of an actuality that exists in matter and must, consequently, be constantly coming to be present in matter. This process of generation is the process of individuation, a process that depends on form.

It is a mistake to think of the process of generation as the form's acquisition of some matter. Nor should we say that the addition of matter to a form does not change form's nature. Both claims suggest that matter is wholly outside of form. Rather, the form of a sensible *ousia* inevitably exists in matter because it is an actualization of matter, and existence in matter entails a plurality of instances. The notion that matter lies outside the form is partly a consequence of the same perspective that takes individuation to be a logical problem. Using the language of logic, we can speak of the relation of form and matter either by noting points of sameness and difference between them or by taking form as some sort of predicate of matter. But the proximate matter of an *ousia* consists of various organs, and these do not retain their nature apart from form. Matter lacks the logical independence to be properly a subject. Rather, matter is the plurality of potential functions that exist as organs and that are unified by the form, the potential of all to function together physically in a characteristic way. Form's existence with many organs, that is, with matter, and its existence in a plurality of composites are ways that form must exist, given its nature. This mode of existence is apt to strike us as odd. It seems to threaten the individuality of form, and in a sense it does. But in another sense, the one that Aristotle fastens on, it does not because form remains a single entity, a single actuality. As I understand them, the central books aim to show us the nature form has and why we should accept the existence of such a peculiar entity.

They lead us away from nature as it presents itself to us initially, the perspective of the *Categories,* to nature as it is in itself, the perspective of form and actuality, a perspective that is, interestingly, akin to the way we know nature. We recognize that the primary *ousia* is not a composite individual but an actuality that exists in various places and times. From the perspective of form, reproduction, development, and the resulting plurality are inevitable aspects of form's manifestation of itself in matter. Only through a plurality of instances can form attain a completeness that imitates the completeness of pure actualities. I am reminded of E. O. Wilson's remark that an individual person is nothing more than a vehicle for genes.[34] Genes and forms differ in crucial respects, but the argument of the central books of the *Metaphysics* forces us to make a parallel gestalt shift away from the primacy of individual composites to the perspective of form. Once we grasp form as an activity that necessarily occurs in matter, the particularity of individuals becomes irrelevant. From the perspective of form, individuals are merely vehicles for form's continued existence, and it is this perspective that reveals the nature of form.

Though it is widely acknowledged that form or essence is Aristotle's answer to the main concern of book Z, "what is *ouisa?*," nearly all interpreters soften this to something like, "form is primary *among* sensible *ouisai.*" The reason is easy to see: form's being *ousia* seems incompatible with Aristotle's view that individual composites are separate and with his view that form cannot exist separately. My account of form enables us to take Aristotle at his word. Form or essence is *ousia,* but it exists with matter and, consequently, in a plurality. Despite this mode of existence, form is one entity because, as an actuality, its end lies in itself. Though form realizes itself in a material plurality, what is realized is just itself, a single function. In contrast, a particular composite *ousia,* though first "for us," is a secondary *ousia;* it is merely an instance of form.

This account of form enables us to understand at last how form can have the two types of unity that generate the classic problem. As we saw, Aristotle argues that the first unmoved mover is both one in number and one in formula because it is an actuality without any matter (Λ 8, 1074a31–37). My claim is that forms of sensibles, actualities that exist with matter in composites, also possess, on precisely the same grounds, both sorts of unity, albeit to a lesser degree. Forms of sensibles cannot be simply one, as an unmoved mover is (H 6, 1045b23), but each is one to the extent to which it is an actuality, and it is an actuality only to the extent that it exists separately from the matter of particular composites (H 6, 1045a36–b4; 1, 1042a28–29). As I said, each is an actuality despite its presence in a plurality of composites because it is its own end. This actuality, a first actuality, is less than that of an unmoved mover, and so too the numeric unity of forms that exist in sensibles is also less. Since this numeric unity lies in an actuality, the differentia that expresses the actuality, the formula of the form, is the formula of something one. This formula of the form is also the formula of form's proximate matter (cf. Θ 2, 1046b8-9). Thus, the formula of an *ousia* does not consist of a part for the form and a part for the matter (as the formula of an artifact or a natural composite does—H 2, 1043a14-18 with a4-5), nor would the formula of the form express the presence of form in matter. Hence, form or actuality is also one in formula. Ironically, though form's numeric unity depends on separating it from all material, form's unity in formula depends on somehow including the proximate matter in the formula. Just as we might expect, matter is, in a way, in the form (as potentiality) and, in another way, outside of the form (as plurality).

Thus, though forms of sensibles lack the degree of unity possessed by pure actualities they can meet the unity requirements for *ousia*. The central books use these requirements to determine the nature form must have, and what emerges is the character of actuality. Actuality is individual without being in a single place or time; it is universal without being properly predicable of individuals (cf. Θ 7, 1049a34-b2). It is one nature inevitably manifested in a plurality. Because *only* such an entity *can* satisfy the unity requirements of *ousia,* it *must* exist.

Are Aristotle's forms the only entities that can meet the unity requirements for *ousia?* Plato tried to make his forms one in both ways. To show that *only* his own forms can meet the requirements Aristotle must show that the Platonic forms cannot. Since Plato's forms are universal, there seems to be no difficulty with their being one in formula (except perhaps for those that are *summa* genera). But Plato thought he could also make them numerically one by positing the universal as separate from sensibles. *Ousia* ought to be separate, but the universal cannot be separate (cf. Z 16, 1040b27-34) because it always depends on something else, that of which it is predicated. It is, by definition, a "one over many"; that is, a predicate. As such, the Platonic form just cannot do what form must, organize and realize matter. No universal could cause the matter to be one because it is not a physical cause. As Aristotle often reminds us, a Platonic form would be unable to cause motion. Moreover, Plato's account of forms is impossible because it makes some constituents of others (Z 14, 1039a24-26). So the Platonic form not only fails to meet the unity requirements of *ousia;* it cannot exist.

Aristotle avoids these problems by recognizing that an actuality existing in a plurality of composites could still be numerically one. With this doctrine, he need not account for the unity of one entity by introducing a separate entity, a procedure that generates the difficult problem of participation. Aristotle's composites do not partake of their form; their form is their actuality, their nature. Thus, Aristotelian form is one and causes unity without existing apart from the composite. Since the composites exist and since no other account of their unity withstands scrutiny, Aristotelian form must exist.

Even so, much in Aristotle's account of it remains problematic. He treats actuality as separate while recognizing that it is not so. He treats form as a nature that is *ousia* while recognizing that it must exist with matter in particular individuals. Despite his claims that form and matter are one, the two remain distinct and their difference seems essential for his account of actuality. Then, there is the fundamental question of whether such an actuality is intelligible at all. All this casts doubt on the unity of *ousia*. Also, form does not seem entirely one because it is itself a potentiality for another (second) actuality and because form can exist both as an actuality and as a potentiality in an undeveloped offspring. So even though they struggle to show that form is one, the central books also show why it fails to be perfectly one. This is not inconsistent: form or essence is more one than accidental composites, genera, physical matter, etc., but less one than an unmoved mover. Because the form of a sensible *ousia* is one, it is a primary sensible *ousia*. Because it is one only to some extent, this form is not a primary *ousia*.

Such a form is not entirely intelligible, but this is due to its nature rather than a deficiency in Aristotle's treatment. Unity is the principle of knowledge (B 4, 999a28–29). Because forms of sensibles are imperfectly one, they are imperfectly knowable. Limited knowability is, I think, Aristotle's point when he makes the well-known remark in the first chapter of Z that the answer to the question "what is being?" is always sought and always puzzling (1028b2–4). Being and *ousia* in sensibles are always puzzling because they are only partially intelligible. We know essence insofar as it is an actuality, but essence manifests itself in a plurality of composites, a plurality that is accidental and thus unknowable. The central books show how sensible *ousia* can be one and thus how it can be known, but they show it to be one only to a degree.

To advert to the unintelligibility of sensible *ousia* certainly seems like a convenient excuse for giving an inadequate account of it. However, Aristotle's *Metaphysics* should be read in the context of Greek philosophy. He had before him the grossly inadequate accounts of the Presocratics and also the arguments of Plato that the sensible world is unintelligible. The accepted beginning of speculation about the sensible world is the problem of the one and the many. In the central books Aristotle is able to use the problem of the one and the many to wrest some intelligibility for the sensible world. In the context of Greek thought, Aristotle's inability to make the sensible world completely intelligible is far less significant than his success in securing some intelligibility for it. For his contemporaries, it is the plurality of the sensible world that poses the greatest obstacles. To find some unity here,

Aristotle advances a complex account of form and essence, an account that succeeded in transforming the terms of the problem. Indeed, one of the obstacles to recognizing the importance of the problem of the one and the many is Aristotle's success. Much of Western medieval philosophy took its start from his solutions, forgetting the problems from which he had begun. Aristotle's failure to account for everything in the physical world left a hole that medieval philosophers filled with God and that modern philosophers filled with physical laws. Yet, the major achievement on which these later developments depend is Aristotle's account of how individual, unchanging essences exist in a world of change and plurality.

This account of being and actuality is neither laid down as dogma nor deduced by argument. Instead, Aristotle supports it by showing the problems that remain unresolved if we do not adopt it, mostly problems involving unity. His doctrines must be true, because they alone seem capable of avoiding greater difficulties. Thus, he argues for his doctrines by drawing our attention to the difficulties. So understood, the central books belong among other works of speculative metaphysics: they argue for the existence of particular entities, actualities. To those who would dispute his conclusions, Aristotle would issue the challenge to advance a better account, an account that both removes the *aporiai* and provides more knowledge of sensibles.

Our inability to give a completely adequate account of sensible *ousiai* points to the existence of higher principles. These eternal causes, the unmoved movers, are also causes of plurality in sensibles; for life reproduces itself in an effort to attain the eternity of the unmoved movers. Yet even these additional principles do not succeed in making sensible being entirely intelligible. As Aristotle says, the question of being will always be puzzling. The central books present an account of the nature of sensible being to the extent Aristotle thinks it can be known, and they also show why, in all likelihood, nothing more can be known.

NOTES

INTRODUCTION

1. Philip Merlan, *From Platonism to Neoplatonism*, 2d ed. (The Hague: Martinus Nijhoff, 1960), p. 2.

CHAPTER ONE

1. Werner W. Jaeger, *Aristotle: Fundamentals of the History of His Development*, trans. Richard Robinson (Oxford: Oxford University Press, 1967), p. 204, maintains that the central books were written before A–E 1, and that Aristotle wrote E 2–4 to connect them to the latter. For a summary and analysis of other reconstructions of how the early (A–E 1) and the central books reflect Aristotle's development, see Giovanni Reale, *The Concept of First Philosophy and the Unity of the Metaphysics of Aristotle*, ed. and trans. John R. Catan (Albany, N.Y.: State University of New York Press, 1980), pp. 199–204.

2. See the preceding note. Even opponents of developmentalism have usually grouped A–E 1 together. For example, Joseph Owens, *The Doctrine of Being in the Aristotelian 'Metaphysics'*, 3d ed. (Toronto: Pontifical Institute of Mediaeval Studies, 1978), pp. 302–3, treats them together in the same chapter.

3. W. D. Ross, I, 351–52, agrees, but he cannot see what Aristotle intends these contrasts to tell us about the nature of metaphysics (*Aristotle's Metaphysics*, 2 vols. [Oxford: Clarendon Press, 1965]—hereafter cited as "Ross"). Christopher Kirwan seems to agree, but he focuses his attention not on the distinguishing marks between metaphysics and the other sciences but on how metaphysics could possibly supply the "what it is" of the subject matters of the special sciences (*Aristotle's* Metaphysics: *Books Γ, Δ, and E* [Oxford, Clarendon Press, 1971], pp. 183–84—cited hereafter as "Kirwan"). As Kirwan mentions, there is no place in the *Metaphysics* where Aristotle tries to supply the definition of an animal to the zoologist. However, this difficulty loses its force if we think in somewhat broader terms. In the central books Aristotle does characterize the "what it is" of sensible *ousiai*. The description he gives of what it is to be a sensible *ousia* is assumed by Aristotle's physics and by his biology, which is, after all, a branch of his physics. The opening discussion in *Metaphysics* E does not, however, aim to show the dependence of the special sciences on metaphysics but to contrast metaphysics with the special sciences.

4. The Greek verb here is singular. The reason is probably not that essence and formula are identical but that to investigate them both belongs to the same activity. As we will see, Aristotle uses the definition to investigate the essence.

5. I argue for this interpretation of book Γ in my "Aristotle on the Possibility of Metaphysics," *Revue de Philosophie Ancienne* IV (1987): 99–131. Although it is not a genus in the strict sense, being is a kind of genus, and this is important in book Γ.

6. Drawing on the *Posterior Analytics*, Owens, *Doctrine of Being*, pp. 291–92, distinguishes the "what is it" and "is it" questions on the ground that the latter

seeks a generic or quasi-generic knowledge while the former seeks the proper differentia of this genus. Because he denies that being is a genus, Owens does not realize how closely this picture fits the *Metaphysics*. He thinks that Aristotle's point is only that both questions fall under metaphysics, and he claims that the "what is it" question plays an insignificant role in the science (pp. 293–94). If, as Owens maintains, being *qua* being signifies (the genus of) *ousia* even in book Γ, then there is not much to be gained by inquiring into what being is. Conversely, if we can see Aristotle undertaking an inquiry into the "what is it" question, we will have reason to doubt that he identifies being *qua* being as the genus of *ousia* in book Γ.

Owens also distinguishes Aristotle's questions from medieval inquiries into existence and essence (292–93).

7. On the most natural reading, this passage (1026a2–3) says that the *formula* has motion and matter. Ross, following Albert Schwegler, *Die Metaphysik des Aristoteles*, 4 vols. (Frankfurt: Minerva, 1960), understands the passage to assert that the formula includes motion and the *thing* has matter. Hippocrates G. Apostle, *Aristotle's Metaphysics* (Grinnell, Iowa: The Peripatetic Press, 1979), translates it as if both motion and matter belonged to the thing. The natural reading is consistent with the parallel passage in K 7 (1064a23–28). The latter speaks only of taking the *formula* with the matter, and Ross and Apostle translate it as if it asserted that the formula includes the matter. Further, the analogy with snub contained in both passages implies that the formula should include matter. Of course, it is obvious that the matter is in the formula only because it is in the thing, and the same could be said of motion. So none of the alternative translations differ significantly.

As we will see, there are a variety of different kinds of matter. The present passage does not say which matter the formula needs to include.

8. W. Jaeger, *Aristotelis Metaphysica* (Oxford: Clarendon Press, 1973), excludes this parenthetical remark from his text.

9. Most current editors follow Schwegler, *Die Metaphysik*, IV, 16, in omitting the "in" from "inseparable" so that the sentence reads, "what is separate but not immobile." The problem with the manuscript reading is the "but." Those who emend the text take it to claim that physics has one character of theology, its objects exist separately, *but* not the other, these objects are movable. On this view, "separate" here does not have the sense that is has earlier in the chapter (independent of matter) but the sense it has at H 1, 1042a28–31 (self subsistent). The manuscript reading is rougher, but possible. (J. D. Denniston, *The Greek Particles*, 2d ed. [Oxford: Clarendon Press, 1970], p. 21, observes that ἀλλά need not be adversative; occasionally, it is "purely connective or progressive." He even cites a passage where ἀλλά is used with μέν in place of δέ and yet carries no adversative sense [p. 6].) It has the virtue of preserving a consistent sense for "separate" throughout the chapter and, as I shall show shortly, the virtue of making Aristotle's argument at this point intelligible. In contrast, Schwegler's emendation precludes understanding this text in conjunction with the preceding arguments for physics and mathematics being theoretical sciences. Further, the very next line of the text (a15) speaks of some mathematicals (presumably the objects of astronomy) as not separate because they are in matter. So immediately after the line under discussion Aristotle again uses "separate" in the sense it had earlier in E 1, independent of matter. Schwegler's emendation would make this line (1026a14) the only one in E 1 where separate meant self-

subsistent. On the other hand, the advantage of the emendation is that it makes the passage more symmetrical. Symmetry would be necessary if the passage were part of a proof of the existence of immobile, separate things. As it is, though, Aristotle's aim here is only to show that such a subject is prior and that it is treated by a theoretical science. Accordingly, I have followed the manuscripts. For a brief review of the literature on this issue see Owens, *Doctrine of Being,* pp. 296-97 n. 44.

10. For support for this rendering of 1026a14 see the reference to Denniston in the preceding note.

11. Kirwan, p. 187, proposes three reasons that changeless and separate things are prior. Drawing on books Z and Λ, and on the *Physics,* he claims that they are prior because they are concrete individuals, *ousiai,* and "unchanged changers." None of these enters into the argument of E 1.

12. Ross I, 222.

13. This is how Pseudo-Alexander explains why the identity of triangle and triangle having angles equal to two right angles is accidental and not essential (Alexander of Aphrodisias, *In Aristotelis Metaphysica Commentaria,* ed. Michael Hayduck [Berlin: George Reimer, 1891], p. 448.27-34—the commentary on books E–N is by a later writer, and I shall cite it hereafter as "Pseudo-Alexander" and the commentary on A–Δ as "Alexander.") Ross, I, 358, disputes this account on the ground that the text speaks only of whether *triangle* and triangle having angles equal to two right angles are other, and not of whether a particular object that happens to be a triangle and triangle having angles equal to two right angles are other. Instead, Ross claims that having angles equal to two right angles is a *per se* accident of the sort described at Δ 30, 1025a30-34; it is known by a science, geometry. Aristotle's point, according to Ross, is that the geometer does not treat the identity of triangle and triangle with this property; the identity or lack of identity is an accident. This cannot be correct, for the identity between triangle and triangle with angles equal to two right angles necessarily obtains. It is not accidental at all. Geometry can demonstrate the identity. On Ross's interpretation the identity scarcely seems an appropriate example to illustrate Aristotle's claim that there is no science of accidents. Moreover, there is no reason to doubt that the generalization of which this identity is an instance can also be known by a science. What obstacle could there be to knowing that *A* and *A with its essential attribute* are identical? This knowledge should belong to metaphysics. In short, Ross's interpretation leads to a consequence that is just the opposite if what Aristotle aims to show here.

Kirwan, p. 191, proposes that the identity is accidental because the expressions "triangle" and "triangle having angles equal to two right angles" cannot be substituted for each other. The result of replacing the latter with the former is an infinite regress and thus babbling. Kirwan needs to assume that Aristotle recognizes use/mention confusions and is pointing one out in the present passage. Even with this highly dubious assumption it remains unlikely that the identity or difference here is accidental in Kirwan's sense. What Kirwan probably has in mind is the case of snub (it is mentioned in *Soph. El.* 31, a text he cites). But snub is a *per se* attribute just as having angles equal to two right angles is. The infinite regress which arises when we try to define snub does *not* arise from a failure of substitution; it is a necessary consequence of the nature or snub (see below 2.4.3). Why, then, should the regress of the triangles arise from an accidental failure of substitution? The sophists may have (mistakenly) thought that an identity of Coriscus and musical Coriscus leads to an infinite regress (at least if Ross, I, 359, is right about 1026b17). But at 1026b11–12 Aristotle's argument needs a genuine accident that cannot be known by a science. It remains unclear, on Kirwan's interpretation, that the identity of triangle and triangle with angles that equal two right angles is truly accidental.

In sum, the lack of an explicit textual reference to a particular triangle seems a small price to pay in comparison with what the other alternatives would exact. Schwegler, *Die Metaphysik,* IV, 21–22, comes to the same conclusion after considering the interpretation later adopted by Ross.

14. Kirwan, pp. 190–1, maintains that Γ and E are inconsistent for this reason. It is preferable to reconcile the two texts if we can.

15. *Commentary on the Metaphysics of Aristotle,* trans. John P. Rowan, II (Chicago: Henry Regnery, 1961), VI. L.2:C 1180.

16. Richard Sorabji, *Necessity, Cause, and Blame* (Ithaca, N.Y.: Cornell University Press, 1980), pp. 3–25. Sorabji supports this position with an analysis of E 3 (pp. 7–13).

17. One place where Sorabji goes wrong is in distinguishing between accidental concomitants that are associated with causes and those that are associated with effects (pp. 5–6). An example of the latter is someone intending to quench his thirst at a well who is attacked on his way there (cf. *Phys.* B 5, 197a32–35). Quenching thirst is not an accidental concomitant; it is the final cause. Failure to pay sufficient attention to causes other than efficient cause contributes to Sorabji's willingness to say that the attack was nonaccidental or uncaused (p. 6).

According to Sorabji, "the case for saying that an accidental meeting . . . has no cause at all is that there is nothing which plays even this indirect explanatory role" (p. 11). Here he assumes that explanation is a wider concept that includes cause; so that if a meeting has no explanation it must have no cause. Earlier on the same page, he had noted (correctly) that not all causes are explanatory. It is consistent with the latter point that accidents might have causes but lack explanations (of the sort Sorabji seeks). The accidental meeting has many causes. What Sorabji seems to be seeking in the way of an explanation is some reason that the meeting *had* to occur. Obviously, an accidental meeting cannot be explained in *this* way. To say that the causes of accidents do not bring them about of necessity is not to say that the accidents are uncaused; it is merely to say that the causes are accidental.

Sorabji has also been criticized by Robert Heinaman, "Aristotle on Accidents," *Journal of the History of Philosophy* XXIII (1985): 316, on the ground that Aristotle does not distinguish the classes of caused and uncaused accidents. The only candidate Heinaman sees for the latter is the chance events of *Physics* B 4–6; they are "end-like results." But no such result need follow from a sequence of events. One could, for example, go to the market and not encounter one's creditor. Hence, Heinaman denies that the uncaused accidents represent any determinate class of accidents. This criticism is unjustified. First, failing to meet a creditor is as much a chance event, an "end-like result" as meeting the creditor: there are an indefinite number of accidents of that trip to the market. So there is no objection to equating the accidents of E 3 with those discussed in the *Physics.* But even if there were, Sorabji would not need a determinate distinction between caused and uncaused accidents. He can assume that the remarks of E 3 need not apply to all accidents. The opening sentence asserts only that there *are* principles that are not in the process of being generated or being destroyed (1027a29–30);

that is, that there are some principles of this sort, accidental principles. From the example Aristotle gives in this chapter, we can safely say that some principles of coincidental meeting are of this sort. Sorabji is wrong to call these latter uncaused accidents, but there is no assertion here that all the principles of all accidents are like these principles of coincidental meetings. For example, Socrates becomes musical through a process in time and at least one principle of such an accident could differ from those of coincidental meetings. So these objections to Sorabji cannot stand.

Heinaman's own arguments to the effect that Aristotle is "irremediably confused" are vitiated by two mistakes. First, he neglects to consider nature or essence, so that a statement like "the father heals" does not seem accidental to him (pp. 317–18). Second, he confuses different sorts of *per se*, so that the inherence of white in a surface seems to him to be not accidental but *per se* (p. 319).

18. Failure to notice this point has caused interpreters of this chapter much unnecessary grief. See Ross, I, 362–63; Kirwan, pp. 195–98. Sorabji, *Necessity, Cause, and Blame*, p. 9, sees the structure, but he is confused about the conclusion.

19. In the *Physics*, Aristotle says of chance and fortune:

> Concerning the manner in which they are causes, each of them belongs among the principles of motion [i.e., the efficient causes] because each is always among causes that are by nature or from thought, but the number of these is indeterminate. (B 6, 198a2–5)

There should be no doubt that what is by chance or by fortune is accidental (*Met.* E 2, 1027a17; 3, 1027b13).

20. In contrast, Arthur Madigan, "*Metaphysics* E 3: A Modest Proposal," *Phronesis* XXIX (1984): 123–36, reconstructs E 3 as a response made by Aristotle's students to objections to the conclusions of E 2. He makes no attempt to compare the inquiry into accidental being with the discussions of other ways of being.

21. Sorabji, *Necessity, Cause, and Blame*, p. 8, claims to find evidence for this at the beginning of E 3, but he shows only that accidents are still under consideration in this chapter and then goes on to speak of accidents as equivalent to accidental causes. This latter assumption underlies Sorabji's claim that an accident is uncaused. He cites 1027b12–14 to support this latter view.

22. Thomas Aquinas, *Commentary on the Metaphysics*, VI, L.3:C 1212, 1215, maintains that the accidental beings are found not to be accidental when traced back to a "common universal cause," for example, a celestial body. This is an attempt to save Aristotle from the assertion of beings not subject to the first principle.

23. Aquinas suggests a similar argument in *Commentary on the Metaphysics*, VI, L.2: C 1176.

CHAPTER TWO

1. This point is often overlooked, but see D. R. Cousin, "Aristotle's Doctrine of Substance," *Mind* XLII (1933): 327.

2. See Owens, *Doctrine of Being*, pp. 390–93; A. Gewirth, "Aristotle's Doctrine of Being," *Philosophical Review* LXII (1953): 588; James H. Lesher, "Aristotle on Form, Substance, and Universals: A Dilemma," *Phronesis* XVI (1971): 169–78.

3. Ross and Jaeger put the passage in parentheses in their editions of the text. Ross, II, 160, thinks the passage only intends to distinguish quality and *ousia*, a view at odds with Aristotle's examples. As he notices, on his interpretation, "three cubits" at 1028a16 does not belong in the discussion. He dismisses this example as one of many Aristotelian "irrelevancies." I take it to be a point against his interpretation.

4. *Notes on Book Zeta of Aristotle's Metaphysics, Study Aids Monograph No. 1,* ed. Myles Burnyeat (Oxford: Sub-Faculty of Philosophy, 1979), p. 1, maintains that Aristotle assumes that the subject of the "what is it" question is a substantial individual. If he were making this assumption, the passage would not be an argument.

5. Jaeger excises this term, "by nature," from his text. If it is genuine, as I think it is, the term indicates that even though we can express the essence of an attribute, the attribute has no essence by nature. (Cf. my discussion of the preceding argument.) The same idea could have been expressed as "*per se* in the proper sense." Indeed, this is what the text must mean even if "by nature" is excised. So even if Jaeger is right in thinking that "by nature" was originally a marginal note, it clarifies the text.

6. This view is enunciated clearly in *Notes on Zeta*, p. 2. There is another, less likely alternative: We could take τῆς οὐσίας in 1028a24 with both *per se* and separable, and render the sentence "For none of these either belongs to *ousia per se* or is able to be separated from *ousia*. . . ." The aporia would then be that the actions signified by the verbs neither belong to *ousiai per se*—so they, unlike the categories (1028a18–20) should not be beings—nor are separable from *ousiai*—so they should be beings. This interpretation assumes that although the categories are clearly beings, whether actions are beings is doubtful. It makes Aristotle's posing of the *aporia* using verbs important as the usual interpretation does not, and the conclusion drawn in 1028a30–31 would have to rest partly on a18–20. However, the usual interpretation is linguistically more plausible.

7. The authors of *Notes on Zeta*, p. 4, think that ὄν ἁπλῶς specifies the complete as opposed to the incomplete being. I cannot see what relevance this distinction would have in this context.

8. Ross, II, 160–61. Owens, *Doctrine of Being*, pp. 320–21, claims that each of the three types of priority mentioned here comes from the three groups described in Δ 11. But, as he puts it, "the correspondence is quite rough."

9. For interpretations different from what I shall propose, see Owens, *Doctrine of Being*, pp. 319–21; *Notes on Zeta*, pp. 4–7.

10. Ross, II, 161, claims that Aristotle confuses the first category and the essence of a thing.

11. This expectation motivates the gloss of Ascelpius, *In Metaphysicorum Libros A–Z Commentaria*, ed. Michael Hayduck (Berlin: George Reimer, 1888), *ad loc.* Gail Fine, "Separation," *Oxford Studies in Ancient Philosophy* II (1984): 35, accepts it; Donald Morrison, "Separation in Aristotle's *Metaphysics*," *Oxford Studies in Ancient Philosophy* III (1985): 136, does not, rightly I think. I shall soon suggest a motivation for accepting the text as it stands.

12. Fine, "Separation," p. 35, maintains that the pertinent type of separation in this passage is what she calls "capacity for independent existence": "A is separate from B just in case A can exist without, independently of, B" (p. 33). Part of the reason she accepts this view is that she also endorses a dubious textual emendation (see preceding note) which leads her to suppose that Aristotle has natural priority in mind here. I shall argue against this latter view shortly. In any case, it a mistake to suppose that a sensible *ousia* can exist without instances of other categories. Its separation from other categories cannot consist of "independent existence." In a footnote, she tries to foist the difficulties with her view on Aristotle (p. 36 n. 19). However, in her reply to Morrison, "Separation: A Reply to Morrison," *Oxford Studies in Ancient Philosophy* III (1985): 163, she "spells out" independent existence as the priority of a particular *ousia* to a particular instance of another category. I think this is right, as far as it goes, but for reasons I am about to explain, it cannot be the final word.

13. Just what a particular instance of a category other than *ousia* is has been the subject of controversy. The lines of dispute are drawn in G. E. L. Owen's "Inherence," *Phronesis* X (1965): 97–105, and J. L. Ackrill's *Aristotle's Categories and De Interpretatione* (Oxford: Clarendon Press, 1979), pp. 74–75. The present argument assumes that particular instances of categories other than *ousia* cannot exist in distinct *ousiai,* a view endorsed by Ackrill. If there is no other way to make sense of this argument (as seems to me to be the case), then we could take it as evidence for this view.

14. Donald Morrison, "Separation: A Reply to Fine," *Oxford Studies in Ancient Philosophy* III (1985): 171, raises problems about different attributes; for example, being heavier than one gram and metabolizing. These are *per se* attributes, not instances of a category other than *ousia*. Hence, they are not relevant.

15. Fine, "Separation," pp. 34–35, distinguishes several types of separation in her useful study. She does not, however, distinguish degrees of separation nor does she notice how Aristotle's insistence that *ousia* be separate alters in meaning. Morrison, "Separation in Aristotle's *Metaphysics,*" p. 126, does not regard the separation possessed by Aristotle's form as a legitimate type of separation.

16. Morrison, "Separation in Aristotle's *Metaphysics,*" pp. 138–41, regards separation as a kind of unity, for he describes separation as a kind of numeric distinctness. He does not pay sufficient attention to the variety of ones or to the complex role of one in other arguments. Because separation need not be defined through the type of numeric unity Morrison has in mind, Aristotle's separation in formula is more than a "face-saving dodge." More on this in the final chapter.

   Fine, "Separation," p. 39, comes close to recognizing a link between separation and unity, for she argues that the most important type of separation, independent existence, implies particularity and is implied by substantiality. Aristotle equates particularity and numeric unity in B 4 (999b33–34), and substantiality is associated with numeric unity, I shall argue. These equations make the positions of Fine and Morrison closer than either of them realizes.

17. Owens, *Doctrine of Being,* pp. 317–18, sees no differences at all between the two passages except that the formulation in Γ is "more elaborate and highly developed."

18. As noted earlier, Ross, II, 161, accuses Aristotle of confusing essence with the first category.

19. "This" (or "this something" as the Greek is often rendered) is often identified
    with the singular; J. A. Smith, "τόδε τι in Aristotle," *Classical Review* XXXV
    (1921): 19; Irving Block, "Substance in Aristotle," *Paideia,* Special Aristotle
    Issue (1978): 60. On the other hand, Harold Cherniss, *Aristotle's Criticism of
    Plato and the Academy* (Baltimore: Johns Hopkins Press, 1944), pp. 351–52 n.
    261, discusses passages where the expression is used of form. Owens, *Doctrine
    of Being,* pp. 386–95, maintains that, although Aristotle does use the expression
    to signify singular, in its primary sense the expression designates an entity that
    is neither singular nor universal, the form. I think that Aristotle signals the
    numeric unity of the singular and of the form when he calls each a "this."
    However, that form is numerically one needs to be shown.

20. I follow the number and order of their presentation in B 2–6. I also count
    1002b11–32 as a separate *aporia* for a total of fifteen *aporiai.* Ross follows B 1
    and counts fourteen *aporiai.*

21. Owens, *Doctrine of Being,* p. 325, also makes this point.

22. Owens, *Doctrine of Being,* p. 326, cites H 1, 1042a13–15 to support this view.
    However, while universal in this passage may refer to the species, there is no
    need that it do so. The passage could be referring to the Platonic notion that
    what is more universal is more of a principle (cf. B 3, 999a21–22; 4, 999a26–
    29). Thus, it is no less ambiguous than the passage under discussion.

23. Ross, I, 310. See also Owens, *Doctrine of Being,* p. 325.

24. Since Aristotle describes the second item on the first list in Δ 8—the causes of
    being, such as soul—by referring to substrate, it might seem that this item ought
    to be called *ousia* in respect of substrate rather than in respect of form. How-
    ever, Aristotle describes it as *present in* something which is not predicated of a
    substrate (1017b15–16). To say that it is in a substrate is not to say that it is a
    substrate. So it cannot be said to be an *ousia* by virtue of its substrate. Later,
    Aristotle identifies this *ousia,* the cause of being, with form.

25. Richard Rorty, "Genus as Matter: A Reading of *Metaphysics* Z–H," in *Exege-
    sis and Argument,* ed. E. N. Lee, A. P. D. Mourelatos, and R. M. Rorty,
    Phronesis, suppl. vol. I (1973): 395–97, recognizes two criteria: (1)
    determinability—the ability to receive logical predicates; and (2) self-reliance—
    the ability to persist through change. Aristotle does describe *ousiai* as *determi-
    nate* substrates (Z 1, 1028a26–27) and as not predicated of other substrates. But
    this is quite different from being able to receive predicates. Some *ousiai,* such
    as the unmoved movers, may perhaps be unable to receive predicates even
    though they are not said of anything else. Further, self-reliance, as Rorty under-
    stands it, is not an assumption but a consequence of Z 7–9. In any case, Rorty
    does not really use these criteria in his explication of Aristotle's argument.

    Ellen Stone Haring, "Substantial Form in Aristotle's *Metaphysics* Z," *Review
    of Metaphysics* X (1967): 309, regards "thisness" as the sole criterion of *ousia.*
    However, she never gives it a fixed sense. During her discussion she equates it
    with separability, completeness, self-containment, and independence (e.g.,
    p. 319). Whenever a new criterion appears in an argument, she deems it a new
    sense of "this." The criteria for *ousia* ought to be clear before Aristotle argues
    that something is or is not *ousia.*

    As I mentioned earlier, Fine, "Separation," pp. 35–36, and Morrison "Sepa-
    ration in Aristotle's *Metaphysics,*" p. 125, both emphasize separation. The
    latter, however, closely connects separation with all of Aristotle's other criteria,
    including unity:

Separation is not one criterion of substance among the others, each serving to help establish the priority relations that structure Aristotle's universe into substances. Instead, separation is the result of, and expresses, the priority relations established by all the other criteria.

26. *Notes on Zeta*, p. 12, mistakenly identifies the reference to first substrate (τὸ ὑποκείμενον πρῶτον) at 1029a1-2 with passages that speak of the "substrate that is first for each thing" (τὸ ὑποκείμενον ἑκάστῳ πρῶτον) at Δ 18, 1022a16-19 and *Physics* A 9, 192a31-32. The substrate that is first for each thing is the matter in which the attributes inhere; this is the thing's proximate matter. Since this matter could be said of another matter, it is apparently not the first but the last matter (cf. *Met.* H 4, 1044a15-18; 1044b1-3; 6, 1045b18). In contrast, the primary substrate is primary because it is not a substrate through something else; others are substrates through it.

27. Malcolm Schofield, "*Metaph.* Z 3: Some Suggestions," *Phronesis* XVII (1972): 99-101, recognizes the distinction, but he denies that what I call "indeterminate matter" is matter. He thinks that the indeterminate result of stripping away all attributes is nothing at all. The one passage that asserts the contrary, the remark "unless the thing defined by them [the dimensions] is something" at 1029a18, Schofield dismisses as an "inept gloss" (p. 99). The interpretation I shall advance is compatible with this text. Schofield's mistake arises from taking Z 3 out of its context: he fails to see the role that the list of Z 2 plays in the discussion. The decisive objection to his interpretation is that bronze, wood, and the other matters do fall under categories, contrary to what Aristotle claims of "matter" at 1029a20-23. Schofield expresses doubts about the meaning of a part of this passage (p. 101); I think, though, that Aristotle intends to say here that the indeterminate matter is not a categorial being. The contributors to *Notes on Zeta*, p. 14, apparently agree. However, their alternative (designated as interpretation A) to Schofield's interpretation also fails to recognize properly the distinction between the material substrate and the completely undetermined matter that figures in this argument.

28. This word is usually rendered as "abstracting." But abstraction, for Aristotle, is just a kind of subtraction. (See M.-D. Philippe, "ἀφαίρεσις, πρόσθεσις, χωρίζειν dans la philosophie d'Aristote," *Revue Thomiste* LVI [1948]: 461-79.) In the present context, rendering the term as "subtraction" enables us to see argument's assumptions more perspicuously, and also to connect Z 3 with the chapters that follow.

29. The Greek word for nothing, οὐδέν, is the subject of puns in the *Parmenides* because it can also be construed as οὐδ᾽ἕν, "not one." It is possible that Aristotle has something like this in mind when he declares that after subtraction, we see *nothing* (οὐδέν) unless it is *something* (τί) delimited by what was subtracted (1029a16-18), a passage that bothers Schofield, "*Metaph.* Z 3," pp. 97-99.

30. Some have taken the opposite approach and moved 1029a33-34 into Z 4. Hans von Arnim proposed this reading of the text, "Zu W. Jaegers Grundlegung der Entwicklungsgeschichte des Aristoteles," *Wiener Studien* XLVI (1928): 39-40; and Owens, *Doctrine of Being*, p. 347, accepts it.

31. Interestingly, Jaeger, *Studien zur Entstehungsgeschichte der Metaphysik* (Berlin: Weidmann, 1912), pp. 61-62; *Aristotle*, pp. 198-99, excludes 1029b3-12 along with two passages on unity, Z 12 and H 6, as later additions to Z-H, though his

grounds for excluding 1029b3–12 differ from his grounds for excluding the other two texts. A virtue of my analysis is that it lets us make more sense of the text as we have it.

32. The contributors to *Notes on Zeta* come to the same conclusion, pp. 16, 11–12.

33. Ross, II, 168.

34. M. J. Woods, "Substance and Essence in Aristotle," *Proceedings of the Aristotelian Society* LXXV (1974–75): 170–71, avoids the first two objections by limiting the linguistic discussion to the first ten lines of the chapter 1029b13–22. He then suggests that 1030a27–28 refer to a second linguistic discussion that immediately precedes these lines. This does not resolve the third problem. Moreover, Woods does not relate this interpretation of Z 4's structure to Aristotle's inquiry into whether essence is *ousia*. See also the assessment of Woods's article in *Notes on Zeta*, p. 27.

35. Ross, II, 166, translates, "the essence of each thing is what it is said to be *per se.*" This is equivalent to my rendering, but it makes the passage more difficult to connect with the discussion that follows in 1029b29 ff.

36. Gareth Matthews, "Accidental Unities," in *Language and Logos: Studies in Ancient Greek Philosophy Presented to G. E. L. Owen,* ed. Malcolm Schofield and Martha Craven Nussbaum (Cambridge: Cambridge University Press, 1983), p. 224, calls them "kooky objects." His discussion of these chapters addresses problems of identity and the semantics of ordinary language. If my interpretation is correct, Z 4–5 treat a problem Aristotle regards as more fundamental: why do these things lack essences? or, to use Matthews's phrase, what is so kooky about kooky objects?

37. Cf. Pseudo-Alexander, p. 467.35–37.

38. Following Ross's text. Jaeger, following the text of Bonitz, brackets εἶναι. For him, the sentence should be rendered, "the white man is white but not the essence of white." By implication, the white man is the essence of white man or, perhaps, the essence of man. Since, though, the identity between thing and essence is not pertinent here, I think the text of the manuscripts should be retained. Although Jaeger does not comment here, he probably has in mind *Categories* 5, 2a29–34. The text in the manuscripts resembles 1029b14–15.

39. Ross, II, 169.

40. More on this point shortly.

41. Ross, II, 169. Aristotle does make similar points in the *Topics*. At E 3, 130b38 ff. he complains of definitions of properties that refer to their subjects: the subject is no clearer than the property to be defined. At Z 1, 139b15–18 Aristotle mentions the mistake of including too much in a definition.

42. Ross, II, 169.

43. Ross, II, 169–70.

44. Two of the other terms also refer to additions of both things and formulae: πρόσεστιν—*Met.* Θ 5, 1047b35–1048a2 speaks of "when" and "how" and the others that must be added to the definition of potency, but at *Politics* Γ 15, 1286a17–18 the term is used to speak of the addition of passions to a man; προσκεῖσθαι—Aristotle is concerned with an addition to a formula when he claims that the definition should add nothing to the formula making clear the *ousia* (*Topics* E 3, 130b25–28), but the term also signifies an addition in things when Aristotle maintains that the primary motion is added to the particular natural motion of each sphere (*De Caelo* B 12, 293a9–11). Προστιθέναι,

though, seems to be reserved for additions of definition (*N. E.* E 9, 1136b3-5; *An. Po.* B 5, 91b26-27).

45. The text here implies that the *Iliad* is "one by continuity." This is puzzling on two counts. First, continuity is one of the main ways that "one" is said (I 1, 1052a16-20). Since what is one has a definition, the *Iliad* ought to have a definition, precisely what is denied in this passage. Second, Aristotle claims elsewhere that the *Iliad* is one by being bound together (H 6, 1045a12-14; *An. Po.* B 10, 93b35-37; *Poetics* 20, 1457a28-30), but this kind of unity differs from continuity (*Met.* I 1, 1052a19-20). Both difficulties vanish once we realize that Aristotle recognizes two kinds of continuity, continuity by nature and continuity by art (*Met.* Δ 6, 1016a4). Being bound together is a kind of continuity (Δ 6, 1015b36-1016a1), but it belongs under the heading of continuous by art. So even though the *Iliad* is one by continuity, it is not thereby among the main ways one is said (I 1, 1052a19-20). It is for this reason that it lacks a definition. The *Iliad* is one by being bound together, but not one by being continuous by nature.

46. The idea that formulae define things rather than terms seems strange when compared with current thinking, but it is Aristotle's view. See T. H. Irwin, "Aristotle's Concept of Signification," in *Language and Logos,* ed. Malcolm Schofield and Martha Craven Nussbaum, pp. 241-66, esp. pp. 245-48. Irwin does not apply this insight to Z 4-5.

47. Of those who have written about Z 4-5, only J. E. Hare, "Aristotle and the Definition of Natural Kinds," *Phronesis* XXIV (1979): 168-79, has recognized that Z 4 intends to argue that all attempts to define white must fail. Hare seems to think that white, like snub, fails to have a definition because its definiens includes white (pp. 170-1). But Aristotle does define white without including it in its definiens (as "piercing color"), and the problem is not that the definiens of white includes white but that it includes *ousia*. Further, Hare does not recognize the differences between formulae of white and of snub and consequently runs together the arguments of Z 4 with the arguments of Z 5 (pp. 175-76). He also neglects the second way something is not *per se,* "not by addition." The subject of Z 4 is accidental attributes and composites, and although the arguments here resemble what Aristotle says about defining "natural things," what emerges from the chapter is that the ontological relation of subject and attribute precludes definition, an issue different from the definition of natural things.

48. Both Asclepius, p. 384.9-21, and Pseudo-Alexander, p. 468.6-26, recognize that the formulae of accidental composites are not *per se* because they fail by addition or the other way, but neither explains why this is the case.

49. Ross, II, 169. Pseudo-Alexander, p. 468.13-26, tries to circumvent the difficulty by supposing that Aristotle refers to what ought (δεῖν) to be added to the formula of a composite. He tries to place both additions in the formula.

50. The way Aristotle poses this question shows that there is a difference between to be a cloak and the essence of cloak. The distinction parallels that between formula and definition. Later (2.4.5), we will see that "to be a cloak" is a secondary essence.

51. Bonitz and Jaeger add τόδε before τι so that the sentence reads, "for an essence is just a this."

52. Montgomery Furth, *Aristotle's* Metaphysics: *Books VII–X: Zeta, Eta, Theta, Iota* (Indianapolis: Hackett, 1985), p. 108, rejects this rendering as impossible, based on Jonathan Barnes's discussion of ὅπερ, *Aristotle's Posterior Analytics*

(Oxford: Clarendon Press, 1975), p. 168. Barnes claims that "Y is ὅπερ X" means X belongs to the essence of Y. It can mean this, as one of the passages he cites shows. However, the other passage he cites, Γ 4, 1007a32–33, need not and probably does not have this sense, for it is parallel to Z 4, 1030a1–2. The latter speaks of the being of white as not belonging to the essence of white man. On the basis of 1007a32–33, "Y is ὅπερ X" could mean, Y is the being of X (cf. *Cat.* 5, 2a27–34). Thus, Aristotle's claim at 1030a3 that essence is ὅπερ something could mean that essence is the being of something, exactly what Ross wishes to express with his translation. Because Furth rejects this approach, and because the claim that essence is ὅπερ something obviously does not assert that the something is contained in the essence, he is left to interpret this passage as if essence were a species of the something. I do not find this intelligible.

53. The text seems to confuse being a this and having a this, for Aristotle moves from the composite's not being a this (1030a4) to the claim that this belongs to *ousia* (1030a5–6). Likewise, is an essence something that belongs to a this or something that a this is? Though Aristotle's failure to draw distinctions here may look like a serious confusion, it does not lead to any real difficulties. In English we speak indifferently of someone's being beautiful and having beauty or of a thing's being one or having unity. In Greek, the same term does duty as both an adjective and a noun. More on "is"/"has" issues later.

54. This is Ross's, II, 170, interpretation of the argument. While he retains the manuscript reading of 1030a3, he equates ὅπερ τι with ὅπερ τόδε τι.

55. See H. Bonitz, *Index Aristotelicus.* 2d ed. (Graz: Akademische Druck-U., 1955), p. 533b36–55 and my n. 83.

56. See Woods, "Substance and Essence," p. 172; Ross, II, 168; Hare, "Aristotle and the Definition of Natural Kinds," p. 170. The last two, and perhaps Woods as well, identify this *per se* with the second sense of *per se* at *Posterior Analytics* A 4, 73a37 ff. However, the latter passage considers a sense of *per se* that is associated with essence. That white inheres in a surface *per se* is not pertinent to the main concerns of Z 4 just because it does not depend on essence. Thus, the second type of *per se* in the *Posterior Analytics* is not under consideration in Z 4. As we will see, Aristotle examines it in Z 5.

57. This sense does not appear in the description at *Posterior Analytics* 73a34 ff. Ross is inconsistent: at II, 168 he asserts that the *per se* at issue in Z 4 is the first sense mentioned in the *Posterior Analytics'* account; at I, 334 he suggests that the *per se* at issue in Z 4 is a different one, the essence discussed at 1022a25–27.

58. This is Ross's view, II, 167. He thinks that surface is the thing added.

59. Woods, "Substance and Essence," pp. 173–74, argues for this interpretation. Hare, "Aristotle and the Definition of Natural Kinds," p. 170, agrees. According to Woods, Ross's interpretation must be incorrect because if we already know that white does not belong to surface *per se,* then it is obvious that white surface does not belong to surface *per se* for the very same reason. This argument is weak. The goal of Aristotle's previous discussion of white is to show that a particular sense of *per se* is not pertinent to the claim that the essence of something is what belongs to it *per se.* Since surface is not the first recipient of white surface, it is *not* obvious that the failure of white to belong to surface *per se* would entail the failure of white surface to belong *per se.* Aristotle's point could be simply that the same criterion that works to show the former failure can also be applied to show the latter failure: to be a surface is neither to be

white nor to be a white surface. Indeed, the Greek particles that introduce this sentence support this interpretation (Ross's). Ἀλλὰ μὴν οὐδέ indicates assent to what precedes and the introduction of a stronger negative condition (see Denniston, *The Greek Particles*, pp. 342–43, 345). οὐδέ at 1029b18 appears parallel to οὐδὲ . . . οὐ at 1029b16. Nevertheless, Woods's interpretation remains possible.

60. Ross II, 168; Woods, "Substance and Essence," p. 174; Hare, "Aristotle and the Definition of Natural Kinds," p. 170; *Notes on Zeta*, pp. 18–19.

61. The authors of *Notes on Zeta*, pp. 18–19, are puzzled about how 1029b19-22 could be a conclusion.

62. *Notes on Zeta*, p. 19, considers two interpretations of this passage that take αὐτό as white, but both assume, following Ross and Woods, that the sentence intends to exclude definiendum from definiens. The interpretation I advance is never considered.

63. Ross, I, 334, incorrectly identifies this latter with the primary recipient of Δ 18, 1022a29-32. Snub is *per se* in a different sense than any distinguished in Z 4. Were this not so, discussion of it in Z 5 would be superfluous.

64. That such *per se* composites are at issue in 1030b28-1031a2 is clear. However, Ross does not clearly distinguish between the treatments of snub and snub nose. D. M. Balme, "The Snub," *Ancient Philosophy* IV (1984): 6, does; but he assimilates the latter to the treatment of snub.

65. This is the most straightforward interpretation of the μέν/δέ opposition in 1030b28-30. There is no good reason to follow Ross (and Balme, "The Snub," p. 6) in taking the εἰ in 1030b30 as beginning an explanation of why snub and concave are not identical. This is already clear. However, even if the hypothetical in 1030b30 were the non-identity of snub and concave, the non-identity of snub nose and concave nose would follow from it and the conditional of 1030b28-30 by modus tollens. There would still be no reason to doubt that snub nose rather than snub is under consideration in what follows.

66. Ross, II, 174.

67. This interpretation follows Balme, "The Snub," p. 6, in taking εἰ δὲ μή . . . in 1030b35 as an explanation for the first alternative mentioned in 1030b32, that snub nose cannot even be said. Balme does not seem to realize that the same consequences follow whether the formula of snub nose is not said at all or contains an element said twice. Ross, II, 174, suggests that the infinite regress could be construed as I have taken it, but he does not connect the regress to the inability to say snub nose suggested in 1030b32. He follows Pseudo-Alexander, p. 478.15-18, in taking 1030b35 to be denying the preceding denial that things of this sort have essences. The latter construes the argument as a *reductio*: if these things do have essences, there will be an infinite regress; so they cannot have essences.

68. Ross, II, 174. He also notes that a corresponding distinction occurs at Z 6, 1031b23-25.

69. Balme, "The Snub," p. 7, dismisses Ross's objection on similar grounds.

70. Russell Dancy showed me the force of this objection. Non-identity is one of the assumptions that Gregory Vlastos, "The Third Man Argument in the *Parmenides*," *Philosophical Review* LXI (1954): 319-49, proposes to generate the third man regress.

71. The regress of Z 5 bears some similarity to the argument at the beginning of the second hypothesis of the *Parmenides* (142c–143a) that shows the inseparability of one and being. Plato begins with the being that is one and then attempts to separate its oneness from its being. However, the one that is separated from the one being also *is,* and the being that is separated from the one being also is *one.* Thus, each of the two components is exactly the same as the original one being. The same separation can be attempted for these two new components with the same results: each will generate two more one beings. This procedure can be carried on *ad infinitum.* This argument can be criticized on the same grounds as that of Z 5: the supposed infinity is bogus without a non-identity assumption. In both cases, though, the regress is intended to show the inseparability of two constituents in a composite.

72. Among the "ones" mentioned in Δ 6, Aristotle includes the one in formula: something is one in this way if its formula is indivisible into another formula that makes clear the same thing (1016a32–34). In this passage, unity of formula depends on the unity of a thing. In Z 4–5 Aristotle uses the unity or lack of unity in a formula to determine whether a thing is one.

73. The distinction of the two modes of investigation is drawn in this way by Schwegler, *Die Metaphysik,* IV, 48–51, and Owens, *Doctrine of Being,* p. 348. Aristotle distinguishes the same two approaches in other texts; for example, the treatment of the infinite at *Physics* Γ 5, 204b6–10.

74. As before, I use quotation marks as delimiters here; they do not imply that Aristotle regards "what it is" as a phrase rather than a thing. My use of "what it is" as a noun is awkward, but it preserves Aristotle's usage.

75. Z 4 probably uses the latter at 1030a21–23 to accent the parallel with τὸ τί ἐστιν. This parallel also suggests two of Aristotle's four scientific questions (*An. Po.* B 1, 89b24–25; cf. 90a1).

76. In Z 1 "what it is" signifies *ousia* in contrast with other categories (1028a11–13). But Z 4 declares that it signifies not only *ousia* and the "this something" but also, in another fashion, each of the other categories (1030a18–20). Further, definition is apparently distinct from "what it is" because Aristotle claims that the two are said in as many ways (1030a16–17). Though Aristotle sometimes seems to use the expression "what it is" to refer to essence or to a part of essence (e.g., *An. Po.* B 3, 90b30–31), this cannot be his intention here because he goes on to support claims about essence by referring to the "what it is." Ross, II, 171, claims that "what it is" can refer to either a part or the whole of the answer to a "what is so and so" question, while essence always refers to the whole answer. In other words, the "what it is" is either a part or the whole of essence. This is inconsistent with Ross's idea that what occurs before 1030a27 concerns what we say rather than the facts; unless, that is, the treatment of a part or whole of essence before 1030a27 falls under the heading of what we say, but the treatment of the whole of essence after this line is a factual inquiry (II, 171, 168). Though I do not agree that 1030a27 marks a transition between a linguistic and factual treatment of essence, my interpretation of "what it is" as the formula is more consistent with this division than the account Ross offers. Moreover, Ross's view of "what it is" is difficult to square with the analogy that Aristotle draws between "what it is" and essence at 1030a29–31 and with Aristotle's claim that "what it is" belongs primarily to *ousia* and then to other categories. For Ross, the latter would be the assertion that all or a portion of essence belongs primarily to *ousia* and secondarily to other categories. What could this mean?

77. Aristotle actually ascribes the view that non-being is a being (though not simply so) to others (1030a25–26). Plato's *Sophist* is the only candidate among extant texts. Plato also regards non-being as not simple but the result of a combination. While the combination of μέγιστα γένη is quite different from the combination of *ousia* and something else of which Aristotle speaks in Γ 2, both accounts agree in taking non-being as some sort of composite.

78. As Ross, II, 168, maintains.

79. A possible, though less likely alternative for the next portion of this sentence is: "since 'is' (ἐστι) is said rightly neither equivocally nor univocally. . . ."

80. Owens, *Doctrine of Being*, pp. 350–51, also maintains that the two express equivalent doctrines. He suggests that "addition and subtraction" is an earlier formulation. For reasons that will soon be apparent, I think that Aristotle had good reasons for using the "addition and subtraction" formulation in this context.

81. Ross, II, 171, following Pseudo-Alexander in part, maintains that addition and subtraction refer to the qualifications that must be added to being in order to say that non-*ousiai* are beings and also to what is taken away from the full meaning of being. A non-*ousia* is not just a being but a being of a certain sort. This interpretation is unlikely. First, it requires that addition be used in a way that is very different from its other uses so far in Z 4. Second, it is inconsistent with Ross's view that this passage belongs to a "factual" inquiry and thus does not describe what we say about being. Third, it is inconsistent with the immediate context of 1030a32–b1. This passage purports to be a justification for the claim in the preceding lines that essence belongs primarily to *ousiai* and in lesser ways to non-*ousiai*. To say that these non-*ousiai* are beings with various additional qualifications does not explain why they have essences. Or does Ross perhaps have in mind that since simple being is *ousia* (1028a30–31), a qualified being is related to *ousia* and has a sort of essence by virtue of this relation? This is not what he says; it is hard to see that it is even consistent with what he says. However, if this is Ross's view, then his position is close to the interpretation I shall advance.

82. Other examples of pluralities composed of things that lack unity appear at *Parmenides* 158b–c and 165a–c.

83. In H 2 Aristotle explains that it is possible to define an accidental composite by giving a formula of its matter, or of its form (the attribute), or of the addition of both (1043a14–19). The latter is the best and most proper definition.

84. The phrase that I render "essence of white man" here is literally "being for a white man." As we saw earlier, Aristotle sometimes speaks as though these two locutions differ. In the present context, though, there can be no doubt that "being for white man" indicates the putative essence of white man because while the issue is whether essence and thing are one, Aristotle considers whether the being and the thing are one (1031a15–21).

85. Ross, II, 176.

86. Ross, II, 176–77; The authors of *Notes on Zeta* endorse this interpretation, pp. 33–35; as does Furth, *Aristotle's* Metaphysics, pp. 111–12.

87. Furth's translation of this line is mistaken. Ross is right.

88. Ross, II, 177.

89. *Notes on Zeta*, p. 35.

90. *Notes on Zeta*, p. 37, claims that this μέν remains unanswered.

91. Ross, II, 177, is right to think that Z 6 contains "covert criticism" of the Platonic forms, but he does not quite see where it lies.

92. ἔτι in 1032a2 does not introduce a new argument; it continues the thought of the γάρ in the preceding sentence. Both sentences offer τὸ ἕν as an example to illustrate the infinite regress.

93. Under the influence of Vlastos's well-known article on Plato's *Parmenides* ("The Third Man Argument in the *Parmenides*"), Woods, "Substance and Essence," pp. 167–80, attempts to reformulate Aristotle's discussion in Z 4–6 in terms of "non-identity" and "self-predication" assumptions. The infinite regress under discussion seems like it would be a prime candidate for Woods's analysis; but, surprisingly, he does not mention it. Perhaps a reason he overlooks it is that the argument makes no "non-identity" assumption. There is no reason to think that these essences differ from each other. Does the lack of a non-identity assumption here cast doubt on the argument? Aristotle does not explain why an infinity of essences is unacceptable, but one reason is the following. If the essence is severed from the thing, there is no way to give the complete essence of the thing. What seems to be the essence turns out to be a thing whose own essence lies in something else. In order to know a thing it is necessary to know its essence. But knowledge of the essence is impossible because it requires knowing an infinity of essences. Understood in this way, the regress does not require that we be able to distinguish the essences but only that the essence of something always lie in something else. Formulating Aristotle's argument in terms of the "self-predication" and "non-identity" assumptions would make it neither more true nor more perspicuous.

94. There may be some hesitation about agreeing that this is the same description as we see in either Z 4 or Z 6 because here Aristotle speaks of what the *Categories* terms "in," whereas in those two passages he seems to have in mind what the *Categories* terms "said of" (2, 1a20–29). Book Z does not use this terminology, and in Z 4 Aristotle contrasts what is primary with attributes that, according to the *Categories,* are "in" *ousiai* (1030a13–14), as the quoted passage does. But the insistence in Z 4 that what is primary be a "species of a genus" shows that Aristotle also contrasts the primary with some of what the *Categories* claims is "said of" primary *ousiai.*

95. Ross, II, 176, describes τὰ καθ' αὑτὰ λεγόμενα as "terms denoting a self-subsistent unity, i.e. either a *summum genus* or a species, either in the category of substance or in some other." He does not compare this unity with what we saw in the preceding chapters.

96. This may be Ross's view, II, 176.

97. Ross, II, 181; Suzanne Mansion, "Sur la composition ontologique des substances sensibles chez Aristote (Métaphysique Z 7–9)," in *Philomathes: Studies and Essays in the Humanities in Memory of Philip Merlan,* ed. R. B. Palmer and R. Hamerton Kelly (The Hague, 1971), p. 75, rpt. as "The Ontological Composition of Sensible Substances in Aristotle," in *Articles on Aristotle: 3. Metaphysics,* ed. Jonathan Barnes, Malcolm Schofield, and Richard Sorabji (London: Duckworth, 1975), p. 80. Furth, *Aristotle's* Metaphysics, pp. 114–15.

98. See n. 73 above.

99. Ross, II, 188, thinks that the referent here is the substratum mentioned in a31. Apostle, *Aristotle's* Metaphysics, p. 332, translates it as "sphere," but his commentary assumes that it is the form. Furth, *Aristotle's* Metaphysics, p. 17, also thinks that Aristotle refers to the form. Form seems the most likely referent

considering the inference drawn in the next sentence (b5–7), especially if Jaeger is right in excising οὐδέ in 1033b5. But the argument will work with either.

100. οἶον. See Ross's, II, 188, remark on this usage.

101. G. E. L. Owen, "Prolegomenon to Z 7–9," in *Notes on Zeta*, p. 44, also notices this difficulty.

102. This, I think, is also the point of 7, 1032b28–30; and it is consistent with the manuscript readings of the passage. The comparison to the stones is difficult but not impossible. See Ross, II, 184–85; *Notes on Zeta*, pp. 57–60.

103. This view is not widely held. Irving M. Copi, "Essence and Accident," in *Aristotle: A Collection of Critical Essays*, ed. J. M. E. Moravcsik (Notre Dame: University of Notre Dame Press, 1968), p. 153, calls the "fixity of the species . . . a casual rather than an integral part of the Aristotelian system." James G. Lennox, "Are Aristotelian Species Eternal?" in *Aristotle on Nature and Living Things*, ed. Allan Gotthelf (Pittsburgh: Mathesis Publications, 1985), pp. 88–89, argues that the form characteristic of a species is not eternal because "it is not the sort of thing that can be eternal, even though it is the basis for predicating eternality of a natural kind and of its members." Were this true, it would violate the principle that that in respect of which things are said to possess a character has that character itself in the highest degree (α 1, 993b24–26). Since Z 7–9 are part of an endeavor to determine the nature of this form, it seems to be premature to decide that form could not be the sort of thing to be eternal without considering the rest of that endeavor.

104. Drawing on the *Generation of Animals*, Lennox, "Are Aristotelian Species Universal?" p. 90, notes that though "new kinds arise . . . they have a natural tendency to revert to the female sort." Rorty, "Genus as Matter," pp. 412–13, compares hybrids to the "heaps" that Aristotle contrasts with what is one in Z 16.

105. Although Z 7–9 do not describe *ousia* as temporally prior, Aristotle speaks of the temporal priority of *ousia* at Z 1, 1028a32–34. This latter passage traces *ousia*'s temporal priority to its separability, but Aristotle may have in mind something similar to the necessary existence of the *ousia* in actuality described in Z 9.

106. Ross, II, 196. Owens, *Doctrine of Being*, p. 360.

107. Ross, II, 196, thinks that the treatment of these questions is interwoven, and he indicates which portions of Z 10 deal with which questions in his paraphrase (pp. 194–95). Furth, *Aristotle's* Metaphysics, pp. 22–27, also accepts this breakdown of the chapter. Later in this section, I shall argue that both questions stem from the same assumption.

108. The authors of *Notes on Zeta*, pp. 79–80, do not consider the possibility that the acute angle is posterior to the right as the intelligible matter is posterior to the form.

109. *Notes on Zeta*, pp. 93, 94; Furth, *Aristotle's* Metaphysics, p. 120.

110. Ross, II, 203. *Notes on Zeta*, pp. 92–93. Ross, II, 205, maintains that the proximate matter must be mentioned "in certain cases."

111. Ross, II, 203–4, points out the dissimilarity in the two cases and accuses Aristotle of faulty reasoning. He thinks that Aristotle should have concluded that the definitions of mathematicals do include matter, namely, space. This is not Aristotle's view of space; but even if it were, Ross's proposal could not apply to numbers. It does not explain why there are distinct forms of numbers.

112. Owens, *Doctrine of Being*, pp. 361-62.

113. The type of priority at issue here is termed priority in *ousia* in Δ 11, 1019a2-4.

114. Ross, I, c-ci, calls the man that is composed of form and matter taken universally the "materiate universal," and he identifies it with the species of the *Categories*. John A. Driscoll, "ΕΙΔΗ in Aristotle's Earlier and Later Theories of Substance," in *Studies in Aristotle*, ed. Dominic J. O'Meara (Washington: The Catholic University of America Press, 1981), pp. 146-48, advances three arguments for this identification. However, his case rests on showing that the species of the *Categories* could not be form. He never considers the possibility that the formal constituent of the universal composite might not be the form, nor does he consider the possibility that the composite universal be neither form nor species. The formal constituent of the composite of formula and matter "taken universally" must itself be universal.

115. See n. 110, and my discussion of this passage in 2.7.2

116. Jaeger deletes τὸ μέρος from the latter of the two passages because it appears in different places in the sentence. Was it perhaps read back into this passage from 1036b30-32?

117. Pseudo-Alexander, Bonitz, and Jaeger (*ad loc.*) all think the passage under discussion and the opening lines of Z 10 deal with the same question, and they accordingly have doubts about whether the passage is correctly placed. Ross, II, 203, defends its position in the manuscripts, but he still translates the problem as if it were the same as the one at the beginning of Z 10. He also finds fault with Aristotle's reasoning, an indication, I think, that he has misinterpreted the issue here.

118. Ross translates this question: "Regarding the objects of mathematics, why are the formulae of the parts not parts of the formulae of the wholes; e.g. why are not the semicircles included in the formula of the circle?" Since a semicircle belongs to the intelligible matter of the circle and is also a part of the circle, the question whether it is included in the formula of the circle could be illustrating the question whether the formulae of the parts are included in the formula of the whole (as Ross thinks), or it could be illustrating the question whether the formula of the matter is part of the formula of the thing (my interpretation). Thus, Ross's interpretation cannot be decisively excluded.

   Furth's rendering of the part of the question that concerns semicircles makes the problem here even closer to the one with which Z 10 begins. I think it unlikely that οἷον means "as" here, as Furth requires (*Aristotle's* Metaphysics, *ad loc.*).

119. Jaeger, *Studien*, pp. 57-58. He also thinks that 1037a10-18 is a later addition (*Aristotle*, p. 199 n. 2).

120. Suzanne Mansion, "La Notion de Matière en *Métaphysique* Z 10 et 11," in *Études sur la Métaphysique D'Aristote: Actes du VIe Symposium Aristotelicum*, ed. Pierre Aubenque (Paris: J. Vrin, 1979), p. 201, thinks that the presence of matter in the sensible composite makes it a "contorted" *ousia* and shows the necessity for a pure form. As we will see, this latter form is more one than the form that is in sensibles. While Z 10-11 show the requirements that essence must satisfy and what it must be like to satisfy them, they do not adequately explain the character of essence. The subsequent development, especially book H, makes essence more plausible. Despite the inherent difficulties, calling the sensible composite "contorted" is an exaggeration.

121. *Studien*, pp. 53–61. Jaeger argues that both were written after the main body of Z–H, placed loosely in the scroll, and later sewn into the text.

122. According to Owens, *Doctrine of Being*, pp. 362–63, Z 12 helps to explain the identity of the composite and its essence by showing the unity of the former. However, there is no mention of the composite in Z 12. Like most commentators, Owens accepts Jaeger's claim that Z 12 and H 6 constitute a doublet and then advances the argument of H 6 as what Aristotle means to say in Z 12. Rorty's claim that the genus is matter and his analysis of Z–H in "Genus as Matter" presuppose the doctrinal identity of the two chapters.

123. Ross, II, 207.

124. Ross, II, 238; Jaeger, *Studien*, p. 60; cf. Rorty, "Genus as Matter," p. 407.

125. Ross adopts an emendation proposed by Joachim and so translates: "But it is also necessary to divide by the differentia of the differentia." This makes the passage smoother, but it is unnecessary.

126. David Balme has pioneered this approach.

127. Owens, *Doctrine of Being*, p. 367 with 326. Ross, II, 164, thinks that Z 13–14 examine the two together.

128. The passage cited assumes that the form has a formula and also asserts that the formula is of the universal. A natural, though not a necessary, interpretation is that form is universal.

129. Michael J. Woods, "Problems in *Metaphysics* Z, Chapter 13," in *Aristotle*, ed. J. M. E. Moravcsik, p. 216, proposes a distinction between universal and what is said universally. Gerald J. Hughes argues for something similar in his paper contained in *Notes on Zeta*, "Universals as Potential Substances: The Interpretation of *Metaphysics* Z 13," pp. 107–26.

130. For example, James H. Lesher, "Aristotle on Form, Substance and Universals," *Phronesis* XVI (1971): 170 n. 7.

131. Owens, *Doctrine of Being*, p. 326, esp. n. 52. Driscoll, "EIΔH in Aristotle's Theories of Substance," pp. 141–43, also argues for such a distinction.

132. Ross, II, 210.

133. Cherniss, *Aristotle's Criticism of Plato*, p. 318.

134. See Woods's criticism of Ross, "Problems in *Metaphysics* Z," pp. 217–18. On the other hand, his criticism of Cherniss misses the mark (pp. 218–19). Woods objects to taking the last line as an argument against the alternative that the universal is the *ousia* of all because the latter was not stated immediately before the last line. But his own remarks on how absurd it would be for anyone to say that the universal is the *ousia* of just one thing make it probable that Aristotle's statement of this mistake in the penultimate sentence (1038b13–14) does not require support and is parenthetical. Woods's own position is that this passage is not intended as an argument against a Platonist but presented to show what the Platonist is committed to (p. 235). The wording of the passage makes this unlikely. Further, in a similar passage later (16, 1040b15–19), Aristotle clearly does argue against Platonism.

Alan Code, "No Universal is a Substance: An Interpretation of *Metaphysics* Z 13 1038 b 8–15," *Paideia*, Special Aristotle Issue (1978): 70, also endorses Cherniss's view that the last line supports the denial that the universal is the *ousia* of all. I think his criticism (pp. 69–70) of the rest of Cherniss's interpretation misconstrues it.

135. Whether the genus is one in form or formula has been disputed. According to Rogers Albritton, "Forms of Particular Substances in Aristotle's *Metaphysics*," *Journal of Philosophy* LIV (1957): 706, the genus is one in form, but the things of which it is the genus, that is, the species, are not one in formula. For example, animal is one in formula, but the species man and horse are not. He concludes that the requirement excludes genera, but not species. In contrast, Woods, "Problems in *Metaphysics* Z," pp. 223–24, denies that the genus is one in form. This is a mistake. At Δ 6, 1016b31–34 Aristotle describes one in species (form) as one in formula and limits one in genus to what falls under the same categorial genus. On this description, animal and all other genera except the *summa genera* are one in species. After criticizing Albritton's argument, Woods goes on to say that 1038b9–16 "leads the Platonist to formulate his position more carefully" (p. 235). He apparently has in mind Albritton's argument against genera satisfying the requirement. Does he now accept Albritton's claim that the genus is one in form, or does he think this is Plato's view? In either case, Woods thinks that Albritton's argument is valid. As I go on to explain in my text, it is not. The genus can be one in formula only if it has a single formula. In exactly the way that genus is one in formula, man and horse are also one in formula: they all have the same generic formula. Woods and Albritton equivocate; they take the genus to be one in generic formula and deny that instances of it are one in the formula of their species.

Also, Woods's interpretation is hard to square with the parallel passage at B 4, 999b20–22 where man is rejected as *ousia* on what looks to be the same ground as 1038b14–15; nor, as I mentioned in an earlier note, does it seem consistent with Z 16, 1040b16–19. I shall have more to say about Woods's view later (4.2.2).

136. This interpretation of the text is advanced by Henry Teloh, "Aristotle's *Metaphysics* Z 13," *Canadian Journal of Philosophy* IX (1979): 81–85. Teloh also comes to the conclusion that both ones in the requirement must be numeric.

137. Owens, *Doctrine of Being,* p. 367.

138. Alan Code, "No Universal is a Substance," p. 68, suggests that this may be the case, but his interpretation of Z 6 differs from what I argued earlier. Hughes, "Universals as Potential Substances," p. 113, suggests that 1038b14–15 might rely on Z 6's identity of thing and essence. But he thinks that this leads to difficulties for Aristotle, and thus that he does not subscribe to it.

139. There are other ways to interpret this passage. I shall argue against them later.

140. Ross, II, 210, and most others miss this.

141. This is a standard translation of the passage. It is the way that Ross, II, 208, understands the text in his commentary; Schwegler and Apostle translate similarly. However, in his translation Ross takes a different approach to the passage. He translates the ἔστι in 1038b19 and b20 as a copula, contrary to the manuscripts. Cherniss, *Aristotle's Criticism of Plato*, p. 318, follows Ross's translation. Ross translates the passage:

> Then clearly it [the universal] is a formula of the essence. And it makes no difference even if it is not a formula of everything that is in the substance.

This rendering implies that the universal is a formula. But Aristotle seems to distinguish the two; for example, he claims not that the formula is the universal but that it is *of* the universal (10, 1035b34-1036a1). Woods, "Problems in *Metaphysics* Z," p. 233, avoids this problem by agreeing with Ross only about the ἔστι at b20 and taking the term existentially at b19. (Woods fails to mention his partial agreement with Ross's translation; he notes only his disagreement with the commentary.) Following Woods, Furth, *Aristotle's* Metaphysics, p. 34, translates the passage,

> Then clearly there does exist some formula of it. And it makes no difference even if it [= the formula of *animal*] is not the formula of all things in the substance [= in *man* or *horse*].

This is an intriguing interpretation. But the obvious objection is that not all universals have formulae. A *summum* genus, for example, could be part of an essence, but it has no formula (Δ 6, 1016b31-1017a2). Schwegler, *Die Metaphysik*, IV, 115, thinks Aristotle has universals like one and being in mind here. Translated in the way that Woods advocates, the passage is falsified by universals that do not have formulae. For this reason, I have adopted the traditional rendering. In any case, the translations of Woods and Ross are compatible with the interpretation that I shall propose. The authors of *Notes on Zeta*, pp. 128-30, canvas possible translations and positions.

142. Even if the alternative translations mentioned in the preceding note are adopted, it remains true that the consequence follows obviously because the universal has a formula.

143. This interpretation of the last lines of the passage resembles Ross's, II, 210. (The excisions Jaeger makes in his text do not affect it.) Pseudo-Alexander, p. 524.25-26, also thinks the argument is a *reductio*, but he takes the absurdity in the last line to be the existence of an *ousia* (animal) of an *ousia* (the universal man). I think that this works less well with what precedes than my interpretation. Another alternative, offered by Woods, "Problems in *Metaphysics* Z," pp. 231-33, is that these lines assert that genera do not meet the requirement that they be proper to individuals in the way that the species do; he accordingly ascribes them to the Platonist. Since I do not see that the species are proper to individuals (see n. 135), I find Woods's interpretation implausible. It seems to me that 1038b20-22's inference that universals will be *ousiai* of things just as man is the *ousia* of man, an inference he takes to be false, suggests that species suffer the very same problems as genera and higher universals.

144. The authors of *Notes on Zeta*, pp. 132-33, remark that, on the usual reading, the argument does not point out an additional absurdity in Plato's position, as we would expect. They also mention difficulties in assuming that the passage defends Plato's position, as Woods supposes. In what follows I shall develop one of the alternative readings of the argument that they propose.

145. Ross, II, 211.

146. Pseudo-Alexander, p. 525.15-16.

147. οὐσία οὐσίᾳ in b29. *Notes on Zeta*, p. 134, mentions another, less plausible, interpretation of this alternative text.

148. Pseudo-Alexander, p. 525.17-18, thinks that the man mentioned here is the individual man. Ross, II, 211, maintains that it is the species man. *Notes on Zeta*, p. 134, mentions both interpretations but leans toward the latter.

149. Cf. *Notes on Zeta*, p. 135. The authors are unsure whether the excluded parts here are *ousiai*; they note that if the parts are, the argument would "place strong requirements on the unity of genuine substances." They apparently doubt that there are such unity requirements.

150. At 1039a30–33 Aristotle is not arguing that the constituents of *ousiai* must be *ousiai*, as the authors of *Notes on Zeta*, p. 137, suppose. Such an argument would require a premise that neither he nor the Platonists would accept, as *Notes on Zeta* also realizes. Instead, Aristotle's point in this passage must be that since the Platonists think some forms are composed of others and since they regard all forms as separate *ousiai*, the constituent forms must also be separate *ousiai*.

151. Aristotle's illustration of numeric unity here, the unity of you with yourself (1039a34), is the same as what he uses at I 3, 1054a34–35 to illustrate sameness in "formula and number." In the latter passage, however, Aristotle ascribes this type of sameness to what has one form and one matter (cf. Δ 6, 1016b31–33).

152. The authors of *Notes on Zeta*, p. 138, think that Aristotle could avoid the problem by specifying the respect in which these characters belong to animal. They also think that the argument relies on ascribing to the Platonists the assumption that the genus is an individual. In fact, the latter is tantamount to the assumption that governs the examination of the first horn of the dilemma, the assumption that genus is numerically one in its instances.

153. Ross, II, 212. Ross's invoking 1038b14–15 in a context where the pertinent unity is numeric unity shows that he too understands the unity of the *ousia* in that passage to be numeric unity, a point I argued earlier. *Notes on Zeta*, p. 139, disputes Ross's interpretation on the ground that it takes the things that are indefinite in number to be the particulars, whereas the text takes them to be species of animal. This criticism cannot be correct: the principle enunciated in 1038b14–15 holds whether the "things" are species or particulars. If universals were *ousiai*, the things could be either.

The alternative interpretations of the indefiniteness advanced by *Notes on Zeta*, p. 139, look promising at first. They take the indefinite things to be species of animal and the absurdity to lie in there being no similarity at all between the various types of animal. However, as the authors note, this interpretation presupposes that the initial assumption (1039b7) is that animal differs in number *and in species*. Since, as 1039a29–30 claims, the animal in various species has the same formula, the numerically different animals cannot also differ in species. Moreover, the lack of similarity between different species of animal is not, in itself, absurd. It is only impossible if we assume in advance that animal is one. The Platonists do indeed make this latter assumption, but if the unity of animal is at issue here, then this argument would be the same as those which follow.

154. Ross, II, 213, inverts subject and predicate here, as does Furth in his translation. Pseudo-Alexander, p. 528.32–33, makes animal itself the subject. Schwegler, *Die Metaphysik*, II, 134 and IV, 120, recognizes that the absurdity lies in animal itself being many; so, too, *Notes on Zeta*, p. 139.

155. Here τε . . . καί indicates the role of 1039b9 in both arguments. There is no need to interpret b9–14 as two arguments, as do the authors of *Notes on Zeta*, pp. 139–40. I do not see any basis here for distinguishing animal and the idea animal, as they do; nor do I see in what such a distinction is supposed to lie.

156. Following the texts of Bonitz, Ross, and Jaeger.

157. This much is explained in *Notes on Zeta*, p. 140.

158. Pseudo-Alexander, p. 531.27–28.

159. II, 215. Ross does not mention that part of the reason it will not work is that Platonic forms are composed of other Platonic forms.

160. Pseudo-Alexander, p. 531.13–14, and Owens, *Doctrine of Being*, pp. 372–73 n. 30, also recognize that these arguments are directed against the existence of Platonic forms.

161. *Notes on Zeta*, p. 144, expresses puzzlement over the argumentative force of Aristotle's claim that sun is an *ousia*.

162. In contrast, Schwegler, *Die Metaphysik*, IV, 126, sees the passage as simply a criticism of Platonists.

163. That these arguments are the same is also noticed by Albritton, "Forms of Particular Substances," p. 705. Without remarking on their identity, Owens, *Doctrine of Being*, pp. 373, 367, explains this passage in the same way he explained 1038b14–15.

164. *Notes on Zeta*, pp. 147–48, proposes as an alternative interpretation that τοῦ ἑνός in 1040b17 is the one itself and that the claim in this sentence is that the *ousia* of the one itself is one. This may seem plausible because of the appearance of ἕν in the preceding line, but this view misconstrues the logic of Aristotle's argument. The Platonic position that is being criticized is that the one itself is an *ousia*. To speak of the *ousia* of the one itself (as *Notes on Zeta* would have it) is thus to speak of the *ousia* of an *ousia*. Further, Aristotle is considering the possibility that the one is *ousia*. The argument is that if it were, then that of which it is the *ousia* (the ἑνός) would also need to be numerically one, which it is not. Accordingly, ἑνός refers to the thing whose *ousia* is offered as the one. *Notes on Zeta* also proposes an interpretation close to the one I have adopted, but it does not recognize the peculiar position of the one in the argument: if one itself is the *ousia* of something, that thing surely has an *ousia* that is one.

165. Pseudo-Alexander, p. 536.33–38, thinks that one and being have a better claim to be *ousiai* because they are more universal than element, and that they are *per se* while principle and element are relatives. *Notes on Zeta*, p. 149, suggests that the reason is that one and being are more familiar. I think a more likely reason that being and one have better claims to be *ousiai* is that being is *pros hen*, a *pros hen* is a kind of *kath' hen* (Γ 2, 1003b11–14), and the latter is a kind of genus. As we saw, being is presumed to have an essence of some sort in the opening chapter of book Z. One acquires its claim to be *ousia* through its close association with being. (Elsewhere Aristotle also speaks of a kind of essence of element and of one and distinguishes them from the things that are elements and are one—I 1, 1052b9–19.)

166. Cf. Pseudo-Alexander, p. 537.4–6.

167. Pseudo-Alexander, p. 537.18–22, reconstructs the argument this way: no universal is *ousia*; *ousiai* can be separate; hence, no universal is separate. This argument is invalid.

168. If this is what the term refers to, the argument would be something like the following: the one *should* not be in many places at once (if it is an *ousia*); a universal is in many places at once; hence, the one is not *ousia*.

169. II, 220. Ross calls it the "truly one."

170. Woods, "Problems in *Metaphysics* Z," pp. 237–38, says it would be absurd "if you could first distinguish individual substances and then notice that the predicate applied to them which supplied a basis for distinguishing them in the first place."

171. Others who have criticized Woods include: Lesher, "Aristotle on Form, Substance, and Universals," pp. 170–74; Driscoll, "ΕΙΔΗ in Aristotle's Theories of Substance," pp. 132–34, 141–56.

172. Parallel distinctions have been endorsed by a number of recent writers: Driscoll, *ibid.*, pp. 151–52; D. K. Modrak, "Forms, Types, and Tokens in Aristotle's *Metaphysics*," *Journal of the History of Philosophy* XVII (1979): 371–72; Michael Loux, "Form, Species, and Predication," *Mind* LXXXVIII (1979): 1.

173. Reale, *The Concept of First Philosophy*, p. 214, also notices that Z 17 expresses a doctrine found in book A.

174. As the authors of *Notes on Zeta* notice, p. 151.

175. The discussion of priority in book Δ presumes a connection between being prior and being a principle, 11, 1018b9–12. Asclepius, p. 449.17–19, appears to take Δ 11 as the source of the assumption that *ousia* is a principle.

176. See Ross, II, 222.

177. Pierre Aubenque, "La Pensée du Simple dans la *Métaphysique* (Z 17 et Θ 10)," in *Études sur La Métaphysique D'Aristote: Actes du VIe Symposium Aristotelicum*, ed. Pierre Aubenque (Paris: J. Vrin, 1979), pp. 75, 88, advances a similar interpretation of this portion of the argument. He compares the question that Aristotle here rejects to that which Plotinus answers by referring to the one. Aubenque also draws on the *Posterior Analytics* to explain Z 17, but he thinks that this work shows that the goal of Z 17, knowledge of simple essences, is unattainable.

178. Furth, *Aristotle's* Metaphysics, p. 125, suggests that the two positions are inconsistent.

179. Ross, II, 224.

180. Schwegler, *Die Metaphysik*, IV, 129, is an exception, but he does not see its significance for understanding the chapter.

181. At 1041a28 the manuscripts assert, "this [the cause] is the essence, so to speak logically (*logikōs*)." This line is excised by Pseudo-Alexander, p. 540.38–39, and by Jaeger, but retained by Ross, II, 223. If it is retained, the following lines would assert that this essence is sometimes the final cause, sometimes the efficient cause, and apparently also (1041b4–9) the formal cause. If it is excised, the following lines would be saying that the cause (of a form's being in a matter) is an efficient, final, or formal cause. Ross makes a case for keeping the line by pointing out that the *Posterior Analytics* treats formal and efficient causes as contained in the definition and that in book H Aristotle does define a house through its final cause. He could have added that we know from the *Physics* that the same nature is the formal, final, and efficient causes.

The authors of *Notes on Zeta*, pp. 152–53, are puzzled about why Aristotle or whoever wrote this line would include "so to speak logically." If "logically" (*logikōs*) here refers to definitions and formulae, as I argued it does earlier, then this phrase makes good sense where it occurs in the text. The definition or formula of the cause is the formula of the essence, and the latter is what we understand when we know the final, efficient, or formal cause. There is, moreover, a particular reason for speaking of the cause "logically" at this point. Someone could object to the inclusion of efficient cause among the causes that are a thing's *ousia* on the ground that, because the efficient cause lies outside of the thing of which it is the cause, it cannot be its *ousia* (see Λ 4, 1070b22–23). Later in the passage Aristotle does exclude the efficient cause as a cause of being (1041a31–32). The efficient cause is the thing's *ousia* only in the sense that efficient cause and essence are one in formula (even for artifacts—Z 7, 1032b11–14, Λ 4, 1070b33–34), and then, as an efficient cause, it is the source of generation or destruction. The final cause can be a cause of being (1041a32) because it is the form or essence. Because both efficient and final causes are effectively identified with essence, Aristotle need not consider them further; and we find that they do not appear in Z 17 after this passage. (As Owens, *Doctrine of Being,* p. 375, puts it, "the efficient and final cause are absorbed into the study of the formal.") In sum, the manuscript reading makes good sense and could well be correct.

182. Ross, II, 224, mentions some alternative readings of the text, but he defends the manuscripts.

183. Owens, *Doctrine of Being,* p. 376, writes that for Aristotle,

> 'to be a definite abiding something' is simply *to be.* 'The form is the cause of a definite something' is the same in meaning as 'the form is the cause of Being.'

G. E. L. Owen, "Logic and Metaphysics in Some Earlier Works of Aristotle," in *Aristotle and Plato in the Mid-Fourth Century: Papers of the Symposium Aristotelicum held at Oxford in August, 1957,* ed. I. Düring and G. E. L. Owen (Göteborg: Elanders Boktryckeri Aktiebolag, 1960), p. 165, echoes this idea when he says, "in his [Aristotle's] view, *to be* was *to be something or other.*" Owen, though, thinks that this is a point about language, about our usage of the verb "to be," whereas Owens takes it to have independent ontological significance.

184. See the critical apparatus in Ross's and Jaeger's texts. For a brief discussion, see Ross, II, 224.

185. Ross, II, 224.

186. In treating the letters as constituents of the syllable, Z 17 seems to be at odds with Z 10. The latter takes the letters to be parts of the formula of the form of a syllable (1035a10–11). Z 17 takes the form of the syllable to be something that is not a letter or composed of letters. An interpretation that could avoid inconsistency is the following. The formula of the syllable could include the letters, just as Z 10 maintains, if the syllable is an artifact like a house (H 3, 1043b4–6) because a definition of an artifact can include its matter and form (H 2, 1043a14–21). Then, the letters would not belong to form, as Z 17 requires, but they would be stated in the formula of the syllable, as Z 10 requires. However, there is nothing in Z 10 to indicate that the syllable is a composite of this sort. That chapter denies that the parts of the formula of the syllable are material parts (e.g., 1035a10–11), and it contrasts the parts of the syllable with the parts of a material composite. A more likely way of reconciling the seemingly contrary uses of the syllable as examples in Z 17 and Z 10 is to realize that the argument of Z 17 does not apply only to material constituents. The letters are

constituents of the form, just as Z 10 implies; but form cannot consist simply of the letters. Their position is crucial, and there must be something else in the form that is over and above the letters. The letters could then be parts of the form, but still not belong to the cause of the syllable. However, even if the argument of Z 17 applies more widely than to material constituents, as it does if the preceding is correct, it still applies *at least* to the material constituents.

187. Schwegler, *Die Metaphysik*, IV, 135–36, calls it fragmentary. Owens, *Doctrine of Being*, pp. 379–80, notes that the book "recapitulates the treatment of Z . . . in six rather loosely connected chapters." Both Schwegler and Owens do, though, emphasize new developments in book H. Owens points out that form is now treated as a this and separate, and Schwegler notes that this book interchanges form and matter with actuality and potentiality. In fact, Aristotle calls *ousia* a this and separate often in Z (e.g., 3, 1029a28;\4, 1030a4–6; 12, 1037b27), and these characters ought to belong to form because it is *ousia*. Likewise, the idea that form is actuality also appears in book Z (10, 1035b14–18; 11, 1036b30–32). Aristotle's discussions of matter in Z 7–11 do not explicitly identify it with potentiality. If anything is new in book H it seems to be this latter identification.

188. So, too, Cousin, "Aristotle's Doctrine of Substance," p. 327.

189. Ross, II, 226.

190. Schwegler, *Die Metaphysik*, IV, 137; Ross, II, 227.

191. This seems to be Pseudo-Alexander's interpretation, p. 546.12–18. He adds that matter is more of an *ousia* than form, at least in this respect.

192. Ross's, II, 226, summary of the text indicates that 1042a32–b8 discusses one of the three substrates mentioned at 1042a27–30.

193. This translation follows the manuscript readings closely. I shall discuss why shortly.

194. This difference does not come out in translations. Ross, Furth, and Apostle translate the former passage as if it contained verbs.

195. Pseudo-Alexander, p. 548.35–37.

196. See Ross's and Jaeger's texts, *ad loc.*

197. Owen, "Aristotle on the Snares of Ontology," in *New Essays on Plato and Aristotle*, ed. Renford Bambrough, (New York: The Humanities Press, 1965), p. 76. He rejects the emendations in a footnote and then advances his own interpretation without drawing attention to the fact that it obviates the need for the emendations.

198. Curiously, Owen considers the possibility that Aristotle intends water to receive the differentia (*ibid.*, p. 81); but he quickly dismisses it on the ground that, were it true, Aristotle's analysis would not show that "for a particular subject 'is' or 'exists' calls for a particular paraphrase." Since it is just this text (1042b25–28) that Owen thinks *shows* Aristotle to be advocating a paraphrase (p. 76), his reasoning is circular.

199. As Ross, II, 227, realizes. Surprisingly, Owen does not cite Z 17. Had he paid more attention to it, he would have seen that the differentia belongs to the matter rather than to the composite.

200. See above, pp. 149–50.

201. It is possible that threshold and ice in 1042b26–28 refer not to the composite but to the form (cf. 3, 1043a29–33). This avoids the interpretative difficulties, but it is an unlikely reading of the text.

202. As Owen says, "*to be* is just *to be something or other*," "Snares," pp. 71, 78 (see also, n. 183). Joseph Owens, *Doctrine of Being*, p. 376, makes the same point. Indeed, it is the theme of Owens's book. As I said in an earlier note, G. E. L. Owen emphasizes the linguistic roots of this doctrine, and Joseph Owens takes it to be the result of the examination of things.

203. Schwegler, *Die Metaphysik*, IV, 139, thinks the discussion of the composite begins at 1043a4 and extends to 1043b4. He recognizes that 1042a26-30 indicate the structure of the discussion. So does Ross, II, 226, 229, but he seems to think that the composite is only mentioned briefly at the end of H 2 (1043a26-28). On the other hand, Furth's characterization, *Aristotle's* Metaphysics, pp. 48-49, of 1042b25-28 as a "false start" in contrast with the "statement of the analysis" at 1043a7-12 reflects his failure to distinguish the different topics under discussion in H 2. The former passage focuses on the differentia, and the latter expresses the same doctrine in terms of the composite.

The difficulty of deciding just where the discussion of the differentia leaves off and that of the composite begins is partially due to our using the same term for both, a point Aristotle makes in the remarks with which H 3 opens.

204. The word συνδυαζόμενον here is usually rendered as "coupled with matter" and understood to refer to the accidental composite; Schwegler, *Die Metaphysik*, IV, 140, and also Ross's and Apostle's translations. But in Z 5 the term signifies the class of things like snub and odd (1030b16; 1031a7), things that belong *per se* in the sense that their definitions include the things to which they belong. This is a class to which natural *ousiai* bear some similarity (E 1, 1025b30-1026a3) and to which accidental composites are analogous. Since the text at 1043a2-4 repeats the characterization of *ousia* as the cause of being in the composite, there would be no point in Aristotle's saying in the next line that neither the differentia nor the composite (συνδυαζόμενον as usually understood) is *ousia*. It is obvious that the composite is not the cause of being in the composite. More likely, the point here is that the differentia is neither an *ousia* nor a *per se* attribute of *ousia*.

205. Echoing Gregory Vlastos's discussion ("Reasons and Causes in the *Phaedo*," in *Plato: A Collection of Critical Essays. I: Metaphysics and Epistemology*, ed. Gregory Vlastos [Garden City, N. Y.: Anchor Books, 1971], pp. 134-37), G. E. L. Owen, "Snares," p. 82, complains about "cause" as the translation of αἴτια. If my analysis is correct, this passage is one place where "cause" is a good translation. Aristotle is not offering an explanation here; he is trying to locate that part of the composite which makes it what it is.

Along the same lines, it seems to me that there is no good evidence that Aristotle aims to analyze the verb "to be" in H 2, as G. E. L. Owen thinks (pp. 69, 91). Aristotle does not intend to speak of paraphrasing predicates. He is talking about the character of things, and the functions that make them what they are. Since being is neither an existential quantifier nor a predicate, Owen's discussion of two kinds of being, pp. 84-92, does not really apply to H 2.

206. Although Aristotle distinguishes actuality and motion at Θ 6, 1048b18-35 and at *N. E.* X 4, 1174a14-23, there are other passages where he calls actualities motions (*Rhetoric* Γ 11, 1412a8-9) and motions actualities (*Phys.* Γ 2, 201b31-32; 1, 210a9-11; Θ 5, 257b5-7; *De Anima* B 2, 417a1-17; cf. Γ 3, 431a6-7), and there are places where he uses the two terms interchangeably (*Gen. Anim.* B 6, 743a26-29; *E. E.* B 1, 1218b36-37; *Met.* Δ 14, 1020b19-23). See also my "Aristotle on Knowledge of Nature," *Review of Metaphysics* XXXVII (1984): 814-15, 821-23.

207. In the text, Aristotle uses different words for the calmness of water and of air: the air rests, and the sea is even. But neither of these belongs uniquely to air or water. So it is unlikely that the examples aim at distinguishing the calmness of air and of water. While the text derives no inferences from the examples, it is plausible that Aristotle mentions two similar differentiae to point up the advantage of including the matter in the definition.

208. In Jaeger's and in Ross's text, the comments on the generation and destruction of composites appear as a long parenthetical remark (1043b14–23). Ross, II, 233, draws attention to the lack of connection with what precedes of the analogy between number and composites (1043b32–1044a11) and also of the summary. He calls the chapter "a collection of ill-connected remarks" (II, 231).

209. This interpretation follows Schwegler, *Die Metaphysik*, IV, 142.

   Although the distinction between actuality and composite is not important for the present inquiry, it is, Aristotle claims (1043a37–b1), important for another inquiry. In which inquiry is this distinction important? According to Pseudo-Alexander, p. 551.30–32, it is dialectic; Thomas Aquinas, *Commentary on the Metaphysics*, VIII. L.3:C 1709-11, thinks that the distinction is important for the inquiry into separate form, the divine. It is more likely that Aristotle has in mind the mathematical examples he has just given, lines and numbers (1043a33–34). Because the form of a line is a number, it belongs to a branch of mathematics different from the branch that investigates lines. Thus, for mathematicals, it *is* important to distinguish form and composite.

210. See Denniston, *Greek Particles*, p. 238. He notes that Aristotle often uses δή, ἄρα, τοίνυν, and οὖν interchangeably.

211. But not for the reason that Ross, II, 232-33, apparently supposes. Aristotle's point here is not that definition of composites is impossible.

212. On this passage, see above, p. 162 and n. 204.

213. Following Ross's interpretation of these lines (II, 232). Pseudo-Alexander, p. 553.7–10, thinks that this sentence disputes those who subtract *matter* from the definition, that is, the Platonists. Though Ross is probably right, it would be entirely consonant with my interpretation of this chapter for Aristotle to be pointing out the mistake of subtracting matter from the definition of a composite.

214. In this discussion Aristotle calls the proper matter the "first matter" (1044a22–23) probably because it is the first matter into which bile is divided. The same designation appears in the manuscripts at 1044a18, but there most editors bracket it on the ground that it conflicts with Aristotle's use of "first" at 1044a16. At 1044a18 and a23 "first matter" refers to the proximate matter, whereas at 1044a16 it designates the ultimate matter.

215. Since the identity of efficient causes that Aristotle speaks about later is an identity in formula (1044a31), their difference should also be a difference in formula.

216. This latter claim (b3–5) seems inconsistent with the claim at *Metaphysics* H 4, 1044a34–35 and with Aristotle's usual view in the *De Generatione Animalium* (A 19, 727b31–33; 20, 729a28–33) that the matter of animals is menstrual fluid. The claim in the *Physics*, though, is more general because it includes the matter for plants, the matter to which the term "seed" most properly applies. Aristotle probably also uses it to describe the matter of animals to avoid having to explain in detail what that matter is.

217. Rorty, "Genus as Matter," p. 394, maintains that the last lines of H 6 state the conclusion of books Z–H. However, he thinks that this chapter treats the issue raised in Z 12, and he does not see any purpose for the last five chapters of book Z (pp. 407-8).

218. Jaeger, *Studien*, pp. 53–61; Owens, *Doctrine of Being*, p. 362; Rorty, "Genus as Matter," p. 407; probably also Furth, to judge by his chapter headings, *Aristotle's* Metaphysics, pp. 30, 57, 131. Marjorie Grene, "Is Genus to Species as Matter to Form?" *Synthese* XXVIII (1974): 57, 62, 65, also thinks that the two chapters enunciate the same views.

219. Aristotle usually denies that what is merely in contact is continuous (Δ 6, 1016a7-9; I 1, 1052a19-20). On the other hand, mere contact could be said to cause a minimal kind of continuity. It is appropriate for Aristotle to mention such an example at this point because he wants to emphasize the need for a cause of unity even where there is very little unity.

220. Rorty, "Genus as Matter." It is also the view of Balme, "ΓΕΝΟΣ and ΕΙΔΟΣ in Aristotle's Biology," *Classical Quarterly* XII (1962): 81–98; and of A. C. Lloyd, "Genus, Species, and Ordered Series in Aristotle," *Phronesis* VII (1962): 67–90, and "Aristotle's Principle of Individuation," *Mind* LIX (1970): 519-29.

221. Ross, II, 207, acknowledges the contrast of *diairesis* and definition derived from material constituents.

222. Ross, II, 238.

223. Rorty, "Genus as Matter," pp. 412-16.

224. For more criticisms of this position see Grene, "Is Genus to Species?" esp. pp. 59-61.

225. Ross, II, 238.

226. For example, D. W. Hamlyn, *Aristotle's* De Anima: *Books II and III* (Oxford: Clarendon Press, 1977), p. 85.

227. Ross, II, 238.

228. Schwegler, *Die Metaphysik*, IV, 154, maintains that the error in these accounts is the supposition that form and matter were originally distinct. Ross, II, 239, repeats his interpretation. This is mistaken; first, because bronze and triangle, for example, could exist apart from each other, and second, because there is not anything obviously absurd in speaking of the communion of things that are never distinct (see, e.g., Z 11, 1036a34-b1).

229. διό at 1045b4 introduces a conclusion about the unity of the composite, a conclusion restated at 1045b19-22. Unless we distinguish these remarks about the composite from the immediately preceding remarks on the essence, 1045b5-6 would just repeat b3-4. As noted, lines 1045a33-b7 are usually understood to belong together.

230. Following the interpretation of Schwegler, *Die Metaphysik*, II, 148 and IV, 155. Most English translators follow Ross in equating these two questions. He renders the sentence, "so that it is like asking what in general is the cause of unity and of a thing's being one," and adds the gloss, "which is an obviously absurd question" (II, 239). Notice that "question" is singular. His "it" can only be the immediately preceding remarks, and he must understand them as dismissing the question, why are actuality and potentiality one? Ross thinks Aristotle regards this question and the question about unity as equally absurd. It is hard to imag-

ine why Aristotle would devote much of Z 17 to the question about unity if he thought it obviously absurd. More on this text later in this subsection.

231. Balme, "The Snub," p. 5, proposes that the identification of form and matter as actuality and potentiality amounts to thinking of an object as if it were "frozen at a moment":

> If an object is considered as at a moment, and not as in the process of changing, it has no matter: what was its matter has been determined *so* at this moment and can therefore be described formally, while its potentiality for further change does not come into question at this moment.

This is Balme's reconstruction. There is no indication in the text that Aristotle intends to introduce a distinction between nature viewed at rest and viewed in motion. (Balme may have in mind some sort of distinction between physical and metaphysical treatments of natures, but his formulation is misleadingly subjective.) Balme's account of H 6's solution to the problem of the unity of the composite seems to be that the matter does not appear in the definition of the composite as matter, but in some formalized way. But this does not explain why the definition is one: for Balme, the definition still consists of a plurality of formalized constituents. It is hard to see that this constitutes any advance over H 2, 1043a26–28, and it seems to be just what Aristotle wishes to exclude at H 3, 1043b4–14. Further, to invoke a particular, subjective way of viewing nature scarcely seems to be appropriate to explain how a composite can be one.

232. Ross, II, 239. See my earlier note 230. Furth, *Aristotle's* Metaphysics, p. 131, is at a loss as to why Ross dismisses this question as absurd. The reason is that Ross is among those who see form and matter as obviously one. But this just highlights Ross's confusion about this passage, for if the question why the composite is one were obviously absurd, even apart from form/matter considerations, then Aristotle would have no need to introduce the latter to solve the former problem (1045a23–33).

CHAPTER THREE

1. On the difference see L. A. Kosman, "Substance, Being, and *Energeia*," *Oxford Studies in Ancient Philosophy* II (1984): 133. Also, *Notes on Eta and Theta of Aristotle's Metaphysics,* Study Aids Monograph No. 4 (Oxford: Sub-Faculty of Philosophy, 1984), p. 49 (this reference was available to me only during the final stages of the preparation of this manuscript). The authors of the latter and Furth, *Aristotle's* Metaphysics, p. 59, seem to think that the potency in the strict sense (κυρίως) encompasses all the potencies discussed in Θ 1–5. More likely this phrase refers to the primary potency to which the others are related (1046a9–11). These others are even less important for Aristotle's inquiry.

2. Probably influenced by Schwegler (*Die Metaphysik*, IV, 157), Ross, II, 240–41, terms this potency "power" and contrasts it with "potentiality," the potency that is most useful; the latter is discussed along with actuality later in Θ. Ross thinks the term "power" captures (a) the necessity of two things and (b) the implication of positive force, though the latter is not always preserved in the various types of potentiality. I think this term is misleading. First, *all* the potentialities

considered in Θ 1–5 come in pairs, but some, such as the rational and nonrational potencies, do not involve one thing acting on another. Second, it is a mistake to think of any Aristotelian potentiality as a positive force. Modern physics sanctions such an idea but for Aristotle potentiality always remains subsidiary to actuality and motion. This is, I think, a central point of Θ 1–5.

3. The variety of potencies Aristotle distinguishes in Θ 1 corresponds closely to those he describes in Δ 12, a point noted by Schwegler, *Die Metaphysik*, IV, 156.

4. See Ross, II, 241.

5. At *Physics* Γ 3, 202a16–b22, Aristotle considers the actuality in agent and patient. He maintains that the actuality of the agent's act is numerically one with the actuality of the patient's being acted upon, though they differ in formula. The formulae differ because the actuality of one thing in another differs from the actuality of one thing by another (202b21–22). On the surface, the *Metaphysics* takes the opposite approach: it claims that the individuals differ but the essence and formula is the same (e.g., Z 7, 1032a32–b14). If the actualities of each differ in formula and essence, then the potentialities should also differ in the same way. However, the differences here may stem from different approaches to similar problems rather than inconsistency. Later in Θ (2, 1046b7–13), Aristotle claims that the same formula can apply to things in different ways. Using this idea, he may have been able to say of the issue in the *Physics*, the actuality of agent and of patient is one both numerically and in formula, though it applies to agent and patient in different ways.

6. Kosman, "Substance, Being, and *Energeia*," p. 138, rejects the suggestion that "what we now seek" could refer simply to what *follows* in book Θ; he thinks it must refer to what precedes, the inquiry into being and *ousia*.

7. Most current discussions of Θ 3–4 concern Aristotle's determinism and whether he endorses the so-called "principle of plenitude," the principle that there are no unactualized possibilities. Jaakko Hintikka, *Time and Necessity: Studies in Aristotle's Theory of Modality* (Oxford: Clarendon Press, 1973), pp. 104, 107–11, thinks he asserts the principle in the first sentence of Θ 4; this is denied by many others, including, Joan Kung, "*Metaphysics* 8.4: Can Be but Will Not Be," *Apeiron* XII (1978): 32–36, and Lindsay Judson, "Aristotle and the Megarians: *Metaphysics* Θ. 3–4" (Paper delivered at the annual meeting of the American Philosophical Association, Eastern Division, Boston, December, 1986), pp. 2–4. I think that other motivations account for the content of these two chapters, but I shall not try to argue this here. Let me simply confine myself to those points that are pertinent to Aristotle's inquiry into being and one.

8. Aristotle's reference to the definition of the potentiality at 1048a2 seems to be at odds with this point and with his earlier suggestion that potentialities and actualities share the same formula. But "definition" here is ὁ διορισμός, a delimitation or boundary. This term is broader than Aristotle's usual term for definition, ὁ ὁρισμός. The passage emphasizes the need to include qualifications in the delimitation of a potentiality. The formula of both actuality and potentiality is the same, but the latter is further delimited with additional qualifications.

9. Aristotle expresses similar ideas at *Nicomachean Ethics* X 4, 1174a14–23. There is an extensive literature on these passages, most of which differs from the interpretation I have just given. Seminal works are Gilbert Ryle's *Dilemmas* (Cambridge: Cambridge University Press, 1954), p. 102, and J. L. Ackrill's "Aristotle's Distinction Between *Energeia* and *Kinesis*," in *New Essays on Plato*

and Aristotle, pp. 125–26. For more discussion of this passage and alternative interpretations, see my "Aristotle on Knowledge of Nature," pp. 815–18.

10. Ross, II, 260, criticizes this argument on the ground that the necessity of a male to give the matter a form does not show the temporal priority of the *male* to the matter; the matter can exist as such without the male. It is rather the female, Ross claims, that is temporally prior to the matter. This is not a very compelling argument, for whatever deficiencies Aristotle may ascribe to women, they are actualities of some sort in respect of the matter.

11. Owens, *Doctrine of Being,* p. 407, also puts the point in these terms.

12. Ross translates, "the good is one of the contraries," and he argues against the interpretation I have adopted (that of Bonitz), II, 267–68. It would be surprising if Aristotle meant to take the good as a particular contrary, as Ross thinks. His usual view is that good, like being, belongs in all genera. Also, the discussion is not about the good, but about the actuality that is good (1051a4–5).

   These remarks on good and bad are in line with the claims that Aristotle makes at the end of I 4 that the contraries are possession and privation and that they are led back to one and many (1055b26–29), and with claims in book Λ about the column of contraries (7, 1072a30–35).

13. Ross's, II, 268, reconstruction of the argument that bad does not exist apart is problematic because he mentions as premises both that actuality is prior to potentiality and that potentiality is prior to the bad. As a result of this interpretation, he accuses Aristotle of an equivocation. The interpretation I have offered is both less problematic and closer to the text.

14. Aristotle locates the object of thought, that is, the unmoved mover and first actuality, in one of the columns of contraries (Λ 7, 1072a30–32). See also the discussion in Λ 10, esp. 1075a13–14.

15. Schwegler, *Die Metaphysik,* IV, 186, thinks that the treatment of truth in Θ 10 does not belong in book Θ because, as E 4 shows, truth in thought falls outside the scope of metaphysics. He thinks it was placed in its present position because it treats "simple and eternal" *ousiai.* In contrast, Owens, *Doctrine of Being,* p. 411, claims, "Θ 10 takes up this topic [truth] against the background of the central books."

16. Jaeger, *Studien,* p. 23, argues that they belong to two distinct and inconsistent versions of E 4. Ross, I, 365, tends to agree.

17. That 1027b28–29 refers to the investigation of simples in Θ 10 is widely accepted, even by those, like Jaeger (*Studien,* pp. 21–23), who think that the text is inconsistent. There is no inconsistency here if Aristotle is not presenting two views of truth but two *kinds* of truth.

18. Ross, I, 128, mentions passages in book A and α that espouse this objective view of truth. I shall quote one of them shortly. Owens, *Doctrine of Being,* p. 412n., mentions this type of truth, but he thinks that in Θ 10 Aristotle intends to dismiss it and to discuss instead truth in thoughts and beliefs. Kirwan, p. 199, also mentions truth in things and cites Δ 29 as an example. He suggests that the claim in E 4 that truth is in thought is inconsistent with Aristotle's view that truth is in things. Again, the appearance of inconsistency results from mistaking Aristotle's different kinds of truth for different statements about truth.

19. Ross, II, 275, excises "most primary" from the text of Θ 10 but suggests that if it is retained, the line should be rendered, "that which is true or false in the most proper sense of those terms." This reading is consistent with the interpretation I am about to offer, but so is the more likely and more natural reading of the text.

20. Editors invariably emend this line to avoid ascribing truth to the things. By substituting τῷ for τό, they make it mean "this depends, in the things, on their being united or divided" (Ross, II, 275). My interpretation avoids the need to emend the text.

21. For a discussion of the question of transcendental truth in this passage and in Θ 10, see Karl Bärthlein, *Die Transcendentalienlehre der alten Ontologie*, I (Berlin: Walter de Gruyter, 1972), pp. 25–33, 45–55.

22. Both α 1 and Θ 10 (1051b22–23) associate being with truth. This looks like a reason to apply the results of the former to the latter; but, on second thought, it might be objected, why should Aristotle only *associate* these two if, as I claim, they are *identical*? The being of α 1 is probably categorial being. There Aristotle points to their similarity. The being of Θ 10 is being as truth, and association is a part of an identification. So the passages are not entirely parallel.

23. Hintikka, *Time and Necessity*, pp. 62–70, maintains that the Greek insistence that knowledge be eternal stems from the formulation of knowledge claims in temporally indefinite sentences. If the things are always the same, temporally indefinite claims about them always have the same truth value.

24. Ross and Jaeger add an extra article to the text to make the first example read like the second: "the white [with] the wood." Also, Ross, II, 276. The difference in the text may hint at the different status of these two compounds, as I describe in my text.

25. For examples of accidental mistakes, see *Posterior Analytics* A 1, 71a31–b5. Someone may be mistaken about whether the particular object before him is a triangle, but that is not the same as being mistaken about what a triangle is. For someone who knows the essence of a triangle, failure to identify instances of it is only an accidental error. In contrast, Ross, II, 277, maintains that accidental errors arise because the essence consists of genus and differentia. His interpretation cannot apply to what is truly incomposite. It would scarcely makes sense for Aristotle to say that incomposites admit of only accidental error if the source of the accidental error is the *plurality* of their constituents. If they had a plurality of constituents, they would not be incomposites. Mistaking a genus reflects a failure to grasp the nature of the incomposite, of which the genus is, we can now say, merely a potential part. Moreover, Aristotle suggests that there can be accidental error in knowledge of *all* incomposites (1051b26–28), not just the ones that are pluralities; but Ross thinks that the *summa* genera are incomposites without parts. I argued earlier against this latter view.

26. There is a lengthy controversy about whether this grasp of incomposites by *nous* amounts to an intuition, that is, to nonexperiential knowledge or whether we can acquire it through experience (see Martha Craven Nussbaum, "Saving Aristotle's Appearances," in *Language and Logos*, pp. 282–83, and the literature to which she refers). Most of the literature in this controversy centers on *Posterior Analytics* B 19. As will soon be apparent, I think both alternatives are mistaken. However, this is not the place to address this literature or *Posterior Analytics* B 19. Instead, my concern is that of Θ 10, not how we come to grasp truth with *nous*, but what we grasp when we grasp such truths.

27. Schwegler, *Die Metaphysik*, IV, 186. Ross, II, 276, thinks that any term in a judgment is incomposite, but that the incomposite *ousiai* mentioned in 1051b27 refer to the pure actualities of Θ 8. Owens, *Doctrine of Being*, p. 413, also identifies the incomposites with the pure actualities. Aubenque, "La Pensée du Simple," p. 79, understands incomposites in Θ 10 as "immobiles et eternels."

On the other hand, a position like the one I shall defend has been advanced by Klaus Oehler, *Die Lehre vom noetischen und dianoetischen Denken bei Platon und Aristoteles,* Zetemata: Monographien zur klassischen Altertumswissenschaft XXIX (Munich: C. H. Beck, 1962), pp. 183–84; Horst Seidl, *Der Begriff des Intellekts (νοῦς) bei Aristoteles im philosophischen Zusammenhang seiner Hauptschriften* (Meisenheim am Glan: Anton Hain, 1971), p. 183; and Enrico Berti, "The Intellection of Indivisibles According to Aristotle, *De Anima* III 6," in *Aristotle on Mind and the Senses,* ed. G. E. R. Lloyd and G. E. L. Owen (Cambridge: Cambridge University Press, 1978), pp. 147–50.

28. Aubenque, "La Pensée du Simple," p. 79, maintains that we are unable to know anything about the simples because we cannot ascribe attributes to them. He is right that we cannot have scientific or demonstrative knowledge about the incomposites. But there is nothing paradoxical in this. In grasping the incomposite by the intellect, we do not know merely its name, as Aubenque thinks—that would just be accidental and we could be mistaken. We grasp it with our intellect when we know its actuality. In principle, it is no more puzzling to say that the *ousia* of a sensible is one and we can grasp what it is than to say that the *ousia* of something eternal and simple is one and we can grasp what it is.

29. Thinking that the sentence applies to the example at hand, Ross renders the last phrase as "numerically single number" in his translation. This is possible; but even if it is correct, Aristotle's point must be more general than just the example of even number that he gives here.

30. Ross, II, 279, is typical. I know of no one who has questioned this interpretation.

CHAPTER FOUR

1. Owens, *Doctrine of Being,* p. 454, complains that in the *Metaphysics* Aristotle does not explain how separate *ousia* is the source of being in other beings. The causation contains two steps: the unmoved mover causes being in sensible *ousiai,* and the latter cause being in all other beings. Aristotle is not explicit about either step; but, if my interpretation is correct, the central books show how the form (of a sensible *ousia*) is the source of being while showing the primacy of form. We could wish for a text where Aristotle made his intentions clear, but this, unfortunately, is true of many of his aims.

2. Owens's book, *Doctrine of Being,* esp. pp. 390–93, seems to have spurred several recent discussions. See Albritton, "Forms of Particular Substances," pp. 699, 704–6; Wilfrid Sellars, "Substance and Form in Aristotle," *Journal of Philosophy* LIV (1957): 688, 696–99; Alan Gewirth, "Aristotle's Doctrine of Being," *Philosophical Review* LXII (1953): 587–88. A very clear discussion of the issue appears in Lesher, "Aristotle on Form, Substance, and Universals," pp. 169–78.

3. Lesher, "Aristotle on Form, Substance, and Universals," p. 178.

4. "Against th[e] great majority of passages in which Aristotle writes as though there were only universal forms," Albritton, "Forms of Particular Substances," p. 707, mentions Aristotle's references to "your form" and "my form" in book Λ (5, 1071a20–29) (see pp. 700–1) and some indecisive indications from the central books. Cherniss, *Aristotle's Criticism of Plato,* pp. 506–7, thinks that Aristotle does not endorse the first position, but should have.

5. For example, Edwin Hartman, *Substance, Body, and Soul* (Princeton: Princeton University Press, 1977), pp. 57-87; Teloh, "Aristotle's *Metaphysics* Z 13," pp. 87-88; A. C. Lloyd, *Form and Universal in Aristotle* (Liverpool: Francis Cairns, 1981), p. 3; and Michael Frede, "Substance in Aristotle's *Metaphysics*," in *Aristotle on Nature and Living Things*, pp. 20-26.

6. "Problems in *Metaphysics* Z 13," pp. 237-38. Hughes, "Universals as Potential Substances," holds a similar view.

7. Owens, *Doctrine of Being*, pp. 398-99, cf. pp. 14-15. His term for what I call "individual" is "singular," and he understands by it the particular instances of a species. He does, in fact, apply the term "individual" to form, but this is a part of his restatement of Aristotle's conclusions in "a more modern fashion." The Greek for my "individual" and Owens's "singular" is καθ' ἕκαστον.

8. Teloh, "Aristotle's *Metaphysics* Z 13," pp. 87-88, mentions the argument of Z 7-8 to support his claim that there are individual forms. He thinks that Aristotle argues that form cannot be in the process of generation or the process of destruction because form "is and is not." Aristotle does speak this way of form, but the passages that Teloh cites (1039b27; 1044b21-23; 1060a23) all concern forms of attributes or forms of artifacts. They do not show that forms of *ousiai* are and are not. Further, as we saw earlier, Aristotle argues in Z 8-9 that even forms of non-*ousiai* exist prior to the generation of the composite in the agent, in a way. Forms of composite *ousiai* must also, and on stronger grounds, exist in an agent prior their realization in composites.

9. Ross, I, c.

10. Albritton, "Forms of Particular Substances," pp. 707-8, also mentions the objection presented in this paragraph.

11. *Ibid.*, pp. 700-1; Frede, "Substance in Aristotle's *Metaphysics*," p. 23. Frede, however, goes on to say,

> But if it should be demanded that there be something about the form in and by itself which distinguishes it from other forms of the same kind, the answer is that there is no such distinguishing mark, and that there is no need for one. (p. 24)

It follows that there is *no* difference between your form and my form! If they are not different, then they are not individual forms; it is contradictory for Frede to say this and yet cite the text from Λ to support individual forms.

Hartman, *Substance, Body, and Soul*, p. 62, views form in the same way. Discussing the passage from book Λ, he remarks in a note,

> The dative['s] . . . singular number indicates that your essence is nobody else's. It does not follow that your essence is different in kind from anyone else's, but only that it is different in number.

Nonsense. Merely to say "my essence" indicates nothing about whether it differs from your essence. Further, how could two essences differ numerically but not in kind? What could make them numerically different? It cannot be their matter; they have no matter. But if they differ in form (τῷ εἴδει), they would differ in kind (τῷ εἴδει). The only feature that could distinguish one form from another in the same species is an accident like being in this particular place or in this particular matter. But such accidents do not belong to form nor do they alter it; so form does not become individual by adding accidents to it. On their view, my form would be the same as yours, and the passage in Λ loses the significance that Hartman and Frede think it has. Their position is just the old "universal form individuated by matter" view with the highly implausible addendum that the form somehow becomes different (it becomes individual) when matter is added to it.

12. Driscoll, "EIΔH in Aristotle's Theories of Substance," p. 144, thinks that Aristotle does have a secondary essence in mind when he speaks of "your form" in book Λ. He thinks that it, the individual's secondary essence, consists of the form plus the distinct matter through which the individual differs from other instances of its species. I agree that this is a secondary essence of a composite individual, but it is not unique to any composite because the essence of the matter is, again, universal. To form a secondary essence that is truly individual, we need to include the accidental attributes.

13. Teloh, "Aristotle's *Metaphysics* Z 13," pp. 81–83, argues that the argument aims to refute the Platonic view (as Aristotle understands it) that form is universal and individual. It does not apply to Aristotle's own universals because they can be one in species but not one in number, nor does it apply to Aristotle's own form which is, Teloh claims, one in number. As we can see, the key premise does apply to Aristotle's form; it just does not exclude this form.

14. Woods, "Problems in *Metaphysics* Z 13," pp. 230–35.

15. Defending a position like Woods's, Hughes, "Universals as Potential Substances," p. 125, makes a distinction between the universal which is a potentiality and the individual which is an actuality. He thinks that "man" can be used in both ways. This avoids the objection that one *ousia* is composed of another, but it is backwards. The form is not a potentiality. Aristotle claims that the form (or species) is the actuality of the composite.

16. Woods, "Problems in *Metaphysics* Z 13," pp. 237–38.

17. Driscoll, "EIΔH in Aristotle's Theories of Substance," defends this distinction (pp. 141–44), and uses it to dispute Woods (pp. 148–52).

18. See Lesher, "Aristotle on Form, Substance and Universals," pp. 170–74.

19. The last of these texts is cited by Hughes, "Universals as Potential Substances," p. 123.

20. This unity does not appear among the ones described in Δ 6, though it bears some similarity to the one in sensible substrate (1016a17–24). The latter belongs to things whose substrate is undifferentiable in form in respect of sensation, such as water or wine. Aristotle surely does not want to give form the type of unity that water has; in the central books Aristotle denies that water is one until it has received a form like being compacted (Z 16, 1040b8–10). Form's unity is much stronger than water's.

21. Also Owens, *Doctrine of Being,* pp. 393, 399; Driscoll, "EIΔH in Aristotle's Theories of Substance," pp. 142–43.

22. Albritton, "Forms of Particular Substances," p. 699n., writes: "I doubt that Aristotle would have understood any better than I do the suggestion that a thing may be neither universal nor particular." This view is echoed by Teloh, "The Universal in Aristotle," p. 77 n. 2. For a very brief defense of this interpretation see Owens, *Doctrine of Being,* pp. xiv–xv.

23. Difficulties with "mass terms" are well known. See Willard Van Orman Quine, *Word and Object* (Cambridge, Mass.: M. I. T. Press, 1960), pp. 90–95.

24. To say that whatever is one in formula is universal creates an some obvious problem. A composite individual like Socrates is one formula because he is one in matter (Δ 6, 1016b31–36). It follows that Socrates is universal! In declaring that the species is what has an essence, Aristotle may have intended to forestall such an inference. That is to say, he may say that the species has an essence rather than that what is one in formula has an essence because only some of the latter entities have essences.

25. See chap. 2, n. 20, above.

26. Compare Z 2, 1028b27–32 and B 1, 995b31–36 with 4, 999a24–b24. The wording of part of the Z 2 passage is close to the fifth *aporia* (995b13–18; 997a34–998a19), and Owens thinks that it asks the same question (but without referring to causes) (*Doctrine of Being*, p. 324). But the fifth *aporia* concerns the number of the genera of being and the position of mathematical intermediates. The passage in Z 2 is more interested in the principles of those genera; it asks, how do these *ousiai* exist and why?, a question about their principles. Consequently, I take it to raise the eighth *aporia*.

27. According to Aubenque, the *Metaphysics* is inherently aporematic and the *aporiai* of book B remain unresolved, as do the puzzles inherent in Aristotle's account of *ousia*. For a brief presentation of the thesis developed at length in his *Le Problème de L'Être chez Aristote,* see his "Aristoteles und das Problem der Metaphysik," *Zeitschrift für Philosophische Forschung* XV (1961): 321–33.

28. Though the two texts where Aristotle nearly makes this claim (1041a28, b8) have been disputed, the point is clear from the rest of the passage.

29. J. L. Ackrill, "Aristotle's Definitions of *Psuchē,*" in *Articles on Aristotle* 4 (New York: St. Martin's Press, 1978), p. 70, rejects what appears to be the account I offer on the ground that it makes nonsense of Aristotle's claim that the same matter could lose its form. On my account, the matter of a living thing that loses its form is so altered that it is no longer the same matter. My response to Ackrill is that the problem is not a reason to reinterpret form or soul; it is rather a problem that Aristotle must face because he insists on both distinguishing matter from form and identifying them. Aristotle is anxious to distinguish the two in order to argue that the form does not contain material parts (Z 10–11) and to dispute Democritus (e.g., *P. A.* A 1, 640b29–641a6). However, the matter excluded from form is that from which the composite comes or that into which it is destroyed (Z 10, 1035a25–b1): it is the matter for generation and destruction. Though present in composites, this matter is not the proximate matter that Aristotle identifies with form and actuality in H 6 (cf. Z 11, 1036b28–32). (In artifacts, the two types of matter are the same, but the consequent lack of unity is just the reason that artifacts are not properly *ousiai.*) The passage that Ackrill cites, p. 69, to show that the same matter can have or lose a form, Z 15, 1039b29, is ambiguous; he probably translates it incorrectly; and, anyway, it refers to the matter for generation. So Ackrill confuses the two types of matter.

If, however, my position is correct, how does Aristotle differ from Democritus? If matter does not persist intact when form is removed, then Aristotle's insistence that to be alive an animal needs more than matter is hard to grasp. Why does he not say that the animal needs a particular kind of matter, Democritus' view? As I understand them, Aristotle's arguments are directed against the particular way that Democritus understood form. Democritus spoke of the arrangement or structure of matter (cf. H 2, 1042b11–15). In arguing against Democritus, Aristotle emphasizes the importance of function. The significance of function is not diminished by recognizing that structure or organization is sometimes itself a capacity to function. A ball, for example, has the capacity to function as such by virtue of its shape, and it is a model for *ousia*. Accordingly, to say that the corpse is not a human being because it cannot function is not necessarily to insist that functioning depends on something besides structure: it is to distinguish function from the matter for generation and destruction.

30. See my "Aristotle on Knowledge of Nature," pp. 825–26.

31. See the contributions to the symposium on the "Principle of Individuation" by Jan Lukasiewicz and G. E. M. Anscombe, *Proceedings of the Aristotelian Society,* suppl. vol. XXVII (1953).

32. See Woods, "Problems in *Metaphysics* Z 13," pp. 237–38.

33. Owens, *Doctrine of Being,* p. 394, calls the problem of the principle of individuation "a very unaristotelian question." Since in the *Metaphysics* Aristotle seeks the nature that all beings somehow share, it would be better to say that the principle of individuation is an unmetaphysical question. It belongs to logic and to physics, disciplines whose principles would today fall under the rubric of metaphysics.

34. Edward O. Wilson, *Sociobiology* (Cambridge, Mass.: Belknap Press, 1976), p. 3.

SELECTED BIBLIOGRAPHY

Ackrill, J. L. *Aristotle's* Categories *and* De Interpretatione. Oxford: Clarendon Press, 1979.

_____ . "Aristotle's Definitions of *Psuchē.*" In *Articles on Aristotle: 4,* edited by Jonathan Barnes et al., pp. 65–75.

_____ . "Aristotle's Distinction Between *Energeia* and *Kinesis.*" In *New Essays on Plato and Aristotle,* edited by Renford Bambrough, pp. 121–41.

_____ . *Aristotle the Philosopher.* Oxford: Oxford University Press, 1981.

Albritton, Rogers. "Forms of Particular Substances in Aristotle's *Metaphysics.*" *Journal of Philosophy* LIV (1957): 699–708.

Alexander of Aphrodisias. In *Aristotelis Metaphysica Commentaria.* Edited by Michael Hayduck. Berlin: George Reimer, 1891. Vol. I, *Commentaria in Aristotelem Graeca.* Prussian Academy Edition.

Allen, R. E. "Individual Properties in Aristotle's *Categories.*" *Phronesis* XIV (1969): 31–39.

_____ , ed. *Studies in Plato's Metaphysics.* London: Routledge & Kegan Paul, 1967.

Annas, Julia. *Aristotle's* Metaphysics: *Books M and N.* Oxford: Clarendon Press, 1976.

Anscombe, G. E. M. "Aristotle: The Search for Substance." In G. E. M. Anscombe and P. T. Geach, *Three Philosophers,* pp. 3–63. Ithaca, N. Y.: Cornell University Press, 1961.

_____ . "The Principle of Individuation." *Proceedings of the Aristotelian Society,* suppl. vol. XXVII (1953): 85–96.

Apostle, Hippocrates G. *Aristotle's* Metaphysics. Grinnell, Iowa: The Peripatetic Press, 1979.

_____ . *Aristotle's* Physics. Grinnell, Iowa: The Peripatetic Press, 1979.

Arnim, Hans von. "Zu W. Jaegers Grundlegung der Entwicklungsgeschichte des Aristoteles." *Wiener Studien* XLVI (1928): 1–48.

Asclepius. *In Metaphysicorum Libros A–Z Commentaria.* Edited by Michael Hayduck. Berlin: George Reimer, 1888. Vol. VI, 2, *Commentaria in Aristotelem Graeca.* Prussian Academy Edition.

Aubenque, Pierre. "Aristoteles und das Problem der Metaphysik." *Zeitschrift für Philosophische Forschung* XV (1961): 321–33.

_____ , ed. *Études sur La Métaphysique D'Aristote: Actes du VIᵉ Symposium Aristotelicum.* Paris: J. Vrin, 1979.

_____ . "La Pensée du Simple dans la *Métaphysique* (Z 17 et Θ 10)." In *Études sur La Métaphysique D'Aristote: Actes du VIᵉ Symposium Aristotelicum,* edited by Pierre Aubenque, pp. 69–80.

_____ . *Le Problème de L'Être chez Aristote: Essai sur la Problématique Aristotélicienne.* 5th ed. Paris: Presses Universitaires de France, 1983.

Bambrough, Renford, ed. *New Essays on Plato and Aristotle.* New York: Humanities Press, 1965.

Bärthlein, Karl. *Die Transcendentalienlehre der alten Ontologie.* Vol. I Berlin: Walter de Gruyter, 1972.

Balme, D. M. "ΓΕΝΟΣ and ΕΙΔΟΣ in Aristotle's Biology." *Classical Quarterly* XII (1962): 81–98.

————. "The Snub." *Ancient Philosophy* IV (1984): 1–8.

Barnes, Jonathan. *Aristotle's Posterior Analytics.* Oxford: Clarendon Press, 1975.

Barnes, Jonathan, Malcolm Schofield, and Richard Sorabji, eds. *Articles on Aristotle: 1. Science.* London: Duckworth, 1975.

————. *Articles on Aristotle: 3. Metaphysics.* New York: St. Martin's Press, 1979.

————. *Articles on Aristotle: 4. Psychology and Aesthetics.* New York: St. Martin's Press, 1979.

Bekker, Immanuel. *Aristotelis Opera.* Rev. ed. Edited by Olof Gigon. Berlin: Walter de Gruyter, 1970.

Berti, Enrico. "The Intellection of 'Indivisibles' According to Aristotle, *De Anima* III 6." In *Aristotle on Mind and the Senses: Proceedings of the Seventh Symposium Aristotelicum,* edited by G. E. R. Lloyd and G. E. L. Owen, pp. 141–63. Cambridge: Cambridge University Press, 1978.

Block, Irving. "Substance in Aristotle." *Paideia,* Special Aristotle Issue (1978): 59–64.

Bonitz, H. *Index Aristotelicus.* 2d ed. Graz: Akademische Druck-U., 1955.

Brody, Baruch A. "Why Settle for Anything Less than Good Old-Fashioned Aristotelian Essentialism." *Nous* VII (1973): 351–65.

Burnet, Ionannes. *Platonis Opera.* 5 vols. Oxford: Clarendon Press. 1973.

Burnyeat, Myles, ed. *Notes on Book Zeta of Aristotle's* Metaphysics. Study Aids Monograph No. 1. Oxford: Sub-Faculty of Philosophy, 1979.

————, ed. *Notes on Eta and Theta of Aristotle's* Metaphysics. Study Aids Monograph No. 4. Oxford: Sub-Faculty of Philosophy, 1984.

Cherniss, Harold. *Aristotle's Criticism of Plato and the Academy.* Baltimore: Johns Hopkins University Press, 1944.

————. *The Riddle of the Early Academy.* Berkeley: University of California Press, 1945.

Code, Alan. "No Universal is a Substance: An Interpretation of *Metaphysics* Z 13 1038 b 8–15." *Paideia,* Special Aristotle Issue (1978): 65–74.

Copi, Irving M. "Essence and Accident." In *Aristotle: A Collection of Critical Essays,* edited by J. M. E. Moravcsik, pp. 149–66.

Cornford, Francis M. *Plato and Parmenides.* Indianapolis: Bobbs-Merrill, n. d.

Cousin, D. R. "Aristotle's Doctrine of Substance." *Mind* XLII (1933): 319–37.

Dancy, Russell. "On Some of Aristotle's First Thoughts about Substances." *The Philosophical Review* LXXXIV (1975): 338–73.

Denniston, J. D. *The Greek Particles.* 2d ed. Oxford: Clarendon Press, 1970.

Driscoll, John A. "ΕΙΔΗ in Aristotle's Earlier and Later Theories of Substance." In *Studies in Aristotle,* edited by Dominic J. O'Meara, pp. 129–59. Washington: The Catholic University of America Press, 1981.

Fine, Gail. "Plato and Aristotle on Form and Substance." *Proceedings of the Cambridge Philological Society* CCIX, n.s. XXIX (1983): 23–47.

_____ . "Separation." *Oxford Studies in Ancient Philosophy* II (1984): 31–87.

_____ . "Separation: A Reply to Morrison." *Oxford Studies in Ancient Philosophy* III (1985): 159–65.

Frede, Michael. "Substance in Aristotle's *Metaphysics.*" In *Aristotle on Nature and Living Things,* edited by Allan Gotthelf, pp. 17–26. Pittsburgh: Mathesis Publications, 1985.

Furth, Montgomery. *Aristotle's* Metaphysics: *Books VII–X: Zeta, Eta, Theta, Iota.* Indianapolis: Hackett, 1985.

Gerson, Lloyd. "Artifacts, Substances, and Essences." *Apeiron* XVIII (1984): 50–58.

Gewirth, Alan. "Aristotle's Doctrine of Being." *Philosophical Review* LXII (1953): 577–89.

Gilson, Etienne. *Being and Some Philosophers.* Toronto: Pontifical Institute of Mediaeval Studies, 1952.

Grene, Marjorie. "Is Genus to Species as Matter to Form? Aristotle and Taxonomy." *Synthese* XXVIII (1974): 51–69.

Halper, Edward. "Aristotle on Knowledge of Nature." *Review of Metaphysics* XXXVII (1984): 811–35.

_____ . "Aristotle on the Possibility of Metaphysics." *Revue de Philosophie Ancienne* IV (1987): 99–131.

Hamlyn, D. W. *Aristotle's* De Anima: *Books II and III.* Oxford: Clarendon Press, 1977.

Hare, J. E. "Aristotle and the Definition of Natural Kinds." *Phronesis* XXIV (1979): 168–79.

Haring, Ellen Stone. "Substantial Form in Aristotle's *Metaphysics* Z." *Review of Metaphysics* X (1967): 308–32, 482–501, 698–713.

Hartman, Edwin. *Substance, Body, and Soul: Aristotelian Investigations.* Princeton: Princeton University Press, 1977.

Heinaman, Robert. "Aristotle on Accidents." *Journal of the History of Philosophy* XXIII (1985): 311–24.

Hintikka, Jaakko. *Time and Necessity: Studies in Aristotle's Theory of Modality.* Oxford: Clarendon Press, 1973.

Hughes, Gerald J. "Universals as Potential Substances: The Interpretation of *Metaphysics* Z 13." In *Notes on Zeta,* edited by Myles Burnyeat, pp. 107–26.

Irwin, T. H. "Aristotle's Concept of Signification." in *Language and Logos: Studies in Ancient Greek Philosophy Presented to G. E. L. Owen,* edited by Malcolm Schofield and Martha Craven Nussbaum, pp. 241–66.

_____ . "Aristotle's Discovery of Metaphysics." *Review of Metaphysics* XXXI (1977): 210–29.

Jaeger, Werner W. *Aristotelis Metaphysica.* Oxford: Oxford University Press, 1973.

_____ . *Aristotle: Fundamentals of the History of His Development.* Translated by Richard Robinson. Oxford: Oxford University Press, 1967.

_____ . *Studien zur Entstehungsgeschichte der Metaphysik.* Berlin: Weidmann, 1912.

Judson, Lindsay. "Aristotle and the Megarians: *Metaphysics* Θ. 3–4." Paper presented at the annual meeting of the American Philosophical Association, Eastern Division, Boston, December, 1986.

Kirwan, Christopher. *Aristotle's* Metaphysics: *Books Γ, Δ, and E.* Oxford: Clarendon Press, 1971.

Kosman, L. A. "Substance, Being, and *Energeia.*" *Oxford Studies in Ancient Philosophy* II (1984): 121–49.

————. "Aristotle's Definition of Motion." *Phronesis* XIV (1969): 40–62.

Kung, Joan. "Aristotle on Essence and Explanation." *Philosophical Studies* XXXI (1977): 361–83.

————. "Metaphysics 8.4: Can Be but Will Not Be." *Apeiron* XII (1978): 32–36.

Lacy, A. R. "οὐσία and Form in Aristotle." *Phronesis* X (1965): 54–69.

Lennox, James G. "Are Aristotelian Species Eternal?" In *Aristotle on Nature and Living Things,* edited Allan Gotthelf, pp. 67–94. Pittsburgh: Mathesis Publications, 1985.

Lesher, James H. "Aristotle on Form, Substance and Universals: A Dilemma." *Phronesis* XVI (1971): 169–78.

Lloyd, A. C. "Aristotle's Principle of Individuation." *Mind* LIX (1970): 519–29.

————. *Form and Universal in Aristotle.* Liverpool: Francis Cairns, 1981.

————. "Genus Species and Ordered Series in Aristotle." *Phronesis* VII (1962), 67–90.

Loux, Michael. "Form, Species, and Predication." *Mind* LXXXVIII (1979): 1–23.

Lukasiewicz, Jan. "The Principle of Individuation." *Proceedings of the Aristotelian Society.* suppl. vol. XXVII (1953): 69–85.

Madigan, Arthur. "*Metaphysics* E 3: A Modest Proposal." *Phronesis* XXIX (1984): 123–36.

Mansion, Augustin. "L'objet de la science philosophique supréme d'après Aristote, Métaphysique, E 1." In *Mélanges de Philosophie Grecque,* offert à Mgr. Dies, pp. 151–68. Paris: J. Vrin, 1956.

Mansion, Suzanne. "La Notion de Matière en *Métaphysique* Z 10 et 11." In *Études sur La Métaphysique D'Aristote: Actes du VIᵉ Symposium Aristotelicum,* edited by Pierre Aubenque, pp. 185–202.

————. "Sur la composition ontologique des substances sensibles chez Aristote (*Métaphysique* Z 7–9)." In *Philomathes: Studies and Essays in the Humanities in Memory of Philip Merlan,* edited by R. B. Palmer and R. Hamerton Kelly, pp. 75–87. The Hague, 1971. Reprinted as "The Ontological Composition of Sensible Substances in Aristotle (*Metaphysics* VII 7–9)," in *Articles on Aristotle: 3,* edited by Jonathan Barnes et al., pp. 80–87.

Matthews, Gareth. "Accidental Unities." In *Language and Logos: Studies in Ancient Greek Philosophy Presented to G. E. L. Owen,* edited by Malcolm Schofield and Martha Craven Nussbaum, pp. 223–40.

Merlan, Philip. *From Platonism to Neoplatonism.* 2d. ed. The Hague: Martinus Nijhoff, 1960.

Miller, Fred D., Jr. "Did Aristotle Have a Concept of Identity?" *The Philosophical Review* LXXXII (1973): 483–90.

Modrak, D. K. "Forms, Types, and Tokens in Aristotle's *Metaphysics.*" *Journal of the History of Philosophy* XVII (1979): 371–81.

Moravcsik, J. M. E., ed. *Aristotle: A Collection of Critical Essays.* Notre Dame: University of Notre Dame Press, 1968.

Morrison, Donald. "Separation: A Reply to Fine." *Oxford Studies in Ancient Philosophy* III (1985): 167–73.

_____ . "Separation in Aristotle's *Metaphysics.*" *Oxford Studies in Ancient Philosophy* III (1985): 125–57.

Mure, G. R. G. *Aristotle.* New York: Oxford University Press, 1964.

Natorp, Paul. "Thema und Disposition der aristotelischen Metaphysik." *Philosophische Monatshefte* XXIV (1888): 37–65, 540–74.

Nussbaum, Martha Craven. "Saving Aristotle's Appearances." In *Language and Logos: Studies in Ancient Philosophy Presented to G. E. L. Owen,* edited by Malcolm Schofield and Martha Craven Nussbaum, pp. 267–93.

Oehler, Klaus. *Die Lehre vom noetischen und dianoetischen Denken bei Platon und Aristoteles.* Zetemata. Monographien zur Klassischen Altertumswissenschaft, vol. XXIX. Munich: C. H. Beck, 1962.

Owen, G. E. L. "Aristotle on the Snares of Ontology." In *New Essays on Plato and Aristotle,* edited by Renford Bambrough, pp. 69–95.

_____ . "Inherence." *Phronesis* X (1965): 97–105.

_____ . "Logic and Metaphysics in Some Earlier Works of Aristotle." In *Aristotle and Plato in the Mid-Fourth Century,* edited by I. Düring and G. E. L. Owen, pp. 163–90. Göteborg: Elanders Boktryckeri Aktiebolag, 1960.

_____ . "Particular and General." *Proceedings of the Aristotelian Society,* n.s. LXXIX (1978–79): 1–21.

_____ . "The Platonism of Aristotle." *Proceedings of the British Academy* LI (1965): 125–50.

_____ . "Prolegomenon to Z 7–9." In *Notes on Book Zeta,* edited by Myles Burnyeat, pp. 43–53.

_____ . "*Tithenai ta Phainomena.*" In *Aristotle: A Collection of Critical Essays,* edited by J. M. E. Moravcsik, pp. 167–90. (First published in *Aristote et les Problème de Methode,* edited by S. Mansion, pp. 83–103. Louvain, 1961.)

Owens, Joseph. *Aristotle: The Collected Papers of Joseph Owens.* Edited by John R. Catan. Albany: State University of New York Press, 1981.

_____ . *The Doctrine of Being in the Aristotelian 'Metaphysics.'* 3d ed. Toronto: Pontifical Institute of Mediaeval Studies, 1978.

Pelletier, Francis Jeffery. "Sameness and Referential Opacity in Aristotle." *Nous* XIII (1979): 283–311.

Philippe, M.-D. "αφαίρεσις, πρόσθεσις, χωρίζειν dans la Philosophie d' Aristote." *Revue Thomiste* LVI (1948): 461–79.

Quine, Willard Van Orman. *Word and Object.* Cambridge, Mass.: M.I.T. Press, 1960.

Randall, John Herman, Jr. *Aristotle.* New York: Columbia University Press, 1968.

Reale, Giovanni. *The Concept of First Philosophy and the Unity of the Metaphysics of Aristotle.* Edited and translated by John R. Catan. Albany, N.Y.: State University of New York Press, 1980.

Rorty, Richard. "Genus as Matter: A Reading of *Metaphysics* Z–H." In *Exegesis and Argument,* edited by E. N. Lee, A. P. D. Mourelatos, and R. M. Rorty. *Phronesis,* suppl. vol. I (1973): 393–420.

_____ . "Matter as Goo: Comments on Grene's Paper." *Synthese* XXVIII (1974): 71–77.

Ross, W. D. *Aristotle.* London: Methuen, 1964.

_____ . *Aristotle's* Metaphysics. 2 vols. Oxford: Clarendon Press, 1924.

_____ . *Aristotle's* Prior *and* Posterior Analytics. Oxford: Clarendon Press, 1965.

_____ . *The Works of Aristotle*. 2d ed. Oxford: Clarendon Press, 1972.

Ryle, Gilbert. *Dilemmas*. Cambridge University Press, 1954.

Schofield, Malcolm. "*Metaph*. Z 3: Some Suggestions." *Phronesis* XVII (1972), 97–101.

Schofield, Malcolm, and Martha Craven Nussbaum, eds. *Language and Logos: Studies in Greek Philosophy Presented to G. E. L. Owen*. Cambridge: Cambridge University Press, 1982.

Schwegler, Albert. *Die Metaphysik des Aristoteles: Grundtext, Uebersetzung und Commentar*. 4 vols. Frankfurt: Minerva, 1960. Reprint of 1847–1848 edition.

Seidl, H. *Der Begriff des Intellekts (νοῦς) bei Aristoteles im philosophischen Zusammenhang seiner Hauptschriften*. Meisenheim am Glan: Anton Hain, 1971.

Sellars, Wilfrid. "Substance and Form in Aristotle." *Journal of Philosophy* LIV (1957): 688–99.

Smith, J. A. "τόδε τι in Aristotle." *Classical Review* XXXV (1921): 19.

Sorabji, Richard. "Body and Soul in Aristotle." In *Articles on Aristotle: 4,* edited by Jonathan Barnes et al., pp. 42–64.

_____ . *Necessity, Cause and Blame: Perspectives on Aristotle's Theory*. Ithaca, N. Y.: Cornell University Press, 1980.

Stokes, Michael C. *One and Many in Presocratic Philosophy*. Washington: Center for Hellenic Studies, 1971.

Teloh, Henry. "Aristotle's *Metaphysics* Z 13." *Canadian Journal of Philosophy* IX (1979): 77–89.

_____ . "The Universal in Aristotle." *Apeiron* XIII (1979): 70–78.

Thomas Aquinas, St. *Commentary on the Metaphysics of Aristotle*. Translated by John P. Rowan. 2 vols. Chicago: Henry Regnery, 1961.

Turnbull, Robert. "Aristotle's Debt to the 'Natural Philosophy' of the *Phaedo.*" *Philosophical Quarterly* VIII (1958): 131–43.

Vlastos, Gregory. "Reasons and Causes in the *Phaedo.*" In *Plato: A Collection of Critical Essays. I: Metaphysics and Epistemology,* edited by Gregory Vlastos, pp. 132–66. Garden City, N. Y.: Anchor Books, 1971.

_____ . "The Third Man Argument in the *Parmenides.*" *Philosophical Review* LXI (1954): 319–49. Reprinted in *Studies in Plato's Metaphysics,* edited by R. E. Allen, pp. 231–63. London: Routledge & Kegan Paul, 1967.

Waterlow, Sarah. *Passage and Possibility: A Study of Aristotle's Modal Concepts*. Oxford: Clarendon Press, 1982.

White, Nicholas P. "Aristotle on Sameness and Oneness." *The Philosophical Review* LXXX (1971): 177–97.

Wilson, Edward O. *Sociobiology: The New Synthesis*. Cambridge, Mass.: Belknap Press, 1976.

Woods, Michael J. "Substance and Essence in Aristotle." *Proceedings of the Aristotelian Society* LXXV (1974–75): 167–80.

_____ . "Problems in *Metaphysics* Z, Chapter 13." In *Aristotle: A Collection of Critical Essays,* edited by J. M. E. Moravcsik, pp. 215–38.

INDEX